ZIMBABWE'S FIGHT TO THE FINISH

This book challenges the Western interpretation that poor governance under President Mugabe is the sole cause of the Zimbabwean crisis. Inherited and highly unequal colonial structures, particularly as applied to land, and the impoverishing impact of an IMF and World Bank conditionally sponsored Structural Adjustment Program (SAP) are considered primarily responsible. Previously the Government managed to balance the peasant capitalist order without comprehensive land redistribution through state controls on prices, wages, finance and trade. Economic liberalization under the SAP, however, exposed the failure of a skewed market to meet majority basic needs, which underpins the current chaos over land. Instead of isolating the country, Western states should help Zimbabwe resolve the land question, which is more likely to secure a democratic and prosperous future.

John L. Moore taught in Zimbabwe during the early 1990s as an Australian Volunteer Abroad and has returned several times since as a researcher in development studies from the School of Social Science and Planning at RMIT University, Melbourne, Australia.

www.keganpaul.com

ZIMBABWE'S FIGHT TO THE FINISH

THE CATALYST OF THE FREE MARKET

John Louis Moore

Kegan Paul
London • New York • Bahrain

First published in 2003 by
Kegan Paul Limited
UK: P.O. Box 256, London WC1B 3SW, England
Tel: 020 7580 5511 Fax: 020 74360899
E-Mail: books@keganpaul.com
USA: 61 West 62nd Street, New York, NY 10023
Tel: (212) 459 0600 Fax: (212) 458 3678
Internet: http://www.columbia.edu/cu/cup
BAHRAIN: bahrain@keganpaul.com

Distributed by:
Turpin Distribution
Blackhorse Road
Letchworth, Herts, SG6 1HN
England
Tel: (01462) 672555 Fax:: (01462) 480947
Email: books@turpinltd.com

Columbia University Press
61 West 62nd Street, New York, NY 10023
Tel: (212) 459 0600 Fax: (212) 458 3678
Internet: http://www.columbia.edu/cu/cup

Printed in Great Britain by Digital Books Logistics Ltd

ISBN: 0-7103-0872-8

British Library Cataloguing in Publication Data
A catalogue record for this book is available from the British Library.

Library of Congress Cataloging-in-Publication Data
Applied for.

CONTENTS

ACKNOWLEDGEMENTS

I would like to thank the Australian Volunteers Abroad program, which offered me an opportunity to spend three years teaching in Zimbabwe. From then on, I owe much to the warmth and generosity of many Zimbabweans but in particular Steve, Bhecki, Max, Janet and Wellington. Without their escort in rural and urban areas and insight into why things are the way they are, I could never have undertaken this work.

I am also grateful to the Institute of Development Studies at the University of Zimbabwe, which allowed me access to all facilities. The staff continually enlightened me about the country and offered much encouragement. Other bodies I wish to thank of similar outstanding expertise include Silveira House, the SAPES Trust, the Zimbabwe Congress of Trade Unions, the Zimbabwe Farmers Union and several Government ministries—Finance, Information and Lands and Agriculture. I also salute the Zimbabwean media for the wealth of information offered, particularly by the *Herald*, the *Zimbabwe Mirror* and the *Financial Gazette*.

I am appreciative of Dr Jock McCulloch's positive support and the fortune of being able to access state of the art services at RMIT University. The editing assistance of Patricia Maher warrants special praise, as does the loving support of my wife, Aer, my mother and sister Katrina throughout the long haul of researching and writing this work.

Map One: Administrative Provinces of Zimbabwe

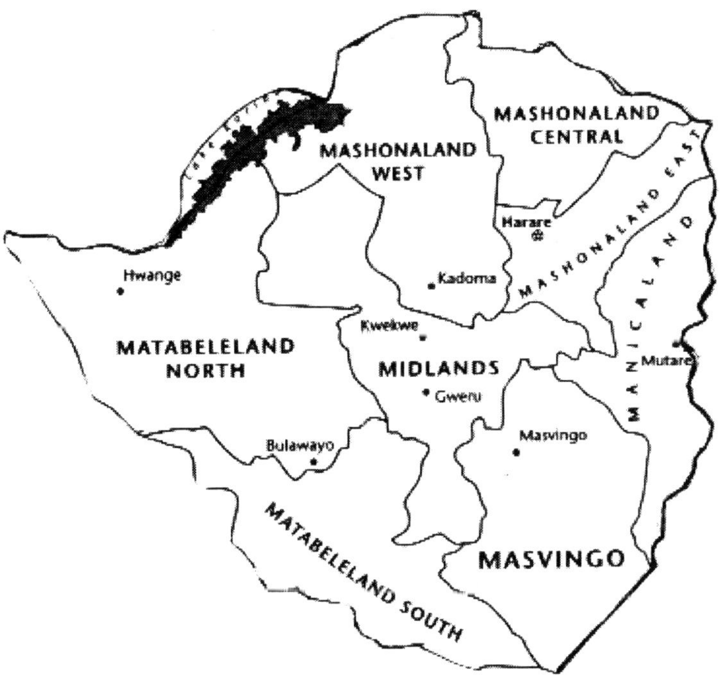

Map Two: The Natural Regions of Zimbabwe

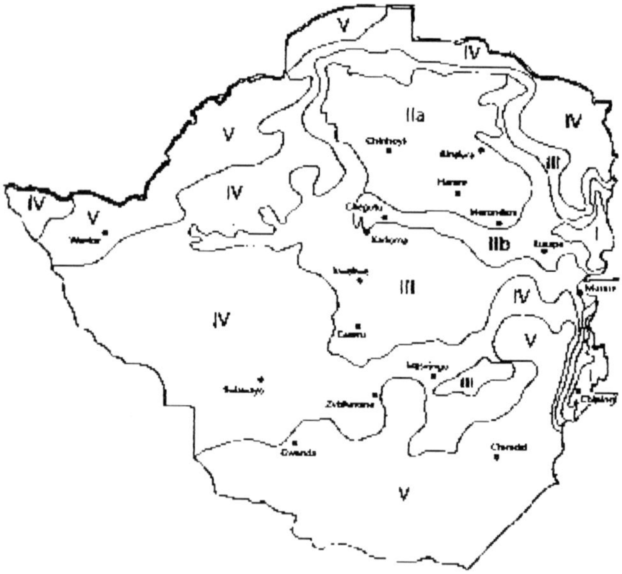

List of Tables and Figures

Figures

Abbreviations

ACCOR	Associated Chambers of Commerce [now ZNCC]
ADB	African Development Bank
AFC	Agricultural Finance Corporation
AGRITEX	Agricultural and Technical Extension Service
AIDS	Acquired Immune Deficiency Syndrome
APIC	African Policy Information Centre
BSAC	British South Africa Company
CBZ	Commercial Bank of Zimbabwe
CCZ	Consumer Council of Zimbabwe
CFU	Commercial Farmers Union
CMB	Cotton Marketing Board
COTTCO	Cotton Company of Zimbabwe
CSC	Cold Storage Commission/Company
CSO	Central Statistical Office
CZI	Confederation of Zimbabwe Industries
DERUDE	Department of Rural Development
DMB	Dairy Marketing Board
DRC	Democratic Republic of Congo
ECA	Economic Commission for Africa
ERP	Economic Reform Programme
ESAP	Economic Structural Adjustment Program
EU	European Union
FAO	Food and Agriculture Organisation
FMB	First Merchant Bank
FPL	Food Poverty Line
GATT	General Agreement on Tariffs and Trade
GoZ	Government of Zimbabwe

GMB	Grain Marketing Board
ICES	Income and Consumption Expenditure Survey
HDR	Human Development Report
IDS	Institute of Development Studies
IFIs	International Financial Institutions [i.e. the IMF/WB]
ILO	International Labour Organisation
IMF	International Monetary Fund
ISI	Import Substitution Industrialisation
LONRHO	London and Rhodesia Mining and Land Company
LSCS	Large-scale Commercial Sector
LTC	Land Tenure Commission
MDC	Movement for Democratic Change
MERP	Millennium Economic Recovery Program
MPSLASW	Ministry of Public Service, Labour and Social Welfare
MLARR	Ministry of Lands, Agriculture and Rural Resettlement
NGO	Non Government Organisation
NOCZIM	National Oil Company of Zimbabwe
NRs	Natural Regions
NRZ	National Railways of Zimbabwe
OPEC	Organisation of Petroleum Exporting Countries
PASS	Poverty Assessment Study Survey
PRF	Poverty Reduction Forum
RBZ	Reserve Bank of Zimbabwe
RISCO	Rhodesian Iron and Steel Company [now ZISCO]
RF	Rhodesian Front
SADC	Southern African Development Community
SAMAT	Southern African Multi-disciplinary Advisory Team
SAP	Structural Adjustment Program
SAPES Trust	Southern African Political Economic Series Trust

SAPEM	Southern African Political and Economic Monthly
SAPRI	Structural Adjustment Participatory Review Initiative
SOEs	State-owned Enterprises
SSCS	Small-scale Commercial Sector
TPL	Total Poverty Line
UANC	United African National Council
UDI	Unilateral Declaration of Independence
UN	United Nations
UNCTAD	United Nations Conference on Trade and Development
UNDP	United Nations Development Programme
USAID	United States Agency of International Development
UZ	University of Zimbabwe
VIDCOs	Village Development Committees
WARDCOs	Ward Development Committees
WB	World Bank
WDR	World Development Report
WTO	World Trade Organisation
ZANLA	Zimbabwe African National Liberation Army
ZANU-PF	Zimbabwe African National Union – Patriotic Front
ZAPU	Zimbabwe African Peoples Union
ZCTU	Zimbabwe Congress of Trade Unions
ZDF	Zimbabwe Development Fund
ZESA	Zimbabwe Electrical Supply Authority
ZFU	Zimbabwe Farmers Union
ZIDS[now IDS]	Zimbabwe Institute of Development Studies
ZIMCORD	Zimbabwe Conference on Reconstruction and Development
ZIMPREST	Zimbabwe Program for Economic and Social Transformation
ZIPA	Zimbabwe Peoples Army
ZIPRA	Zimbabwe Peoples Revolutionary Army
ZISCO	Zimbabwe Iron and Steel Company
ZNCC	Zimbabwe National Chambers of Commerce

‘Done because we are too many’,
Thomas Hardy, *Jude the Obscure*.

INTRODUCTION:
Making Sense of the Chaos

By the year 2000, after a decade of worsening national poverty, Zimbabwe's development crisis had deepened. In an apparent bid to destroy rather than salvage the present economy, the Government sanctioned land invasions of white farms—traditionally a mainstay of agricultural output and exports—and then went on to designate about 93% of white-owned land for state appropriation. Drought coincided with the land turmoil that the country now faces famine, not to forget an HIV-AIDS scourge, rampant inflation and debt, fuel and power shortages, war in the Congo and global isolation. The ruling party—the Zimbabwe African National Union–Patriotic Front [ZANU-PF]—suppresses any voice of dissent, whether from the main opposition party—the Movement for Democratic Change [MDC]—the press, the judiciary or the general public. Indeed, the March 2002 presidential election results fell short of legitimacy—in urban areas where ZANU-PF had little support, a shortage of polling stations and time denied many voters their democratic right.

From the West, the common view among politicians, diplomats, aid organisations and the media is that Zimbabwe's crisis is due to poor governance. A recent article in the US diplomatic broadsheet *Foreign Affairs*, for example, by the President of the Washington based World Peace Foundation, Robert Rotberg, put the blame on one man and one man alone:

> ... kleptocratic, patrimonial leaders—like President Robert Gabriel Mugabe... are the ones largely responsible for declining GDP levels, food scarcities, rising infant-mortality rates, soaring budget deficits, human rights abuses, breaches of the rule of law, and prolonged serfdom for millions... [2000:47].

In this view, the President's personal quest for survival and prestige destroyed the economy. His decisions to grant lavish pensions to war veterans in November 1997 and send the military into the Democratic Republic of Congo [DRC] in August 1998 are considered illustrative, whereupon on both occasions the currency plunged, inflation soared and investment collapsed. Mr Mugabe then politicised the land issue, the argument runs, to recover popularity, which entailed proposing a draft constitution that reputedly enabled the state to 'confiscate land without compensation'. When the electorate rejected this draft in February 2000, he 'incited' war veterans and ZANU-PF supporters to defy the High Court and invade white farms. Until 'despots' like him abide by 'good governance and sensible economic policy', insists Robert Rotberg [2000:60], they deserve to be ostracised. Over the years, he maintains, the world community—African and Western leaders alike—including the two International Financial Institutions [IFIs], the International Monetary Fund [IMF] and World Bank, have been far too 'forgiving' of his sort.

From Robert Rotberg's perspective, which typifies that of the West, resolution of the Zimbabwean crisis simply depends on replacing Mr Mugabe with a leader who respects 'good governance and sensible economic policy'. The first concept is equated with the norms of Westminster—the rule of law, separation of powers and parliamentary democracy—and the second refers to the 'Washington Consensus'—state fiscal rationalisation [retrenchment, cutbacks, cost recovery, privatisation] and liberalised market regimes over wages, prices, trade and finance [Williamson, J., 1993:1329-1336]. To bring Zimbabwe back into the fold, the Western development community presently applies a freeze on non-humanitarian aid, debt relief, investment and trade concessions, which the US Congress recently made official by passing the Zimbabwe Democracy and Economic Recovery Act. The assumption is that the outcome sought—referred to as *neo-liberal*—is entirely appropriate and works, only that a perceived tyrant stands in the way.

For the sake of all Zimbabweans, the Western interpretation and approach to the crisis needs to be critically examined as to whether it offers a lasting solution. To begin with, a fundamental question concerns the true origins of the crisis. Is Mr Mugabe the real problem or is it an agrarian structure that allows an extreme minority of foreign companies and individuals to enclose the most fertile lands when over half the population can barely survive from barren and overcrowded plots? And upon one of the world's most inequitable agrarian bases, a second fundamental question concerns the feasibility of liberal democratic and free market aid conditionalities. On grounds that the Zimbabwean Government has failed to fulfil democratic and free market ideals, is Western disengagement resolving or fuelling the crisis?

In a divided polity, the stakes have become exceedingly high. Over 60,000 families, according to official sources [cited in *The Zimbabwe Mirror*, 4-10/05/01], have settled on white farms while in the Congo, the military defends mining, agricultural and timber concessions on behalf of the ZANU-PF hierarchy. The advent of an MDC government, as sought by the West, promises to restore private property and withdraw from the Congo, which conceivably could provoke another civil war—the country's fourth following three during the Rhodesian era. Ideally, at this juncture, Western powers, notably the UK and US, should help resolve the national question of land and livelihood that has characterised Zimbabwe's modern history.

In truth, the roots of the development crisis go beyond governance and derive from non-viable structures of class and production established under Rhodesian settler colonialism. Two initial land wars—the War of Dispossession in 1893–1894 and the first *Chimurenga*[*] of 1896–1897—and systemic state-sponsored racial privilege deprived the African agrarian sector of an adequate resource base and entrapped the majority in a demographic and environmental crisis. Thereon, despite substantial manufacturing growth based on import substitution, the structural base proved too reliant on white consumption and foreign capital to pull African society out of the poverty trap, let alone overcome an problematic dependency on primary exports relative to capital imports. Tragically, after the second *Chimurenga* of 1966–1980, at the behest of the UK and US, the Lancaster House settlement denied the nationalists full sovereignty over the land issue, which compromised political and economic development.

[*] *Chimurenga* is the Shona word for war of liberation.

Against this background, the current agrarian upheaval is primarily an outcome of alarming rises in national poverty during the early 1990s. An economic crisis preceded political turmoil, which contradicts the perception of the Western media that Mr Mugabe is solely responsible for the economic slide. The actual catalyst of the development crisis can be traced to the impact of an IMF and World Bank recommended and conditionally sponsored Structural Adjustment Program [SAP], which from 1990 served as the conduit of the 'Washington Consensus' and the policies of state fiscal rationalisation and market liberalisation. By mid-decade, according to the Central Statistical Office [CSO] [1998a:36], the prevalence of people below the poverty line increased from 52.8% to an astonishing 75.6%. The subsequent explosion of the land issue and the military's entry into the DRC were as much about changing the dynamics of an impoverished economy as any quest of ruling party figures for personal advantage.

Prior to the SAP, the Government managed to balance the peasant – capitalist order without comprehensive land redistribution through inherited state economic controls, which—in essence—contained the capacity of highly skewed market forces to reach socially unsustainable equilibrium levels in regard to life's basic essentials [Stoneman, C., 1993:91-93]. In a heavily import-dependent and oligopolistic economy, controls on prices and the exchange rate countered inflation; centralised wage setting secured a reasonable living wage; controls on imports and capital repatriation protected domestic industry and countered external imbalances; and interest rate controls kept domestic liquidity cheap to finance fiscal deficits. The peasantry in turn received the benefit of relatively low inflation, a stable urban remittance base and, most significantly, subsidised food, education, health care and farm inputs.

Yet, outside the public sector, private investment and employment creation remained stagnant, which really signalled the urgency of comprehensive land redistribution to broaden the dimensions of the national market. Instead, a confluence of elite international and national class forces—Western states, the IMF and World Bank, multinational companies, white farmers and, crucially, allied capitalists among the ZANU-PF hierarchy—pushed to deregulate the economy upon notions that state controls and welfare gains came at the expense of investment and growth. Advocates promised that global market integration—in effect, the removal of controls over prices, wages, interest and exchange rates, exchange allocation, capital and import flows—would deliver sustained rises in export-oriented and labour intensive investment. To release and encourage savings for a private investment, tight monetary policy [i.e. positive interest rates] and state fiscal rationalisation [i.e. retrenchment, cutbacks, higher 'user fees' and sales of State-owned Enterprises] formed a vital part of the adjustment rationale.

The Government thus embarked upon the SAP, anticipating a doubling of external financial support over the first five years [GoZ, 1991a:24]. From the outset, however, the domestic damage of state cost recovery and other measures—currency depreciation, high interest rates, deregulated import flows and liberalised price and wage setting—overwhelmed the external stimulus gained. In accord with the structural base, the beneficiaries comprised a minority of mainly white-owned tradable enterprises, predominantly geared to the limited fortunes of primary commodities. Otherwise, a stagflation crisis of high inflation and low growth wrecked havoc on the living wage and inward-oriented enterprise including most State-owned Enterprises [SOEs], peasant farmers and many manufacturing concerns. Worse still, the national budget—upon a rising debt interest bill and shrinking revenue base—succumbed to a spiral of debt accumulation wherein cost recovery measures failed to correct the deficit and selling indebted SOEs offered no real salvation. In turn, the state fiscal crisis carried terrible ramifications on the country's health and education.

Paradoxically, by highlighting apparent positives, a mid-1990s World Bank report really disclosed fundamental weaknesses:

> Wage rates for garment machine operators in Zimbabwe are one-tenth of those in Hong Kong... In a few years, Zimbabwe has become the third largest supplier of imported cut roses to Europe, and the fourth largest supplier of cut flowers. Similarly, there has been a significant increase in the export of fresh off-season vegetables such as mange-tout peas, sugar snap peas, cherry tomatoes and baby sweetcorns [WB, 1995 vol. 2: 133, 3].

In reality, as purchasing power collapsed, the increased export bias of irrigated large-scale farms and associated exposure of national food needs to a drought prone smallholder base contributed to unprecedented food inflation and food insecurity. Similar to horticulture, although the tourist industry grew fourfold in US dollar terms within five years [RBZ, 1997b:24], the benefits fell well short of compensating the damage of an enhanced wealth divide and more impoverished national economy.

'We all underestimated the social impact of the program', to quote an anonymous Western economist [cited in *The New York Times*, 05/07/00], 'and when we recognised it, we didn't get our act together quickly enough to help'. Indeed, as foreign exchange levels hit critical lows in late 1997 and militant war veterans compelled the Government to deliver gratuities as well as land, IMF and allied creditors for reasons of 'poor governance' imposed a boycott. The currency crashed on November 14, known as 'Black Friday', whereupon a hyper stagflation spiral offered the MDC fertile ground. Entry into the Congo added to the Government's legitimacy crisis yet by then, IMF intransigence and a perceived 'Westernised' local opposition had fired the cause of militant nationalists. The draft constitution did not deny compensation for designated lands but affirmed state discretionary power to determine the amount. In any case, the negative referendum result signalled immediate action on the land front, which despite all has clear aspiration. The Agricultural Minister, Joseph Made:

> Zimbabwe will ensure that agricultural production is never again in the hands of a few who underutilise or hold to ransom the nation in terms of food security, employment creation and economic growth [cited in *The Age*, 21/11/01].

At the forefront of globalisation, IMF and World Bank conditionally sponsored SAPs are applied throughout the developing world and their economic record is generally no better than Zimbabwe's. As M. Weisbrot, R. Naiman and J. Kim [2000] demonstrate, a simple comparison using UNDP data of the period 1960 to 1980—a time of state management—with the period 1980 to 2000—the era of market liberalisation—reveals that since 1980 virtually every developing country except China experienced lower GDP per capita growth rates and living standards. Sub-Saharan Africa fared the worst: GDP per capita grew by an average of 36% over the first period and then *fell* by an average of 15% over the second [Weisbrot, M., Naiman, R., and Kim, J., 2000:7]. Meanwhile, in respect of trade—supposedly a boon of SAPs—Africa's world share fell from about 4% in 1979 to a miserable 1.5% [IMF data cited in *The Guardian Weekly*, 06-12/06/02]. The above authors concluded dramatically:

> In short, there is no region of the world that the Bank or Fund can point to as having succeeded through adopting the policies that they promote—or in many cases, impose—upon borrowing countries. [They are understandably reluctant to claim credit for China, which maintains a non-convertible currency, state control over its banking system and other major violations of IMF/World Bank prescriptions] [Weisbrot, M., Naiman, R., and Kim, J., 2000:8]

In a candid moment, an IMF official concurred:

> ... too many countries, and nearly one-fifth of the world population, have regressed in relative and sometimes even absolute terms. This is arguably one of the greatest economic failures of the 20th Century [IMF press conference, 04/12/00, cited in Centre of Concern, 2000:2].

The advent of globalisation, as pioneered since the late 1970s through policy-based credit, stemmed from accumulated financial power by the West to apply an open door policy toward world trade and investment. Multinational companies—mostly based in the West—are the primary beneficiaries, which quickly exploit the opportunities of expanding markets [via import liberalisation], cheap labour [via liberalised wage setting], commodity inputs [via currency devaluation] and investment outlets [via privatisation]. By contrast, most developing countries lack a transnational capacity to exploit global opportunities while the trade and investment stimulus delivered from the West rarely compensates for the withdrawal of state protection. In fact, rich countries are net recipients of wealth from the poor through debt service, profit repatriation and a trade nexus of mostly appreciating manufactured Western exports relative to depreciating commodity-based Third World exports.

Such is the outcome of world power inequalities that presently sees the US and European Union [EU] demanding universal free trade regimes when they themselves protect their markets. Indeed, after introducing a 30% tariff on US steel in March 2002, the Bush administration approved a farm subsidies bill worth an estimated

US$180 billion over ten years, which is almost equal to what the EU spends on agricultural subsidies [*The Guardian Weekly*, 16-22/05/02]. Simultaneously, the President vowed to almost double the US aid budget, largely via the IMF and World Bank, so as to continue the spread of 'free trade'. In both institutions, Western states through capital subscriptions wield the most voting power. As of 1993 in the World Bank, for example, the 'big five'—the US and UK, Japan, Germany and France—held 39% of votes while forty-five African countries controlled 4% [George, S., and Sabelli, F., 1994:14-15, 208].

Meanwhile, the IMF/World Bank and other leading development organisations advance globalisation under the pretence that SAPs deliver poor countries a higher standard of living and foster democratic governance. For example, a study by Sahn, Dorosh and Younger [1997:248,256]—funded by the pro-market United States Agency of International Development [USAID]—claimed that SAPs are 'distributionally progressive' toward the poor and future research should focus on ways to promote democracy to prevent numerous rent-seeking governments from reversing the policies. Yet the poverty record of SAPs defies this analysis, which suggests that governments reverse the policies to regain democratic legitimacy. In fact, imposed from above and often devoid of a mandate, SAPs invite authoritarianism and deny a meaningful choice over macroeconomic policy. Ultimately, as foreign capital tends to be favoured at the expense of nascent indigenous enterprise, the policies undermine the national economic sovereignty needed to sustain a legitimate democratic contract between state and society, which creates potential for political instability.

True, governments consciously choose to adopt the policies but then, in a circle, most lack an autonomous economic base—sustained by a strong indigenous bourgeoisie—to resist the pull of Western finance and neo-liberal policies. The fact that Malaysia, for instance, had been acquiring such a class over the decades, notably under state protection, enabled the country to put up a hitherto solitary defence from the developing world. In turn, Malaysia's experience affirms the need of an inward-oriented development state in Africa—not one disposed toward autarchy as such but prepared to facilitate and protect the rise of a vibrant indigenous private sector, which may eventually better exploit external trade and investment opportunities.

The Malaysian challenge came amid the Asian crisis of 1997–1998 when previous liberalisation drives of the IMF and World Bank subjected the region to destabilising flows of Western speculative capital, which forced several countries to accept IMF 'bail-out' loans. The Malaysian Prime Minister, Dr. Mahathir Mohamad, remained defiant:

> It is no exaggeration to say that the IMF demands on Indonesia were largely responsible for the riots and uprisings that led to the downfall of President Suharto. Fortunately, Malaysia did not take the IMF's bitter medicine, we considered the medicine more dangerous than the disease... The pressing question today is not whether, or how, we can fine-tune the mechanisms applied by the IMF: bluntly stated, the real issue is whether we will willingly allow our economies to be governed by a 'doctor with only one pill for every illness' and by a bunch of yuppies with no sense of history or human responsibility [Mohamad, M., 1999:20].

The outspoken Dr. Mahathir acted swiftly to eradicate what he believed to be a recipe of disaster. While the state imposed currency and capital controls, the prospective vanguard of the neo-liberal economic and good governance agenda, Anwar Ibrahim, was persecuted and jailed. Although short of Western democratic standards, the Malaysian people at least, as I later substantiate, went on to experience the strongest and least indebted recovery in the region.

Even the prospect of an IMF and World Bank sponsored regime can worsen political conflict. In many countries where the regime has taken hold, a circle of economic and political failure can begin: deterioration of majority livelihood, enrichment of minorities, shrinkage of the economy, increased speculative activity, political destabilisation, reduced investment and so on. The following quote from the deputy chairman of the Standard Bank's investment division in Johannesburg, Sakumzi Mocozoma, seems universally applicable:

> There is a sense of frustration that the government has done everything that international capital has asked of it but the political cost of that has not been rewarded and in some ways has even been punished by speculation against the rand. In retrospect, I think we were a bit naïve [cited in *The Guardian Weekly*, 06-12/09/01].

The countries most vulnerable appear to be dominated by large peasantries, reliant on a narrow range of tradable industries and susceptible to wealth polarisation, particularly along ethnic lines. Indonesia, Ecuador, Zambia, Rwanda, Peru and Nepal are cases in point. Another is Papua New Guinea where the Morauta Government recently managed to quell an army mutiny and serious civil disturbances over state rationalisation and the influence of foreign advisors [*The Australian*, 24-25/03/01; *The Age*, 27/06/01; *The Guardian Weekly*, 22-26/03/01]. In Zimbabwe, most acutely, the entrenched structural causes of poverty and the impact of market liberalisation combined with disastrous consequences.

I first outline the structural conditions established under Rhodesian colonialism and then concentrate on state economic controls under Ian Smith, which in the skewed context proved valuable development tools. At Lancaster House, ascendant Western finance wrought a toll on Zimbabwean sovereignty, which ultimately set the road to economic liberalisation. I then turn to the global arena to assess the debate about SAPs with reference to African performance in the 1980s, which is then contrasted with the significant but threatened welfare advances delivered under Zimbabwean state-directed 'macro populism'. Three chapters discuss the local impact of the SAP through real life households under the following themes: agricultural market liberalisation, family poverty in communal areas and urban informal business. The breakdown of the national political economy is the final focus.

1

Rhodesian Political Economy, 1890–1962

Four phases of Rhodesian political economy are considered, namely, primitive accumulation 1890–1930, the 'two pyramids' 1930–1953, 'partnership' 1953–1962 and UDI 1962–1980. I discuss the first three here and devote the next chapter to the fourth. Throughout *all* phases, Rhodesian development remained a complete paradox: the sources of growth—African dispossession, settler nationalism, external demand and white luxury consumption—were also the sources of structural constraints that crystallized in the recession of the late 1970s. A skewed domestic class structure formed the root of economic ills—not the so-called 'closed' economy, as is the want of the orthodox economists of the World Bank and IMF. State intervention released a dynamic of national economic growth far greater than elsewhere in sub-Saharan Africa [excluding South Africa]. Ultimately, market distortions emanated from racially based capitalist classes that denied black entrepreneurs access to the resources and services necessary to add to the country's wealth and develop the national market.

The process of brutally converting the land and labour resources of native economies into market commodities is what Marx called 'primitive accumulation', which he considered the starting point of capital generation [Marx, K, 1978 ed, vol.1, pt.8: 668-669]. Rosa Luxemburg in *The Accumulation of Capital* [1913] argued modern capitalism was engaged in a 'fight to the finish ... with every historical form of natural economy' in order to usurp the land, labour, minerals, flora and fauna for capitalist development [1951 [ed]:369-371].[1] In the settler colonies of Southern Africa violent assaults were perpetrated against indigenous people to make way for capitalist agriculture and industry. The experience was less violent in the areas of indirect rule but no less revolutionary. Either way, to quote Colin Leys [1995:45], whether by direct assault or by the gradual encroachment of capitalist relations of exchange, 'the result was to destroy the precolonial economies and the social orders based on them, without putting in their place economies or social systems capable of defending themselves against world market forces'.

In March 1938, Godfrey Huggins, the then Prime Minister of Rhodesia, inadvertently defined the nature of unbalanced or uneven development:

> The Europeans in this country can be likened to an island of white in a sea of black, with the artisan and the tradesman forming the shores and the professional classes the highlands in the centre. Is the native to be allowed to erode away the shores and gradually attack the highlands? [cited in Rifkind, M.L., 1972:56]

His answer to the latter question was an illusory 'two-pyramids' or two separate societies each with a monopoly over occupations. Earlier the Land Apportionment Act of 1930 officially divided the country according to race and sanctioned the concentration of the economy's main productive asset in the hands of a white minority. The Act effectively entrenched a deformed structural base marked by highly inequitable wealth accumulation.

Allocated marginal and inadequate land, African reserves converted to 'sink areas', that is, lands beset by environmental and demographic crisis bereft of any real autonomous development prospect. In turn a dispossessed and impoverished population deprived the country of the national market needed to sustain embracive endogenous development. The consequent external orientation of the capitalist base reinforced uneven development and the vulnerability inherent to world market fluctuations and foreign capital imperatives. The protection of white class status via laws of racial discrimination perpetuated an ongoing interest in African oppression to ensure supplies of cheap labour and an absence of competition; discouraged intensive land use and production innovation; and enticed luxury consumption amid conditions of relative mass deprivation [Brenner, R., 1977:84].[2]

Yet given a settler-focused capitalist development state and exogenous stimulants, namely, white immigration, world export demand and foreign direct investment, Rhodesia obtained drive especially while the latter factors lasted. Indeed, based on agriculture and mining, external stimulants enabled by the 1960s a higher GDP contribution from manufacturing than both the former. But the prospect for sustained and balanced development had been eliminated. The monopoly of white labour over skilled employment pushed up production costs beyond African purchasing power while the export focus of white farmers often left the country short of food and industrial inputs. The savings base and domestic market only expanded in so far as white society was enriched. Without an inclusive rural–urban dynamic, the national economy could only grow in spurts and forever tend toward saturated markets and recession. Inevitably, the 'trickle down' remained inadequate to pull African society out of poverty, which proved the nemesis of colonial Rhodesia.

The interests of domestic and international capital generally coincided but a disjuncture emerged in the 1950s during the so-called 'partnership' era under Prime Minister Garfield Todd [1953–1958] and his successor Edgar Whitehead [1958–1962]. The post World War II boom in manufacturing, largely fuelled by international capital, and the corresponding rise of African nationalism created an interest amongst liberal-minded industrial classes to promote a productive black agrarian bourgeoisie and a skilled, less migrant-prone urban workforce. A golden opportunity surfaced to strengthen the national market and the agricultural sector as a whole but such a venture, at the bare minimum, depended on repeal of the Land Apportionment Act—an issue that Whitehead fought the 1962 election on and lost. The white farming community and labour aristocracy were not prepared to court the competition of an African middle class and thus voted for the reactionary Rhodesian Front.

Ian Smith's subsequent Unilateral Declaration of Independence [UDI] in 1965 and comprehensive resort to state economic controls managed impressively to harness foreign capital to serve national development goals but only for a while. He opted to work within the skewed class structure and market, which continued to pose chronic limits on balanced development. In a paradox, as much as settler nationalism was an economic strength, it was a weakness. As access to productive resources continued to accord to race, African oppression remained a concomitant of development, which ultimately courted war. Yet the challenge of overcoming the economy's deformed structural base lay less in a victory over racist ideology as it did over the ruling class structure based on land segregation and the interests of dominant capital. Such comprised the key elements of Rhodesia's development and underdevelopment.

1.1 Primitive Accumulation 1890–1930

Once the Rudd concession to mine Mashonaland had been deceitfully obtained off the Ndebele king, Lobengula, Cecil Rhodes founded the British South Africa Company [BSAC], which received a Royal Charter to colonise Zimbabwe. The BSAC's Pioneer Column entered the country in 1890 and met little resistance forging the *colonial belt*.[3] The Shona, the colonists said, wanted their protection from the Ndebele raiding parties from the southwest. The African population was estimated at 530,000 and the land they cultivated at about 500,000 acres out of a total land area of near 100 million acres [Government of Southern Rhodesia, 1955:1]. The BSAC claimed the Rudd concession and the purchase of the land concession in 1891 from the German, Edward Lippert, gave it the legal right to *sell* away African land once surveyed.[4] Later, a Judicial Committee in 1918 concluded candidly that the land belonged to the Crown through 'right of conquest'.

'The fuelling of Rhodes's adventures' was one of the 'last great speculative splurges' of the nineteenth century [Bond, P., 1998:44]. The BSAC's overestimation of the country's gold reserves precipitated a boom on the London money market in speculative land and mining capital. Contrary to expectations, however, there was no 'second rand': the alluvial deposits had been mined by the Africans and remaining deposits were scattered and of low quality. Well before the speculative bubble finally burst in April 1903, Rhodes knew that unless the 'subordination of production to speculation ceased', to use Giovanni Arrighi's words [1973a:184], the colony would collapse and the BSAC's huge investment in rail unrecovered. In the long run, export-oriented settler agriculture would have to be promoted while the mining industry needed to maximise output and minimise costs, particularly African wages. In the short run, Rhodes and the BSAC decided to ransack the Ndebele economy to increase access to land and labour.

Lobengula provided the pretext in 1893 when a Ndebele raiding party at Fort Victoria disturbed Mashona labourers. Starr Jameson, the BSAC administrator, said to Rhodes:

> The serious part is that every native has deserted from the mines and farms ... There is no danger to whites but unless some shooting is done, I think it will be difficult to get labour ... [cited in Ranger, T., 1985:93].

In the ensuing 1893–1994 *War of Dispossession*, a BSAC force of 1,135 white troops killed 1,000 Ndebele troops, pursued Lobengula to his death, plundered some 90,000 cattle and were awarded 6,000 acres and 20 gold claims each for their efforts [Martin, D., and Johnson, P., 1981:45-46; Phimister, I., 1988:9-10]. The BSAC's subsequent land commission created the first African reserves at Gwai and Shangani where the Ndebele were relocated [Rifkind, M.L., 1972:53].

The BSAC administration then resorted to taxing the African economy, which all households, rich or poor alike, had to pay either in cash, kind or labour.[5] Africans were to pay for their own brutal colonisation that entailed land encroachments, livestock seizures, forced labour and violent native police. In March 1896, propelled by ancestral anger believed to be expressed in drought and rinderpest and locusts plagues, the Ndebele rebelled followed by the Shona in June. The uprising dragged on until October 1897, killed 10% of the white population and threatened the collapse of the BSAC administration. At the behest of Rhodes, the Ndebele surrendered while most Shona leaders were killed or executed [Rasmussen, R.K., and Rubert, S.C., 1990:299].[6] On the basis of an 1897 British Government report, authored by Sir Richard Martin, the land assigned to African reserves expanded and reached 20% of the total land area in 1902 [about 20 million acres] while the remaining 80% was open to purchase by any race [Rifkind, M.L., 1972:53].

According to Kingsley Garbett [1966:116], from thereon the 'traditional political system ceased to exist' and African chieftainship was reinvented. Before colonisation, 'power rather than entitlement' had been the key to chiefship: prime land, warriors, wives, cattle and slaves, especially female, were the key determinants of wealth [Ranger, T.O., 1993:356; Schmidt, E., 1996:33-35]. Once conquered, these powers of chiefs became virtually defunct as people moved freely about the reserves, unassigned land or stayed on ancestral lands in exchange for rent or labour services to the new European owners. Most sought to develop the peasant option, that is, the production and sale of crops to the mining compounds and towns in order to pay tax and buy consumer items. While some chiefdoms remained intact, the Administration split others up and elevated kraalheads as chiefs [Garbett, G.K., 1966:117]. A 'bogus traditionalism' evolved to use Terence Ranger's phrase [1993:382], or an 'ideology of communal tenure' to borrow Angela Cheater's [1990], that chiefs held land in trust for everyone and promoted equality. This was contrary historical truth and in reality, chiefs and headman had become appendages of state colonial policy in the reserves.

The resilience of African farmers frustrated the endeavours of white capitalist agriculture to gain a foothold in the domestic market as a necessary financial precondition for export production. Again in the words of Giovanni Arrighi [1973a:193]:

> ... the expansion of the mining industry and of tertiary activities without a comparable development of capitalist agriculture generated a demand for, and tended to raise the price of, African produce, and this discouraged African participation in the labour market at the wage rate fixed by 'the tradition of the subsistence wage'.

Whether on land claimed by Europeans, unassigned or within the reserves, a productive African peasantry produced 90% of the country's total marketed output in 1904 [Phimister, I., 1988: 68]. The backbone of peasant resistance was the work of African women upon whom the patriarchal relations of production were based [Schmidt, E., 1996:3]. Households quickly moved into the cash crops demanded by European markets such as maize, groundnuts and sunflower and many managed to invest in cattle and ploughs.[7]

An economic war of survival ensued, wherein the colonial administration sought to crush the African agrarian economy. Forced labour [foreign and local], tax, settler immigration and ongoing land dispossession comprised the major weapons. The fine tuning of *chibaro* by the Rhodesian Native Labour Board, set up in 1903, covered the labour shortage from the poorer peasantries of Mozambique, Northern Rhodesia and Nyasaland [Arrighi, G, 1973a:198; van Onselen, C, 1976:101, 123].[8] The announcement by the BSAC directors in 1907 of the 'white agricultural policy' in response to disappointing gold production officially marked a phase of collusion in international and domestic capital to generate a capitalist agricultural export surplus. The rapid rise of white immigrants, their desire to oppress Africans at all costs and the economies of scale acquired eventually spelt the end of vibrant peasant agriculture. The administration offered settler farmers loans to purchase land, free extension services, subsidised fertiliser and stock as well as marketing infrastructure.[9]

From an estimated number of 1,500 in 1891, white immigrants flowed into Rhodesia and totalled 11,000 in 1901, 23,600 in 1911, 33,600 in 1921 and 49,900 by 1931 [Rasmussen, R.K., and Rubert, S.C., 1990:93]. The number of white farmers spiraled from 300–400 in 1904 to 1,324 in 1911, and to 2,040 in 1914 [Phimister, I., 1988: 60]. The vast majority of settlers were English-speaking from South Africa and Britain and mostly single men of working class and lower middle class origin. 'Short on capital, education, and skills', to quote Elizabeth Schmidt [1996:9], they perceived their aspirations for improved status and wealth to be 'deeply threatened by the prospects of African competition, whether as independent agricultural producers or as skilled artisans and clerks'. In the global arena, despite being nursed by international capital, rural and urban whites displayed an economic nationalism and class solidarity from the outset. They saw themselves as 'battlers' against the shareholders of London and sought self-government, which they attained through a restricted franchise in 1923.

By 1910 the external and internal effects of settler agriculture began to be felt: 90,000 kilos of tobacco were exported that year [Cole, D.L., and Cole, J.S., 1994:234] and for the first time settler farmers comprehensively undercut African maize prices by almost 50% [Schmidt, E, 1996:66]. The heavy tax burden upon African farmers began to significantly bite [Arrighi, G., 1973a:197].[10] As cheap foreign labour flowed into the colony, white farmers grew more aggressive and intensified evictions of African tenant farmers. The proportion of the African population residing in the reserves increased from 54% in 1909 to 59% in 1914 to 64% in 1922 [Arrighi, G., 1973a:202]. Most white farmers began to seek a fundamental structural division: to put the native farmer 'so far away from railways and markets that the white trader will not be able to buy from him and compete with the white farmers'

[District Official cited in Phimister, I., 1988:65]. The Native Reserves Commission of 1914 adhered to these demands and by 1920 the favourably located and best quality land in the reserves, amounting to one million acres, was removed [Schmidt, E., 1996:69].[11]

In addition to finance[12] and later manufacturing, multinational corporations also became big investors in Rhodesian agriculture and mining. The two biggest conglomerations, the London and Rhodesia Mining and Land Company [Lonrho] and Anglo-American Corporation [AAC] were founded in 1909 and after World War I respectively. AAC became linked with three other corporations, 'united by interlocking holdings and directorships', namely, the BSAC, De Beers and Tanganyika Concessions [Arrighi, G., 1973b:355]. Other British–South African multinationals soon followed and all became major landowners in Rhodesia involved in ranching, tobacco, sugar, forestry and citrus. The Imperial Cold Storage and Supply Company, Liebigs Ltd, Lonrho and Triangle Ltd, for instance, acquired over one million acres of ranching land each and over 60,000 head of cattle [Tandon, Y., 1990:83]. Triangle Ltd also bought vast estates in the southeast and founded the sugar industry while AAC purchased the citrus, and later, sugar estates of Mazowe and the Hippo Valley respectively.

The BSAC leased out many of the small and scattered mines, which enabled settler capital to acquire about a 50% share in the country's gold production [Stoneman, C., 1978:64]. This was the one exception to the general preserve of multinational capital in the mining industry. Between them Lonrho and Anglo-American asserted dominance over copper, coal and later nickel and remained heavily involved in iron and chrome [Rasmussen, R.K., and Rubert, S.C., 1990:22]. Later, the British multinational, Rio Tinto, invested in gold, copper and nickel while American capital through Union Carbide and Foote Minerals also acquired stakes in the mining industry, particularly chrome. Turner and Newall, another British firm, came to dominate Rhodesia's long-fibred asbestos industry. Rhodesia offered up to 50 kinds of minerals for commercial production, platinum, silver, mica, lithium and gemstones among them.

The external stimulant of World War I arrested the downward pressure on crop prices, which prolonged the viability of peasant agriculture but also boosted that of the capitalist sector, particularly through maize and beef exports. The post-war slump in maize and beef prices by over 50% between 1920 and 1923 is identified by Giovanni Arrighi [1973a:207] as the turning point from which peasant agriculture never recovered. The tax burden became unpayable and migration to the reserves accelerated while the reverse flow of labour to the towns caused wages to fall below 1904 levels. In the reserves, an environmental crisis preceded the demographic as declining yields became the general rule brought on by extensive plough cultivation and the movement of peoples into less fertile areas. The consequent surfacing of a land shortage, over-stocking and soil erosion prompted the state in 1926 to appoint the ex-missionary E.D. Alvord as Agriculturalist for Natives in the Native Affairs Department [NAD] [Kramer, E., 1998:85].

Table 1.0 *The Land Apportionment Act 1930*

Category	Acres	Hectares
European Areas	49,149,174	19.9 million
Native Reserves	21,600,000	8.7 million
Native Purchase Areas	7,464,566	3.0 million
Forest Area	590,500	240,000
Unassigned Area	17,793,300	7.2 million
Undetermined Area	88,540	36,000
Total	96,686,080	39.1 million

Source: Rukuni, M., 1994:18.

To cut off the minute potential for a competing African agrarian bourgeoisie, the settler state passed the Land Apportionment Act of 1930, which ended the non-racial land market outside the reserves.[13] The Act officially cemented the structural determinants of African poverty, that is, the environmental and demographic constraints, which until the present have crippled indigenous agrarian and small-scale industrial development. In total, as Table 1.0 shows, African land comprised about 11.7 million hectares of which 8.7 million belonged to the reserves under customary or communal tenure and the remaining 3.0 million to Native Purchase Areas under freehold tenure. By contrast, Europeans—about 5% of the population—gained access to half the country, about 19 million hectares.

Settler colonists and multinational companies enclosed the prime cropping land and vast tracts of ranching land while three quarters of land assigned to Africans was relatively remote, drought-prone and subject to food deficits. A high prevalence of poverty was assured but the depth would vary depending on geographic location and varying degrees of population pressure, environmental decay, wage employment opportunity and community land inequality. Given rain dependency, location in relation to Natural Region [NR] [Appendix 3 and Map 1] wielded an immediate impact on production and wellbeing. Within the locale, community and livestock population relative to total land available would have a decisive bearing—while within the family, the number of dependents relative to the arable holding allocated and employed wage earners would be crucial.

Sir Morris Carter, the chairman of the 1925 Land Commission responsible for land apportionment, concluded:

> However desirable it may be that members of the two races should live together side by side with equal rights as regards the holding of land, we are convinced that in practice, probably for generations to come, such a policy is not practicable or in the best interests of the two races, and that until the Native has advanced very much further on the path of civilisation, it is better that the points of contact in this respect between the two races should be reduced ... [Carter, M, 1925 cited in Rifkind, M.L.,1972:54].

In reality, contrary to apartheid visions, the fortunes of the African and European sectors were intrinsically interlinked. Labour migration had already replaced peasant agriculture as the economic basis of rural life [Moyo, S., Moyo, N.P. and Lowenson, R., 1985:29]. By 1932 African income derived from agriculture accounted for less than 20% of the total compared to 70% in 1903 [Arrighi, G., 1973a:206-207]. Ian Phimister [1988:141-142] records that the number of African men engaged in some form of wage labour had doubled in a decade from about 20% in 1922 to 46.4% in 1932. 'By 1933', Charles van Onselen concludes [1976:119], 'Rhodesian employers were being so well served by 'market forces' that the Rhodesian Native Labour Board was disbanded'. Primitive accumulators, as John Iliffe writes [1987:277], 'turned the world upside down' from the pre-colonial one where land was abundant and labour scarce to one where labour was abundant and land and work were scarce.

1.2 The 'Two Pyramids' 1930–1953

The collapse of world markets during the Great Depression caused a fall in Rhodesia's export revenue by 50% between 1929 and 1931. Cattle export earnings declined from £340,000 in 1930 to £49,000 in 1931 while a similar trend applied to maize and mining exports. The slump in tobacco prices from 1928 drove out three-quarters of growers. The land market crashed, rail revenue declined by half and agricultural production fell by 30% across the board [All data cited in Bond, P., 1998:50-51]. The agrarian bourgeoisie demanded state intervention to regulate crop prices and to break the monopoly of international capital over marketing, particularly that of the United Tobacco Company. There were also calls for a national central bank to curtail the drain of financial surpluses through the two international banks, Standard and Barclays, to their London headquarters.[14]

No serious friction, however, emerged between domestic and international capital until after World War II when global capital regained ascendancy. During the Great Depression, as world trade and investment slowed, local capital accumulation based on import substitution became inevitable. Animosity towards foreign capital did not go beyond rhetoric, particularly as foreign interests were increasingly prominent in the recovery of gold exports.[15] When in opposition, for example, Godfrey Huggins denounced Prime Minister Moffat's refusal to rescind the BSAC's hold over mineral rights as non-Rhodesian but within a year after his electoral victory in 1933 purged his Government of autarchic elements [Rasmussen, R.K., and Rubert, S.C., 1990:129,211; Bond, P., 1998:61-62].[16] Huggins merged his Reform Party with Moffat's Rhodesian Party to form the United Party [subsequently United Federal Party] and won a renewed mandate in 1934. Over the next two decades, Huggins accommodated the interests of international finance and adopted the British currency board system in 1940, which did little to enhance state autonomy over the money supply and capital flows [Bond, P. 1998:53-54].[17]

Nevertheless, the experience of the Great Depression offered settler nationalists a context to revise the state's economic role to one of prioritising more the interests of local capital. Many felt that foreign investors could not be expected to provide the infrastructure to lead market demand and create investment opportunities. The anomaly of a racially based class structure, specifically, the all-white agrarian bourgeoisie, labour aristocracy and state bureaucracy, assured that the rise of a capitalist development state went hand in hand with African repression. To secure the future of white living standards, the state passed four legislative acts, namely, the Maize Control Act [1931], the Cattle Levy Act [1931], the Industrial Conciliation Act [1934] and the Native Registration Act [1936], which together with the Land Apportionment Act made up the 'two pyramids' framework. Although Moffat passed three of these, his Government bore the brunt of popular discontent in the 1933 election. Huggins promised to strengthen the framework.

After World War II, a disjuncture between international and domestic interests arose out of the contradictions of uneven development, which eventually culminated in Ian Smith's UDI. The paradox was that the import substitution strategy launched by the state lacked a strong internal dynamic because the African rural economy remained mired in poverty. The reliance on an external dynamic increased the country's exposure to international capital, which reasserted economic dominance after the war, particularly in the fast growing manufacturing sector. In turn, as the nationalism and militancy of black working classes grew, the manufacturing bourgeoisie sought to break the economic hold of the white agrarian and labour aristocracy. A competing black agrarian base and a more stabilised as well as skilled urban labour force would improve national conditions of supply and demand and counter the radicalisation of African nationalism. This then marked the beginnings of 'racial partnership', otherwise dubbed a *neo*-colonial solution, which threatened the racial privileges of settler society.

1.2.1 The 'Pyramids' Framework

The Maize Control Act [1931] established the predecessor of today's Grain Marketing Board [GMB], the Maize Control Board, which introduced a system of price subsidies to keep European maize production viable. Between 1929 and 1931 the export price of maize collapsed and though the local price was marginally higher both were below the European costs of production. White farmers feared that African farmers, who had the benefit of free family labour, would force them out of the local market. The Maize Control Board thus offered an artificially high local price, the profit of which white farmers reaped, while the vast majority of African farmers, being without transport, were left to the mercy of white middlemen [Schmidt, E., 1996:75]. Huggins's amendment in 1934 gave the Board monopoly control over all maize and allowed a two-tier price system. White farmers received prices 40% higher than world prices while African farmers and the largest white producers received minimal prices after the Board covered the losses [Rukuni, M., 1994:22].

In similar fashion, the Cattle Levy Act [1931], as amended in 1934, forced African cattle owners to pay a levy on the slaughter of all cattle for domestic consumption in order to subsidise the export stock drawn exclusively from white farms [Phimister, I., 1988:184-185]. The Native Registration Act [1936] aimed to tighten up the Pass Law by prohibiting African trade in European areas, which effectively reinforced African dependency on low mining and agricultural wages. While the marketing of crafts and trinkets was sometimes permitted, vegetables, chickens, eggs and other foodstuffs could only be sold in African locations [Arrighi, G., 1973b:347-348].

To further restore white agriculture and relieve white unemployment, the Huggins Government embarked upon major public works [roads and irrigation] and set up the Electrical Supply Commission in 1936. The state provided subsidised credit facilities and passed the Farmers Debt Adjustment Act [1935].[18] The Tobacco Marketing Board was created in 1936 to enhance the collective bargaining power of growers although international monopoly buyers continued to predominate [Arrighi, G., 1973b:345]. The Dairy Marketing Board [1931] was established under Moffat while the Cotton Marketing Board [1936], the Cold Storage Commission [1937] and the Pig Industry Board [1937] were all created under Huggins. The function of all these parastatals, otherwise referred to as State-owned Enterprises [SOEs], was to regulate and secure white farm income through price subsidies and controls over supply.

The Industrial Conciliation Act [1934], as amended in 1937, by not recognising Africans as 'employees' and prohibiting wage fixing below white rates, effectively debarred Africans from Trade Union activity as well as entering into skilled employment. This act entrenched the white labour aristocracy and the highly inequitable wage structure, which constrained the country's economic development. Africans working in towns could hardly afford the cost of rent let alone buy a house. Low African purchasing power debilitated black housing development, which had lasting repercussions on urban poverty.

Unless white farmers required the labour, evictions of African sharecroppers on white farms intensified, which amounted to about 100,000 between 1931 and 1945 [Arrighi, G., 1973a:212; Martin, D., and Johnson, P., 1981:53-54]. In recognition of the need to increase the carrying capacity of the Reserves, Mr Alvord started the centralisation scheme in July 1929, which aimed to replace the extensive system of shifting cultivation with intensive settled agriculture. Through enlisting the support of traditional authorities, arable and grazing areas were to be separated by a road and a line of village huts. Africans were very suspicious of the state's motives: many thought the line of huts made taxation easier and increased yields off a smaller land area would justify future land deprivation [Kramer, E., 1998:91]. By the mid-1930s, despite evidence of fatter cattle in some areas, with only one-fortieth of the budget spent on white agriculture at his disposal [Arrighi, G., 1973a:211], Alvord's scheme had little impact. By 1936 only 590,075 acres out of near 22 million had been centralised [Kramer, E., 1998:98].

In fact, increasing population pressure and African resistance guaranteed failure. The centralisation scheme assumed the average African small holder to be commercially oriented when state repression assured most were not. Male labour migration and a subsistence orientation, based on extensive farming [abetted by the plough and maize[19]] and the exploitation of female and child labour, was the norm among households. Without fertiliser, marketing infrastructure, irrigation and other services required for settled intensive agriculture, centralisation threatened to reduce and fragment the family land holding and, therefore, the basis of subsistence. State policy contradicted itself: the two pyramids framework by marginalising African development only reinforced an unsustainable reliance on extensive cultivation and the patriarchal family mode of production. Environmental and demographic crisis got worse: between 1930 and 1945 while the reserve land area remained fixed the African population increased by 40% and overstocking reached margins of 45% [Dunlop, H., 1972:2; Government of Southern Rhodesia, 1955:2].[20]

The failure of the state and traditional authorities generally to secure the future sustainability of the commons deterred agricultural investment in the reserves. The greater incentive for most was to get out of the reserves and buy land in the Native Purchase Areas. Not many managed to do so: only 9,000 by the 1960s according to William Duggan [1980:235]. For the rest, investment in education took priority over agriculture: enrolments at mission primary schools rose from 87,000 in 1936 to 117,000 in 1943 to almost 180,000 in 1947 [Arrighi, G., 1973a:211]. Clearly, many households regarded education and acquired employment opportunity to be their main escape route out of poverty.

Under the state's import substitution strategy food processing and beverages, leather products, construction materials, household consumer goods, rail and associated subsidiaries had emerged as the main manufacturing industries. In 1938, there were 299 registered manufacturing enterprises employing 17,500 people with a net output worth £2 million [Handford, J., 1976:130]. The overall bias of the economy towards mineral and agricultural exports remained dominant. Most manufacturing industries were oriented to the local market, which meant that African agricultural stagnation posed severe constraints on expansion. Any rural–urban growth dynamic was confined to an economic base mainly geared to a small white population of 55,000 in 1936 [Handford, J., 1976:66], about 3,000 of whom were farmers [Rukuni, M., 1994:19], and the limited buying power of 254,000 Africans formally employed [Arrighi, G., 1973b:351; Handford, J., 1976:66]. Over 60% of the latter were employed in white agriculture and domestic service and received paltry wages [Handford, J., 1976:66].

1.2.2 Industrial Take-Off

The Second World War provided the necessary external stimulants—trade and white immigration—that lifted the economy out of the rut. Rhodesia supplied air bases for British forces during the war while the scarcity of imports boosted demand for local materials [chrome, asbestos and cotton] [Arrighi, G., 1973b:350]. The world shortage of foodstuffs provided a ready export market for white agriculture and immigrants flowed in: the white population rose from 69,000 in 1941 to 82,400 by 1946 [Rasmussen, R.K., and Rubert, S.C., 1990:93]. The state launched major investments: both the Rhodesian Iron and Steel Company [RISCO], based at Que Que [Kwe Kwe], and the first cotton and wool textile plants, based at Gatooma [Kadoma], were established during the war. The advent of these strategic industries deepened linkages between agriculture, manufacturing and mining, which generated investment opportunities in food and agro-processing, household goods, clothing, metallurgy, transport, building and so forth. Total African wage employment shot up to 377,000 by 1946 [Arrighi, G., 1973b:351] and manufacturing employment more than doubled.

The same external stimulants continued after the war. The worldwide shortage of American dollars stimulated demand within the British Empire for the Rhodesian exports of tobacco, gold, chrome, asbestos, beef and sugar. The signing of the 1948 and 1949 Customs and Trade Agreement with South Africa provided a significant boost to textile exports [Handford, J., 1976:13; Bond, P., 1998:67]. The prospect of an attractive suburban lifestyle lured many immigrants, mainly from Britain, and the white population increased to 136,000 by 1951 [Rasmussen, R.K., and Rubert, S.C., 1990:93]. By then, two-thirds of the white population lived in towns and over half in Salisbury and Bulawayo [Godwin, P., and Hancock, I., 1993:20]. Although most of the real wealth was generated outside the towns, in mining and agriculture, most Rhodesians were employed in industry, commerce and the service sector [Beach, D., 1994:174].

Foreign capital also poured in—enticed by the developments in national infrastructure, a liberal tax regime on profit repatriation and spooked to an extent by the 1948 Afrikaner nationalist victory in South Africa. In fact, Rhodesia became the main destination for foreign capital in the region. From a total of £13.5 million in 1947, foreign direct investment rose to £50.7 million in 1951 [Arrighi, G., 1973b:351]. Between 1946 and 1954 two-thirds of a national investment total worth £300 million stemmed from foreign sources [Astrow, A, 1983:8; Bond, P., 1998:73].

Over the same period, total public or state debt increased from £27 million to £137 million, which was divided almost equally between foreign and local sources [Handford, J., 1976:41]. The London bond market was the main credit source but multilateral lenders, such as the World Bank, the US Export-Import Bank and the Commonwealth Development Corporation, increased in importance. Projects included the expansion of rail, iron and steel, electricity and the establishment of Central African Airways and the Posts and Telecommunications Corporation [PTC]. The construction of Kariba dam, which the World Bank underwrote, usurped the bulk of the state's loans during the 1950s.[21]

Between 1945 and 1955 real GDP growth averaged 10%, mainly propelled by commercial agriculture followed by manufacturing. The number of white farms almost doubled from 3,669 in 1945 to a peak of 6,255 in 1955 [Rukuni, M., 1994:19]. Most invested in tobacco, which tripled in output, quadrupled in value and became the country's number one export—accounting for about half of export revenue—and the biggest employer of African labour [Astrow, A., 1983:8; Bond, P., 1998:68-69; Rasmussen, R.K., and Rubert, S.C., 1990:359]. Manufacturing averaged 24.4% annual growth over 1944–1948 and by 1955 output had undergone a tenfold rise and the sector became the third largest employer after white agriculture and domestic service [Phimister, I., 1988:254; Duggan, W.R., 1980:233].[22] RISCO received lucrative orders from Japan and America and by 1960 Rhodesia assembled its first car [Handford, J., 1976:132]. Labour unrest, however, was the order of the day as urban living conditions for Africans were unsanitary and minimum wages were generally below the poverty line [Sibanda, M.J.,1989:44-45].

The manufacturing sector's share of GDP rose from 9% in the late 1930s to 15% by the early 1950s while the share of mining fell from 25% to 10% [Arrighi, G., 1973b:352-354]. The trend reflected increased competition from the Zambian Copperbelt and South Africa, falling gold prices, increased mechanisation and reduced employment.[23] The overall output of the mining industry expanded though and the sector retained its key export status [asbestos, gold, chrome, nickel, copper] [Astrow, A., 1983:8].

The Rhodesian economy became the 'preserve of international capital' [Phimister, I., 1988:222]. In all three sectors of mining, agriculture and manufacturing two-thirds of total net operating profits accrued to multinationals [Arrighi,G., 1973b:353, 357; Clarke, D.G., 1980:31]. Once mining had been saturated, foreign capital expanded agricultural operations and diversified into manufacturing and came to dominate both. In manufacturing, only 9% of firms, mainly the British–South African multinationals already mentioned, accounted for 67.8% of the gross value of manufacturing output [Arrighi, G., 1973b:353]. Similarly, in agriculture, 75% of total corporate profits and 61% of gross capital formation accrued mostly to the same companies [Duggan, W.R., 1980:238]. According to Ian Phimister [1988:298], 'the wave of mergers and takeovers of local firms by international companies placed an important section of the domestic bourgeoisie in intimate alliance with foreign capital'.

1.2.3 The Contradictions of Uneven Development

Skewed racial wealth distribution imposed chronic limitations on economic development, which eventually caused a conflict of interests between domestic rural capital and foreign industrial capital. The focus of white farmers away from domestic to external markets, evident in the shift from maize to tobacco, encouraged an indifference for balanced internal development and, therefore, a bias towards uneven development. In fact, the white agrarian class along with the labour aristocracy had a vested interest in maintaining cheap African labour supplies, eliminating black competition and thus cutting down the national market. As the number of white farmers increased over the post-war years, for example, another 85,000 African tenant farmers were evicted from white farms and relegated to bare subsistence [Arrighi, G., 1973a:352; Martin, D., and Johnson, P., 1981:53-54]. The Government added four million acres to the African land area under the category Special Native Areas but most of it was already occupied [Dunlop, H., 1972:3, footnote 38; Bhebe, N., 1989:56].

At the same time, white agriculture failed to meet the total input requirements of manufacturing or the food needs of the country generally [Duggan, W.R., 1980:233; Shopo, T.D., 1986:226-227].[24] In regard to maize, for example, between 1949 and 1953 African and white farmers on average produced 37% and 41% of national requirements respectively while 22% had to be imported [Government of Rhodesia, 1955:12]. While the Government managed to maintain a relatively cheap food policy, via price subsidies, it recognised the absurdity of an agricultural economy having to import food. Further, the monopoly of white labour over skilled employment enforced high wages and the high turnover of African migrant labour also proved costly. While food and other input shortages fostered an interest within the manufacturing sector for a viable African agriculture, 'mass production and the high capital intensity of operations' created an interest in a more skilled, less expensive and stable African industrial workforce without 'tentacles' in the soil [Arrighi, G, 1973[b]:358; Dunlop, H., 1972:3].

By the early 1950s, for want of purchasing power and infrastructure, capital lacked productive investment outlets beyond the colonial belt or the main highway of towns forged by the Pioneer Column. The formation of the Central African Federation in 1953 relieved financial saturation somewhat but being a highly tenuous arrangement failed to avert a serious recession in the late 1950s. In fact, from the outset, the Federation was built upon sand, as Southern Rhodesia had no authority over constitutional negotiations between Britain and the African nationalists of Northern Rhodesia [Zambia] and Nyasaland [Malawi].[25] From an industrialist's point of view, the undeniable imperative was to break the class alliance between white farmers and the labour aristocracy to enable a more efficient agricultural sector, access to a broader pool of skilled labour and an enlarged national market. The successful nationwide strike led by the African Trade Unions in 1948 made the case more urgent.

The Native Land Husbandry Act of 1951, formulated under Huggins, comprised the attempt to resolve the country's development question. On paper the Act confronted the challenge to open up a 'huge market for agricultural and household requisites ... to the great benefit of trade and industry generally' [Government of Southern Rhodesia, 1955:13]. The stated aims were to stabilise the African workforce in the towns through wage increases and double the cash income of African agriculture through a 50% increase in output.

The Rhodesian state now faced a profound dilemma. At the very least, broad-based development required ending racial privileges but the Government could not easily do so without risking electoral defeat. Thus instead of confronting the primary cause of economic stagnation—the class structure based on race and land segregation—the Native Land Husbandry Act attacked secondary elements—African labour migration and customary land tenure—over which the state could more easily exercise power. The chief evils identified were the 'deadweight of the communal system of land occupation' and 'the large mass of migrant workers'. The former, the Government complained, instilled no individual interest in the conservation of public resources while the latter 'turn to illicit unions' and 'dabble' in some paid occupation and reserve agriculture tending 'to be grossly inefficient at both' [Government of Southern Rhodesia, 1955:2,4,14].

Under the Native Land Husbandry Act, the era of partnership would entail a direct state assault on the very method of straddling town and country Africans relied on as a way of coping with land segregation and low urban wages. As a result, African nationalism, in the words of George Nyandoro, the leader of the African National Congress, 'received the best recruiter ... ever' [cited in Bhebe, N., 1989:58]. Through the Trade Unions initially and then the mass nationalist parties, African leaders were able to capture the interests of migrant worker and peasant in a single agenda.

1.3 The Partnership Era 1953–1962

One of Rhodesia's most progressive leaders, Sir Garfield Todd, drew his support for partnership from urban-based and liberal-minded industrial and professional groups. Todd envisaged a thriving non-racial agrarian and industrial capitalism. 'We do not want native peasants', he said. If 100,000 families were absorbed in industry 'we can begin to cope with what is left ... and give each family 150 or 200 acres on a 99 year lease' [Todd, G., cited in Arrighi, G., 1973b:362]. Without major reform to the structures of property and wealth, however, through broad-based and state-managed land redistribution, Todd could only dream. In reality, drawing on British policy in Kenya, 'partnership' merely proposed a *neo*-colonial solution, that is, the removal of racial barriers in a bid to obtain the allegiance of an African middle class. Although comprising no fundamental threat to the existing economic order, many settlers perceived the agenda internationally driven, which would inevitably hand power to the African nationalists at the expense of their status and privilege.

'Partnership' ended up a casualty of the distorted production and wealth base, which lurched toward comprehensive crisis in the 1950s. On the one hand, within the constraints of land segregation, the Native Land Husbandry Act threatened to make landless over 100,000 families in order to make way for a black rural bourgeoisie while on the other, an economic recession destroyed the prospect of absorbing these people in industry. As African nationalism gathered momentum, Todd and his successor, Whitehead, sought to broaden the franchise, the provision of African education and then, finally, to repeal the Land Apportionment Act. Meanwhile, the forerunner to the Rhodesian Front, the Dominion Party—formed in 1956 as a right-wing breakaway from the United Federal Party—campaigned on a nationalist platform, the central themes being the primacy of settler interests over foreign and African repression. In broad terms, settler and international interests collided over the prospect of a *neo*-colonial solution, which saw the Rhodesian Front claim victory in the 1962 election.

1.3.1 The Native Land Husbandry Act

The key rationale of the Native Land Husbandry Act, to recall, was to enlarge the national market through the establishment of a black agrarian bourgeoisie and a stabilised and skilled urban workforce. The Government assumed that in rural areas an expanded production and income base would follow the allocation of land to permanent farmers while in urban areas, higher wages would automatically flow from improved labour productivity and the reduced influx of labour from the reserves. As to the mechanics of implementation, the Act effectively sought to 'freeze the numbers of people inside and outside the reserves' by forcing town workers to decide to which class they belonged—the urban proletariat or the agrarian bourgeoisie [Duggan, W.R., 1980:229]. Within the constraints of land and racial segregation, however, such a feat of social engineering could not be achieved without undermining African livelihood generally. Opposition united town and country, which caused the Act to collapse from the beginning.

In rural areas, the land allocation powers of traditional authorities, chiefs and headmen, were to be stripped and invested in

Native Commissioners. Rural families considered permanent cultivators were to be allocated a 'standard area' of land over which the head of the household would receive tenurial rights. Table 1.1 shows the recommended standard area according to an average family of two parents and three children. The land holding allocated was supposed to be large enough to support a marketable surplus in stock and crops and the size varied according to local rainfall and number of family members. Polygamous husbands, for instance, were entitled to an extra third of the standard area for each additional wife. Single men over age 21 were entitled to a standard area while single women were not. In fact, women generally received a raw deal: widows, divorcees, deserted mothers, providing they had dependants, were entitled to only one-third of the standard area [Gaidzanwa, R., 1988:6].

Table 1.1 *Standard Family Holdings Recommended by the Native Land Husbandry Act*

Rainfall Zone [inches]	Livestock Holding [number of cattle]	Arable Holding	Acres Required Per Family
28+	6	8	70
24-28	6	8	80
20-24	10	13	160
16-20	15	14	390
-16	20	15	620

Source: Government of Southern Rhodesia, 1955.

Those with livestock above the number prescribed for their area would be forced to de-stock. Households with a land holding larger than the standard area were to be brought down to equal the standard area while households below were to be brought up. Titles to the standard area could be sold but not subdivided or attached to debt. No person could own more than three times the standard area. To enforce conservation, the state imposed penalties including fines and convictions. 'All have rights to reside', the *New Rhodesia* asserted [17, 959, 08/12/50], 'but a right to destroy the land is withdrawn'. All titleholders were considered responsible for sound farming practice, such as crop rotations and anti-erosion measures to protect vleis, springs, sponges, marshes and stream banks.

In terms of having an impact on the national economy, all came to naught within the constraint of land and racial segregation. In rural areas, to quote M. Rifkind [1972:59] 'it was no use for Government officials to stress that the scarcity of land required de-stocking. The Africans merely pointed to millions of acres of unused European land'. Nonetheless, according to Ngwabi Bhebe [1989:56-57], in Matabeleland South people were forced to dispose of 21,538 head of cattle; in Masvingo 13,645 head; and in Manicaland 15,259 head. Meanwhile, the absence of secure urban land rights and the lack of affordable housing contradicted the major thrust to create a stable workforce. The Government's own inquiry into urban affairs, conducted by R.P. Plewman in 1958, for example, condemned the continued tendency to treat the towns as a European preserve and recommended the immediate application of black freehold tenure, non-racial industrial centres and African representation on town councils [cited in Rifkind, M.L., 1972:58].

The Government's Quinton Report of 1960 on the 'resettlement of natives', however, dealt the most telling blow. If each of the 346,261 families entitled to land rights were to be allocated a standard area, the report revealed, only 235,000 could be catered for within the African land area [i.e. native reserves, special native areas and purchase areas] [Quinton Report cited in Dunlop, H., 1972:5]. The remaining 111,261 families would effectively be made landless without rights in the towns or the country. All along, therefore, the Government had to ignore the conditions of its own Act. The size of the recommended standard areas were reduced, sometimes below subsistence requirements, overstocking and cultivation in grazing areas had to be tolerated and the provision of private grazing land dropped altogether [Dunlop, H, 1972:7; Duggan, W.R., 1980:233, Bhebe, N, 1989:56]. The Quinton Report concluded the obvious:

> Your Committee does not believe that the [Land Apportionment] Act can, or should, in the best interests of the country, remain in force for much longer ... land in general, whether urban or agricultural, should be purchasable by anyone irrespective of race or colour ... [Quinton Report, 1960, as cited in Rifkind, M.L., 1972:60].

The Government narrowed its focus on elite reserve and purchase area farmers to develop the native middle class. In the case of the latter, as land could be put up as collateral, credit was seen as the means to incorporate these farmers in the mainstream economy. Both state and private credit facilities were established.[26] Yet without countering the disparities in marketing and production infrastructure as well as pricing and interest rates, 'the infusion of credit', writes Patrick Bond [1998:103-104], 'would neither raise the competitive standing of black farmers in relation to whites, nor achieve sustainability [in the form of regular repayments] on its own terms'. By 1964, 10,000 credit recipients in the purchase and reserve areas were in arrears and £500,000 remained outstanding in unpaid loans.

Opposition to the Native Land Husbandry Act crossed the full spectrum of African society: traditional authorities [i.e. chiefs, headmen, kraalheads], women and migrant labourers, whose land rights were directly threatened, were all openly hostile. The discontent notwithstanding, the World Bank forwarded a £2 million loan in support of the Act in 1960 and serious riots broke out in subsequent years [Bond, P., 1998:74; World Bank web site, www.worldbank.org]. After altering land use patterns of more than 50% of the reserve land area without conceivable gain [Drinkwater, M., 1989:288; Brand, C, 1994:54], the Act was finally suspended by Rhodesian Front in 1962.

1.3.2 Economic Stagnation and the Failure of 'Partnership'

The economic crisis manifested as one of reversed financial flows, which 'turned against Southern Rhodesia in the form of interest, dividends, and profit repatriation' [Bond, P., 1998:74]. The problem reflected less the hold of foreign capital than the inability of the skewed class structure to generate enough productive investment outlets to retain it. Ascendant global capital had simply run its course in Rhodesia. Although manufacturing output rose by 88% over 1954–1961, the domestic consumer market expanded by only 70%. A Government economic inquiry concluded: 'the problems inhibiting the further expansion of manufacturing are deeply rooted in the small dimensions of the domestic market' [Advisory Committee, 1961, as cited in Bond, P., 1998:75]. Indeed, according to a 1959–1960 study on the black

African market, expenditure of employed Africans was preoccupied with the bare essentials only—on average 46% went on food alone [cited in Handford, J., 1976:161]. Inevitably, by the late 1950s, fixed capital investment sharply declined and capital outflow averaged 8.4% of GDP per year [Bond, P., 1998:74].

Apart from the nexus of saturated domestic markets and profit repatriation, not to forget the burden of foreign debt service, the trend of financial outflow also reflected a growing trade deficit strongly propelled by excessive luxury imports. Easy hire-purchase credit for whites was too readily available: out of a total white population of about 220,000 in 1960, for example, the number of court summonses for debtors rose from 11,700 in 1956 to 22,000 by 1959 [Bond, P., 1998:77]. In 1958, mainly through informal methods of 'persuasion' [Bond, P., 1998:70-73], banks were encouraged to crack down on loans including for personal and professional use. The country, however, found it easier to omit the import of strategic capital goods, according to Patrick Bond [1998:77] who quotes the May 1960 edition of *Property and Finance*, than ' ''motor cars or toilet preparations'' '. The Government remained disinclined to impose reserve and liquid asset requirements on the financial sector or resort to direct controls on exchange allocation and luxury imports, apparently for fear of alienating commercial banks but probably more so, the white electorate.[27]

Other than accentuating social unevenness, the economy was really going nowhere. The Government tried to encourage building societies, for instance, to invest in a housing scheme for urban blacks but demand remained chronically sluggish. White labour wielded a monopoly over the housing industry, which pushed costs way beyond majority purchasing power. Overcrowding remained the general rule in black urban areas and African workers naturally clung to rural ties. Meanwhile, excess liquidity flowed into property speculation, hire purchase and the construction of luxury apartments and offices in Salisbury's CBD [Bond, P., 1998:86-88, 101-102]. The exodus of capital got progressively worse: external payments peaked in 1964 at £25.9 million—'a figure exceeded by capital inflow in only six of all preceding years' [Stoneman, C., 1978:67].

In terms of breaking down the racial barriers, the partnership Governments could only tinker at the seams. A 1954 amendment to the Land Apportionment Act established a multiracial university and allowed African lawyers to have offices in the city. This first concession to the African elite provoked a storm of protest from white rural and labour interests, which no doubt contributed to the formation of the segregationist Dominion Party [Rifkind, M.L., 1972:57]. An amendment to the Industrial Conciliation Act proposed in 1954 sought to recognise African Trade Unions and apply to blacks the same wage setting machinery as that applied to whites. After a delay, the amendment was watered down in Parliament and dual standards continued to apply in the labour market [Arrighi, G., 1973[b]:362; Bhebe, N., 1989:62-63]. More successfully, the Todd Government undertook a sixfold increase in expenditure on African agriculture and doubled the student intake of African schools [Arrighi, G., 1973:360-361].[28]

Table 1.2 *Land Apportionment 1930–1962*

Land Apportionment	**1930**	**1950**	**1962**
		[million acres]	
Native Reserves	21.6	20.9	
Special Native Area		3.8	40.2
Native Purchase Areas	7.5	5.7	4.2
Total African	29.1	30.4	44.4
Unreserved Land		------	5.
European Land	49.2	48.0	36.9
Unassigned Land	17.8	17.5	------
Other [game reserves]	0.6	0.8	9.9
Total –All Land	96.7	96.7	96.7

Source: Dunlop, H., 1972:1.

As recognised by the Quinton Report, any semblance of national development required repeal of the Land Apportionment Act and the establishment of a non-racial land market. In 1961, a modestly reformist constitution—negotiated in London between the Whitehead Government and African leaders of the National Democratic Party—enlarged the African franchise and commenced a slow process of land desegregation. The reserves and special native areas were combined to form the Tribal Trust Lands and a category of unreserved land was created open to any race. These adjustments, as Table 1.2 shows, usurped all unassigned land, reduced European land by about 11 million acres and expanded African land to half the country.

In any case, the Rhodesian Front soon reversed the trend once elected in December 1962. Formed the previous March when the Dominion Party merged with other right-wing groups, the Rhodesian Front inherited a strong grassroots base mainly among the white farming community but also in urban areas where many whites feared blacks flooding towns and undermining living standards [Rasmussen, R.K., and Rubert, S.C., 1990:304]. 'Rhodesia First' comprised the winning campaign slogan, which effectively meant constitutional independence from Britain in order to uphold land apportionment and white supremacy.

In theory at least, a *neo*-colonial solution, which no doubt was in the wings under the United Federal Party, posed no real threat to the privileged position of whites and foreign capital. As long as an African government upheld existing property rights partnership between black and white would still be one of 'horse and rider' to quote Huggins [cited in Astrow, A., 1983:11]. The same point is made by both Arrighi [1973[a]:213] and van Onselen [1976:117]: once the era of white primitive accumulation was won, free market forces tended to entrench the prevailing structures of wealth distribution. In 1962, however, the Rhodesian Front and the white electorate trusted neither an African capitalist elite nor free market forces to secure the future of white interests. Logically, the African nationalist agenda had to entail a counter strategy of primitive accumulation to broaden the production base, ever more so in a stagnant free market economy that failed to deliver blacks an adequate 'trickle down' and decent living standard.

The Rhodesian Front thus opted to repress African nationalism and comprehensively regulate the operations of the free market. The former path met with the dead end of war but the latter gained the economy a new lease of life. Following the UDI in 1965, assisted by white immigration and ironically, international economic sanctions, Government willingness to trap capital inside the national economy and create investment opportunities found space for deeper import substitution, albeit based largely on the 'South African luxury goods model' [Bond, P., 1998:68]. The rift between foreign and settler capital over a non-racial capitalism proved neither permanent nor fatal. In fact, as discussed next, foreign investors adjusted well to a more endogenous development strategy, which characterised UDI.

Inevitably though, upon a deformed structural base of land and racial inequity, any economic strategy would fail in the long run to overcome the constraints of uneven development. By the late 1970s, the limits of the skewed market were again reached and capital, particularly foreign, sought a more outward orientation via the removal of sanctions. In any case, the more the war dragged on, the prospect of a radicalised African government loomed ever closer, which evoked more urgently the imperative of a non-racial capitalism to keep the structural base of the socioeconomic order more or less in tact.

2

The Skewed Fortune of the UDI Economy

At its core, the Unilateral Declaration of Independence [UDI] on 11 November 1965 was an assertion of settler autonomy over the country's destiny. The action put imperial powers, such as the UK and US, and African nationalist leaders in a subordinate position and postponed the sought after political solution of a black government upholding the status quo. Ian Smith accurately predicted the reaction of foreign capital to the UDI but underestimated that of the African nationalist movement. Despite the trade sanctions, multinationals accommodated the settler regime while the African nationalists took up arms to overthrow it. As the war intensified and African forces threatened to overhaul the class basis of settler society, a negotiated settlement to safeguard the interests of large-scale capitalism became increasingly vital. The UK and US courted the Patriotic Front leaders at the Lancaster House conference in 1979, which produced a constitution that effectively entrenched existing property rights.

The UDI and resulting trade sanctions boosted the Import Substitution Industrialisation [ISI] strategy adopted by the Rhodesian Government, which saw local manufactures explode from about 600 to 6,000 products [Mlambo, A.S., 1997:29; Bond, P., 1998:117]. Keynesian economic thought underlined the policy framework, which emerged from the Great Depression to dominate world development discourse [Polanyi, K., 1944:100]. The major weapons included state fiscal policy [taxation and expenditure] and regulation over interest and exchange rates, wages, prices, investment, capital and trade flows. According to John Waterbury [1999:324] ISI was a 'politician's dream' going hand in hand with authoritarianism The state had discretionary power to redistribute wealth and overrule parity to world market value, via price subsidies or trade controls, to protect and stimulate local enterprise. In fact, global market forces tended to be subordinate to the national economic interest, not the other way round as is the case today [Bienefeld, M., 1989:9-41].

Many Zimbabweans look back at the UDI years with envy—household goods were cheap, money had value and jobs were available. The benefits offered were really 'crumbs off the table' of white prosperity but vital to welfare nevertheless. At a fundamental level, broad-based growth was not really on offer in an economy where real development only revolved around a minority white community. After 1975, the economy went into decline constrained by wealth concentration, war, white emigration and widespread poverty. Of central importance to all these outcomes was the skewed agrarian base, which harboured gross inefficiencies among white commercial farmers, a generally pitiful wage regime and worsening environmental and demographic crisis for the rural peasantry. By the 1970s, Africans, that is, 95% of the country's population, paid only 0.6% of total income tax while African agriculture as a whole contributed barely 5% to the GDP [Handford, J., 1976:54,95: Astrow, A., 1983:65].

Clearly, the economy required comprehensive structural reform centred on land redistribution to enable an indigenous private sector to broaden the production and income base. Within the military wings of ZAPU and ZANU, that is, ZIPRA and ZANLA respectively, Marxist ideological schisms known as the March 11 Movement and the Zimbabwe Peoples Army [ZIPA] promised to avoid creating a Zimbabwe where white rulers were simply replaced by black privileged classes. The political leadership of the two main parties, namely, the Patriotic Front, absorbed the discourse of revolutionary socialism yet never allowed it to gain hegemony within the movement [Moore, D., 1991:495]. In reality, party leaders were prepared to compromise with the Anglo-American alliance, which accomplished political self-rule at Lancaster House but practically limited land reform to the redistribution of abandoned land only [Astrow, A., 1983:136].

The disappointing outcome was equally the result of altered dynamics in the global political economy, which had given rise to unprecedented Western financial power. By the late 1970s, within anti-communist imperatives, core industrialised states began to push forcefully for state 'roll back' in the developing world in favour of open and unregulated markets. The key instruments to implement what became a *global strategy* of economic liberalism were the two International Financial Institutions [IFIs], namely, the IMF and World Bank, and the chief weapon was debt, specifically, loan conditionality, which tied the release of credit to desired policies [Ould-Mey, M., 1994:323]. In this vein, a Zimbabwe Development Fund proposed at Lancaster House—otherwise referred to as the 'Kissinger billion' [Moyo, S., 1995:105-106]—swayed the Patriotic Front to accept a constitution that protected property rights and market sovereignty over land redistribution [Tshuma, L., 1997:41].

Besides the land question, the Lancaster agreement paved the way for international powers to attack state sovereignty over macroeconomic policy. Post-1975 economic decline, according to the World Bank [vol.2, 1995:116], largely attributed to trade sanctions, foreign currency shortages, price controls, the pegged exchange rate and high budgetary deficits, which manifested after the 'easy phase' of import substitution. Within the deformed structural context, however, the state-directed macroeconomic regime, as outlined in the next two sections, achieved a strong record of national development. The focus of the World Bank overlooked the deeper cause of a plutocracy that skewed development and ignited war, which I discuss in the third section. In all likelihood, had land, income and nationalism been less concentrated and racially based, the UDI boom years would have gone on. I end with the shift in global political economy and the Lancaster agreement, which tragically undermined Zimbabwe's prospects for long-term equitable development.

2.1 Founding Features of the UDI Economy

Being a 'resort to force' [Beach, D., 1994:181], the UDI ultimately meant war. Britain's refusal to intervene militarily encouraged both settler defiance and the African leadership to move beyond a simple reliance on the mother country to bring about majority rule [Astrow, A., 1983:39]. In

August 1963, the Zimbabwe African Peoples' Union [ZAPU]—formed in 1961 after the National Democratic Party was banned—split, resulting in the formation of the Zimbabwe African National Union [ZANU]. Differences over political strategy originally caused the divide: only later in the heat of war did it manifest on Shona-Ndebele tribal lines.[1] In 1964, Ian Smith imprisoned the main leaders for a decade hoping for disarray. Yet regardless, from Zambia and later Mozambique, both parties gradually waged war, which by the 1970s amounted to a communist-inspired strategy of peasant mobilisation. Meanwhile, Rhodesians supported UDI not so much to uphold 'Western civilisation' but simply out of 'fear for their jobs, land and lives' [Beach, D., 1994:181].

Britain opted for economic sanctions to resolve the Rhodesian question, which involved boycotts on the country's access to export, import and capital markets. In mid-1966, the United Nations Security Council ruled that Britain could use force to maintain a naval blockade of Rhodesia's port at Beira, Mozambique, and by May 1968 made sanctions mandatory upon members rather than voluntary. In terms of world trade, Rhodesia appeared a 'sitting duck': black-ruled Zambia and Britain itself were by far the most important export markets in 1964 and in terms of imports, Britain was the main source, which included vital supplies of petroleum and machinery. Following destruction of the country's four biggest foreign exchange earners [i.e. tobacco, asbestos, gold and tourism], Harold Wilson, the British Prime Minister, and other experts predicted the rebel state would be brought to its knees in 'a matter of weeks rather than months' [Wilson, H., cited in Bond, P., 1998:120].

At first, the odds of survival seemed completely against Rhodesia. In anticipation of war, whites were leaving the country in droves: 50,000 emigrated between 1961 and 1964 [Godwin, P., and Hancock, I., 1993:17]. International capital had lobbied intensely to avoid the UDI outcome and 'wanted nothing of a new regime which would attract international sanctions, market closures, higher trading costs, financial stringency, political instability and world hostility' [Clarke, D.G., 1980:29]. Nonetheless, the country emerged as one of the world's 'boom economies' according to the May 1972 London *Economist* [cited in Handford, J., 1976:29-30]. Between 1966 and 1974 the state presided over a low inflation economy that generated a real average growth rate of between 7.5% and 9% [Handford, J, 1976:64; Mlambo, A.S., 1997:29; Bond, P., 1998:117].

With trade havens provided by South Africa and Mozambique until 1974, sanctions simply failed to destroy the economy. Of Rhodesia's main exports, the only truly effective sanction was on tobacco, which saw the country's share of world trade decline from about 27% before the UDI to 10% by mid-1972 [Handford, J., 1976:106]. In regard to essential imports, especially oil, agro-machinery, transport equipment, chemicals and rubber, trade sanctions forced adjustments but did not cut off inflow. During the voluntary phase before 1968, for instance, imports from Germany, Japan, France and Italy were up 62%, 62%, 222% and 24% respectively [Handford, J., 1976:20,21]. At best, sanctions forced trade routes under cover; increased transport costs; and pressured international reserves. At worst, African workers bore the brunt of adjustments while sanctions provided the drive for import substitution and new export markets, which became major sources of growth in the UDI economy.

State measures to trap capital inside the national economy outmanoeuvred the British Government and secured ample resources to finance investment. Only a 'matter of hours' before the UDI more than half of the fixed and liquid Rhodesian reserves in London were 'whisked away'. At the Government's behest, British-controlled banks in Rhodesia—Barclays and Standard—put their foreign currencies in South Africa 'and it appeared this helped them to extend credit against blocked accounts' [Handford, J., 1976:18,50]. The Reserve Bank received enhanced exchange control powers to overview the suspension of debt service obligations on non-South African capital, prohibition of profit remittance from multinational companies to the UK and the freezing of non-resident bank deposits [Clarke, D.G., 1980:29,108; Bond, P., 1998:121]. In effect, Rhodesia defaulted on Rh$82.6 million worth of public debt owed to the London bond market and the World Bank, which saw external repayments decline from 7% to 4% of GDP [the equivalent of about £12.3 million per year] [Stoneman, C.,1978:72].[2]

Foreign companies faced a stark option: either they could cease business in the country or comply with the regime and accept their status as 'directed' companies under Rhodesian legislation. Parent multinationals generally chose the latter path: they divested responsibility to their local subsidiaries and instructed them to locally re-invest profits [Clarke, D.G., 1980:29]. This was a convenient arrangement for both the Rhodesian Government and parent multinationals. While the state effectively harnessed foreign capital to serve the national economy, parent multinationals could counter charges of unethical business relations with a racist regime. They blamed the continued export and import of their Rhodesian subsidiaries on 'lost control' yet retained a long-term grip on their assets in the advent of the country returning to legality.

Similarly, new regulations required foreign banks to take on a 'domestic complexion' in policy, which stimulated a keener interest in local productive investment outlets and the development of a secondary financial structure, such as finance houses, insurance and investment trusts [Clarke, D.G., 1980:107]. South African/Dutch capital grew in importance evident in the establishment of Rhobank of which the Netherlands bank of South Africa [i.e. Nedbank] had a 62.5% share and the Rhodesian Government 32.5% [Stoneman, C., 1978:71].

State appointed committees encompassing representatives from Treasury, the Reserve Bank, industry and commerce dealt with foreign exchange allocation, tariffs and import quotas, which were key strategic weapons under import substitution. Foreign exchange applications, for example, were assessed on criteria that concerned the adequacy of existing capacity; the ability to manufacture at competitive prices and acceptable quality; employment potential; the net foreign exchange benefit [i.e. expected export earnings minus recurrent import commitments]; and the impact on state revenue [Handford, J., 1976:138-139]. Through additional applications of tariffs and import controls, the state identified investment opportunities and simply relied on the parsimonious nature of capital to take advantage. In short, pragmatism ruled rather than ideology.

In the words of John Handford—a Rhodesian Front economist:

> The state decided what developments were needed, dangled the carrot of big profits in front of private enterprise, ensured that those profits would eventuate through virtual monopolies created by tariff and quota policy, and then let human nature take its course [1976:41].

Hostes Nicholle, the Secretary for Internal Affairs, concluded vehemently:

> UDI was a blessing in disguise. We were soon manufacturing a large range of industrial products to meet local needs which were previously satisfied by imports ... The strength of our position soon revealed itself because we became masters in our own house through the good fortune of sanctions which had so effectively removed the villains who had previously manipulated our development and had dictated our progress through the fraudulent device of international finance [1971:2].

'Trade and investments flowed into Rhodesia', to quote Yash Tandon [1990:85], 'like water through a sieve'. Multinationals exploited the regional trade and investment conduits and leapt 'joyfully into the sanctions breach' [Handford, J., 1976:134]. For example, despite the closure of Lonrho's oil pipeline from Beira and the Feruka refinery, the five petroleum companies, namely, Shell, British Petroleum, Mobil, Caltex and Total kept petrol flowing via South Africa [Handford, J., 1976:23; Clarke, D.G., 1980:128]. Turner and Newall registered operations in South Africa under another company name—Southern Asbestos—and within two years asbestos exports had recovered fully [Handford, J., 1976:23-24]. With help from the 'Byrd' amendment[3], Union Carbide, Anglo-American, Lonrho and Rio Tinto all expanded export operations during the UDI including chrome, gold, copper, nickel and coal [Astrow, A., 1983:58; Stoneman, C., 1978:69-70]. The list could go on but secrecy clouds multinational operations during the UDI [Clarke, D.G., 1980:31].

The state and multinationals dominated investment. Between 1966 and 1976, the share of foreign capital in total investment rose from 25% to 37% while the share of the public sector rose to account for 44% [Stoneman, C., 1978:68,72]. In real terms, state investment underwent a 169% rise wherein budgetary outlays prioritised capital expenditures, particularly infrastructure such as rail, roads, power and water. The state-owned Industrial Development Corporation provided a channel for the Government to buy up shares—worth R£1.8 million by the mid-1970s—in various enterprises that spanned, among others, textiles, metallurgy, pharmaceuticals, paper and chemicals [Handford, J., 1976:138].

In the face of world hostility and local 'red terror' an appeal to patriotism spurred the economic nationalism of the white community, whether linked to local or foreign enterprise. 'We were involved in an economic war', to again quote Mr Nicholle [1971:3], 'and it was a question of work or die'. Some whites found the Rhodesian Front odious but still rallied to the cause of pioneering new markets on 'both sides of the Atlantic, the Iron Curtain and throughout Africa, the Middle East, and Asia' [Godwin, P., and Hancock, I., 1993:55]. In recognition, the Government awarded Independence Commemorative Decorations [ICDs]. Geoff Ellman-Brown and Jock Malloch, for example, received ICDs for 'sanction busting', as did the so-called 'Scottish Mafia', namely, N.H.B. Bruce [Reserve Bank Governor], D. Young [Treasury] and later, D. Smith [Finance Minister from 1976] for protecting the currency and reserves [Godwin, P., and Hancock, I., 1993:26,54]. By 1969, Rhodesia offered whites a living standard and lifestyle arguably better than the industrialised world, which largely explains the reversal of the net white migration loss [Appendix I].

2.2 National Economic Development during the UDI

By the late 1970s, the value and output of mining had tripled and doubled respectively and the sector's share of GDP rose from a low of 6% before the UDI to 8% [Stoneman, C., 1978:69]. Commercial agriculture was hit hard by tobacco sanctions—earnings fell from Rh$70 million in 1965 to $30 million by 1971—which was largely responsible for the decline in the sector's share of GDP from 16.9% to 12.4% over the UDI [Handford, J., 1976:97; Rukuni, M., 1994:27]. On the other hand, the output of other commodities, notably beef, wheat, cotton, maize, soya beans and coffee increased by 250% and their value rose from Rh$103 million in 1965 to $223 million by 1971 [Astrow, A., 1983:72, footnote 74; Handford, J., 1976:97]. Because of its strategic importance in replacing imports, the manufacturing sector became the centrepiece of the UDI economy and its share of the GDP reached 24% by the late 1970s, up from 18% before the UDI [Stoneman, C., 1978:69; Astrow, A., 1983:14].

The ISI strategy arguably got the best out of the racially skewed economy. A strong domestic growth dynamic deepened the linkages between the main productive sectors of commercial agriculture, mining and manufacturing. Even so, the distorted agrarian base, which no doubt was at the crux of the war, had to claim the economy as a victim at some point. By the late 1970s, accustomed constraints prevailed—limited African 'trickle down', relative mass impoverishment, saturated white consumer markets and worsening balance of payments pressures. The overriding imperative was broad-based structural reform, especially in the agrarian sector, far less to dismantle the state-directed macroeconomy. Indeed, the ISI strategy, as the Rhodesian Government demonstrated for white society, offered an African government vital weapons to contain inflation, orient welfare expenditures and, if combined with structural reform, reignite a rural-urban dynamic on behalf of the indigenous population

2.2.1 The Manufacturing Hub

For a while, at least, high profits in manufacturing were there for the taking in an overall buoyant economy that offered entrepreneurs, via sanctions, import controls and repressive labour laws[4], a captive domestic market and cheap labour supplies. Indeed, as manufacturing grew at an annual rate of 12% between 1966 and 1974, the volume of output rose by 110%, gross fixed capital formation by 524% and profit ratios by 75% [Astrow, A., 1983:14; Handford, J., 1976:141]. The number of firms employing more than ten people increased from 665 in 1965 to 1,036 by 1970 and the range of products increased from 1,059 in 1967 to 3,837 three years later [Bond, P., 1998:123-124]. Colin Stoneman [1978:71] points out that the 'general picture' of the UDI economy 'in almost every sector was of one or two multinational firms operating in a monopoly situation with a number of small domestically owned firms picking up what crumbs were to be had'.[5]

In an economy heavily dependent on raw commodity exports and capital imports, there was broad scope for import substitution to add value to production and exports as well as counter import reliance. Before the UDI, virtually all the country's fertiliser requirements, for instance, were imported, as was a broad range of metal and textile products. One quarter of Rhodesia's private consumption relied on imports—the main items being foodstuffs, beverages, household and recreational goods [Handford, J., 1976:16]. Figure 1 provides a list of import substitution manufactures during the UDI.

The import of consumer items as a percentage of total manufactured imports fell from 27% in 1964–1965 to 11% by 1981–

1982 [Riddell, R.C., 1990:347]. The state simply clamped down on imported goods for the white luxury market and encouraged local production. In 1970, for instance, industrial enterprise received about 90% of foreign exchange while only 10% went toward retail 'shop' items [Astrow, A., 1983:14-15; Handford, J., 1976:165]. By 1971, white suburban homes could be furnished entirely by local goods [Handford, J., 1976:141]. Besides washing machines, air conditioners, electric heaters, toothpicks and the like, as listed in Figure 1, the state encouraged production of carpets, books, assembled cars, coloured film and scotch whisky. Suddenly also, as Patrick Bond [1998:123] points out, supermarkets offered 'fifteen varieties of hair shampoo, five lipsticks, seven varieties of swimming pool paints and ten varieties of pet food'.

Figure 1 *UDI Import Substitution Industries*

Foodstuffs: bread, meat processing, fruit and vegetable processing, fruit canning, cube sugar, biscuit making, high protein animal foods, almonds, dried apricots, breakfast cereals.

Textiles and Clothing: tallowed cottons, sewing thread, handkerchiefs, ties, uniforms, shirts, dresses, interlinings, shorts, suits, jackets, underwear, knitwear, stockings, pantyhose.

Wood: paper and pulp, paper recycling, high-quality furniture, lollipop sticks, meat skewers, matches, pegs, cocktail sticks, medical spatula, hangers, rolling pins.

Chemicals, Non-Metallic Mineral Products: textile chemicals, fertiliser, detergents, brake fluids, cleaning chemicals, disinfectants, bactericides, paints, shampoos, starch, shoe white, pharmaceuticals, plastic items, containers, glass, cement, hinges, moldings, cap fillings, ballpoint pens, polythene bags, air purifying blocks.

Metal Products: copper piping, steel tubes, sheeting, nuts and bolts, vehicle parts, air conditioners, washing machines, refrigerators, deep freezers, electric heaters, aluminum cables and frames, office furniture, stainless steel, locks, sawmilling machinery, spray irrigation, arms and ammunition, battery fittings.

Source: Handford, J., 1976:134–135.

As cotton increasingly replaced tobacco in the agricultural sector, the textile industry was an obvious choice for Government support. In less than a decade, cotton production expanded by 1,000% while African smallholders, mainly upon virgin soils in the recently opened Gokwe region, increased their share of total output to about one-quarter by the mid-1970s [Mariga, I.K., 1994:220]. The Industrial Development Corporation and Whiteheads Limited, which Lonrho bought in 1967, launched major investments in clothing, textiles and footwear. The number of cotton gins increased from two to six and by 1968, some 400 new investment projects saw the import of men's clothing virtually cease [Handford, J., 1976:136].

Other major 'sanction busting' initiatives involved the establishment of fertiliser and aluminum enterprises. At a cost of Rh$17 million, the fertiliser plant at Que Que [Kwe Kwe] built by Sable Chemicals, a South African company, was the largest single investment during the era. By the early 1970s, Rhodesia became self-sufficient in nitrogenous fertiliser but remained import dependent for potash supplies. Although the Government subsidised the factory to keep costs down, the savings in foreign exchange outweighed the expenditure [Handford, J., 1976:30,103,137]. In 1969, Rhodesia's first aluminium factory came into production, which saved an estimated £500,000 a year in foreign exchange [Handford, J., 1976:138].

About half of gross manufacturing output, value added, employment, capital stock and exports derived from just three subsectors, namely, food, chemicals and metal products [Riddell, R.C., 1990:338]. The share of intermediate and capital goods subsectors in total output actually surpassed the contribution of foodstuffs during the UDI, which distinguished Rhodesian manufacturing from elsewhere in sub-Saharan Africa [Riddell, R.C., 1990:341]. Over 1966–1974, chemicals and petroleum products, non-metallic mineral products, metals and metal products and transport equipment grew on average by 9.4%, 13.4%, 13.2% and 5% respectively [Ndela, D.B, 1986:143]. The gross output of metals rose 240% while that of steel trebled, which saw a 30% increase in RISCO's labour force [Handford, J., 1976:141, 143]. Turner and Newall invested in an asbestos mill at Shabani [Zvishavane]; nickel processing commenced from scratch [Ndlela, D.B, 1986:148]; and Alfa Romeo, BMW, Daihatsu, Peugeot and Ford all restarted car assembly plants. Output of pharmaceuticals rose in importance while that of plastics more than quadrupled.

2.2.2 Anomalies of the Agrarian Sector

The state focused on the development of large-scale capitalist agriculture, which accounted for 80% of total agricultural output and 95% of marketed sales [Chavunduka, G.L., 1982:35]. Although production in the African sector is said to have increased by 297% over the UDI, most was consumed in-house but still failed to cover population increases [Astrow, A., 1983:72, footnote 74]. African farmers in the freehold Purchase Areas, who numbered 8,600 in 1975, accounted for one-third of African sales [Duggan, W. R., 1980:235; Handford, J., 1976:96]. The Government regarded African agriculture as a 'bottomless pit' [Nicholle, W.H.H., 1971:8] and sought to promote a growth dynamic between commercial agriculture and manufacturing to absorb Africans in employment. To a real extent, the dynamic took root but was inevitably ruined by the skewed agrarian base. The maintenance of land segregation on racial lines involved an enormous opportunity cost of idle land, an extensive production bias, non-utilisation of skilled African farmers and the costly protection of numerous inefficient white farmers.

Table 2.0 *Land Apportionment 1962–1969*

Land Apportionment	**1962** [million acres]	**1969**
Tribal Trust Lands	40.2	39.9
Native Purchase Areas	4.2	3.7
Total African	44.4	43.6
Unreserved Land	5.4	-----
European Land	36.9	38.7
Unassigned Land	------	-----
Other [game reserves]	9.9	14.2
Total – All Land	96.7	96.5

Source: Dunlop, H., 1972:1.

Over 60% of the African population, some 600,000 families according to the 1969 census, lived in the reserves or Tribal Trust Lands [TTLs]. Between 1960 and 1973, the population in these areas increased by 60% [Dunlop, H., 1974:184] but the available land area, as determined by the Land Tenure Act of 1969, was actually reduced while that to Europeans—less than 5% of the population—increased. As evident in Table 2.0, the Act added 1.8 million acres to the European area, abolished the unreserved category open to all races and reduced the Purchase Areas by 500,000 acres and the TTLs by 300,000. A report by the secretary of agriculture in 1967–1968 recorded that only 5% of African farmers used fertiliser, less than half owned cattle, 8% owned scotch carts and over two-thirds could not feed themselves [cited in Dunlop, H., 1974:181]. Annually, maize output usually fell short of subsistence needs by some 40% [Astrow, A., 1983:65].

In September 1970, Hostes Nicholle responded to a motion put by an African MP[6] that Africans lacked sufficient land to develop:

> Even if the whole of Rhodesia were allocated for African occupation, it is clear that with the rate of population increase, and the rate of despoliation, we would not only be in the position now expounded by the movers of this motion within less than 25 years, but far worse ... There would be no money to build dams or to put in the development projects supplied by the European sector of the Rhodesian economy ... it should be clear that the answer to African advancement is not more land, but firstly increased production from the land that he has, and secondly the development of projects which will open up opportunities for commercial and industrial employment ... [cited in Handford, J. 1976:93-94].

Rhodesians, Peter Godwin and Ian Hancock [1993:314] noted, 'acquired a harmful habit of lying to themselves and to each other'. In this case, Mr Nicholle adheres to the illusion of a non-racial meritocracy wherein the white man showed natural economic and cultural superiority. John Handford [1976:7] provides another example: 'The idea that the Land Apportionment Act prevented the mass of the African population from raising their incomes as farmers is a complete lie'. The outlook defies historical reality in that the African agrarian crisis, as outlined previously, has direct roots in the primitive accumulation of white colonists.

As to the subsequent population explosion, which also undermined long-term agricultural prospects, so-called natalist and anti-natalist schools of thought differ over whether it accords to colonialism's benevolence or malevolence. Natalism, outlines John Iliffe [1989:165-169], is based on demographic transition theory, which views African population growth a result of pre-colonial high fertility rates and the positive impact of colonialism in reducing mortality rates through medicine and ending tribal war and famine. Anti-natalism, on the other hand, sees the increase largely as a response to declining material fortunes under colonial rule. In this view, African smallholders, to sustain livelihood, intensified their resort to a patriarchal mode of production, which meant maximising family population, ideally through polygamy, in order to 'squeeze' family labour. In Rhodesia's case, the natalist position encounters difficulty over the brutal nature of colonial oppression, the constant poverty struggle, the high prevalence of polygamy where land was available early on and the delayed reach of colonial medicines until mid-20th century in many areas [Iliffe, J., 1989:167;Beach, D., 1994:173].

Whatever the case, given the extent of demographic and environmental constraints, a full-scale commercialisation of the Tribal Trust Lands, as the Rhodesian Front believed, would only hasten decline. Renowned scholars offer credence to the perception that peasant economies are not suited to sustained productivity increases [see Amin, S., 1964:23-46; Brenner, R., 1976:30-75; Cooper, F., 1993:147-148; Leys, C., 1996:135-142]. Apart from the dearth of land and overpopulation, the development of productive forces are considered hampered by kinship obligations, land fragmentation, sporadic labour shortages and difficulties in maintaining the common grazing. Underneath the racial facade, Hostes Nicholle was right to imply that the future of national development rested on the capitalist agrarian sector. Land, labour, capital and technology could more easily be harnessed into productive designs to generate a surplus, feed an expanding urban populace, provide manufacturing with the necessary inputs as well as a growing market for consumer and capital goods.

A sustained subsistence economy centred on local food production and consumption was really the best general option for the Tribal Trust Lands. Although the Rhodesian Front professed this aim, land dispossession defied it and few positive measures were undertaken. In fact, after abolishing the Native Land Husbandry Act, the Government simply ignored African agriculture and allowed an era of 'laissez faire' to reign: grazing lands were encroached upon, households reverted to shifting cultivation and conservation works were ignored [Dunlop, H., 1972:7]. Only with the rise of security imperatives in the late 1960s did the state attempt to arrest economic decline in a bid to counter growing support for the guerrillas. From thereon, by default, 500 kilometres of roads including bridges were constructed in rural areas per year— mainly to gain the Rhodesian military access [Godwin, P. and Hancock, I., 1993:131]. The Tribal Trust Land Development Corporation [TILCOR] was established in 1968 but its operations were seriously hampered by budgetary constraints.[7]

The main approach was 'community development', which put the onus of rural administration and development on African councils and traditional authorities. The African Councils Act of 1957 created 220 councils and granted rights to raise taxes from a poverty-stricken base. The Tribal Trust Land Authority Act of 1967 and the African Law and Tribal Courts Act of 1969 restored respectively the powers of chiefs and headmen to allocate land and hear minor criminal cases. Chiefs were also made ex-officio members of African councils, conscripted on the Government payroll and received access under the 1969 constitution to 10 Senate seats [Kriger, N.J., 1992:74]. According to Dunlop [1974:183], the policy of attempting to perpetuate what remained of tribal society was as much in the nature of an imposition of an 'alien culture' as the introduction of Western style institutions. Outside the royal lineage, that is, among numerous 'stranger' clans, clan-based chiefships often lacked the authority or legitimacy to enforce land management.

More successfully, the Government promoted capitalist agricultural development through a 100% increase in expenditure to encourage less reliance on tobacco and a greater domestic orientation [Handford, J., 1976:48]. The distinguishing feature of the period, in contrast to the 1980s and beyond, was that the large-scale commercial sector became less of an export enclave. 'There is no doubt', writes Handford [1976:97], 'that one of the strengths of the Rhodesian economic position in the years after UDI was the country's ability, almost complete, to feed itself'. Abundant food supplies were an integral feature of industrial growth in Rhodesia, as they were during the British industrial revolution [See Brenner, R., 1976:66]. The state founded new industries in bananas and wheat while previous public investments in agricultural technology enabled the spread of cotton and higher yields for maize, wheat, groundnuts and rice. The most spectacular technical advance was the SR 52 hybrid maize seed, which created two shoots instead of one.[8]

The Rhodesian Front claimed that drought was a bigger economic enemy than sanctions. In January 1965, the Sabi-Limpopo Authority [SLA] was established with the purpose of building irrigation networks from the Sabi, Lundi and Limpopo rivers, which trap over half the country's rainfall though the southeastern lowveld. For Mashonaland, the Farm Irrigation Fund, a soft loan facility, was established in 1966. By 1975 about 300,000 hectares [750,000 acres] of SLA estates around Chiredzi plus another 8,000 hectares of private farms in Mashonaland were brought under irrigation [Rasmussen, R.K., and Rubert, S.C., 1990:317; Rukuni, M., 1994:29].

The infrastructure enabled Rhodesia to counter import dependency for wheat, which stood at about 95% before the UDI. By the mid-1970s, over 75% of the national wheat requirements were being produced locally, which saved about Rh$20 million in foreign currency per year, and self-sufficiency was attained later in the decade [Handford, J., 1976:59; Rukuni, M., 1994:29]. Among the prime beneficiaries of the irrigation projects were multinational landowners, such as Anglo-American Corporation [UK-SA], Triangle Ltd [UK-SA] and Tate and Lyle [UK], who ran vast sugar and citrus estates.

The country transformed into a regional maize exporter: earnings totalled Rh$34 million between 1968 and 1973 [Handford, J., 1976:28,113]. Maize silos, which numbered three after a new 85,000-ton capacity silo was built in mid-1972, seemed ever full despite regular droughts [i.e. 1965–1966, 1967–1968, 1971–1972 and 1972–1973]. Rhodesia produced about double domestic requirements of 500,000 or so metric tons and excess stocks were needed to avert famine. Beef output also expanded—exports underwent a 180% increase by 1973, consuming about 40% of the off take [Handford, 1976:109]. Sugar, coffee and tea were other major exports while sunflowers, soya beans, groundnuts, potatoes, sorghum, green beans, rice, fruits and dairy produce were mostly consumed domestically. From a position of importing some 90% of bananas before the UDI, the country became self-sufficient in this fruit subsequently [Handford, J., 1976:116].

Over the UDI, as Table 2.1 shows, the percentage of agricultural output absorbed by the manufacturing sector increased sevenfold. As a proportion of total manufacturing inputs, the share of domestic agriculture doubled between 1965 and 1975 and by another 50% by 1981–1982. The manufacturing subsectors, namely, foodstuffs, tobacco and beverages, consumed 90% of the agricultural inputs while the consumption of cotton by the textile subsector steadily increased during the 1970s to take a 21% share of total agricultural inputs [Riddell, R.C., 1990:364].

Table 2.1 *Agricultural Output and Manufacturing Inputs, 1965–1982*

	1965	1975	1981/82
% of agricultural output used as input by manufacturing sector	12.8	31.1	43.9
% of commercial agricultural output used as input by the manufacturing sector	16.0	38.6	59.2
% of inputs used by manufacturing sector originating in the domestic agricultural sector	9.7	20.4	29.2

Source: Riddell, R.C., 1990:364.

The reverse relationship, however, namely, the agricultural sector's absorption of manufacturing inputs was not so healthy. As revealed by Table 2.2, the rate of commercial agriculture's absorption of manufactures remained relatively stagnant at 42% to 43% during the UDI, which was less than 10% of *total* manufacturing output. The chief agricultural input manufactures were stock feeds [31%], fertilisers and chemicals [54%], machinery [11%], transport equipment [3%] and paper and packaging [1%] [Riddell, R.C., 1990:366]. To a real extent, the sluggish demand for manufacturing inputs reflected production constraints inherent in land segregation and class privilege, which curtailed the rural-urban growth dynamic.

Table 2.2 *The Supply of Material Inputs to the Agricultural Sector, 1965–1982*

	1965	1975	1981/82
% of inputs provided by manufacturing sector	42	43	48
% of inputs directly imported	9	7.5	10.4
Inputs from manufacturing to agriculture as a percentage of total manufacturing output	3	6	7

Source: Riddell, R.C, 1990:365.

To begin with, vast tracts of prime land in the European area were simply going to waste. Out of the seven million arable acres available to Europeans in the best Natural Regions [i.e. I, II and III] only about 1.25 million were being cropped in the mid-1970s [Dunlop, H., 1974:184]. Most white farmers lacked innovation and remained very reluctant to diversify away from tobacco [Dunlop, H., 1972:12].[9] This forced the Government to uphold an expensive tobacco quota system, which amounted to Rh$100 million in price support between 1965 and 1973 [Handford, J.,1976:105]. Although the stockpile was gradually exported, the expenditure represented a huge opportunity cost. In any case, according to the Rhodesian National Farmers' Union, 60% of white farmers could not cover their combined operational and fixed costs [Astrow, A., 1983:59; Godwin, P., and Hancock, I., 1993:27]. Out of 6,250 white farmers in 1972, for example, the average debt per farmer was between Rh$15,000 to $19,000 and only 1,090 farmers could pay tax [Handford, J., 1976:102-103].

The expansion of agrarian productive forces to help drive urban industrial development effectively relied on the 2,000 or so efficient commercial farmers. To broaden the wealth base and, therefore, the rural–urban dynamic, there was ample space to carve the sector up into smaller units for more intensive farming, let alone opportunity to facilitate the entry of the best of African agrarian entrepreneurs. Such a move, however, required the Rhodesian Front to shed the idea that only whites knew how to farm.

2.2.3 The Balance of Payments

Until the mid-1970s, foreign exchange earnings increased by an average of 11% per year and by 1972 export revenue in real terms was a fraction under pre-UDI levels [N.H.B. Bruce cited in Handford, J., 1976:31]. As evident in Appendix 4, except for 1968, Rhodesia maintained a trade surplus over the UDI years. Favourable movements in world commodity prices underlined the success, as did a pegged exchange rate, a strong Rhodesian dollar and low inflation.

Tourism remained the country's third to fourth largest foreign exchange earner. Between 1965 and 1972 tourist income, predominately from South Africa, rose by 150%, which was greater than Rhodesian travel expenditure abroad [Handford, J., 1976:24,30,31]. Behind Argentina and South Africa, Rhodesia became the third most popular tourist destination in the Southern Hemisphere. However as the war intensified tourist income declined by 50% in 1973 and the ongoing survival of the industry depended on state subsidies [Astrow, A., 1983:62].

Agriculture and mining both accounted for a 30% to 40% share of exports while manufacturing accounted for the remaining 20% to 30%. As a proportion of total exports, the share of manufactures [including cotton lint and ferro-alloys] progressively weakened during the UDI, particularly after 1975. The ratio of manufactured exports to the sector's gross output, for example, fell from 26% in 1965 to 18% by the late 1970s. There occurred, though, a marked shift in the composition of export manufactures, which saw the share of foodstuffs, clothing and footwear decline from about 30% in 1964–1965 to 13% in 1982–1983 while that of value-added metals and textiles double to 45% and 22% respectively [Riddell, R.C., 1990:346-346].

Manufacturing in Rhodesia still remained a net importer and could only source 34% of inputs from within the sector [Riddell, R.C., 1990:344]. As a developing country, such a predicament is expected. Pointedly though, over the UDI, import trends reflected strong domestic growth: 86% of imports comprised intermediate inputs and capital [i.e. machine-based] goods [Riddell, R.C., 1990:347]. Of greater concern was the overall ratio of processed to raw exports, which changed little over time. Rhodesia remained locked into the lower valued position of being a raw commodity exporter. This was the case, for example, for mineral and 90% of cotton exports. While trade sanctions did not help the cause of export manufactures, especially given the loss of markets in Zambia and Malawi, Rhodesia's location on a poor continent and worldwide protectionism were the more formidable obstacles.

With the initial reduction of foreign debt service, Rhodesia's current account balance received a considerable fillip [Handford, J., 1976:24; Stoneman, C., 1978:79]. The growing dominance of South African capital, however, entailed a cost: between 1966 and 1976 new foreign investment at $350 million was exceeded by outflows of $490 million in property income [See Stoneman, C., 1978:71-72,78-79]. From 1973, as evident in Appendix 4, invisible transactions [i.e. payments for services, transfers and investments] sharply escalated. The economy's fortunes deteriorated in 1973 and 1974 when Zambia and Mozambique closed their borders and OPEC hiked the price of oil by

300%.[10] All trade had to be directed through South Africa at higher freight cost and lengthy delays subject to rail congestion. The sharp rise in investment payments included the servicing of 'secretive' foreign loans to finance the war [Astrow, A., 1983:59, footnote 22].

2.2.4 Macroeconomic Management and Welfare

Upon so narrow a production base, the Rhodesian economy was particularly vulnerable to a crisis of *stagflation*, that is, a combination of high inflation and stagnant growth, wherein the African populace at large could suffer famine. The potential crisis stemmed from exclusive structures of production and wealth shaped as they had been by settler and foreign capital. Therein, a confluence of political and economic distortions prevailed: an authoritarian state, an impoverished [food insecure] national market, a problematic dependency on commodity exports relative to capital imports and monopoly-controlled or oligopolistic production circuits. Under such conditions, a laissez-faire approach combined with an exogenous shock, whether import price hikes, falling commodity prices or drought, could easily let loose a spiral of stagflation fuelled by currency depreciation, rising production costs, capital flight and a rapidly shrinking domestic market.

Although short of resolving these structural weaknesses, the ISI strategy at least went some way toward containing the stagflation potential and balancing the peasant-capitalist order. Discretion over macroeconomic controls allowed the state to simultaneously strengthen the productive capacity of capitalist classes and redistribute some wealth, albeit crumbs, to the African populace. Thus, alongside fiscal stimulus, controls on imports, foreign exchange allocation, prices and interest rates delivered production incentives to the agrarian and industrial bourgeoisie as well as greater employment opportunities and cheaper essential goods for Africans. An appreciation of the high growth economy during the UDI explains the contemporary conundrum that most Zimbabweans look back at the period as a time of relative prosperity.

The Rhodesian Front, however, mistakenly assumed that the benefits of a strong macroeconomic environment, namely, low inflation and expanded employment opportunity, compensated for gross inequities in wealth and welfare. To Ian Smith, Rhodesia's natives were the happiest in the world, all they wanted was a 'full belly and a large family' and be ruled separately by their chief or kraal head [Godwin, P., and Hancock, I., 1993:47]. No matter the macroeconomic performance, there could be no peace, let alone sustained and balanced growth, while a privileged minority monopolised the country's resources and sought Africans 'only as labourers, not as consumers' [Duggan, W.R., 1980:237]. The state spent about 20 times more per capita on education and health for whites than blacks [Mlambo, A., 1997:55]. The rationale was ruthless: whites generated the wealth and, therefore, their lives were of more value [See Handford, J., 1976:38-40].

All would come to grief, the official argument ran, if investment in the African social sectors retarded state fiscal capacity to stimulate production and employment among the formal sectors. Accordingly, the bulk of state expenditures had to be directed at the taxpaying, voting and most productive part of the population, the whites. In this way, policies that were rooted in capitalist class formation became effective in terms of race [Beach, D., 1994:178]. After expenditure on economic services to the formal sectors, which usurped over three-quarters of budgetary outlays between 1965 and 1973 [Handford, J., 1976:57], next in importance was white welfare, then, African welfare and last of all, African agriculture.

Fundamentally, the welfare of too many relied on the generation of wealth by too few. As shown in the 1980s, a fiscal re-orientation could expand the African welfare net but then, like the Rhodesian Front, the IFIs and capitalist classes argued that the social gains were unsustainable because they undermined capital expenditure and, therefore, economic growth. Lasting fulfilment of African welfare needs required a greater growth potential in the economy, which in turn depended on structural reform to enlarge the capital base. Unable to contemplate this prospect, the Rhodesian Government chose to maximise state capital investment to maintain growth and then deliver whites health and education services on a par with the industrialised world to ensure continued reproduction—leaving Africans the scant revenue leftovers.

John Handford [1976:189,191] maintains that the UDI economy generated more for African health than elsewhere in Africa, evident in lower rates of infant and maternal mortality, leprosy, diphtheria, tuberculosis, smallpox and ratios of blacks to doctors and hospital beds. In reality, Africans relied on the mercy of church missions to deal with numerous illnesses related to poor sanitation and nutrition. The policy of 'community development' shifted the onus of heath delivery on to the African Councils, which effectively enabled the state to rationalise funds as grants to Councils were delivered 'commensurate to their effectiveness' [Handford, J., 1976:57]. The state regarded missions politically subversive and progressively reduced grants, which combined with falling contributions from American and European congregations saw the Church gradually subside from the forefront of African welfare. The element of charity also faded: state fees for health and education had been officially introduced in 1963 and 1964 respectively.

The Government aimed to spend 2% of GDP on African education, which was generally maintained. By 1980, 7% to 8% of African children of the 15 to 19 age group; 20.6% of the 30 to 40 age group; 34.6% of the 45 to 59 age group; and 51% of the 50 to 60 age group had had no formal education [Mlambo, A., 1997:56].[11] Primary retention rates and access to secondary education were extremely poor. Out of a base intake at primary school usually a third of Africans completed the full course and out of those only 12.5% graduated to secondary school [Martin, D., and Johnson, P., 1981:58; Mlambo, A., 1997:55].

As intended, macroeconomic performance did more for African welfare than health and education services. The reality of diminishing returns in the reserves meant low inflation and employment opportunity were crucial factors in African livelihood. Between 1965 and 1972, inflation averaged a mere 3.3% while the economy generated 131,000 new jobs in manufacturing and agriculture alone. The state-directed macroeconomic regime, based essentially on price and trade controls, underpinned the performance, which within the structural context fulfilled the potential for an endogenous dynamic. Of course, the capital-labour regime delivered paltry wages but to an important extent, state price and trade controls contained inflation and kept basic essentials affordable.

In 1972, formal African wage employees totalled 848,000: domestic service employed 109,000; manufacturing 113,000 [up from about 69,000 in 1965]; commercial agriculture 336,000 [up from about 250,000]; mining 54,500; and other industry [e.g. retail, health, education, construction] the remaining 235,100 [Handford, J., 1976:72; Astrow, A., 1983:28, footnote 30]. Relative to over 100,000 new labour entrants each year, job creation at an average of 30,000 new annual positions was not enough but the percentage of the population employed, as per Appendix 5, reached record proportions during the UDI.

The Agricultural Marketing Authority [AMA], established in 1967, coordinated the pricing behaviour of the main agricultural SOEs or parastatals, namely, the Grain Marketing Board [GMB], Cotton Marketing Board [CMB], the Cold Storage Commission [CMC] and the Dairy Marketing Board [DMB]. The final decision on producer and consumer prices was taken at Cabinet level [Chavunduka, G.L., 1982:124]. The objectives of price policy were to safeguard against the bankruptcy of commercial agriculture, encourage diversification away from tobacco and provide cheap food to the consumer.

In some cases, parity to world market value was overruled to serve the national interest in terms of food security or foreign exchange needs. The local consumer prices of maize and beef, for example, were usually subsidised below export parity to promote food security. The producer price of wheat was subsidised above import parity to stimulate production, save foreign currency and recover investment costs in irrigation. The local price of cotton was subsidised to stimulate the textile industry, as was the price of fertiliser to reduce agricultural production costs. It was cheaper, for instance, to import bread and fertiliser but that required foreign currency, the supply of which was scarce. In any case, unless such strategic infant industries were nurtured, they were unlikely to emerge in an international division of labour that many argue was already entrenched at the turn of the 18th century [See Waterbury, J., 1999:330].

The quest by the AMA, on the one hand, to offer producer prices sufficient to stimulate production, and on the other, sell at a low wholesale price for the consumer, inevitably resulted in market disequilibrium evident in parastatal losses. The fiscal burden of subsidy payments to either an oligopoly of millers to keep retail prices low or parastatals to cover trading losses steadily increased after 1976. The economy's deteriorating terms of trade following the oil crisis hampered the export operations of the GMB, CMB and CSC, which until then had covered the losses [Chavunduka, G.L., 1982:126-131].

Proponents of economic liberalisation, such as the Chavunduka Commission [1982:137-9] and the World Bank [1989:91], advocated the rapid phasing out of 'blanket' food subsidies on the grounds that they were too costly and benefited urban free riders more than the rural poor. In the absence of structural reform to give the rural population a land base to obtain basic food security, food subsidies were a welfare concession to the peasantry, which could not as a whole produce their own food, or relied on buying food to grow cash crops [Handford, J., 1976:101]. As a taxpayer's burden, the subsidies were a measure of wealth redistribution. The notion of urban free riders was somewhat imaginary: most urban Africans, even amongst the highest elites, sent remittances to rural kin. In this respect, the removal of food subsidies would undermine their capacity to do so with far reaching consequences.

In regard to trade controls, the importance of state management over tariffs, import and foreign exchange allocations in stimulating growth and employment has been highlighted. The other element was exchange rate management, which helped sustain that growth rate and, along with price controls, contain inflation. Despite the persistent lobbying from orthodox economists, mining companies and commercial farmers to devalue, the 'Scottish Mafia' maintained a strong currency.[12] The gains in international competitiveness from devaluation that free market theorists supposed were not necessarily achieved on the African continent. Nullifying factors included consequent increased transport costs, the chain reaction of retaliatory devaluations of other African currencies and the price elasticity of commodity export markets. The reluctance to devalue reflected a pragmatic grip on economic reality.

The cause of industrial development required a strong currency, which outweighed the interests of commodity exporters for a devalued currency. As the hub of the UDI economy, the manufacturing sector consumed the most imports and was the second largest employer. Import demand was inelastic as about 70% of the sector's intermediate and capital inputs were imported. A rise in import prices following devaluation would raise production costs, induce a fall in domestic demand and increase the price of exports, which could then wipe out the intended effect of devaluation [Riddell, R.C., 1990:377]. Prudent exchange rate management was, therefore, essential to contain inflation and preserve African employment.

A price control order of 1974 and the formation of a Consumer Council also helped to counter a certain crisis of stagflation precipitated by the OPEC oil price hikes. The former only allowed companies to pass on 20% of rising costs to consumers while the latter policed prices [Handford, J., 1976:167-168]. Oligopolies were forced to search for productivity gains to compensate for rising costs rather than simply increase prices. The management of inflation was thus conceived to be not simply a function of monetary policy but also of power realities in the economy, which amounted to another important African welfare concession. In the 1990s, for instance, the sole resort to tight monetary policy to fight inflation had dire social consequences. Over the 1970s, as Appendix 5 reveals, annual inflation jumped from a low of 3% to 9% yet relative to overseas rates at the time, inflation was contained in Rhodesia despite the onset of war budgetary deficits.

2.3 The Nature of the Economic Crisis

Aside from a radical strategy to enlarge the capital base, nothing could stop the economy from moving headlong into decline. Indeed, as from the mid-1970s, GDP growth turned negative [Appendix 5] and contracted by nearly 14% [Astrow, A., 1983:59]. Although complaints abounded about foreign exchange access, the fixed exchange rate, import protection and budget deficits, none of these factors were the real cause. In fact, unprecedented levels of import self-sufficiency had been attained and several manufacturing subsectors, such as metals, furniture, textiles and foodstuffs, were generating net foreign exchange surpluses [Bond, P., 1998:126]. The crisis manifested as a classic case of overproduction underlined by capital intensive investments and a shrinking white market [Bond, P., 1998:128-131]. Like in the late 1950s, excess capital lacked investment outlets beyond the mainstream markets for want of infrastructure, skilled labour and purchasing power. In simple terms, the skewed dimensions of the domestic market now turned against the economy.

The state's refusal to 'fragment' labour—meaning to break the monopoly of white artisans over skilled employment—held down African earnings, wasted manpower and denied opportunities [Godwin,

P., and Hancock, I., 1993:25, 127; Handford, J., 1976:74]. In 1972, for example, 112,000 non-Africans earned a total of Rh$409.3 million while 848,000 Africans earned a total of $285.9 million [Handford, J., 1976:79]. In 1977, white wages averaged Rh$513 per month compared to $49 for Africans. A 1975 study by R.C. Riddell and P.S. Harris titled *The Poverty Datum Line* concluded 80% of black urban workers received incomes below the line while 85% of commercial farm workers 'did not earn half the amount necessary to reach it'. In contrast the *European Expenditure Survey* of 1975–1976 conducted by the CSO revealed that the average income of white households rose by 88% between 1968–1976 [All data cited in Godwin, P., and Hancock, I., 1993:127, 134]. About 92% owned cars, one in every six a swimming pool and 89% lived in luxurious houses [Handford, J., 1976:165; Godwin, P., and Hancock, I., 1993:31, footnote 58].

Table 2.3 *African and European Expenditure Patterns*

Item	% of African Budget	% of European Budget
Foodstuffs	51.1	22.5
Drink and Tobacco	6.5	6.0
Clothing and Footwear	10.1	7.2
Rent, Fuel and Light	15.1	20.8
Household Stores	4.7	7.0
Transport [inc. own vehicles]	4.5	12.3
Servants Wages	Not applicable	5.5
Personal Care and Health	1.6	Inc. in other items
Miscellaneous	6.4	18.7
	100.0	100.0

Source: CSO data, 1972, cited in Handford, J., 1976:166.

Beyond the basic essentials, as Table 2.3 displays, the consumption base relied heavily on the white market, which inevitably meant recession once white migration realised net losses after 1975 [Table 2.4].[13] Between 1976 and 1979 the employed African workforce fell from close to a million to less than 800,000 [Astrow, A., 1983:65]. The downturn may have been countered had the Government redesigned land holdings and fragmented labour to increase African purchasing power. A 10% increase in African earnings in 1972, for instance, would have injected an extra Rh$28.6 million into local markets [Handford, J., 1976:79]. Unfortunately, the boast that development depended on the 'guiding hand of the white man' or one white immigrant created seven jobs [Handford, J., 1976: 63,74] was all too true.

The Government did attempt to redress uneven development: budget outlays for African housing, for example, doubled in 1975 from Rh$30 million to $60 million [Handford, J., 1976:198]. By then, however, the war began to divert funds at an increasing rate. Over 1975–1980, as the cost of waging war quadrupled and the budget deficit rose to 15% of GDP, budget outlays to the Rhodesian military increased from 20.3% to 37% [Godwin, P., and Hancock, I., 1993:131; Astrow, A., 1983:150; Bond, P., 1998:138].

Table 2.4 *White Migration Trends in Rhodesia, 1975–1979*

Year	Immigrants	Emigrants	Net Migration
1975	12 425	10 500	+1 935
1976	7 782	14 854	- 7 072
1977	5 730	16 638	- 10 908
1978	4 360	18 069	- 13 709
1979	3 416	12 973	- 9 557

Source: CSO data cited in Mlambo, A., 1997:34.

Meanwhile, African rural administration, the tourist industry, commercial farming in the northeast and mining exploration progressively collapsed [Astrow, A., 1983:63].[14] Guerrilla forces exploited peasant discontent over land not only between black and white but also between 'royal' and 'stranger' clans. Indeed, among such households, holdings could vary from 1 to 100 hectares [Kriger, N.J., 1992:60-63; Astrow, A., 1983:72, footnote 76]. Promising a new democratic order after the war, the guerrillas generally wrecked havoc. People were obliged not to pay dues to the Councils, which paralysed operations. In Mutoko, one out of three chiefs and six out of fifteen headmen were killed [Kriger, N.J., 1992:104]. By 1980, about half the number of primary and secondary schools had been destroyed or forced to close [Astrow, A., 1983:153]. With domestic markets expended and property threatened, multinationals sought the removal of sanctions and began to switch their allegiance to the African nationalist parties. In 1978, Lonrho publicly backed the Patriotic Front [Astrow, 1983:63].

2.4 The Resurgence of Foreign Power

In 1976, the late Mozambican President, Samora Machel, commented on the subtle change in US policy after Vietnam:

> You do not try to fight against national liberation wars, you sought to subvert them, and instead of trying to protect the rights of privileged minorities individually, you sought to protect the overall rights of capitalism [cited in Martin, D., and Johnson, P., 1981:236].

In Rhodesia, the then US Secretary of State, Henry Kissinger, sought to 'co-opt the program of moderate evolutionary reform, that is to say majority rule, and minority rights' [Kissinger, H., 1979, cited in Martin, D., and Johnson, P., 1981:235]. After persuading Ian Smith with South African help to concede majority rule within two years in September 1976, Carter's victory forced Kissinger to withdraw but already the course of Anglo-American diplomacy had been set. The Lancaster agreement of 1979 achieved the aim, namely, a constitutional Bill of Rights that guaranteed majority rule, judicial independence and universal civil rights. A World Bank managed Zimbabwe Development Fund [ZDF] worth US$1.5 billion, as Kissinger forecast in late 1976 [Martin, D., and Johnson, P., 1981:254-55, 272], proved a crucial inducement against 'white flight' and African intransigence.

In effect, as Samora Machel warned and Kissinger intended, the liberation struggle was seriously truncated. The protection of private property had been 'mediated by the ideology of human rights' [Tshuma, L., 1997:42] while the ZDF forewarned of binding the country to a Western agenda of economic liberalism through debt [Stoneman, C., 1978:74,76]. True, Zimbabweans received civil rights yet, as Ken Booth [1991:321-322] notes, 'liberty without economic status is propaganda'. When an elected government is without unequivocal sovereignty to gear the economy around majority interests and needs, there is no real liberty. Within international and national spheres, two elite trends made such an outcome possible, namely, unprecedented Western financial power and the Patriotic Front's suppression of liberation goals. I briefly review each before returning to conclude on the Lancaster agreement.

2.4.1 The Ascendancy of Western Finance

Since World War Two, the maintenance of an open door policy of free trade and investment has been central to American interests [Williams, W.A., 1972:232-233; Strange, S., 1988:78].[15] When devising the post-war order, the then US State Department Planning Staff, according to original documents, perceived the colonial periphery as a 'source of raw materials and a market' and the main threat as 'nationalistic regimes', which interfere with 'our resources', a 'climate conducive to private investment' and a 'reasonable return' [cited in Chomsky, N., 1991:14; 1997: 12-129]. Such core economic interests of the US and European allies have not changed over time but the financial power to enforce them grew enormously. The advent of developing world indebtedness offered the Western alliance increasing 'power to shape the structures of global political economy within which other states, their political institutions and their economic enterprises have to operate' [Strange, S., 1988:24].

In no small part, the debt crisis and consequent Western financial power to enforce economic liberalism stemmed from the failure of the International Monetary System [IMS], negotiated at Bretton Woods in 1944, to regulate the supply of world liquidity. Over 1969–1972, for example, mainly on the back of US trade and budget deficits, the supply of US dollars—the world's principal international reserve—doubled from US$79 billion to $159 billion—'an increase as large as in all the previous centuries taken together' [Triffin, R., 1978:304]. Credit creation from the Eurodollar market added impetus, which with the deposit of OPEC revenues rose from US$75 billion in 1970 to $1,000 billion by 1984 [Strange, S., 1988:106-107]. The mass of capital saturated Western markets and, apart from the Asian 'tigers', showed little inclination to directly invest under an ISI regime, not to mention a communist state [See Gill, S., and Law, D., 1988:148-150]. Instead, vast sums translated into sovereign debt: in sub-Saharan Africa, for example, total external debt shot up from US$9.9 billion in 1970 to $109.2 billion by 1980 [ADB, 1995:222-225].

In Western economies, excess liquidity accommodated demand inflation, which by the late 1960s launched into the realm of cost inflation. On the one hand, cost pressures derived from world commodity agreements and cartels, which apart from oil encompassed sugar, coffee, tin and other minerals [See Gill, S., and Law, D., 1988:292-294], while on the other, centralised industrial interaction between big corporations and Trade Unions succumbed to a wage-price spiral, that is, 'the upward pressure of wage settlements on prices, the upward pull of prices and living costs on wages' [Galbraith,

J.K., 1987:267]. As a strategy primarily conceived to combat the deflation of the Great Depression, Keynesianism had no ready answer to the new inflation other than fiscal contraction, higher taxes and wage-price controls [Galbraith, J.K., 1987:266-270]. Monetarism, however, offered a more palatable direction especially from a financial perspective. The leading advocate, Milton Friedman, argued inflation always reflected movements in the money supply, which necessitated monetary contraction, specifically, higher interest rates to inhibit bank leading and resulting credit creation.

America and Britain strongly adhered to the prescription, which by the early 1980s began to bring down inflation but at the expense of a global recession and a more impoverished developing world. In both the US and UK unemployment reached double-digit levels, which eventually arrested the wage-price spiral through weakening Trade Union bargaining power. Meanwhile, higher interest rates converted the developing world into a net exporter of capital through debt service alone, excluding profit repatriation and capital flight [Gill, S., and Law, D., 1988:152; George, S., 1993:179]. In collective bids to recover hard currency, developing countries created commodity gluts, which caused the collapse of prices and most commodity agreements and cartels, even the weakening of OPEC [Gill, S., 1993:271].

The cost-push sources of Western inflation were thus brought under control but a lasting victory required resolving the crisis of excess liquidity through enhancing the global mobility of capital [Bienefeld, M., 1989:9-41; Strange, S., 1988:108; Amin, S., 1994a:33-39; Ould-Mey, M., 1994:321-322]. This imperative underpinned the quest for global adjustment, that is, the 'rolling back' of state-directed economies in favour of open market forces. World indebtedness enabled the power agents in the world economy, namely, the Group of Seven* [G7], to commence the adjustment process by lending money in exchange for the desired policy reforms. Over 1975–1980, the G7 progressively coordinated their approach and eventually designated the IMF and World Bank 'as the central authority for exercising the collective power of capitalist nation states over international financial negotiations' [cited in Ould-Mey, M., 1994:323]. In 1983, the US Secretary of Treasury, Donald

* The G7 is composed of the USA, the UK, Germany, France, Italy, Japan and Canada.

Regan, announced 'a broad international strategy' in which the IMF was the 'linchpin' [cited in Ould-Mey, 1994:323].

Evident in any World Bank or IMF publication since the late 1970s, a theoretical rationale drawn from the neo-classical or neo-liberal school presents Structural Adjustment Programs [SAPs] as being in the best interests of poor countries. The 1980s development record in Africa and elsewhere, however, as I discuss in the next chapter, suggests that the policies better serve the rich via export markets, investment outlets and cheap import sources. John Keynes—a leading architect of the Bretton Woods system—hoped that the two IFIs created would adopt a supra-national approach toward world monetary stability, credit provision and a liberal trading order [George, S., and Sabelli, F., 1994:34-35]. Instead, they ended up beholden to the open door policy, which reflected the fact that members of the Western alliance were the chief capital subscribers with the highest voting power [Gill, S., and Law, D., 1988:90-91; George, S., and Sabelli, F., 1994:14-15,208]. As a result, the West wielded unprecedented power over the world economy, which ultimately spelt the end of the Soviet bloc [See Callinicos, A., 1991:94], let alone a true liberation of Zimbabwe.

2.4.2 The Shortfall of Lancaster House

In an endeavour to get the international community to lift sanctions, Ian Smith heeded Kissinger's advice and established a transitional government run by a multiracial executive council. By insisting, however, that the new constitution guarantee white control of defence, law and order, the public service and 25% of parliamentary seats, he only lured the moderate 'internal' African parties, which had no control over the war. Known as the 'internal settlement' of 'Zimbabwe Rhodesia', the arrangement led to the election of the United African National Council [UANC], led by Bishop Abel Muzorewa, which formed the country's first black Government in April 1979.[16] Although committed to repeal laws of racial segregation over land, health and education [Martin, D., and Johnson, P., 1981:271], the Frontline States* and the exiled or 'external' parties of ZANU and ZAPU could never recognise a Government in which

* The Front Line States were Zambia, Mozambique, Tanzania, Botswana and Angola.

Rhodesians retained control over the military and police. The war greatly intensified—33% of total deaths occurred in 1979 alone [Kriger, N.J., 1992:92,113]—which no doubt countered an inclination among Western powers, particularly Margaret Thatcher's UK, to recognise the Muzorewa regime [Martin, D., and Johnson, P., 1981:302].

The Frontline States and the 'external parties' commanded real power over the war and the fate of settler society but only used it to obtain a better deal from the Anglo-American alliance concerning the safety of their military forces. Largely at the behest of the Frontline States, the ZANU and ZAPU leadership formed the Patriotic Front to bring about a quick diplomatic end to the war. From the Geneva conference in late 1976 through to Lancaster House in late 1979, a key priority related less to the land question than simply, as Robert Mugabe put it, to 'whose army will be in control' before a free election [cited in Martin, D., and Johnson, P., 1981:268]. Although less acute than in the 'internal' parties, a populist-elitist or peasant-capitalist divide still applied to the 'external' parties. Indeed, as a 'struggle within the struggle', a broad 'bourgeois-Marxist' ideological gap manifested between political and military wings [Moore, D., 1991:481-488], which saw the former use force to bring military ranks into line with a confined liberation agenda.

The Marxist ideological challenge came from the March 11 Movement and the Zimbabwe Peoples Army [ZIPA], which both emerged from the military wings of the ZAPU and ZANU, namely, ZIPRA and ZANLA. Unlike the political leadership, most guerrillas were politicised with Marxist ideology after having been trained by the USSR and China [or by allied countries]. The first challenge occurred in Zambia on March 11, 1971, when a group of guerrillas from ZIPRA detained the Moyo and Chikerema factions in ZAPU. They demanded a congress to shift the interests of the party away from bourgeois elitism to those of soldiers, workers and peasants [Nyangoni, C., and Nyandoro, G., 1979:171-184]. Fearful of the socialist rhetoric, the Zambian Government arrested the cadres and imprisoned them for three years [Stoneman, C., and Cliffe, L., 1989:38].

The challenge of ZIPA was more long-lived and far-reaching. Its formation was ironically instigated by the Frontline States in late 1975 to create a united military leadership to intensify the armed struggle [Astrow, A., 1983:94,106]. Adopting the Chinese method of encircling the towns through the countryside, ZIPA went from strength to strength on the battlefield. In the camps in Mozambique, Wampoa College was established—a Marxist-Leninist school to train cadres in the methods of peasant-based revolutionary socialism [Moore, D., 1991:493]. Like the March 11 Movement, ZIPA wanted the politicians to be answerable to the military and believed that Zimbabwe's freedom could only be attained from total war, not from negotiations with either the settler regime or foreign powers. The Anglo-American initiatives of 1977, for example, were regarded by ZIPA as nothing but an 'imperialist plot ... to sabotage our revolution' [cited in Astrow, A., 1983:105].

Its autonomous existence posed an obstacle to the quest of the Frontline States and Patriotic Front to reach a compromise with the Anglo-American alliance. In early 1977, the ZIPA leadership was arrested and several hundred cadres murdered [Astrow, A., 1983:107]. At the forefront was Robert Mugabe, who took on board ZIPA's ideological discourse:

> The leadership must be warned that unless it can keep ahead of its followers, in its ideological education, it cannot justifiably continue to lay any sustainable claim to leadership [Mugabe, R., cited in Moore, D., 1991:494].

Revolutionary ideology made potent military strategy and propaganda to gain the support of the peasantry. Marxism-Leninism became the official ideology of the Zimbabwean state, albeit delivered by a bourgeois class that would 'multiply their appeals to the left for calm, while on their right they scan the horizon' [Fanon, F., 1963: 69].

Mixed messages were sent on the land question. At one point in 1978, Robert Mugabe promised an 'entirely new socialist arrangement' that would 'dismantle' the white farms [cited in Astrow, A., 1983:140]. Later in the year he qualified: 'you cannot start off by nationalising everything. You have to take into account the realities of the situation' [Mugabe , R., cited in *Zimbabwe News*, 10, 6, 1978:3]. In October 1976, Joshua Nkomo appeared to sum up the true position: 'The homes, farms and businesses of whites in Rhodesia need not be at risk in a nationalist Zimbabwe provided whites respected the new laws and accepted the inevitability of a non-privileged status' [cited in Astrow, A., 1983:146, footnote 40].

At Lancaster House, apart from the security issue, the concessions offered did not differ greatly from those of Ian Smith. Subject to parliamentary amendment in ten years time, the Lancaster constitution assured for whites 20% of the parliamentary seats and protection of existing property rights, which encompassed the best half of the country. Section 16, the declaration of rights, to be upheld by an independent judiciary, prohibited outright state nationalisation of land; restricted land redistribution to market transactions; and confined state designation to under-utilised land upon payment in foreign currency [Stoneman, C., and Cliffe, L., 1989:30-31; Moyo, S., 1991: 9-14; Tshuma, L., 1997:39-47]. The Patriotic Front raised objections that the constitution undermined state sovereignty to redress land inequity and, therefore, the purpose of the war. Land redistribution through the market would bankrupt the government, the African nationalists argued, while the foreign currency stipulation accorded whites the status of foreigners and meant the state had to import land from its own country.

From above, the Patriotic Front faced formidable pressure. The Frontline states, whose economies were being destabilised by the war, threatened to withdraw the guerrilla sanctuaries while the UK indicated that sanctions on the Muzorewa Government may not be renewed [Stoneman, C., and Cliffe, L., 1989:31; Martin, D., and Johnson, P., 1981:315]. Still reluctant, the American undertaking to finance at least one-third of the US$1.5 billion Zimbabwe Development Fund [ZDF] finally broke the deadlock [Tshuma, L., 1997:41]. The promise went a long way to alleviate the Patriotic Front's fears over how to meet the people's 'great need' of land even though, as Joshua Nkomo later admitted, no-one really knew 'how much they would put up' [cited in Tshuma, L., 1997:41].

Regretfully, the ZDF turned out a 'bribe' as it never eventuated [MacGarry, B., 1994:17; Moyo, S., 1995:105-106; Bond, P.,1998:341]. One of the reasons surely related to the inherited state-directed macroeconomy especially in the light of the soon to be released World Bank report authored by Elliot Berg, *Accelerated Development in sub-Saharan Africa: an Agenda for Action* [1981]. Indeed, a sum like the 'Kissinger billion' could not go to a country with the wrong policies, which the West argued failed to create an 'enabling environment' for investment. The Rhodesian experience of ISI, however, indicates the contrary. Without the help of international 'donors', Zimbabwe acquired one of the most diversified and least indebted African economies, which the IFIs considered 'under-borrowed' [Kadhani, X.M., 1986:107, footnote 14]. Nonetheless, following Zimbabwe's membership to the IMF and World Bank in September 1980, the process of undermining what proved in the structural context an appropriate macroeconomic strategy commenced immediately.

In one of the world's most unequal societies, the Lancaster settlement tragically denied state autonomy to attend to the real cause of the crisis, namely, the agrarian base, which offered uneven development only. By cementing the continued dominance of settler and foreign capital, the agreement assured that an emergent African bourgeoisie would exploit the state to acquire interests in a highly skewed socioeconomic order. From the outset, there was limited potential for democratic and prosperous development and, therefore, little chance of counteracting Western imperatives. Many elements within the military preferred a 'fight to the finish' to give the African state unequivocal power to redesign the country. Otherwise, the question begged whether the sacrifice of 27,350 lives and the displacement of over a million people during the war had been in vain [Astrow, A., 1983:151; Mlambo, A., 1997:35].

3

The African Experience of SAPs and the Global Debate

At the time of Zimbabwe's independence, most African countries had already adopted Structural Adjustment Programs [SAPs], sponsored by the two International Financial Institutions [IFIs], the IMF and World Bank. Until the present, the economic benefits promised have largely eluded the continent, and along with other Asian and Latin American countries under the same policy regime, the experience can be one of disintegration. This chapter seeks to uncover why SAPs fail in certain countries. A major purpose is to update the reader on the status of these programs in the dialogue between North and South and to put the plight of Africa and Zimbabwe in a global context. In the following sequence, I introduce the controversy surrounding SAPs; review their rationale and impact in Africa; provide a critique of SAPs in relation to the African crisis; and assess the impact of the Asian crisis on the global debate with reference to Malaysia. The African experience gives poignancy and credence to an alternative route, which I outline in the concluding section.

Karl Polanyi [1944:132] provides a useful paradigm, which captures the underlying dynamics of a country's political economy. In a bid to control the 'legal mechanisms' that decide the extent of market freedom over trade and how the value of land, labour and money is determined, class forces engage in a continuous power struggle centred on 'two organising principles', namely, *economic liberalism* and *social protection*. A broad political divide tends to manifest between groups with interests in the international economy and tradables, who tend to favour *economic liberalism*, on the one hand,

and groups with interests in the national economy and non-tradables, on the other, who tend to favour *social protection.*[1] Current advocates of the former principle comprise a most powerful bloc that encompasses Western states, global institutions of finance and commerce, multinationals and export oriented farmers and industrialists. In contrast, advocates of protection comprise a poorer stratum of society including wage labour, small-scale industrialists and the bulk of peasant farmers. The position of the political class is pivotal and over the last twenty years, as the rise of SAPs reflects, liberalism has won general support.

Since the aforementioned World Bank report authored by Elliot Berg [1981] opened proceedings, SAPs are based on the assumption that state interference is to blame for the internal and external imbalances that plague African economies. Initially, SAPs focused solely on economic policy reform, particularly removal of state controls over trade, exchange, finance, prices, wages and investment. By the late 1980s, SAPs also focused on political reform—the key thrust being to foster 'good governance', which refers to a Western model of liberal democracy based on the rule of law and separation of powers. SAPs embrace, therefore, not only the principles of liberal economy but also of liberal democracy.

Either indebted and fiscally bankrupt states adopt SAPs or they forgo concessional credit from the IFIs and Western states as well as the chance of debt rescheduling [Chossudovsky, M., 1997:51]. Widespread global indebtedness across Africa, the Pacific, Latin America, Asia and the former Soviet bloc has enabled core states to use *loan conditionality* or 'policy-based' lending as the key weapon to spread the policies of economic liberalism. The agents of power, the G7, coordinate the global strategy of liberalism, otherwise called the 'Washington Consensus' [Williamson, J., 1993:1329-1336], while their instruments, the two IFIs, implement it through SAPs. These programs are the frontrunners of globalisation, which according to the author of *The Lexus and the Olive Tree* [1999], Thomas L. Friedmen, means the creation of a 'world without walls' [cited in *The Age*, 03/12/99]. If trade and commerce flow more freely across the globe, spreading a 'universal consumer culture', and country political systems 'increasingly resemble one another' [Fukuyama, F., 1992:xiv-xv], then, this directly reflects the global application of SAPs.

Many analysts view the advent of a more unified global political economy as beneficial for humankind. As the Berlin Wall tumbled, Francis Fukuyama [1989:3-18] claimed the new era a triumph of liberal democratic principles, which to him signified the 'end point of mankind's ideological evolution'. The 'good news', he later wrote [1992:xiii], is that virtually all societies now nurture the liberal ideals of individual liberty and freedom, which drove the French and American revolutions. Others like Anne Krueger, the director of the Centre for Research on Economic Development and Policy Reform at Stanford University, claim that globalisation 'has brought, and is bringing, great benefits to most of the world's population' [cited in *The Australian*, 11/10/00]. 'Evidence that economic growth', she continues, 'through trade liberalisation has delivered tremendous increases in living standards in poor countries is overwhelming'. During recent protests against the World Trade Organistion [WTO], the World Economic Forum and the IFIs, a persistent theme in the popular press is that the protestors misunderstand the advantages of free trade for thc world's poor [*The Australian* 5/09/00; *The Age*, 9/09/00].

Such arguments rest heavily on the export economies of East Asia, which over recent times witnessed the number of people subsisting on less than US$1 a day fall from 452 million to 278 million [*The Guardian Weekly*, 20/04/00]. Yet, pointedly, East Asian countries, whether Japan, Taiwan, South Korea, Singapore or Hong Kong, never adopted a laissez-faire market strategy as is being currently applied in Africa. In fact, most country trade regimes have been models of state regulation encompassing import protection, foreign exchange allocation, production incentive frameworks and public welfare [See Stein, H., 1995:31-52; Kim, K.S., 1995:87-144;Brautigam, D., 1995145-181].

While the era of globalisation has created prosperity, the wealth divide and poverty have grown alarmingly. The 2000 Human Development Report released by the UNDP observed that global inequalities had increased in the 20th century 'by orders of magnitude out of proportion to anything experienced before' [UNDP cited in *The Guardian Weekly*, 6/07/00]. In 1993, the richest countries with some 15% of the world's population controlled close to 80% of total world income while some 56% of the world's population in the low income countries [including China and India] received approximately 5% [Chossudovsky, M., 1997:38]. The 1998 Human Development Report concurred:

20% of the global population in that year accounted for 86% of consumption [cited in *The Age*, 10/09/98; *The Guardian Weekly*, 20/09/98]. The same report revealed that while the number of undernourished Africans increased from 103 million to 215 million over the last 20 years, the 15 richest people on earth had accrued more wealth than the total GDP of sub-Saharan Africa.[2]

The anomaly is that for many developing countries undergoing SAPs more capital in the form of debt service, import payments and profit repatriation seems to flow out than in. In the 1990s, according to the African Economic Report 1998 by the UN based Economic Commission for Africa [ECA], at about US$30 billion per year, sub-Saharan Africa now spends more on debt service than health and education [ECA 1996, via APIC, 8/05/98].[3] Yet more children are currently out of school than in 1990 and 24.5 million out of a world total of 34 million HIV-AIDS cases are in Central and Southern Africa [*The Guardian Weekly*, 9/12/99; UN/Harvard AIDS Review cited in *The Age*, 12/07/00]. While the internal and external structural constraints that underline the debt crisis existed before SAPs, the point is that these programs have helped expose poor countries to the inequities of the international trading and financial order.

The countries most vulnerable are dominated by peasantries—found across sub-Saharan Africa, South and Southeast Asia and Central and Andean America [Waterbury, J., 1999:335]—with weak domestic markets and a strong dependence on a narrow range of primary exports. The international trading environment—characterised since the 1970s by a downswing in prices for raw material exports and a upswing in prices of manufactured imports from the West—has worked against these countries [Mandaza, I., and Sachikonye, L.M., 1991:4-5]. The result has been debt and SAPs, which then force ruling Governments to expose fragile indigenous businesses and rural populations to fierce global forces of value, competition and speculation. A circle of development failure can get under way: economic decline leads to political instability, which continues to ensure economic failure [Bienefeld, M.A., 1995:118-121]. Although professing otherwise, SAPs can militate against the development of liberal democracy because they override the sovereignty of the state and local society to determine their own development priorities.

Indeed, the poor record of SAPs has recently inspired various IMF/World Bank staff members and consultants to question the ruling orthodoxy. The turning point seems to have been the Asian crisis in mid-1997 when the 'crisis five'—Indonesia, Malaysia, The Philippines, Thailand and South Korea—experienced massive capital flight that destabilised the whole region. While the popular press blamed the crisis on Asian governance, specifically, 'cronyism', a group of economists in the November 1998 edition of the Cambridge Journal of Economics argued that it had more to do with the progressive loss of state control over the financial system as a result of previous liberalisation drives recommended by the IMF and World Bank [cited in *The Guardian Weekly*, 6/12/98].

Figure 2: Wilcox's View of IMF Sponsored Structural Adjustment in Indonesia

Taken from *The Age*, 19/05/98.

The case of Indonesia, for example, inspired a stunning criticism from the then World Bank Chief economist, Joe Stiglitz. In return for 'bail out' loan, the IMF attached a standard list of adjustment conditions such as removal of food subsidies, currency devaluation and budget cutbacks. The negative impact of these measures, according to the Indonesian Central Bureau of Statistics [cited in *The Weekend Australian*, 4-5/07/98], witnessed an extra 32 million people fall below the poverty line to give a total of 79.4 million poverty-stricken out of a total population of 202 million. Stiglitz wrote: 'IMF economists frequently lack extensive experience in the country. They are more likely to have first-hand knowledge of its five-star hotels than of the villages that dot its countryside' [cited in *The Australian*, 19/04/00].

The Malaysian Prime Minister, Dr Mahathir Mohamad, denounced the 'one size fits all' policy prescriptions as 'deeply flawed' and went on to preside over a strong economic recovery under alternative policies. To some extent, the Malaysian experience vindicated criticism that orthodox 'austerity measures' tended to confirm rather than alleviate the economic crisis. Signs of new thinking have become evident, not least because of the embarrassing protests that presently seem to trace all major meetings of the IMF and World Bank. Yet the real power agents, the G7, remain reluctant to embrace change, most probably because the material benefits SAPs deliver to the industrialised world are too substantial. These programs are still presented as the panacea to economic and political decline in poor countries and I turn now to examine their rationale and record in Africa.

3.1 The Record of SAPs and the Evolving Rationale

Neo-classicism or neo-liberalism provides the economic and political rationale to apply SAPs. The roots of this school of thought lie with free market economists, particularly Frederick von Hayek [1944] and Milton Friedman [1980] from the University of Chicago [Galbraith, J.K., 1987:249-250].[4] 'Rational choice' theory, otherwise referred to as the 'new political economy' or the 'new institutionalism', emerged later as a political version of neo-liberalism. At the forefront was the work of both Robert Bates [1981] and Douglass North [1981], which focused on the political economy of poor countries—specifically the way 'different institutionalised rules affect the behaviour of rationally choosing individuals seeking to maximise their given material welfare preferences' [Leys, C., 1996:80]. Their research conclusions, that ISI policies are sources of corruption, have been important political weapons for the IFIs to legitimate SAPs in Africa beyond just economic theory. First and foremost though, SAPs reflect neo-liberal economic principles and I review the economic rationale before the political.

3.1.1 The Economic Rationale

'The main factors', the World Bank noted, 'behind the stagnation and decline were poor policies—both macroeconomic and sectoral—emanating from a development paradigm that gave the state a prominent role in production and in regulating economic activity' [1994a:20]. The ISI strategy is thus seen as the primary cause of the crisis, not external factors, whether oil shocks, the debt crisis or declining commodity prices [WB, 1989:25-26; 1994a:21-24, 55-56]. State controls on prices, wages, imports, exchange and interest rates are considered to distort market value, which then causes failure in resource allocation and integration with the world economy [WB, 1989:27-29; 1994a:20-23]. Fiscal and current account deficits eventually, blow out, the Government falls into a debt trap, public services deteriorate and the economy descends into a trough of stagnation.

The central contention is that an artificially low cost of goods and services, whether through subsidies, overvalued exchange rates or undervalued interest rates, burdens the state fiscus and creates conditions of excessive domestic demand, which in turn keeps inefficient producers in business, encourages imports as opposed to exports, drains foreign exchange reserves and constrains investment. By encouraging import dependent and internally oriented enterprises, ISI policies are believed to perpetuate the reliance on commodity exports, and therefore the vulnerability of African economies to external shocks. In 1980, for example, 88% of Nigerian export value was derived from oil, 93% of Ugandan from coffee, 57% of the Sudan from cotton and 89% of Zambian from copper [Gill, S., and Law, D., 1988:282].

To turn the economy around, African governments must submit to an international law of market value, as implied from the following quote:

> World experience demonstrates that the countries with the highest growth rates have kept their exchange rates competitive, avoided excessive protection to manufacturing industry and under pricing their agricultural products, kept interest rates positive and real wages in line with productivity, priced utilities to recover costs, and avoided high and accelerating inflation by following disciplined fiscal and monetary policies ... [WB, 1989:5].

Herein lie the key economic conditionalities of SAPs: an open trade regime, liberalisation of market forces to determine the value of goods, labour and money and financial prudence. To overcome state fiscal deficits, a standard SAP seeks to rationalise the public sector through disciplined monetary and fiscal policy, civil service retrenchment, privatisation of State-Owned Enterprises [SOEs] and cost recovery on public services including health and education. To correct current account deficits, SAPs advocate removal of wage and price controls, financial deregulation [i.e. market determined interest rates] and trade liberalisation [i.e. market-determined exchange rates and deregulation of imports, capital flows and foreign exchange allocation]. SAPs generally favour a shift from direct to indirect tax as well as reductions in company and trade taxes.

The rationale is that the free reign of market forces will release a strong dynamic of export-led growth. On the demand side, tight monetary policy and fiscal discipline is expected to shift consumption and investment back into line with actual income, counter inflation and release resources for productive investment [Nyawata, O.I., 1988:92]. Although the withdrawal of the state will cause an overall contraction in domestic demand, significant growth impetus from export markets is expected to more than compensate [WB, 1989: 4-14; 1995 vol. 1;13]. On the supply side, market-determined rates of exchange, interest, wages and prices alongside the deregulation of imports, foreign exchange and profit remittance are expected to attract foreign and induce local investors to capitalise on export opportunities [Bird, G, 1996:492]. Currency devaluation, for example, is believed to stimulate export demand and foreign investment; higher interest rates are expected to boost savings and reserve credit for viable entrepreneurs; and higher prices and lower wages will alleviate the profit squeeze. Meanwhile, privatisation of SOEs should reduce fiscal pressures on the state, create investment opportunities and increase competition.

Stand-by credit facilities promised by the IFIs and other donors are a critical part of any adjustment package to help the country buy imports as well as to ensure that the Government follows through on the reforms. Since the mid-1980s, in recognition that adjustment measures such as retrenchment and increased user fees have an austere impact on the poor, stand-by credit is also for welfare 'safety nets' [ADB, 1995:239]. Some social hardship, though, is considered a necessary but temporary cost. Once stabilisation is achieved, that is, the emergence of sustainable fiscal and current account deficits, strong economic growth is expected to override the social costs.

The fundamentals of neo-liberal orthodoxy—domestic demand restraint [i.e. monetary discipline, fiscal balance], open free trade and laissez-faire market forces—comprise the ruling philosophy of the IFIs [Leys, C, 1996:80; Bird, G., 1996:491, 493, 495, 503]. During the Reagan years, the IMF and World Bank both underwent centralisation to install these principles in dealings with all client countries [See George, S., and Sabelli, F., 1994:112-134]. Tightly monitored recruitment procedures and an absence of genuine research autonomy ensures that publications from both institutions never deviate from the accepted orthodoxy [See also Leys, C., 1996:26]. Whether contracted to consultants or done in house, the IFIs always specify 'the types of research that it will regard as legitimate and capable of generating valid results' [George, S., and Sabelli, F., 1994:193].

Nicholas Stern, a former Professor at the London School of Economics and Chief Economist of the European Bank for Reconstruction and Development, and currently Chief Economist of the World Bank, investigated the extent of intellectual freedom amongst World Bank staff. He concluded:

> Researchers are not free to follow intellectual inspiration. They are under constraints of designated priorities ... Further, there is quite a strong hierarchy and the atmosphere is much more deferential than one would find in universities. There is an understandable concern with what superiors will think of conclusions [cited in George, S., and Sabelli, F., 1994:198].

In this light, data gathered by the African Development Bank[5] [ADB] is considered of greater neutrality than that of the IFIs. Although the ADB is dependent on the financial subscriptions of core industrialised members and a propagator of SAPs, African member states have majority voting power on the Board of

Directors. In contrast to the IFIs, therefore, where the interests of core industrialised members are relatively unchecked, the ADB Group is forced to balance more the interests of both African and non-African members, which has resulted in a far more objective and less ideological appraisal of SAPs.

3.1.2 The Economic Record

Table 3.0 *Africa's Economic Performance, 1965–1994*

Indicators	1965-73	1974-79	1980-85	1986-93	1990-94
Population Growth Rate	2.7	2.9	3.0	3.0	3.0
Average Growth Rate of GDP	5.7	3.5	1.8	2.5	1.9
Average Growth Rate of Per Capita GDP	3.0	0.7	-1.1	-0.5	-1.1
Average Growth Rate of Agricultural Output	2.7	3.0	1.5	2.7	2.1
Average Growth Rate of Manufacturing Output	7.3	6.7	5.2	2.5	1.3
Investment/GDP [average]	16.5	20.9	16.3	15.6	15.3
Average growth Rate of Investment	9.6	6.9	-4.8	1.2	0.8
Savings/GDP [average]	16.2	19.7	14.9	13.8	12.7
Average Growth Rate of Exports	8.2	2.6	0.4	3.0	0.6
Average Growth Rate of Imports	7.4	6.2	-2.4	-0.7	0.4
Fiscal Balance/GDP	-	-5.4	-9.0	-8.7	-4.8
Average Rate of Inflation	5.8	13.8	18.8	21.7	27.2

Source: ADB, WB and UNDP data as cited in ADB, 1995:223.

A careful glance at Table 3.0 reveals that for most African countries the economic crisis commenced after and during the first and second oil shocks between 1973 and 1979 when OPEC increased the price of oil by some 550%. Import costs escalated accordingly, which alongside falling export demand and commodity prices saw the outbreak of large current account and fiscal deficits. Africa's total external debt jumped from US$9.9 billion in 1970 to $109.2 billion by 1980 while average debt service as a percentage of exports followed suit from 5.3% to 17.2% [ADB, 1995:222-225]. The 'officialisation' of most of this debt in the hands of the IFIs emerged as a key underlying factor for the spread of SAPs throughout Africa. The IFIs increased their ownership of the debt by either buying out private creditors on the 'secondary market' or receiving the debt from Western governments after private creditors had provisioned it off against tax [Chossudovsky, M., 1997:21-22; George, S,1992:87].

From 1980 onwards—the era of SAPs—Table 3.0 indicates that African economies generally failed to regain the growth rates obtained before the first oil crisis over 1965–1973 under ISI policies. In fact, surface figures display a very poor economic record: of higher inflation; declining or stagnant average growth rates of investment, savings, manufacturing output, exports, imports, overall GDP and GDP per capita; and a continued average growth rate in agriculture below the population rate. Despite significant currency devaluation, attractive tax concessions and the deregulation of wages, imports and prices across the continent, SAPs did not deliver on their major draw cards of greater investment, trade and macroeconomic stability.

Table 3.1 World Market Share of Africa's Traditional Exports

	1970	1980	1991	% Change
Cocoa	80.3	72.5	67.2	-16.3
Coffee	26.4	22.4	15.0	-43.0
Cotton	30.7	15.0	16.0	-47.7
Rubber	7.4	4.1	4.6	-37.8
Timber	13.4	11.0	7.2	-46.6
Copper	1.5	4.2	2.2	47.0
Iron Ore	12.5	6.5	2.5	-79.7

Source: UNCTAD data [various years] cited in ADB, 1995:357

The aggregate flow of foreign direct investment to Africa fell to US$2.2 billion in 1990—a decrease of 50% since 1989 and slightly more than what Portugal received in the same year [Mkandawire, T., 1994b:194]. By 1993, total foreign direct investment in Africa declined to US$1.8 billion while communist China received $26 billion alone [ADB, 1995:300]. In regard to trade, the world share of sub-Saharan Africa fell from 2.1% in 1987 to a mere 1.9% in 1997 while that of the least developed African countries fell from 0.6% to 0.3% [ECA, via APIC, 5/08/98]. Since 1970, as Table 3.1 shows, Africa lost world market share in all major export commodities except copper [ACB, 1995:356].[6] In most countries, current account deficits markedly deteriorated due to a worsening trade balance and rising external debt service. The continent's external debt rose from US$109.2 billion [32% of GDP] in 1980 to $249.6 billion [85.6% of GDP] in 1988 then to $349 billion by 1997— about 68% of which was in the 'official' hands of the IFIs [ADB, 1995:225, 1996:5; ECA 1998, via APIC, 8/05/98]. Debt service as a percentage of export earnings varied between 20% and 35%, which remained a real impediment on investment and growth.

The World Bank attempted to argue 'countries that improved their policies had improved growth, while those with deteriorating policies suffered further declines in growth' [Kiguel, M., and Jones, C., 1995:8]. Scholars maintain that the results of this line of inquiry are too inconclusive [see Logan, B.I., and Mengisteab, K., 1993:8-11]. To the African Development Bank [1995:229], the absence of improved investment rates even among the strongest reformers, such as Ghana and Tanzania, indicated that any increased capacity utilisation merely reflected higher import levels fuelled by increased IFI credit rather than any significant increase in productive capacity. In any case, as the World Bank conceded, irrespective of weak or strong reformers economic performance was generally inadequate to reduce poverty.

3.1.3 Broadening the Rationale

The central issue over SAPs is whether the poor performance reflects a failure of policy implementation or of the policies themselves. Indeed, out of the 266 IMF programs negotiated worldwide over 1980–1990, for example, 52% broke down in that the recipient Government disbanded the program and reversed the policies [Bird, G., 1996:488].[7] Significantly, once the IMF suspends credit all other creditors including the World Bank automatically follow. In Africa, the reform areas identified as subject to little or no progress included privatisation, financial policy, trade liberalisation and public sector management [Kiguel, M., and Jones, C., 1995:8-12]. As the 1980s progressed, the IFIs echoed the arguments of the 'rational choice' school that the reluctance of African states to fully implement SAPs reflected political failure on the part of leaders, not economic failure of the policies [see WB, 1997a:99].[8] One World Bank report [WB, 1989:6] called for a 'political renewal' to make the policies of economic liberalisation succeed. The rationale behind SAPs moved beyond pure economics into the realm of governance.

The 'rational choice' interpretation of African political economy presently legitimates the efforts of the IFIs to continue liberalising political and economic systems in Africa. The basic assumption is that African states have been hijacked by rapacious ruling elites and treated as domains to distribute largesse for political ends. The Weberian traits imposed upon the state—'impersonality of office and the uniform application of rules'—were 'interpenetrated', writes Crawford Young [1994:237-238], 'by a radically different set of operating mores, characterised as prebendalism'. The work of Jean-Francois Bayart [1993] consolidates this view further, particularly by its tendency to 'reduce African politics to personal accumulation and patronage, devoid of ideals, struggles for justice [and] notions of equality' [Szeftel, M., 1998:221].

Any persistence of economic controls, whether import protection, state allocations of foreign exchange or price subsidies, is perceived to reflect the ambitions of governing elites for power and wealth. In the words of Robert Bates [1994:18,25]:

> With demand exceeding supply, those who command power over the allocation of the good give it to some and withhold it from others. Government intervention in industries and markets can thus be used to create organised followings—groups of persons who owe their individual fortunes to discretionary or personalistic acts by those in power.

According to 'rational choice', the system of a quid pro quo explains why African states display a reluctance to undertake the necessary domestic demand management and stabilisation measures to offset fiscal and balance of payments deficits. Instead, a nasty cycle of self-destruction takes hold as 'the interventions that yield clientelism, patrimonialism, and corruption promote as well fiscal deficits and trade imbalances' [Bates, R., 1994:25].

The 'impulse for reform' remains generally muted amongst the public because the majority, being producers of non-tradables, acquire vested interests in continued protection and subsidies. 'Few mass movements have arisen', Bates observes [1994:25], 'demanding less government intervention, fewer social programs, less spending or less regulation'. Foreign involvement is thus perceived necessary to break the internal 'political deadlock'. Domestic calls for reform are largely confined to the producers of tradable—commercial farmers and multinational companies—who have an interest in the deregulation of exchange rates, foreign exchange allocation, imports and profit remittance. Although a minority, their voice is powerful, as Bates admits [1994:26], because 'it is backed by international agencies and foreign capital'. There are no qualms about whether the policies are right, or of overriding the democratic sovereignty of African states. Any resistance or reversals by governing elites are simply regarded as attempts to retain or restore rent-seeking opportunities [See Sahn, D.E., Dorosh, P.A. and Younger, S.D., 1997:247-252].

The key thrust of SAP political conditionalities is to create the so-called 'rational state'—one subject to the rule of law, transparent policy making, an efficient bureaucracy, responsible government and active civil society [WB, 1994b:vii]. Loan conditionalities thus incorporate a range of variables beyond economic policy such human rights, contained military expenditure, multipartyism and parliamentary democracy. These are seen to be consistent with the Bank's mandate to promote sustainable economic and social development. In practical terms, the governance agenda aims to turn around the abysmal record of SAPs through a more selective approach of 'identifying' reformers rather than 'creating' them [Dollar, D., and Svensson, J., 1998:4]. According to the World Bank's own research, successful SAPs accord to Governments that act within a democratic consensus [Dollar, D., and Svensson, J., 1998:15]. The Structural Adjustment Program Review Initiative [SAPRI] launched by the Bank in November 1997 should be seen in this light.[9]

3.2 The Political and Economic Failure of Loan Conditionalties in Africa

Historically, the period of 'creating' reformers initially relied in many cases on authoritarian regimes. The earliest SAPs pioneered in Africa, for instance, were all through dictatorships in Ghana, Nigeria and Malawi [Mkandawire, T., 1994a: 167-168]. In Latin America, Chile provides the clearest example of the nexus between SAPs and authoritarianism. In 1973, a US supported coup marked the commencement of Pinochet's murderous military junta and a SAP, which by 1990 witnessed 40% of the population living in poverty

[See Bello, W., 1994:42-45].[10] True, old Cold War dictatorships have now fallen but arguably, such a trend is more the result of civil resistance against the authoritarianism behind SAPs than any liberalism.

Now that the era of 'creating' reformers has passed, the present approach is to 'identify' the promising candidates. The selection of favoured clients is politically loaded and has arguably increased global inequality and exacerbated instability within some societies. Inevitably, the more economically diversified and politically cohesive countries receive the most support. The more fragile and divided states, on the other hand, which often reverse the policies because of higher poverty, can be left to rot under an 'aid freeze' until a 'better' governance regime emerges. As 'good governance' is equated with the implementation of neo-liberal policies, the key question raised is whether the new regime represents the ideals of the oppressed or the material interests of the power brokers in the world economy. If the latter case prevails, the distortion is enough to guarantee ongoing economic and political strife.

The global hegemony of neo-liberal orthodoxy tends to reduce democratic procedures to an 'exercise of futility' [Ould-Mey, M., 1995:145], particularly in societies where the welfare of large peasantries depends on strong state intervention. Zambia is a classic case where the fall of one Government and the rise of another resulted in continuation of the same IMF policies that local people had rebelled against.[11] Similarly, an IMF sponsored plan to 'dollarise' the currency in Ecuador, dramatically brought down the Mahaud Government in January 2000, only for it to be replaced by another that went on to implement the same plan.[12] In such cases, 'top down' insistence on neo-liberal policies militates against meaningful democratic development. In the end, the model of 'governance' offered is a 'truncated democracy' in that the freedoms inherent remain subordinate to the imperatives of global capitalism [Mkandawire, T., 1994a:163]. As true self-determination is curtailed, the political system loses the capacity to represent the people.

The neo-liberal ideological stance of the World Bank and IMF thus manifests as a form of indirect political interference and really stretches the bounds of their respective charters to promote in-country development and international stability. At the April 2000 summit of the Group of 77—an international organisation that represents 80% of the world's population—most members resented the apparent subservience to the G7 for open and unregulated markets and supported Fidel Castro's appeal to regain a 'fighting spirit' [*The Guardian Weekly*, 20/04/00]. As African economies deteriorate, the denial that SAPs compound demand and supply side constraints increasingly appears dogmatic. According to Sayre Schatz [1996:240] to blame these structural problems on poor governance is a 'fundamental misconception'. Of course, corruption may contribute to the malfunctioning of African economies but the 'fundamental problem', he continues [1996:242], 'lies in the economy itself'.

3.2.1 The Nature of the African Crisis

The economic crisis manifested as a stagnant dependency on primary exports and capital imports but the disarticulation between African peasantries and modern capitalism formed the underlying cause [Breman, B., 1992:191; Mhone, G, 1995:69]. During the colonial era, because of unbridled commercialism, Government neglect and rising demographic and environmental pressure, African agriculture—a sector that still accounts for over 60% of the population in many countries—went into 'atrophy' [Mhone, G, 1992:20-23]. Other than 'state-conferred privileges and monopolies', there was little scope for African entrepreneurs to accumulate capital [Leys, C., 1995:45]. Deprived of thriving local markets, the modern industrial sector operated as an enclave, precariously relying on world commodity markets for its growth [Mengisteab, K., and Logan, B.I., 1990:449-452]. As the African agrarian base wilted, the onset of mass consumerism to fulfil basic needs could not be sustained by the 'excessive extroversion' of the continent's economies [Mengisteab, K., 1992:83; Cummings, R.J., 1992:31-32].

African nationalists turned to state enterprise as the central channel to increase wealth and address colonial inequities [Mkandawire, T., 1994b:206-209]. There is validity in the rational choice view that capital accumulation through the state merely benefits members and friends of the political class. Yet a sole focus on the exploitation of public office overlooks the underlying causes of poor economic and political performance. These are embedded in the structures of class and production, which sustain privileged elites alongside dependent peasantries. Most people are caught up in hand to mouth agriculture while monopoly enterprises exploit the scant investment opportunities available. As long as the indigenous economy fails to broadly flourish, no matter what the macroeconomic policy, whether of a capitalist or socialist orientation, state corruption, limited 'trickle down' and elite luxury consumption amid mass deprivation will remain features of the African landscape.

In most economies, the central contradiction is that 'social need and market guided allocation of resources do not necessarily correspond' [Mengisteab, K., 1992:84]. If the majority of population fails to assert effective demand, market forces simply bypass their needs and reach an equilibrium suited to a minority [Sen, A., 1990:189-203; Streeton, P., 1993:1293; Stoneman, C., 1993:93]. Contrary to the 'rational choice' school, state interference is required for the most basic of economic reasons, not least hunger. Between 15% to 73% of rural households in the major grain producing areas of Mali, Somali, Senegal and Zimbabwe, for example, are net buyers of stable grain and only between 22% to 48% are net sellers [Staatz, J.M. and Eicher, C.K., 1990:26]. State provision of public goods, employment, subsidies on basic necessities and farming inputs became pivotal factors in African economies to keep people above the poverty line and sustain domestic forces of supply and demand. Inevitably, a paternal and rent seeking relationship evolved between African states and peasant communities. Again, though, this should be seen as a political manifestation of a given structural predicament rather than an outright cause of economic crisis.

There is evidence, as Paul Kennedy [1994:194-195] uncovers, that African governments have shown a reluctance to encourage the rise of local capitalist classes. This anomaly is not simply the result of political ambition on the part of leaders to sustain patrimonial links. What is not fully appreciated by 'rational choice' is the great political dilemma that besets African states. The support of local capitalism—to recall Rosa Luxemburg's thesis [1951 [ed]:369-371]—involves an assault to lessen the hold peasant communities have on land, labour and handicraft industries. The survival needs of peasants and capitalist entrepreneurs are in conflict: those of the former are linked to the provision of subsidies and ongoing state paternalism while those of the latter to the onset of a 'fully commoditised economy'. The failure to encourage local capitalism, therefore, as well as the subversion of the 'rational' state, relates as much to the social quest to protect the livelihoods of peasant households as it does to preserve channels of political support.

Nevertheless, the economic emancipation of Africa rests far more on the rise of indigenous capitalist classes than it does on state enterprise. Scholars have long stressed that the emergence of an autonomous national bourgeoisie, or indigenous 'anchor class', to use Ibbo Mandaza's preferred term [1995:31; see also *The Zimbabwe Mirror*, 14/01/00], is a crucial factor in widening the cycle of production, employment and consumption. The challenge is for the state to interact with local entrepreneurs and broaden the base for the primary accumulation of capital [Leys, C., 1996:164]. Yet such in turn calls for bold structural reform, as I outline in the final section, which confronts inherited colonial land structures, institutions and bureaucracies. Irrespective of the ideology, any attempt to work within is likely to fail as the agrarian programs of village collectivisation and tenure reform in Tanzania and Kenya demonstrate respectively [Okoth-Ogendo, H.W.O. 1993:247-273].

Although 'rational choice' thinkers misinterpret the reasons why state economic controls persist, their conclusion that the patrimonial nexus between rulers and peasant communities needs to be overcome to make way for indigenous capitalism is pertinent. Indeed, unless this is achieved the continent is likely to remain forever dependent on so-called 'donors'. The point of issue is over the type of development strategy advocated, whether state or market-led. The problem with 'rational choice' is that it seeks a market cure from an unviable structural base wherein there is great disharmony between free market forces and social need. The end result is chaotic: with an ironical vengeance, the worst features of African economies and governance appear to surface.

3.2.2 The Turmoil of SAPs

SAPs represent a 'top down' assault on the peasantry and any allied government. Virtually overnight, households are made to submit to a global law of market value, the imperatives of export production and capitalist productive relations. Within the constraints of land and infrastructure combined with demographic and environmental pressures, the survival of many rural households is directly threatened. Global markets for palm oil, groundnuts, cocoa and coffee are increasingly the preserve of large-scale enterprises in Malaysia, USA, Brazil and Egypt [Leys, C., 1996:185] while the prospects for cotton also look dismal with the recent arrival of Pakistan, India and China on the world market [WB, 1995 vol.2:99]. Meanwhile, without candidly acknowledging the radical implications on peasant societies, 'rational choice' theorists including the World Bank maintain a persistent emphasis on the desirability of private property rights.[13] The unpopular intention is to hasten the processes of land and labour commodification, propelled by capitalist classes, and force non-viable households to disband and release land and labour. Nothing less than complete commercialisation is sought, which inevitably entails destruction of the final vestige of traditionalism—communal land tenure.

In a real sense, SAPs harbour an English style development route of gradual land enclosure and absorption of excess labour in towns and commercial farms. Paradoxically, however, by demanding state withdrawal from the domestic economy and exposure to the global economy, SAPs simultaneously diminish the prospect of a successful repeat of the English scenario. The domestic and global domains are dangerously idealised: the former as one of imminent entrepreneurs when people generally are without the wherewithal; and the latter as one of free and fair trade when in fact it is heavily regulated by core states and multinational companies. The policies of demand restraint and submission to export-led growth strip African economies of an adequate growth dynamic and expose them to their greatest vulnerabilities shrinking domestic markets and reliance on a few commodity exports. Under additional loan conditionalities of import liberalisation and a passive stance toward wealth redistribution, the advent of a healthy indigenous capitalism is extremely remote. The most likely consequences are increased landlessness, unemployment and political turmoil [Leys, C., 1996:137-138].

The World Bank and other interested creditors spend considerable sums on poverty studies that conclude 'adjustment has not worsened poverty' [Kiguel, M., and Jones, C., 1995:8-12]. A USAID funded study on adjustment in ten African countries, for example, claimed that the poor are 'small net gainers' and the biggest financial losers are ruling elites [Sahn, D.E., Dorosh, P.A. and Younger, S.D., 1997:247].[14] The simple reality, however, is that the sudden pursuit of fiscal balance, particularly the imposition of 'user fees' and retrenchment, carries an instantaneous socioeconomic cost upon many rural households in terms of health, education, output and income [ADB, 1995:234].[15] At the same time, macroeconomic deregulation results in currency depreciation, import competition, rising interest rates, high inflation and falling real wages. Only a select range of rural households and formal enterprises escape the dire struggle to survive. Meanwhile, the only cost upon governing elites is political popularity: otherwise, SAPs create plenty of opportunities to obtain privileged access within the marketplace [Szeftel, M., 1998:233]. Popular methods include hoarding foreign currency and imported goods in anticipation of rapid appreciation, or pursuing private trading opportunities to defraud peasant producers.

The attained export orientation comes at significant social cost and then exposes the economy to the vagaries of commodity markets. Because the import content of production and consumption is so high in African economies, the inflationary impact of currency devaluation is 'explosive' [ADB, 1995:348]. Thus, to obtain real export incentives for cocoa, kola nuts and pineapples, somewhat analogous to a dog chasing its tail, the Ghanaian economy underwent currency depreciations of 68% per year over the 1980s to keep competitive over an average inflation rate of 44% [ADB, 1995:369]. Although a rural minority capitalised on higher producer prices, anti-inflationary measures caused a depression in the non-export sectors, which engaged the majority. Informal markets became flooded, particularly as the state's deficit reduction program saw 50,000 people retrenched.[16] In the end, a 100% rise in cocoa output over 1983–1989 was accompanied by a decline of 48% in the world price and a 30% negative shift in the terms of trade [Logan, B.I., and Mengisteab, K., 1993:19]. By 1990, the trade deficit had increased to US$334 million, up from US$60 million since the start of the SAP in 1981, and external debt had risen from US$1.7 billion to US$3.5 billion [Bello, W., 1994:45-50].

The failure of the global economy to deliver benefits seriously questions whether fiscal austerity and macroeconomic deregulation bears any fruit at all. As already noted, greater foreign direct investment continues to elude the continent while higher commodity prices and expanding markets for export manufactures are yet to eventuate. An unfair reality of globalisation, via SAPs, is that African obedience to open markets for foreign imports and market-determined equilibrium value is not fully reciprocated in industrialised countries. At a deep level, the persistence of an illiberal trading order puts a cloud over the feasibility of enforcing internal reform in Africa without complementary reform in the external sphere [Logan, B.I., and Mengisteab, K., 1993:11]. Indeed, the failure of global demand to compensate for the fall in domestic demand makes African recession inevitable. The emergence of a more liberal and concessionary trading order, on the other hand, entails making more farmers and manufacturers in the developed world redundant—a prospect relevant governments do not embrace warmly. As it stands, globalisation is delivering them benefits in the form of financial returns, cheap commodities and additional markets.

The uneven prosperity of the era is reflected in the rise of multinational companies from about 7,000 in 1970 to 39,000 by 1995, of which about half are from four countries—the USA, Japan, Germany and Switzerland—the UK seventh on the rung [UN World Investment Report 1996 cited in The Age, 23/07/98; see also Lang, T., and Hines, C., 1993:34]. At the November 1999 WTO meeting in Seattle, according to the December 1999 issue of Africa Recovery by the UN [APIC dispatch, 22/01/00], African, Latin American and Caribbean delegations claimed that 70% of the wealth generated from trade liberalisation flowed to developed countries. They also pointed out that subsidies on Western food exports amounted to US$250 billion per year while tariffs on manufactured products entering industrialised markets from developing countries were four times higher than those imposed on such goods from core states.[17] One of the great ironies of the SAP era is that Africa, according to US Congressional Records [cited in Ould-Mey, M., 1995:135], emerged as one of the fastest growing agricultural markets for the US.[18]

Meanwhile, African transformation is expected to occur on the back of commodity exports, which according to some analysts 'makes no sense at all' [Browne, R.S., 1992:80]. Between 1970 and 1997, according to the World Bank report Can Africa Claim the 21st Century? [2000], the cumulative losses in the terms of trade for non-oil African commodity exporters amounted to 120% [APIC dispatch, 16/11/00]. In 1985–1986 alone, the export earnings of the region fell from US$64 billion to US$19 billion [UNCTAD, 1988, cited in Logan, B.I., Mengisteab, K., 1993:12].

The reality is that buying and selling power in world markets is heavily concentrated amongst multinationals. In the mid-1990s, for example, five companies were reported to control 77% of the cereal trade; three companies 83% of the cocoa trade; four companies one-third of manufactures; and similar concentration was evident in minerals [Greider, W., 1997:21; Lang, T., and Hines, C., 1993:35-36]. The concurrent pursuit of export strategies by African states accentuates the perils of flooded and colluded markets. The wide extent of demand elasticity assures little is gained from currency devaluation except the social costs of imported inflation and heavier debt burdens. The apparent domestic incentive to replace more expensive imports with local substitutes is often nullified by technological incapacity, which a weaker currency tends to reinforce [Browne, R.S. 1992:76].

The failure of SAPs to attract productive investment is a major point on which the policies backfire. The reality is that direct investors focus their attention on domestic markets that are growing, stable, and possessed with reliable infrastructure, like those found mainly in the industrialised north, to some extent Asia and decreasingly so in Africa.[19] Where home markets are stagnant or declining, liberalisation of financial and capital controls tends to invigorate portfolio investment, particularly speculative dealings in currency, property and share markets. African countries are particularly vulnerable, especially Zimbabwe, where global speculative capital during the 1990s proved a significant factor in economic instability.

Africa's general experience of SAPs has been one of economic contraction—higher debt burdens, inflation, unemployment, inequality and poverty, of which escalating rates of HIV-AIDS are a symptom. Meanwhile, the IFIs are the 'net recipients of resources from the developing countries' [Chomsky, N., 1997:131], which carries a serious ethical indictment on the policies of internal fiscal stringency and tradable goods promotion. The governance agenda provides no panacea, because political reform is tied to the same set of policies that results in this inequitable financial order. According to US intelligence sources, sub-Saharan Africa presently displays signs of 'implosion', as about half of the region's forty-eight states are embroiled in conflicts [cited in The Age, 26/08/00]. In certain circumstances, where wealth disparities accord to ethnicity, heightened socioeconomic stress under SAPs can exacerbate political instability. 'It can hardly be irrelevant that before the outbreak of genocide in Rwanda in 1994', writes Colin Leys [1996:25], 'per capita incomes had fallen by 50% in one year as a result of a collapse in coffee prices, followed by a drastic rise in food prices imposed by an IMF and World Bank SAP'.[20]

Paradoxically, however, the IFIs brand any government that resists or reverses the reforms corrupt and undemocratic. In reality, SAP reversals in poor countries often reflect attempts to restore macroeconomic management [i.e. budget allocations, financial policy, import liberalisation, price controls etc] to the sphere of democracy between local society and the state and away from the sphere of autocracy between the state and the IFIs [Ould-Mey, M., 1995:145; Schmitz, G.J., 1995:70; Moore, D.B., 1995:18; Bienefeld, M.A., 1995:108]. In any case, as mentioned, ruling elites do not need to reverse SAPs to restore rent-seeking opportunities. Corrupt governance has deeper roots in the structures of economic failure than the type of macroeconomic regime. A basic truism is that unless the local economy thrives, wealth seekers will always be tempted to exploit public office for private ends [Himmelstrand, U., 1994: 23-24]. The road to better governance in Africa would seem to lie in alternative policies that aim to reform the structural constraints and create space for an indigenous sector to prosper.

To some extent, the weak points of globalisation, namely, free trade hypocrisy, the worsening debt crisis, an enlarged wealth divide and destabilising speculative activity are shifting global public support against the neo-liberal orthodoxy. A significant event was Malaysia's denouncement of IMF prescriptions during the Asian crisis and successful adherence to an alternative route.

3.3 The Malaysian Challenge: Is the Tide Turning?

In global terms, the onset of SAPs in the late 1970s accompanied and added impetus to the shift away from productive to portfolio investments [See Strange, S., 1986:1-3]. In the early 1990s, many Asian countries liberalised their financial and capital markets. The changes were largely in response to international pressure and provoked a flood of speculative capital seeking short-term gains in real estate, shares and currency dealings [Stiglitz, J., cited in *The Australian*, 19/04/00].

As markets became flooded and the banking system overstretched, the float of the Thai baht in July 1997 precipitated panic. 'Just as suddenly capital flowed in', Joe Stiglitz wrote [cited in *The Australian*, 19/04/00], 'it flowed out' causing currencies and economies to plummet across the region. Amid the chaos, currency speculators were reported to have made fortunes, Soros Fund Management, for example, to the tune of US$1.6 billion [*Sydney Morning Herald*, 31/10/97].

The IMF and Western countries maintained that the crisis reflected fundamental weaknesses in the Asian financial and corporate systems caused by a lack of separation between business and government [Stanley Fischer, IMF deputy Director, cited in *The Australian*, 19/10/99]. Currency traders were viewed as an integral part of the free market system and 'equilibrium' value. The head of Soros Fund Management, George Soros, however, seemed at variance with this view:

> ... as I told the US Congress, financial markets behaved more like a wrecking ball, swinging from country to country. It is difficult to escape the conclusion that the international financial system itself constituted the main ingredient in the meltdown process [Soros, G., cited in *The Age*, 30/11/98].

Nonetheless, in a bid to 'restore confidence', South Korea, Indonesia, the Philippines and Thailand all negotiated 'bail out' loans with the IMF in exchange for standard 'austerity' measures centred on monetary and fiscal contraction as well as further trade and capital liberalisation.

In the words of the Prime Minister, Dr Mahathir Mohamad, Malaysia followed the 'Frank Sinatra' road [cited in *The Austrialian*, 22/10/99]. At first, the quest to assert state authority over global market forces lacked coherency. Rhetorical threats to ban currency traders—whom the Prime Minister labelled 'self-serving rogues' and 'criminals'—and control foreign share trading, only fuelled capital flight, falling share prices and a 40% crash in the local currency [i.e. the ringgit] [See *The Australian*, 6-7/09/97]. Meanwhile, Soros responded with hypocrisy: 'Dr Mahathir is a menace to his country'; and regarded the threat to ban currency trading 'so inappropriate that it does not deserve serious consideration' [cited in *The Australian*, 27-28/09/97]. But on September 1 1998, Malaysia's threats were given substance: the Government pegged the ringgit against the US dollar, removed the currency from international trading and imposed controls on the repatriation of foreign speculative capital.[21]

The aim, according to Bank Negara, the country's central bank, was to 'regain monetary independence and insulate the Malaysian economy from the prospects of further deterioration in the world economic and financial environment' [cited in *The Australian*, 2/09/98]. No restrictions applied on the flow of foreign direct investment. 'The changes are directed at containing speculation on the ringgit', Bank Negara continued, 'and at minimising the impact of short-term capital flows on the domestic economy'. In effect, the measures enabled the Government to lower interest rates without risking another currency plunge, stimulate lending and restart an economy that for the first time in 13 years had registered negative growth.

The defiance of neo-liberal orthodoxy came at an economic and political price: the measures deterred prospective foreign direct investors[22] and entailed a domestic political purge, which damaged the country's prospects for long-term political stability. The day after the controls were imposed, Dr Mahathir sacked the Governor and deputy of Bank Negara as well as the Finance Minister, Anwar Ibrahim—the symbol according to the then US Vice-President, Al Gore, of the country's democracy movement or 'reformasi'. Anwar's pro-IMF stance was well known: he had vowed earlier to root out 'cronyism' and proceeded to implement an IMF style austerity program, which saw a 20% reduction in Government spending and the shelving of several big-ticket projects. A lot was at stake, the Prime Minister later said [*The Australian*, 22/10.99], as the approach 'threatened to destroy the fabric of modern Malaysia'. Whether a fiction or not, he regarded Anwar an external agent undermining the economy and coherency of the state in what he considered at the time an 'economic war' with 'Western syndicates':

> They [i.e. foreign powers] look for credible puppets ... They gave open support to the attempt by the puppets to paralyse the race which is the backbone of the national Government. This is what is happening. It is clear that an attempt to colonise the country was made. It has failed this time. But there is no guarantee that another attempt won't be made again [*Mahathir, M., cited in The Age, 14/12/98*].

Anwar was politically crucified: tried and convicted of corruption and sodomy, he received 15 years imprisonment and has since become a rallying point for democratic reform. He claimed himself a victim of a political conspiracy at the highest order driven by vested crony interests that were threatened by his austerity program [*Guardian Weekly*, 13/09/98].

On the economic front, many orthodox analysts regarded the economic measures 'staggeringly inept' and predicted 'spectacular failure'. The Government's stance, however, was soon vindicated: after contracting by 6.7% in 1998, the economy rebounded with a 5.4% positive growth rate in 1999, 11.9% in the first quarter of the year 2000 to average out at 8.7% per annum [*The Age*, 30/11/00]. The performance was underpinned by low interest rates and inflation, strong domestic demand and phenomenal surges in export manufactures, which ushered trade surpluses for twenty consecutive months [*The Australian*, 9/08/00]. The state-led investment push into the cheap markets of Asia, Africa and Latin America, often spurned by others, continued to be of prime significance [*The Age*, 5/10/00].[23] But fundamental to the recovery, according to the International Trade and Industry Minister, was a stable and competitive exchange rate:

> The pegging of the ringgit against the US dollar brought about certainty and predictability for the business community [Rafidah Aziz, cited in *The Australian* 3/08/99].

At an IMF meeting, the Japanese Finance Minister, Kiichi Miyazawa, hailed the capital controls a success and advised they be 'evaluated positively as one positive response when a country faces the danger of sudden capital flight' [cited in *The Australian*, 29/09/99]. To Joe Stiglitz, Malaysia offered a general lesson:

> I hope that the recovery ... will bring with it a renewal of self-confidence that allowed the region to forge three decades of unprecedented growth, stability and poverty reduction, based not on the dictums of the Washington Consensus but a deeper understanding of their own economies and societies [cited in *The Australian* 20/10/99].

The relatively debt-free and strong Malaysian recovery directly challenged neo-liberal orthodoxy. The IMF maintained that the capital controls made little difference and, if anything, deterred direct investment relative to the other 'crisis' economies [Stanley Fischer cited in *The Australian*, 19/10/99]. In contrast, however, Indonesia descended into absolute chaos and the Thai economy—a key strategic IMF pupil—experienced a deep contraction of 10% in 1998. If Indonesia and Thailand, Dr Mahathir argued [*The Australian*, 5/02/99], 'had not been forced to raise their interest rates to squeeze credit they could have managed their economies better'. Pointedly, the Thai Government since 1998 has been allowed to run up a budget deficit to stimulate the economy in classic Keynesian fashion [*The Guardian Weekly*, 24/02/00].

In the developing world, many Governments such as the Zimbabwean regard Malaysia as a model to emulate. Dr Mahathir cautions that the favourable trade balance and domestic capacity to finance development limits Malaysia's relevance elsewhere [*The Australian*, 5/02/99]. In terms of investment, trade and tourism, he insists, the country is more globally engaged than the US. Nonetheless, on behalf of the South, he lambastes the IMF as 'too rigid' and for seeing the world only 'from the view of Europe and the US' [*The Australian*, 7/03/00]. As for currency traders:

> Their reform is much more needed than ours ... I don't see the need at all for currency trading. They take out money but pay tax to no one. I don't understand why there is a reluctance to curb currency trading ... The ringgit will remain pegged until the international system finds a way to stop currency traders devaluing currencies at will [*The Australian*, 1/02/99. 3/09/99, 14/07/00].

On the down side, the strength of the Malaysian economy, that is, the extent of global engagement, is also a weakness. Japan and the US alone take up about 45% of the country's exports, two-thirds of which are electrical goods such as disk drives, computer chips, microwave ovens and TVs. A severe downturn of the American and Japanese economies is likely to embroil Malaysia and all outward trade economies that could well imperil the globalisation project itself. To retrieve the confidence of direct investors, an easing of capital controls appears imminent but while about to 'blow a kiss' to international finance, Dr Mahathir has reservations:

> Absolute globalisation unguided by rationality and sound judgement is perhaps the greatest danger to the world at the dawn of our new century [The Australian, 28/02/01].

The experience of the Asian crisis provoked other incidents of recalcitrance amongst IFI staff besides that of Joe Stiglitz. The first draft of the World Development Report [2000], for example, written by consultant Professor Ravi Kanbur from Cornell University, admitted that the prescriptions of balanced budgets, free trade and externally oriented growth had failed to reduce poverty [*The Guardian Weekly*, 22/07/00; APIC dispatch 21/07.00]. A fresh approach was called for that put greater emphasis on progressive taxation, social spending, income security for the poor and capital controls to stem speculation. Another example is Horst Koehler, the new Managing Director of the Fund, who apparently said at a recent IFI meeting in Prague that he could no longer force developing nations to adopt trade liberalisation that rich countries like the US had not yet undertaken [*The Guardian Weekly*, 30/09/00].

The G7, however, continue to lag behind the impetus for change and hold steadfast to neo-liberal prescriptions. In apparent fear that developing countries may have used the World Development Report to justify efforts to reintroduce controls and redistribute income, the US Secretary of Treasury, Larry Summers, rewrote Professor Kanbur's draft, which provoked his resignation in June 2000 [*The Guardian Weekly*, 21/09/00].[24] Debt relief and increased market access in the West are used by the G7 as carrots to secure and deepen liberal reforms in poor countries. For example, the 'Africa Growth and Opportunity Act', passed by the US Congress in the late 1990s, allocates trade preferences and debt relief to countries that demonstrate a commitment to market oriented reforms and human rights [APIC dispatch 9/09/97, 13/07/99]. Similarly, the G7's 'fast track' US$23 billion debt relief initiative passed at the Cologne meeting in June 1999 and the promise of Britain and Germany to cancel bilateral debt in response to the Jubilee 2000 campaign only applies to countries faithfully undergoing SAPs [*See The Guardian Weekly*, 9/09/99, 30/09/99, 7/10/99, 6/01/00, 9/11/00]. As mentioned, over 60% of Africa's debt is owed to the IFIs and whether they can themselves engage in meaningful debt relief largely depends on the US Congress.

3.4 Toward an Alternative in Africa

The African Development Bank [1995:237] observes that while governments may after implementing a SAP 'point at some progress in the fiscal and monetary areas, as well as in their balance of payments, few could, with any degree of confidence, point to a significantly improved situation for their poor and vulnerable groups'. The basic dilemma of African political economy is that the measures perceived necessary to restore the economy—fiscal balance and macroeconomic deregulation—do not accord to the welfare interests of the mass peasantry. A successful SAP merely resuscitates the outward orientation of an oligopolistic enclave, which on average only employs about 15% of the labour, while poverty remains endemic and continues to stymie industrial growth [Mhone, G., 1995:66]. In this context, 'it is not obvious', write Kidane Mengisteab and Bernard Logan [1990:439], 'that economic efficiency and growth should be the priorities of African states'. Short-term goals of efficiency and growth may have to be sacrificed in favour of a longer-term strategy to overcome the structural predicament

Any alternative strategy to SAPs must rest on a different philosophy, one that measures development objectives 'by what is happening to people, not what is happening to GDP, the balance of payments or the budget deficit' [Browne, R.S., 1992:75]. In this respect, the Organisation of African Unity [OAU] and the Economic Commission for Africa [ECA] have advocated inward oriented basic needs strategies in which macroeconomic variables are rightly relegated a servile role in a quest to boost local food production, small-scale industry, housing, health and education [See Cummings, R.J., 1992:29-46 and Browne, R.S., 1992:71-86]. A general consensus exists amongst these bodies that such a growth trajectory depends on a symbiotic expansion of home markets and indigenous entrepreneurial classes. Although the envisaged role of the state in alternative frameworks parallels the World Bank's [1989:5-6] emphasis on promoting an 'enabling environment' for investors through the provision of infrastructure, human capital, a legal framework and stable macroeconomic policies, a fundamental difference is that economic controls are regarded as legitimate policy weapons.

Beyond the minorities who benefit from export markets, the failure of globalised economies to adequately clothe, feed and accommodate the majority puts great pressure upon states to realign policies around peoples' needs rather than export enclaves. Some 'delinkage' from the world economy is likely to come, as Samir Amin [1994b:334] points out, more by 'default' than by 'design', which nonetheless involves a switch from serving global to home markets. Even so, if an inward orientation is to be sustainable, African governments and societies must face squarely the challenge to broaden the primary accumulation of capital and give rise to an anchor class. Put simply, the days of a generating a national economy from peasant agriculture are long gone.

Africa can take some solace from the Japanese path of industrialisation, emulated to a large extent by South Korea and Taiwan, which did not involve peasant annihilation or a laissez-faire market approach. Indeed, the Asian trajectory of a proactive state in pursuit of agrarian class reform, financial stability and the promotion of import substitution, capital goods industries, non-traditional exports and strategic foreign investments, strikes at the heart of the neo-liberal orthodoxy [Mhone, G., 1995:71,75-83]. Despite the World Bank's attempt in the East Asian Miracle study [1993] to reconcile such contradictory evidence by isolating export promotion and education as the 'be all' factors, the pivotal macroeconomic role of the state in facilitating economic emancipation in Asia remains of concrete relevance to Africa [Bienefeld, M.A., 1995:96,101]. Yet Africa's road of agricultural transition will differ from Asia, as the particularities of wet rice production [i.e. the high grain to seed ratio, the suitability of small fields and the availability of irrigation], which allowed the survival of many Asian family-based cultivators, cannot easily be replicated [See Breman, J., and Mundle, S., 1991:xviii-xix; Byres, T.J., 1991:41-64].

The advent of an anchor class 'is primarily a political proposition' [Kennedy, P., 1994:196], which in Africa must comprise bold initiatives of agricultural reform and the abnegation of export-led growth. The former area involves bringing more land under capitalist productive relations in order to create space for an indigenous capitalist class to improve agricultural productive capacity. The latter area concerns a strategic use of state economic controls in order to improve the position of indigenous investors vis-à-vis transnational capital and encourage emergent enterprises to focus on the production of necessities—food, housing, transport and machinery. Progress in both areas hinges on intense political struggle, which entails the disruption of old class alliances, the creation of new ones, and the reorganisation of land use [Mhone, G, 1995:68,75,80].

The needs of rising capitalist classes and the peasantry will conflict, particularly over land. In contrast to the impoverished export-led scenario under SAPs, however, a domestic-led dynamic is likely to offer higher growth rates, lower inflation and overall greater employment opportunity. Further, the state retains discretionary power to mediate over the socioeconomic transformation and muddle its own way through. Indeed, a mixed land tenure pattern based on a selection of certain areas for commercial agriculture and others for sustainable subsistence production is a likely compromise to balance diverse sociopolitical interests.

The livelihoods of many rural households are at stake and a genuine democratic order is essential to ensure that outcomes are equitable and legitimate. There is, though, an unfortunate catch 22, in that a truly national liberal democratic order is only likely to eventuate after the anchor class has brought more land and labour of the peasantry under capitalist productive relations. The class itself generates the capital base for the state to invest in public utilities [i.e. cheap food, housing, health and education]; it diverts entrepreneurs away from state channels of exploitation; it demands accountable government; and it provides the political and economic autonomy to resist external interference and, therefore, sustain a lasting democratic pact between state and society. In contrast to the 'top down' scenario of SAPs, the road to better governance of an inward growth strategy is from the 'bottom up'.

In some shape or form, this very trajectory has been at work in Malaysia and the consequent rise of the national bourgeoisie was the defining factor, which enabled the state to withstand the 'onslaught of globalisation' [*The Zimbabwe Mirror*, 16/02/01]. Since the commencement of SAPs, African societies are showing the reverse and the gap between the ideal of equity and advancement and the reality of inequity and poverty has widened dangerously. What were Zimbabwe's chances to avert a similar fate?

4

The Demise of a Macroeconomic Compromise

The ZANU-PF Government espoused a 'popular socialist' agenda, which according to the *Growth with Equity* [1981] statement aimed to overcome:

> … economic exploitation of the majority by the few, the grossly uneven infrastructure and productive development of the rural and urban and distribution sectors, the unbalanced levels of development within and among sectors and the consequent grossly inequitable pattern of income distribution and of benefits to the overwhelming majority of this country … [cited Sachikonye, L.M., 1995b:184].

The Transitional National Development Plan [1982–1985] and the First Five Year Development Plan [1986–1990] emphasised the importance of state intervention to 'purposefully direct development' in industries 'strategic to socioeconomic development', such as housing and capital goods, which could lift employment, living standards, the export base and reduce the import bill [GoZ, 1982, 1986, cited in Lehman, 1990:54; Kadhani, X.M., 1986:102;Ndlela, D.B., 1986:156-157].

In an economy overwhelmingly concentrated in non-African hands, these documents elucidated the 'pleasant ends desired' but not 'the means of getting them' [Stoneman, C., 1988:53]. As of 1980, outside communal areas, the state only controlled 16% of productive capacity while whites and Asians [28%] and foreigners [56%] controlled the rest [WB, 1995 vol.2:115]. Worse still, given excess industrial capacity of some 30% [Riddell, R.C., 1990:379], the private sector's local investment horizons were largely static. Despite high savings and liquidity levels, the underlying inclination was to pursue speculative ventures in share trading and CBD property development rather than invest in the industries 'strategic to socioeconomic development'. Even development called for the state to initiate a process of indigenous 'primary accumulation through simultaneous rural and industrial transformation' [Mhone, G, 1995:70], which entailed trading off short-term efficiency goals for a long-term gain of indigenous ownership, especially of prime land [Kadhani, X.M., 1986:118].

The Lancaster House constitution, however, fatally weakened the new Government's autonomy over land redistribution and, therefore, the potential for a dynamic linkage between agrarian change and industrial growth to establish itself. The market held sovereignty over the price of land, which bound redistribution to state fiscal capacity. Critically, market conditions of a dominant state buyer saw land values rise by 40% in US dollar terms over the 1980s [Moyo, S., 1995:123] while renewed links with the world economy, via the removal of sanctions on trade, credit and aid, saw debt payments rise 'sixty-fold' [Riddell, R.C., 1990:368]. Other pressing fiscal priorities in welfare, defence and agriculture soon overtook the land program, more so given the international community's unwillingness to fund land purchase [not to forget the empty ZDF]. By the end of the 1980s, land redistribution failed to impact on the agrarian class structure—less than 5% of rural households benefited [Moyo, S., 1995:266].

Popular socialism, however, was not totally devoid of substance or success. In the absence of structural reform, state economic regulation formed the basis of an important political compromise. Without seriously threatening the profits of monopoly capitalism, market freedom to determine interest rates, prices and wages as well as source imports and repatriate profits at will was denied [Stoneman, C., 1988:48]. Put together, the controls contained inflation and current account deficits and guaranteed a relatively cheap supply of domestic liquidity to finance budgetary deficits. In the interim, the peasantry received access to affordable health care, education and food while the Minimum Wages Act [1980] granted the highest real wage increases to the poorest sections of the workforce.[1] The budget deficit became the primary domain of wealth redistribution as well as employment creation, which had positive ramifications on African household economies through strengthening the exchange of food items and income between rural and urban kin.

Although welfare measures effectively balanced the peasant–capitalist class order and sustained Government legitimacy, they offered little in terms of resolving the aforementioned structural problem of investment. Despite an initial surge of growth [1980–1982] and late recovery [1987–1990], productive private investment remained sluggish, which underlined negative GDP per capita growth rates [1982–1984, 1986–1987] and stagnant employment levels [Appendix 7]. In turn, stagnation bolstered the push to liberalise the economy advocated by what amounted to a transnational bloc that crossed the spectrum of commerce, industry and capitalist agriculture. Led in large part by the two IFIs, national and international economic elites predictably overlooked their skewed monopoly over productive resources as a chief cause and blamed the crisis on the domains of popular socialism, namely, state economic controls and high recurrent expenditures.

The IFIs maintained a relentless criticism that the resort to state controls and budget deficits caused 'financial disintermediation' [Ncube, M.N., 1994:180]. The key point is that the distortion of market forces below equilibrium value [via consumer price controls/subsidies and fixed interest rates] and above [via fixed wage and exchange rates] created excessive home demand and a capital-intensive investment bias, which favoured protected and inward-oriented enterprises devoid of export drive and innovation [WB, 1995 vol.2:115; 1997b:2]. Meanwhile, budget deficit financing is seen to divert private sector liquidity toward non-productive ends, such as a top-heavy civil service, inefficient SOEs and public debt service [IMF, 1997:6-9; WB, 1995 vol.2:16]. In the end, being at the expense of private investment, poverty reduction is 'not matched by a commensurate increase in average incomes' and is thus considered unsustainable [WB, 1995 vol.2:29].

To the World Bank, the problem of excess industrial capacity could easily be resolved by integrating with the global economy:

> Much of Zimbabwe's growth over the past thirty years has come from the pursuit of self-sufficiency in manufacturing and agriculture. This has meant that output and employment growth has not been commensurate with the magnitude of investments undertaken ... Zimbabwe must look outwards in its quest for sustained growth and poverty reduction. The

> growth in domestic demand will not be sufficient to fully utilise existing capacity and provide a basis for rapid growth [WB, 1995, vol.1:13].

The passage exemplifies the ahistorical and dangerous reasoning behind the push to deregulate the economy, upon which the World Bank and the IMF conditioned their credit. An external orientation is considered able to compensate for the need of internal structural reform and therein a more embracive endogenous growth dynamic, the absence of which had already caused two civil wars. Even then, as implied, there is little regard for the state to at least moderate the lack of mass purchasing power through the budget deficit which in reality became crucially linked to the maintenance of national welfare, infrastructure [via the SOEs] and social stability. External constraints of impoverished and war-torn regional markets and protected industrialised markets are ignored. The EU market, for example, was subject to non-tariff barriers [rules of origin clause, quota systems], tariff barriers [the Common Agricultural Policy] and restrictions under the GATT orbit [the Multifibres Arrangement and the Blair House Accord], all of which seriously hindered African exports [Onwuka, R.I., 1989:77-78; Hewitt, A., 1989:290; Grilli, E.R., 1993:162; Watkins, K., 1994a:65].

Inside Zimbabwe, the key wielders of economic power—white capitalist classes—could not be counted on to resist liberalisation. The economic regulations that industrialists and farmers, as Tor Skalnes [1993:420] observed, 'had earlier advocated under the banner of economic nationalism were now denounced by those same people as unworkable socialism'. Although the white population fell from 232,000 in mid-1979 to about 80,000 by 1990 [Godwin, P and Hancock, I., 1993:315; see also Appendix 1], the remnants, along with multinationals, dominated the output of agricultural, mining and manufacturing tradables. Under an African state, whites increasingly disliked controls on prices, wages and imports but particularly resented those over foreign exchange. Direct access to the hard currency earned from exports offered a sure way to protect wealth and a European standard of living. Economic liberalisation, therefore, accorded to the material interests of white capitalist classes while notions of African emancipation through land redistribution and state regulation remained fundamentally contrary.

Any chance of counteracting the global strategy of economic liberalism rested on the emergence of a new patriotic pact between the state and an indigenous 'anchor class' to champion UDI-style the cause of national development through the necessary controls. A thriving African private sector was likely to harbour a class interest for continued economic protection and democratic accountability as well as generate an economic base for the state to override the interests of white capitalist elites. Yet the Lancaster House constitution disallowed the thorough overhaul of colonial land structures required to create space for an autonomous African bourgeoisie. Instead, a state-based bourgeoisie led by ZANU-PF increasingly acquired stakes in the skewed economy, which went hand-in-hand with a bigger interest in political hegemony than structural reform. The embedded trends of authoritarianism and 'embourgeoisement' were ultimately responsible for the adoption of the SAP in 1990 [Dashwood, H., 1996:33-34, 41-44]. After all, like white capitalist counterparts with exporting enterprises, the ZANU-PF politburo stood to gain in an open economy.

In the end, economic liberalisation offered no prize at all: state regulation was actually holding the fragile society together. In the opening section, I elaborate on the rationale for structural reform as an ideal development strategy. The realities of the Lancaster agreement and macroeconomic constraints are then highlighted, which circumvented Government capacity to attend to the structural roots of an evolving national agrarian crisis. The third section discusses IMF and World Bank involvement in the economy during the 1980s, which discouraged a real resolution and assisted in the demise of what was in the circumstances a popular macroeconomic comprise. The final section concludes on the distorted domestic political development that inevitably accompanied the failure to enact structural reform. The country's leaders eventually courted the neo-liberal policy agenda and committed the fatal mistake of liberalising the economy before resolving its potential to spawn a stagflation spiral and greater mass impoverishment.

4.1 The Case for State-led Structural Reform

Just as the state had been pivotal in setting up the prevailing socioeconomic structure, it remained so for purposes of reform. In Zimbabwe, any development strategy worth its salt needed to resolve the national land question. The increased utilisation of prime land toward low cost intensive production, the World Bank belatedly admitted [1995 vol.2:102], offered the 'greatest potential' source of growth. Early post-war South Korea and Taiwan demonstrated that increased agricultural productivity facilitated by land reform was an effective way to stimulate industrial enterprise [Brautigam, D.A., 1994:117-119; Moyo, S., and Skalnes, T., 1990:18]. Land redistribution in Zimbabwe was no less fundamental to enlarge the national market and generate the industrial growth required to counter trade constraints and help divert excess liquidity away from non-productive speculative pursuits. The net gains included defusing the potential for another civil war and the rise of an African 'anchor class', which as argued in the previous chapter, is a necessary foundation toward building a democratic society.

Table 4.0 *Farm Sector Share of Natural Region and Percentage of Population in 1980*

LAND CATEGORY	NATURAL REGION					Total Hectares 1980	% of POP 1980
	I %	II %	III %	IV %	V %		
State inc. NPs	16	6	12	18	23	5,877,000	-
Communal Areas	13	21	39	50	49	16, 335,000	54.1
SSCS	-	4	4	4	2	1,477,081	1.5
LSCS	71	69	45	28	26	14,386,604	21.0
Total	100	100	100	100	100	38,075,685	76.6

Source: Chavunduka, G.L., 1982:23, 63-64.

As it was in 1980, the country's land structures were simply flawed:

> The Natural Regions designated for intensive production are currently being farmed extensively, whereas land that should only be utilised in an extensive manner is being farmed and grazed intensively [Weiner, D., Moyo, S., Munslow, B., and O'Keefe, P., 1984:39].

The prime Natural Regions [i.e. I and II], as Table 4.0 displays, overwhelmingly belonged to the large-scale commercial sector. Therein, a handful of multinational companies owned about 61% of the land; 6,000 individual farmers about 34%; and the state the remaining 5% [Moyo, S., 1995:84; IMF, 1997:8]. Meanwhile, over half the total population—about 4 million people in 1980—languished in communal areas, 74.2% of which were located in the driest Natural Regions of IV and V [Moyo, S., 1995:84]. Out of a total of 700,000 households, beyond the 100,000 or so *kulak** households, at least 330,000 suffered from a land shortage in that access to land was either non-existent or below subsistence requirements [Moyo, S., 1995:5,118; Bratton, M., 1994:72]. In addition, the number of squatters in urban and rural areas was recorded at 500,000 nationwide, 70,000 in Manicaland alone [Moyo, S., 1995:119; Astrow, A., 1983:182].

Although the large-scale sector accounted for 90% of agricultural output and 40% of total exports [IMF, 1997:8], large tracts of prime farming land lay idle. A 1984 study, for example, concluded that one-third to a half of the net arable land on a national scale and less than half in Mashonaland, Zimbabwe's grain basket, was being utilised both for cropping and fallow [Weiner, D., Moyo, S., Munslow, B., and O'Keefe, P., 1984:28, 22]. Sam Moyo [1995:13], a leading authority on the issue, claimed that commercial farm sizes, which averaged about 1,728 hectares, were generally beyond the financial and managerial capacity of owners to fully exploit. Lionel Cliffe [1986:43] in an FAO funded study argued that this situation reflected the historical evolution of the large-scale sector, which accorded more to political factors concerned with white income security than 'economic logic'. While a few thousand farms embodied efficient economies of scale, the extensive production systems of most fostered high import reliant cost structures.

There was considerable scope for the state to redistribute land without having to destroy white farms and the 271,000 jobs they provided in 1980, which represented about 25% of the formally employed [Cliffe, L., 1986:42]. Somewhere over 6 million hectares, as a conservative estimate, was unutilised or underutilised.[2] Most were located in the poorer Natural Regions of IV and V in 'large contiguous blocks' mainly suitable for grazing. In areas of higher agricultural potential [NRs I, II and III], according to a study by

* *Kulak* is the Russian term for rich peasant.

Michael Roth and John Bruce, about 3.5 million hectares were underutilised 'if crop production is more efficient than livestock grazing or wildlife management' [1994:113]. Otherwise at least 1.2 million hectares could be safely redistributed in these regions without disturbing stock production. Importantly, though, the best land was spread haphazardly over many farms and available in small parcels.

Land reform in Asia was largely confined to legal measures, which by granting full property rights to those already cultivating the soil eliminated a non-productive gentry [Moyo, S., 1995:74]. In Zimbabwe ninety years of colonial dislocation meant physically relocating people and building up infrastructure from scratch in some areas. The state also confronted a complexity of socioeconomic demands that ranged between destitute groups requiring land for reasons of basic survival through to *kulak* peasants and other elites requiring it for purposes of capitalist development. Inherent was a serious class conflict over land, which in the final analysis could only be resolved if the state accepted a dualism in agriculture and made land available for both subsistent as well as commercial purposes. Logistically and ideally, this meant carving out the small tracts of unutilised commercial land from the prime regions into viable units for capitalist farming and adding where possible the large tracts of commercial land in the poorer regions to communal areas or creating new areas for subsistent farming.

To suit varying class needs, different systems of land tenure and allocation were in order. For capitalist farming, given the need of large capital outlays and the reality that banks lend on the basis of collateral [Mswaka, T.E., 1994:14-15], security of tenure through alienable freehold or title deeds is 'an essential element of commercial success' [Rukuni, M., 1998:4]. Where a land holding is made a market commodity, the least arbitrary means of allocation, to concur with the World Bank [1995 vol.2:100], would be to allow the market to select the proprietors. The state could well assist indigenous buyers by fixing an affordable land price and as Rhodesia did, after an initial outlay, provide a lease to buy arrangement. In any case, out of the 162,000 families the Government planned to resettle in 1982, the overwhelming majority required land for reasons of basic livelihood—a purpose for which communal tenure was entirely appropriate. If land was to be comprehensively added to communal areas, depending on the local situation in the aftermath of the war, either a legitimate chiefship or 'people's committee' provided ideal channels of allocation.

The national exigency would be to ensure that on a sustainable basis areas meant for commercial or subsistence purposes performed their respective functions of enlarging the capital and employment base and providing people with basic social security. In areas designated commercial, freehold tenure alone was no guarantee to stop the resort to household relations of production— 'set primarily within the cultural context of marriage and reproduction, rather than hiring practices' [Cheater, A., 1986:73]. As the experience of the small-scale commercial sector [formerly the Purchase Areas] attests, there are inherent dangers of household population outgrowing the land available, which then results in land fragmentation and debilitated productive capacity.[3] If the function of freehold land is to maximise profit, employment and production, then capitalist relations of production based on wage labour are appropriate. Conversely, in areas designated for subsistence, within demographic constraints, an unbridled commercial exploitation of common property by privileged households was not only unsustainable on environmental grounds but also clashed ethically with the rationale of the tenure system. The overriding priority was to ensure that land use sustained majority welfare over the long term.

In new freehold areas, support in the form of seeds, breeding stock, advice, marketing and processing from the state agricultural bureaucracy and white farmers was paramount to help entrench capitalist productive relations. To encourage a reliance on wage labour, a ban on polygamy would be desirable. In expanded communal areas, long-term preservation of the commons—to echo the conclusions reached by Cliffe [1986:76, 80-81, 93] and the Land Tenure Commission [GoZ/LTC, 1994 vol.1:44]—depended on genuine community empowerment. During the brief time after the war, for example, when wartime 'people's committees' were relatively autonomous of party and state, they demonstrated an impressive capacity to resettle people and attend to village welfare and development [Kriger, N.J., 1992:215; Tshuma, L., 1997:86]. In other areas, clan-based traditional authorities remained strong and had the support of the people, in which case their ongoing inclusion in local resource management was vital.

If land reform were to balance the national imperatives of subsistent livelihood and capital accumulation, positive ramifications on the macroeconomy were likely to follow. The colonial inheritance of African rural decline imposed enormous fiscal burdens on the state, via SOEs, in the form of resettlement costs, food relief and consumer and producer subsidies. If land redistribution was to significantly enhance the carrying and productive capacity of communal areas, the corollary was less community dependency on the state budget. The advent of a prosperous local food economy, for instance, could markedly reduce resettlement and health maintenance costs as well as stimulate home industries [i.e. beer brewing, brick making, dressmaking, food processing]. According to Earl Scott's study, such enterprises had potential to generate 'reliable income to supply ... basic needs and make significant contributions to wellbeing' [1995:204].

Meanwhile, an overhauled large-scale sector would serve as the primary domain for an indigenous agrarian capitalism to intensify production and re-ignite a rural–urban growth dynamic. According to the World Bank [1995 vol.2:105-105-108] about 1.5 million hectares of land obtained from prime Natural Regions would suffice to create an extra 50,000 to 70,000 farms, benefit 250,000 to 350,000 family members and generate 130,644 jobs in ten years. Indeed, if such a growth trajectory was obtained, *kulak* peasants and non-resident communal 'free-riders' could well relieve communal areas of capitalist exploitation by entering the freehold sector where tenure, the agro-potential of the land, surrounding infrastructure and expertise was much better suited to sustain such a purpose.

State economic controls would continue to offer vital weapons for the Government to stimulate indigenous enterprise and markets as well as encourage foreign capital to diversify and deepen linkages among the formal sectors. 'The most effective tool', according to the former Chief Economist of the Confederation of Zimbabwe Industries [CZI], Roger Riddell [1990:386], 'to alter the pattern of relative investment is the foreign exchange allocation system'. Through targeted allocations, the development of selected subsectors can be prioritised and investment horizons broadened.

A core strategic aim was to foster a greater articulation between mining and manufacturing through an expanding capital goods sector. Thus, instead of exporting over 80% of the country's mineral wealth in raw or semi-processed form, the challenge was to process more minerals and ultimately widen the manufacture of machinery, spare parts and other intermediate inputs. Although initially requiring capital-intensive investments, a growing capital goods sector generates labour-intensive upstream linkages with other lead sectors such as agriculture, telecommunications, transport, energy and construction [Ndlela, D.B., 1986:148-151]. State industrial planning remained pivotal if the economy was to generate productive investment outlets, employment and a value-added export capacity. The aim should be to deliberately counter the tendency of market forces to reinforce the reliance on commodity exports and capital imports.

If any such strategy of 'self-sustaining industrialisation' was to eventuate, the state required unequivocal power to comprehensively overhaul colonial land design in one swoop through appropriation of underutilised land only upon payment for the investments undertaken. That the state was under a moral obligation to pay for the land value was dubious, as market appreciation, to accord with the principles of Henry George[4], rested more on the toil of African labour than any single white owner. Although many had paid for the land value, deprivation of recompense in this respect was no more unjust than how the land was originally obtained through 'right of conquest'. In any case, the overriding imperative was to resolve the national land question lest more lives were to be lost in yet another civil war.

Needless to say the foregoing is hypothetical, as the Lancaster constitution for the entire decade required the state to effectively 'import' appropriated land at market prices paid in foreign currency. For reasons of political legitimacy, the market should determine the indigenous proprietors of freehold farms but should not have held sovereignty over the Government's quest to resolve the national question, which is where I depart from the World Bank view. The constitution set the framework to preserve the socioeconomic order and thereby secured the same distortions that beset Rhodesian political economy [Stoneman, C., 1988:45; Moyo, S., 1991: 9-14; 1995:108].

4.2 The Tyrannies of Circumstance

In a *catch-22*, being bound to state fiscal capacity, land redistribution was hostage to the underlying structures of class and production, which remained too narrow to generate enough wealth for the Government to enact a comprehensive transfer. The highest rate occurred within the first three years of independence when ZANU-PF's revolutionary socialism remained fresh and the economy boomed in response to favourable agricultural seasons, large increases in minimum wages and the lifting of trade and credit sanctions. The simultaneous outbreak of internal and external imbalances, however, undermined state fiscal capacity and spawned dependency on the prevailing order, which IMF and World Bank credit further encouraged. The argument that economic woes stemmed from state regulation, buoyed by local lobby groups, such as the Whitsun Foundation[5] and the Commercial Framers Union [CFU], obviated the need for land reform and justified protection of the agrarian export base as well as a market-driven process [Moyo, S., 1995:54-55].

In parallel, a basic needs-oriented land redistribution subsided from the forefront of agrarian policy. Initially, the program targeted the poorest people, such as squatters, unemployed and war refugees [Mhishi, S.G., 1995:9] but by mid-decade, as the debate broadened to assess the relative efficiencies of peasant and capitalist framers, settler selection hardened and squatters were evicted. The land issue became subordinate to the interests of agrarian capitalism and surfaced as a contest between white and black elites. Within frozen land structures, the state promoted a black capitalist class and focused on peasant productivity and land use [Drinkwater, M., 1989:290-291]. The rational choice view gained sway in that low peasant productivity attributed less to a land shortage than an absence of market incentives, technical deficiencies in land use and 'backward' practices such as labour migration and subsistence production [Tshuma, L., 1997:72-75]. An intensified commercial orientation replaced land redistribution as a way to combat poverty, which over the short-term offered benefits but over the long-term greatly exacerbated the African agrarian crisis.

4.2.1 Macroeconomic Realities

In March 198I, the Zimbabwe Conference on Reconstruction and Development [ZIMCORD]—attended by forty-five nations, fifteen UN agencies and ten aid societies—marked the re-opening of links with the world economy, which the IMF affirmed the following month through release of a 'honeymoon' tranche of US$37.5 million [Appendix 8]. Western credit did not come unattached: out of the Z$2 billion pledged at ZIMCORD only Z$103 million was earmarked for land redistribution [Stoneman, C., 1988:60, footnote 18] while about 30% of every bilateral loan was tied to the purchase of imports [Chimombe, T., 1986:132; see also Lehman, H., 1990:61; Astrow, A., 1983:163]. The discipline of UDI-style macroeconomic management soon broke down. Externally, to meet demands of foreign creditors, low current account deficits could no longer be sustained by continuing the default on Rhodesian debt, strict import rationing and restrictions on profit repatriation while internally, low fiscal deficits could no more be maintained at the expense of neglecting African welfare interests.

Thus, over 1979–1982, as the Government honoured Rhodesian debt and eased restrictions on domestic expenditure, import consumption and capital repatriation, the current account deficit rose almost nine-fold to Z$533 million and the budget deficit reached 9.4% of GDP [Appendix 6 and 7]. Besides rising all-round outflows of service, income and transfer payments, the external deficit was compounded by the onset of negative trade balances. By 1983, net foreign reserves had declined by Z$500 million since 1979 [Kadenge, P., Ndoro, H., and Zwizwai, B., 1992:171]. To cover both the internal and external shortfalls, within three years, the country's foreign debt almost trebled and debt service obligations jumped by 300% [Appendix 7].

Declining world consumption and prices for raw and semi-processed goods largely underlined the poor trade performance. Trends in export manufactures were also disappointing. The ratio of manufactured exports to gross manufacturing output continued to fall over the late 1970s and early 1980s. In every subsector, except metals and textiles, the export to gross output ratio was less than 10%—down from 14% at the beginning of UDI [Riddell, R.C., 1990:345-346]. As a major market and transport hub for Zimbabwe's export manufactures, South Africa's conversion from a friend to foe and pursuit of destabilisation in Mozambique was reputed to reduce transit trade in the order of 25% [Stoneman, C., 1988:55]. At much greater cost, 55% of exports and 80% of imports had to pass through Mafeking and Beit Bridge. The shortage of foreign exchange and high transport costs constrained the capacity of enterprises to penetrate overseas markets. For the time being, given an upswing in domestic demand, the home market offered high profits, which the state import regime and cost-plus pricing formula protected.

Gross investment as a percentage of GDP declined from an average of 27% in the mid-1970s to about 20% during the 1980s [ILO/SAMAT, 1995:11; WB, 1995 vol.2:11]. Despite a healthy savings rate, which averaged 20% of GDP [WB, 1995 vol.1:9], the private sector remained inclined to disinvest, evident in falling fixed capital formation and share of gross investment from 19.8% and over 12% of GDP respectively in the early 1980s to 11.9% and 8% by mid-decade [GoZ, 1991a:2; Gibbon, P., 1995:8]. Thereon, fixed private investment began to improve yet total new foreign direct investment remained sluggish [Gibbon, P., 1995:8]. The capital goods sector was terminally flat while vast sums of capital flowed into luxury building renovations, city property speculation and the Zimbabwe Stock Exchange [ZSE]—one of world's the fastest growing. Indeed, quite unrelated to real production, as Patrick Bond [1998:225-263] documents, industrial and mining share indexes underwent an eighteen-fold increase over the decade while city land values rose between 455% and 1,488%.[6]

The public sector increasingly accounted for the formation of GDP: between 1980 and 1990, state expenditure ranged from 34% to 53% of GDP while state consumption rose from about 9% to 24% [Chidzero, B., 1993: 42; IMF, 1997:6]. Capital outlays, as a percentage of total state expenditure, fell from a peak of 24.2% in 1975 to less than 10% by the late 1980s. Overwhelmingly then, budget outlays went on recurrent purposes, namely and in order of importance, wages and salaries, education, defence, transfers to SOEs, debt service and health [Kadhani, X.M., 1986:116; Nyawata, O.I., 1988:108; CSO, 1997c:53]. The tax revenue base rose from 28.3% of GDP in 1984 to 37% by 1989, which was high by international standards but still inadequate to cover the budget deficit [Ncube, M.N., 1994:178; WB, 1995 vol. 2:17].

Total employment in public administration rose from 128,200 to 230,300 [Raftopoulos, B, 1992 No.55:59] while wages and salaries, as a percentage of recurrent expenditure, increased from 27% to 41.4%, which represented one-third of total formal sector earnings [Riddell, R.C., 1990:374; Chidzero, B., 1994:283; IMF, 1997:8]. Within two years of independence, education and health expenditure underwent increases of 140% and 74.5% respectively [Zvobgo, R.J., 1986:341; Bond, P., 1998:344]. As a percentage of GDP, education expenditure increased from 4.9% in 1980 to 6.5%

in 1987 [about one-fifth of budgetary outlays] while that for health, from 2.2% to 3.1%, which in real per capita terms represented a 48% rise [UNDP/PRF/IDS, 1998:25, 32-33; WB, 1996:27; Agere, S.T., 1986:364].

Defence expenditure, after initially falling in 1980, sharply escalated to usurp about one-fifth of the budget. Acts of South African sponsored sabotage in Mozambique forced Zimbabwe to deploy 15,000 troops to defend trade routes [particularly the oil pipeline], which cost an estimated US$3 million per week [Mlambo, A.S., 1997:48]. The Government also catered for 200,000 Mozambican refugees over the decade, which despite assistance from Oxfam and UNHCR represented a huge drain on resources. In the regional context, the dissident outbreak in Matabeleland, led by disgruntled ex-ZIPRA guerrillas, comprised a genuine internal security threat.[7] In early 1983, the President sent in the North Korean trained 'Fifth Brigade', composed largely of ex-ZANLA guerrillas, so that the rebels 'do not become as systematically organised as UNITA and RENAMO' [Mugabe, R., cited in Weitzer, R., 1990:164, footnote 110]. Until the signing of the ZANU-ZAPU Unity Accord in December 1987, thousands of innocent lives were lost in what is referred to as *Gukurahundi* [Fifth Brigade war].

Table 4.1 Accumulated Deficits of SOEs, 1980–1987
Z$ millions

SOE	Accumulated Deficit
Agricultural Marketing Authority*	1,584
National Railways of Zimbabwe	607
Zimbabwe Iron and Steel Corporation	500
Zimbabwe Electrical Supply Authority	474
Air Zimbabwe	358
Post and Telecommunications Corporation	207
Zimbabwe Mining Development Corporation	200
National Oil Corporation of Zimbabwe	161
Zimbabwe Broadcasting Commission	107

Source: WB data cited in Riddell, R.C., 1990:401, footnote 71.

* The AMA consisted of the Grain Marketing Board [GMB], the Cold Storage Commission [CSC], the Dairy Marketing Board [DMB] and the Cotton Marketing Board [CMB].

Transfer payments to SOEs, as a percentage of total spending, rose from 7.8% to 13% and interest payments on public debt grew to absorb 14% [ILO/SAMAT, 1995:12-14; Riddell, R.C., 1990:371; CSO, 1997c:53]. Combined SOE losses accounted for 28% of net foreign loan liabilities by 1987 [Riddell, R.C., 1990:371] and, as a percentage of the budget deficit, increased from 22.5% in 1980 to a peak of 58.5% in 1985, thereafter declining to below 40% [WB, 1991:7]. Poor performance of SOEs, according to Jeffrey Herbst [1989:73-80], stemmed from the relegation of economic rationality to political imperatives of African 'kingdom creation'. Maybe so but the uneven economy also invoked an imperative to regulate SOE operations as a way to offset structural deficiencies on the supply and demand side [Riddell, R.C., 1990:363,374, 387]. By no coincidence, being well placed to integrate the peasantry, the AMA incurred the most debt [Table 4.1] through capital expansion and provision of producer/consumer subsidies. In the domains of steel, fuel, transport and power, as much as formal enterprise benefited from subsidies through contained costs and improved export competitiveness; the peasantry did through enhanced capacity of urban kin to remit income.

4.2.2 The Extent of Land Reform and Large-Scale Commercial Trends

As of the late 1990s, over 70% of resettlement land purchased and almost the same percentage of people resettled was accomplished within the first five years of independence [Mhishi, S.G., 1995:7; Moyo, S., 1995:121]. The state gained 3,324,880 million hectares of land for resettlement in the 1980s: 2,780,863 hectares were purchased from the large-scale commercial sector, 2,247 hectares was state land and 541,770 hectares was derelict land [Moyo, S., 1995:121]. The number of white farm owners was reduced from about 6,000 to 4,600 odd and the large-scale sector's share of the total land area from 47% to 32% [Moyo, S., 1995:121; Roth, M, and Bruce, J., 1994:61; CSO, 1997a:145]. However, as Table 4.2 indicates, the large-scale sector retained the lion's share of the prime Natural Regions while the land released on the market, as Table 4.3 reveals, was generally the least productive—up to 80% was located in the driest regions.

Table 4.2 *Farm Sector Share of Natural Region and Percentage of Population in1992*

LAND CATEGORY	NATURAL REGION					Total Hectares 1992*	% of POP 1992
	I %	II %	III %	IV %	V %		
State^	8.5	0.5	2.2	18	21	5,478, 000	0.37
Communal Areas	20	22	39.3	50	47	16, 350, 000	51.40
SSCS	1.4	4	7.4	4	2	1, 238, 700	1.63
LSCS	65.9	63	33.6	22	24	11, 213, 400	11.30
Resettlement	4.2	10.5	17.5	6	6	3,290, 000	4.10
Total	100	100	100	100	100	37, 570,100	68.8

Source: Adapted from Moyo, S., 1995:85; CSO, 1992:28.

By decade end, 52,000 families, comprising over 400,000 people, had been resettled on about 2.7 million hectares [Bratton, M., 1994:77; Tshuma, L., 1997:70]. Of the area settled, 91% was devoted to model A, about 6% to model B and the remainder was shared between model C and D [Bratton, M, 1994:77].[8] Meanwhile, in what became known as the 'tenant farmer' scheme, vacant large-scale farms under state leasehold were transferred to black tenants among which politicians, military leaders and senior civil servants featured prominently [Moyo, S., 1994:38; 1995:266, 113-116; Tshuma, L., 1997:60, 66]. The Western media viewed with distaste Government efforts to establish a black large-scale capitalist class, even though for the previous 90 years the Rhodesian state had done the same for whites. Double standards notwithstanding, the opportunity cost was immense: only 500 households gained land as opposed to over 30,000 smallholders [Moyo, 1995:262].

Land purchase amounted to US$38.6 million by 1987 [Bratton, M, 1994:78-79] of which about half came from the UK [Moyo, S., 1995:124]. Although the EU met the costs of resettlement, which totalled US$70 million by 1984 [Bratton, M., 1994:79], the Government simply could not afford

* Note that among data sources total hectares per sector differ. These figures, as well as in the tables above and below, are approximate only.

^ State includes state-run farms and National Parks.

comprehensive land redistribution. Over the 1982–1985 drought period, for instance, Z$111.1 million was spent on food relief, which no doubt underlined a 52% cut in land purchase funds and rationalisation of the lead Ministry involved [Tshuma, L., 1997:58; Drinkwater, M., 1989:287-288].[9] Between 1986 and 1989, land offers totalling 1.15 million hectares were rejected on the grounds that land prices were too high and farm sizes too small to enable economies of scale in resettling people [Roth, M., and Bruce, J., 1994:124].

Table 4.3 *Distribution of Farm Sectors According to Natural Region*

SECTOR		NATURAL REGIONS					
		I	II	III	IV	V	TOTAL
Large-scale Commercial	[000ha] %	200 1.8	3,690 32.8	2,410 21.5	2,430 21.7	2,490 22.2	11,200 100
Small-scale Commercial	[000ha] %	10 0.7	240 17.4	530 38.4	500 36.4	100 7.3	1,380 100
Communal Areas	[000ha] %	140 0.9	1,270 7.8	2,820 17.2	7,340 44.8	4,780 29.3	16,350 100
Resettlemen t Areas	[000ha] %	30 0.9	590 17.9	1,240 37.7	810 24.6	620 18.9	3,290 100
State	[000ha] %	10 2	10 2	160 32	60 12	260 52	446 100

Source: GoZ, 1992, cited in Mukora, C.M., 1993:42.

The CFU made no offer for a broad-based land distribution: the argument forwarded stressed that large farms crucially sustained foreign exchange levels and displayed superiority over smallholders in all crop yields except cotton [Moyo, S., 1995:98]. Such data merely highlighted the absence of demographic and environmental constraints as well as disparities in soil quality, use of irrigation, fertiliser and other inputs. Not surprisingly, as Table 4.4 shows, the commercial sector overwhelmed crop sales— about an average of 80% accrued to large-scale farmers [Weiner, D., 1988:74]. While the dominance pointed to the real economic dependency of the state and the precarious plight of land reform, production and employment trends indicated that the sector was becoming more of an export enclave and offered the domestic economy little in the way of dynamic drive.

Table 4.4 *Summary of Sales by Farm Sector of Major Crops*[*], *1976–1990 [Z$ millions]*

Year	Communal/ Resettlement[^]	Commercial[#]	Total
1976	18.2	225.4	243.6
1979	12.2	249.2	261.4
1980	22.0	350.1	372.2
1981	63.7	518.2	581.9
1982	65.0	484.7	549.7
1983	45.6	451.1	496.7
1984	103.2	603.5	706.7
1985	224.8	856.8	1,081.6
1986	221.9	960.5	1,182.4
1987	124.1	765.2	889.3
1988	301.2	1,066.1	1,367.3
1989	294.6	1,228.5	1,523.1
1990	232.5	1,649.7	1,882.2

Source: CSO, 1997b: 167.

With the exception of wheat and cotton, there was a marked shift away from controlled non-tradables—maize, sorghum, ground nuts, sunflower, beef, milk—toward uncontrolled tradables—tobacco, horticulture [vegetables, cut flowers, citrus], poultry and wildlife products [meat, hides, tourist services] [WB, 1995 vol.2:86-87, 92-93]. Increased mechanisation and sharp reductions in farm employment accompanied the trend [Table 4.5], despite a declining share of wages in total agricultural output value from 36% over 1980–1983 to 25% over 1988–1991 [WB, 1995 vol.2:94]. Improved export demand from the mid-1980s saw a rise in the number of casual workers, later found to be among the most deprived people in the country [See Mugwetsi, T. and Balleis S.J., P., 1994]. The total cropped area remained constant at about 650,000 hectares, suggesting that the extensive production bias was retained [Moyo, S., 1995:95]. The export power of the sector did not outweigh the rationale or belie the scope to intensify production and re-ignite a domestic growth dynamic.

---

[*] Major crops: maize, groundnuts, sorghum, soyabeans, coffee, wheat, cotton, tobacco, sugar and sunflower. Also mhunga, rapoko, beans and rice as from early 1984.

[^] Output recorded from resttlement schemes commenced 1982.

[#] Commercial includes output from the small-scale commercial sector.

Table 4.5 *Employment Trends in the Large-scale Commercial Sector, 1976–1989*

Year	Owners, Occupiers	Permanent Employees	Seasonal Employees	Total Employees
1976	6,211	233,873	73,352	307,225
1979	4,932	230,523	56,302	286,825
1980	4,926	-	-	271,291
1981	4,859	-	-	242,149
1982	5,206	164,044	56,184	220,228
1983	5,091	154,738	61,275	216,013
1984	4,934	162,325	54,580	216,905
1985	5,163	147,842	66,399	214,241
1986	-	-	-	-
1987	4,264	137,746	82,241	19,987
1988	5,281	137,154	90,472	227,626
1989	5,560	136,860	110,294	247,154

Source: Roth, M., and Bruce, J., 1994:169

Technical preoccupations about land use efficiency and the extent of utilisation—made more complex with the advent of 'environmental' uses [i.e. game ranching, forestry and eco-tourism]—confounded the application of a land tax and repeal of subdivision laws in a bid to break up the large-scale sector [Moyo, S., 1995:112]. The *Draft National Land Policy* in 1989, for example, concluded that there were no 'acceptable criteria for defining the expected land use capability of the existing different classes of land in order to facilitate the determination of underutilisation' [GoZ, 1989, cited in Tshuma, L., 1997:37]. A way out, according to Roth and Bruce [1994:124-128], was not to apply a tax on underutilised land per se but simply on the 'assessed value of the land'. A fixed property tax, alongside a liberal subdivision policy, had potential to force land prices down and pressure the least efficient owners to either sell unused land or make it more productive. The opportunity missed, Roth and Bruce [1994:59] concluded, had a lot to do with 'the persistence of land concentration'.

In reality, the land program had succumbed to macroeconomic difficulties, dependency on the large-scale sector and both black and white ruling class interests. After the 1982–1984 drought period, for example, the AFC rescued a number of indebted white farmers to the tune of Z$100 million rather than force foreclosure [Stoneman, C., 1988:50]. The imperatives of capital accumulation within the prevailing land structures held sway, which in the light of the large-scale sector's export bias inevitably meant a greater reliance on the peasantry to meet national food needs. The Chavunduka report [1982:3, 12] captured the essence of the state's outlook:

> The prime objective of agricultural policy must be to encourage all farmers to become commercial farmers. The assumption, implicit or otherwise, that the communal will remain at subsistence production levels is not appropriate ... In the past, policy concerning the communal areas has been guided by a series of widely held but ill-founded myths. The most pervasive of these is that the communal farmer is unresponsive to the economic incentives.

4.2.3 An Evolving Agrarian Crisis

The rationale of agrarian policy was to overcome agricultural dualism—to 'integrate the commercial and communal ... into a national system' [GoZ, 1982, cited in Moyo, S., 1995:113]—through extending the reach of state marketing services, the agricultural bureaucracy and agro-business concerns. Given the overall dearth of land in communal areas, an intensified commercial orientation based on family productive relations would only add to demographic pressure while tenurial and local governance regimes, being remotely vested in the state, could not ensure an equitable or sustainable use of resources. Indeed, by decade end, commercialism completely backfired: communal areas were increasingly unable to meet subsistence requirements and comprised bigger fiscal drains. Processes of community resource commodification, skewed wealth concentration and environmental degradation were exacerbated, which progressively undermined general livelihood and compounded land constraints.

In both communal and resettlement areas, the Government distrusted village governance systems. The Communal Lands Act of 1982 vested title of the land in the President and the power to allocate and administer in District Councils subject to consultation with the Minister for Local Government and traditional authorities [Tshuma, L., 1997:89; GoZ/LTC, 1994 vol.2:152-154]. Meanwhile, the wartime 'people's committees' were replaced with Village and Ward Development Committees [i.e. VIDCOS and WARDCOs], which remained exempt from the state payroll and without real power other than to devise development plans for Council consideration [Makumbe, J.Mw., 1996:45].[10] Among the array of actors, no one could clearly say who was in charge over land, whether the kraalhead, headman, chief, the VIDCO or WARDCO, the Council, the Minister of Lands or Local Government.

USAID and the World Bank were the leading financiers behind the expansion of the GMB marketing and AFC credit networks respectively [Breslin, E., 1994:84; Bond, P., 1998:318]. Between 1980 and 1985, the number of GMB depots/collection points in communal areas rose from three to 148 and credit allocation increased eightfold [Mudimu, G., 1994:24; Kwaramba, S.G., 1994:42; WB, 1995 vol.2:89]. Combined with price incentives, a fourfold rise in fertiliser use and new technologies released by AGRITEX, the market share of smallholders in maize, cotton and sunflower increased from about 7% to over 50% [Rukuni, M., 1994:33]. From 1985 on, however, the above stimulants went into reverse: producer prices declined, AFC credit and GMB marketing operations were rolled back and crop yields stagnated [WB, 1995 vol.2:89-92]. By 1991, per capita output of the country's food staple [i.e. maize] had fallen by 25% while rural population rose by 25% and urban demand for maize by 40% [Jayne, T.S., and Rukuni, M., 1994:375, 377, 379]. Food insecurity was estimated to affect 420,000 rural households and malnutrition, 33% to 36% of all children under five [WB, 1995 vol.2:78; Mudimu, G., 1994:30].

An important study on the maize market by Tom Jayne [1991] from Michigan State University—partly financed by USAID—blamed deteriorating food security on the centralised marketing system. During the 1980s, the country was divided into two separate trading zones: Zone A comprised of large-scale commercial areas; and Zone B comprised of smallholders. From both Zones, all grain had to be sold to the GMB, which then sold about 77% of an annual intake at subsidised prices to a cartel of four industrial millers*, who then produced super-refined or roller maize-meal before selling to retailers countrywide [Jayne, T.S., Chisvo, M., and Rukuni, M., 1994:294]. The prevention of trade between the Zones, Jayne argued, undermined private trading networks and the development of a small-scale milling industry, which could offer a cheaper, less refined and more nutritious 'straight-run' maize-meal [Jayne, T.S., Chisvo, M., and Rukuni, M., 1994:292]. In another study, Edward Breslin [1994:89,99] concurred pointing out the

* National Foods, Blue Ribbon Foods, Midlands Milling Company and Triangle Milling Company.

co-existence of hungry people living next door to GMB silos overflowing with grain.

Tom Jayne and USAID became the leading proponents of grain market liberalisation, which the Government adopted as part of the SAP in the 1990s. In essence, the policy simply meant allowing private traders to shift grain freely around the country and for small millers to process maize at market prices. The net outcomes expected were cheaper maize-meal and improved food security, which in turn would relieve the GMB of price subsidy payments and help farmers diversify into non-food crops. Ironically, USAID sought to retrieve in the 1990s the private trading networks it helped destroy in the 1980s through funding the GMB's expansion. Nonetheless, as I discuss in the next chapter, the rationale dangerously idealised the role of private traders and diverted from the simple contradiction that the livelihoods of too many depended on too small a land area. According to Sam Moyo [1995:270], as of the late 1980s, 30% of communal households were basically landless, 60% had access to two hectares or less while 10% had five hectares or more. Most households simply did not have enough land to balance their food and income requirements and often sold themselves short before accustomed droughts [1981–1982, 1983–1984, 1986–1987, 1991–1992].

A reliance on a rain dependent and mostly remote peasantry to meet urban food requirements was precarious from the outset. National food security should have been a primary function of the irrigated large-scale sector but, as mentioned, this was becoming increasingly disarticulated. The GMB performed a vital strategic role amongst the peasantry, which militated against profit maximisation. In order to secure national food needs and help people meet school, health and other expenses, the GMB maintained an immense infrastructure and offered better buying *and* selling prices than private traders. Inevitably, the parastatal incurred losses—67% related to the marketing of maize—and relied on state subsidies that averaged Z$43.2 million per year [Takavarasha, T., 1994:165, Muir, K., 1994:48]. Fundamentally, the GMB and the AFC for that matter were protagonists of a commercial project that was flawed by land shortages, not the type of marketing system. The real answer to national food insecurity was not liberalisation but comprehensive land reform.

Within land and demographic constraints, the greater pursuit of commercial surpluses spawned a generalised crisis of household reproduction characterised by heightened socioeconomic inequality and environmental degradation. Households advantaged by land and often by additional factors, whether lineage, remittances, cattle ownership or polygamy, literally dominated resource utilisation and usurped commercial benefits [Moyo, S., 1995:155-156,199]. The top 10%, Jackson and Collier [1988:20,34] concluded, controlled 40.4% of cereal production, 83% of marketed produce and 41.7% of the total income while the bottom 25% controlled as little as 3.5% and 4.3% of production and income respectively [see also Cousins, B., Wiener, D., and Amin, N., 1992:7; GoZ, 1991a, annex 111:6; Chipika, S., and Chisvo, M., 1997:42]. Those with the least land were the poorest; among which young men and separated or divorced women were disproportionately represented [Moyo, S., 1995:165].

The clearing of an additional 20% to 30% of the communal land area in the 1980s [WB, 1995 vol.2:88] reaped extra crops but also higher levels of erosion and desertification. Demographic pressure, a 'shocked' Land Tenure Commission noted [GoZ/LTC, 1994 vol.1:28], caused people to 'reside in grazing areas, stream banks, steep slopes and mountain tops'. The general failure of grazing schemes had dire ramifications on the health of livestock and vulnerability of animals to drought [GoZ/LTC, 1994 vol.2:75]. A classic 'tragedy of the commons' appeared to manifest— courted in a tenurial and local governance regime unable to regulate commercial exploitation. In the words of Lionel Cliffe:

> Where individual livestock owners have access, for as many beasts as they can manage to accumulate, to common pasture and there is no communal mechanism for controlling livestock numbers or the use of the grazing land, then it is not in any one individual's interest to curb numbers, as they will not gain advantage by conserving grazing unless others do the same. This contradiction between public and private interest in a context where there is increased land pressure, but where the customary system cannot respond to the new situation is the one undoubted area where the structural character of the indigenous farming system needs modification [1986:28].

There was real fear that the same scenario was underway in resettlement areas and in so far as households on freehold allotments had outgrown available land resources, the small-scale commercial sector was not immune [GoZ/LTC, 1994 vol. 2:70,85,87; ILO/SAMAT, 1995:72]. In the circumstances, AFC credit proved an instrument of indebtedness: by

1990 about 80% of loans in communal areas, 77% in resettlement areas and 68% in the small-scale sector were in arrears [Bond, P., 1998:320-326; Takavarasha, T. and Sibanda, L., 1994: 20].

In communal areas, several official studies proposed an internal reorganisation. The Riddell Commission [1981] recommended measures of land consolidation reminiscent of centralisation in the 1930s while the Chavunduka Commission [1982:62-63] and the Government's *Communal Lands Development Plan* [1986] advocated tenure reform in line with the Native Land Husbandry Act of the 1950s [Drinkwater, M., 1989:290-291; Brand, C., 1994: 53-77]. Authored by a Dr L.T. Chisike, the Plan read, in Lawrence Tshuma's words, 'like a colonial manifesto':

> Among the many problems inhibiting the developments of these areas are… poor land husbandry techniques, poor veld management, overgrazing and soil degradation, rural-urban migration, part-time farming … Fundamental to the rapid destruction taking place is the system of land tenure and the fact that all natural resources are there for the taking, free of charge. Government should be given the right and power to change the structure of land holdings to improve land productivity … The land tenure system should place control over the agricultural land in the hands of those who actively farm and manage the land and who get an income from it … [MLARR, 1986, cited in Tshuma, L., 1997:94-95; Ranger, T., 1993:376].

True, the tenure system could not sustain capital accumulation, as it offered no investment incentive to replenish the commons. Yet there was simply not enough land to enable tenure reform or re-organisation without dispossessing various households of their land and cattle. The Ministry appeared locked in a time warp in that the dearth of land had already undermined state initiatives in the 1930s and 1950s. Many had not forgotten, Michael Drinkwater [1989:304] warned, and did 'not want their land once again re-planned and re-organised for them'.

The major issue ignored concerns the feasibility of commercialisation in communal areas. The Chavunduka Commission [1982:435] insisted that such areas must make a 'net contribution to the economy' but then later observed the encroachment of commerce entailed 'costly ecological consequences'. Indeed, such was the case in the 1980s while commercial benefits eluded the majority and forced the Government to sink millions of dollars worth of food subsidies [Moyo, S., 1995:15-16, 124]. In what still was a labour reserve economy, the state lost sight of the number one priority in peasant agriculture, namely, to ensure a subsistent livelihood for the majority. A land distribution to resuscitate communal areas and decentralisation aimed at empowering village authorities to manage the commons may have helped counter the agrarian crisis. Instead, despite in many instances the proximity of resettlement land, the state conducted the land program 'independently of the situation prevailing in communal areas' [GoZ/LTC, 1994 vol.1:62].

4.3 'Macro-populism' and the IFIs

Yet, to a vital extent, the welfare oriented macroeconomic regime compensated the peasantry for the lack of land redistribution and forestalled an absolute crisis of survival for many. In a similar pattern to land reform, the Government made the greatest progress in improving African welfare within the early years of independence. Thereon, as internal and external imbalances set in, the IFIs gained greater leverage in the economy. Until 1990, the Government adopted piecemeal the recommended policy prescriptions in a state-regulated stabilisation program. The gains in African living standards were whittled away to a degree but nothing in comparison to what happened when the state relinquished the commanding economic heights.

At a cost of US$546.6 million [excluding interest], the World Bank was engaged in about 15 projects over the 1980s while the IMF approved only two stand-by credit arrangements worth US$337.5 million [excluding interest] [Appendix 8]. At the macro level, the IMF was intolerant of centralist management and suspended almost half of the second loan on account of policy recalcitrance. At the sectoral level, the World Bank also asserted neo-liberal policy conditionalities but the Government cooperated more at this level, which explains the Bank's ongoing involvement.

Through the budget deficit and centralised wage fixing, the living standards of the poor received an unprecedented boost. By 1985, primary, secondary and tertiary enrolments escalated by 232%, 330% and 399% respectively while the number of rural health centres increased by 58%, which offered free services for those earning below Z$150.00 per month. [Zvobgo, R.J., 1986:338; Dashwood, H.,

1996:36]. Between 1980 and 1982, average real wages rose by 22% [Table 4.6] and workers in manufacturing, agriculture and mining received the highest increases. Technical, professional and managerial civil service personnel, on the other hand, experienced relative or net falls in disposable income, which provoked white retirement en masse [Kanyenze, G., 1996:58]. The state unilaterally announced wage rises every May Day until 1985 when the Labour Relations Act began dismantling the corporate-style industrial pact in favour of collective bargaining.[11]

Table 4.6 *Trends in Average Real Consumption Earning, 1980–1990*

SECTOR	1980	1982	1984	1986	1988	1990
Agriculture	100	164	143	137	130	130
Mining	100	130	113	103	113	116
Manufacturing	100	116	109	103	101	103
Electricity	100	110	90	93	96	94
Construction	100	120	107	98	85	78
Finance	100	103	85	87	89	93
Distribution	100	115	92	94	88	85
Transport	100	108	79	82	80	90
Public Admin.	100	89	66	63	62	61
Education	100	59	69	73	77	82
Health	100	102	79	85	81	90
Domestics	100	115	82	100	92	82
Other Services	100	107	84	81	76	80
Total	100	122	100	102	101	103

Source: UNDP/PRF/IDS, 1998:25.

The phenomenal growth rates of 10% obtained over 1980–1981, fuelled by surges in domestic demand and import consumption, were accompanied as noted by internal and external imbalances. In mid-1982, Bernard Chidzero, the Finance Minister, negotiated a US$300 million 'bail out' loan with the IMF, which came attached with the standard rationale and prescriptions. To induce an investment cum export-led recovery, policies recommended included exchange and wage rate depreciation, ongoing deregulation of import and capital flows and domestic demand compression [i.e. tight monetary policy, deficit reduction]. The Government devalued the currency by 40% within 18 months, almost doubled interest rates, allowed real wages to depreciate, froze state employment creation and cut back expenditure to the order of US$200 million [Chimombe, T., 1986:138;Bond, P., 1998:344].

As captured in Appendix 7, a severe recession ensued over 1982–1983 partly caused by the foreign exchange crisis but more so, by the potent combination of drought and the policies of demand restraint—a scenario repeated in 10 years time under the SAP. Despite benefiting a few mineral and agricultural exporters, currency devaluation proved a net drain on foreign exchange through increasing the cost of imports as well as debt service. The inflation rate rose sharply, which along with import sources received impetus from the removal of price subsidies on basic necessities and public utilities.[12] Meanwhile, real wage levels were kept below parity, which some employers criticised for damaging local markets [Kanyenze, G., 1996:56]. In circumstances of eroding purchasing power, restrictive monetary policy bore little relation to inflation and appeared to only encourage the shrinkage of domestic markets and GDP [Kadenge, P., Ndoro, H., and Zwizwai, B., 1992:176; Bond, P., 1998:367].

One factor in the collapse of the IMF program was the Government's refusal to further reduce the budget deficit in the midst of drought and an external threat [Lehman, H., 1990:62]. The final catalyst—an act of greater recalcitrance—was the suspension in March 1984 of profit repatriation on pre-1979 company investments [Stoneman, C., 1988:56]. Thereon, the Government pursued a state-regulated road of stabilisation wherein external deficit containment was the main focus. The key components included export promotion [i.e. managed exchange rate depreciation on a two-tier basis, incentives for non-traditional exports], import compression, prudent debt management and intermittent capital controls.[13] A limit of 10% of GDP was placed on the budget deficit wherein the Government continued the resort to domestic financing and maintained expenditures. Price controls contained inflation but did squeeze profits, which was countered at the macro level by real wage depreciation [Table 4.6] and at the micro level, by efficiency gains within companies.[14]

Meanwhile, the World Bank remained heavily engaged. In all service sectors, the Bank displayed an ideological commitment to a market solution, that is, to allow market forces to determine the price of public utilities so as to help SOEs recover deficits. Other underlying themes of Bank credit detected by Patrick Bond [1998:281,356,358, 364-365] included a bias toward subcontracting foreign as opposed to local companies and the lucrative employment of foreign consultants.[15] The deeper contradiction, though, between theory and reality—of seeking a market solution from a defunct market—was the more significant constraint on project success. Put simply, conditionalities based on subsidy reductions and higher charges, which were attached to loans for housing, electricity, rail and micro-credit, curtailed the capacity of service providers, whether building societies, ZESA[16], the NRZ, the AFC or SEDCO[17], to extend beyond the top end of the market.

Housing provides a clear example. Through respective loans worth US$43 and $50 million, the World Bank and USAID encouraged a reliance on building societies to meet low-income urban housing needs, which coincided with a budget cut for public housing from Z$88.9 million to Z$47.2 million over 1982–1985 [Auret, D., 1995:23]. High-income groups emerged as the chief recipients of housing credit as well as the main beneficiaries of World Bank and USAID projects [Bond, P., 1998:279]. People generally could hardly afford the cost of rent, let alone a housing bond at realistic rates of interest. While urban population underwent massive increases—by 237% in greater Harare between 1975 and 1987—housing construction barely met 11% of the need. The national housing backlog, which excludes unregistered lodgers and squatters, rose from 37,000 in 1980 to 240,000 by 1985 [Auret, D., 1995:23-24]. The opportunity forgone was to exploit the country's self-sufficiency in building materials and high levels of bank liquidity, via the budget deficit, to finance a state charge in public housing.

Loans to replenish the manufacturing base [IBRD and IDA 3268] and foster an increased export orientation [IBRD 3272] achieved greater success, which probably attributed to the Bank adopting a more pragmatic than ideological stance. Of some influence was a 1982 commissioned report by the American consultant, Doris Jansen, which—although drastically recommending the closure of ZISCO—concluded upon the Bank's own Domestic Resource Cost [DRC] method that Zimbabwean manufacturing was globally competitive [Riddell, R.C., 1990:349-350; Stoneman, C., 1988:57].[18] The finding temporarily turned the Bank's attention away from macroeconomic policy to every day export constraints such as access to markets and foreign exchange. Toward these ends, the Bank set up a US$70.6 million Export Revolving Fund and the Government an Export Incentive Scheme, which offered exporters a 9% price subsidy and tax incentives. These initiatives, according to a survey of 38 firms by Joseph Muzulu [1996], directly changed the incentive structure beyond domestic markets.

The response was swift: non-traditional export manufactures, such as paper products, non-metallic minerals and transport equipment, experienced rises of 68% in 1984, 33% in 1985 and continued expansion thereafter [Riddell, R.C., 1990:347,354]. The average growth rate of *total* exports for the 1980s—at 9% in US dollar terms—was largely propelled by export manufactures, which grew by 55% overall and gained an increased share of total exports from 29% to 36% [WB, 1995 vol.2:118; ZCTU, 1996:60]. The dependency on African markets, notably South Africa, for all export manufactures declined from 41% in 1984 to 34% in 1986 [Riddell, R.C., 1990:350].

Nonetheless, the Bank discontinued its successful line of credit in 1987 on account of the Government's non-compliance with market policy [Stoneman, C, 1993: 90-91]. The Bank insisted that a market-determined exchange rate and deeper currency devaluation were needed to boost export demand, reduce import consumption and encourage labour intensive techniques and use of local inputs. Firm level evidence, as provided by Muzulu [1996:37-39], suggested that such theoretical assumptions had little basis in reality. Most firms had exhausted labour-intensive methods and local substitutes for imported inputs were unobtainable. Other than induce higher inflation, deeper currency devaluation would militate against the capital-intensive investments needed to obtain the economies of scale, product range and quality required to penetrate export markets. As to future export demand, this seemed to hinge less on currency depreciation than improved political relations with the USA[19], more open Western markets, higher regional import capacity and less Western export 'dumping'.

Since parting with the IMF in 1984, the Government achieved notable success on both external and internal fronts. By decade end, capital controls, trade promotion and tight import compression converted negatives on the trade and current accounts into positives

[Appendix 6]. Internally, the health status of the population seemed also to turn around. Between 1980 and 1990, the percentage of children immunised against common diseases rose from 25% to 86%; life expectancy at birth increased from 56 to 62 years; and under five infant mortality and malnutrition per 1,000 births declined from 86 to 49 and 37 to 26 respectively [WB, 1995 vol.2:49; Ministry of Health, *The Herald*, 7/4/99]. Beyond health expenditure, improved social indicators reflected a macroeconomic strategy that relative to the 1990s protected the currency, contained inflation, expanded African employment and assured national food security during drought years without resort to imports [Stoneman, C., 1993:94]. A necessary feature was the budget deficit, which presided over a respectable 4% average GDP growth rate in the late 1980s [CSO, 1997c:4].

Table 4.7 *External Debt Repayments, 1985–1990*
Z$ millions

Year	1985	1986	1987	1988	1989	1990
Government	264.6	418.9	621.2	584.5	571.0	773.6
SOEs	278.6	269.8	236.0	264.4	239.8	306.0
Private	39.5	27.5	31.5	27.9	38.8	63.6
Total	582.7	716.2	888.7	876.8	849.6	1,143.2
Interest	259.8	250.7	254.5	274.0	308.1	445.5
Capital	322.9	465.5	634.2	602.6	541.5	697.7

Source: RBZ, 1994.

Therein, the Government managed to service debt, both external and domestic, without any rescheduling. Table 4.7 shows the hefty amounts repaid to external lenders, which largely stemmed from the undisciplined acquisition of debt over 1980 and 1982. Then, as a percentage of total external debt, Zimbabwe owed 85% to private creditors but by 1988 this figure had dropped to 36%. Thus, as time progressed, most of the external debt was owed to official creditors, mainly the IMF and World Bank, which saw the former alone receive US$254 million in repayment over 1986–1988 [All data cited in Lehman, H., 1990:62, 69 footnote 59].

Table 4.8 captures the growing reliance on domestic debt to cover the budget deficit, which by 1990 represented about 60% of *total* debt. The resort to domestic liquidity made sense: domestic debt service, being in local currency and at negative interest rates, was significantly cheaper than external debt service, which at higher interest rates saw Zimbabwe pay out more hard currency than what was received [MacGarry sj, B., 2000:4]. Indeed, prudent debt management since 1984 was behind the decline in the debt service ratio from the peak of 1987 [Appendix 7].

Table 4.8 *Summary of Central Government Accounts, 1985–1990 Z$ millions*

Year	1985	1986	1987	1988	1989	1990
Total Revenue inc. Grants	2,353	2,848	3,405	3,974	4,703	6,011
Total Expenditure inc. Net Lending	3,064	3,539	4,371	4,871	5,822	7,148
Overall Budget Deficit	-711	-692	-966	-898	-1,119	-1,138
Financing						
Abroad	489	211	211	148	129	202
Domestic	222	481	786	748	990	936
Government Debt Outstanding	4,639	5,450	6,552	7,923	9,460	11,318

Source: CSO, 1997[c]:50.

In fact, the economy was far from collapse, which suggests that outright external dependency was less a factor behind the adoption of the SAP than the emergence of a supportive political coalition. The bone of contention, which provided the political capital to deregulate the economy, was the failure to counter the stagnant percentage of the population employed [Appendix 7]. 'The fact that increasing numbers of young graduates and school leavers walk our streets with the intellectual equipment', Bernard Chidzero stressed in 1987, 'but without jobs and unable to find a role to play in the economy, strikes at the very heart of society' [cited in Dashwood, H.S., 1996:40].

The recovery of private investment during the late 1980s, which witnessed a 7% per annum increase in the capital stock [WB, 1995 vol.1:6], displayed an anti-employment bias. The IFIs argued that such was the consequence of 'large legislated increases in minimum wages' and the subsidising of capital-intensive investment costs through negative interest rates, overvalued exchange rates and tax write-offs [WB, 1995 vol.1:4,6]. Although enormous sums were sunk into tradable enterprises, such as commercial farming, textiles and packaging, the World Bank [1995 vol.2:120] maintained that the investment surge disproportionately benefited inefficient industries such as ZISCO, the CSC, large-scale milling and transport companies and, therefore, reflected 'resource misallocation'.

Although state-led stabilisation, the World Bank admitted, succeeded in containing imbalances, 'it clearly resulted in an environment which was not conducive to employment creation and sustained economic growth' [1995 vol.2:11]. Market forces should be granted the sovereignty, came the inevitable conclusion, to determine the true cost of goods and services as well as allocate foreign exchange and repatriate capital. A complete rationalisation of the state through fiscal deficit reduction was a key pivot of the market reform because such would release liquidity, ease pressure on deregulated interest rates and enable the Government to focus on 'productive' expenditures. A market-driven resource allocation, the IFIs promised, would deliver export stimulus, labour-intensive investment and price competition that would eventually override the short-term costs of higher inflation, external debt and retrenchment. As a starting point, the Government issued a new investment code in April 1989, which aimed to make the country more attractive to foreign investors.[20]

On offer, though, was really an under researched export optimism and much less a practical remedy to overcome the structural problems of investment or inflation; in other words, the private sector's proneness to excess capacity, speculative activities, capital repatriation, stagnant import dependency and monopoly control.[21] In this light, the mopping up of excess liquidity by the Government, via the budget deficit, accomplished more economic and social good than harm. Resolution of the economy's plight went far deeper than any question of macroeconomic policy and related internally, to the concentration of wealth and externally, to similarly scant regional markets and further afield, protected industrialised markets.

4.4 The Undemocratic Roots of the SAP

The Economic Policy Statement Bernard Chidzero [1994:277-288] delivered to the Parliament on 26 July 1990 officially symbolised the convergence of interests between the state, bourgeoisie and the IFIs for the full array of market reforms. Save only for a shared reticence between the Government and the CZI over import liberalisation, support was unanimous among the elites to reduce the budget deficit, particularly welfare expenditures, and dismantle controls over foreign exchange allocation, prices and wages including restrictions on labour dismissals [Sachikonye, L.M., 1995b: 188, 190-191]. Only by means of a virtual dictatorship could 'macro-populism' be suddenly abandoned in favour of a market strategy that centred on the investment interests of about 4% of the population. The matter was never clearly put to the people in the 1990 election: the peasantry, organised labour and even the ZANU-PF rank and file were marginalised during the design of the SAP [Sachikonye, L.M., 1995a:46-47;WB, 1996:iv].

Undemocratic political development reflected the absence of an autonomous 'anchor class', which as argued could have served as the backbone of national wealth creation and liberal democratic governance. Instead, African entrepreneurs, in Patrick Bond's words, 'met racism and 'old boy networks' in the corridors of finance on the one hand, and on the other, a stagnant economy which offered few opportunities for accumulation' [1998:217].[22] Inevitably, they distinguished themselves by 'utilising the state as a basis for accumulation and class formation' [Raftopoulos, B., 1992 No. 54:62]. The consequence was immediate and comprehensive democratic demise driven by the need of the state-bourgeoisie to protect privileged positions and shut other petty factions out [Mafeje, A., cited in Mandaza, I., and Sachikonye, L.M., 1991:7].

The problem was not the desire of the state-bourgeoisie to accumulate wealth but the fact that the quest was structurally reduced to indigenising a highly skewed economic order, which carried the concomitant of political repression. The goals of the entrepreneurial class amounted to acquiring the farms, houses, businesses and managerial posts left vacant by whites and generally forcing inroads into monopoly capitalism, via SOEs and joint ventures with foreign capital. A leadership code attempted to restrict 'accumulation from above' but stood no chance when minorities outside the state were left free to 'amass fortunes' [Mandaza, I., 1991:29]. In 1989 Robert Mugabe [1989:358] acknowledged the existence within ZANU-PF of 'a minority, but very powerful bourgeois group which champions the cause of international finance and national private capital, whose interests thus stand opposed to the development and growth of a socialist and egalitarian society'.

Indeed, led by a core entrepreneurial group within ZANU-PF, the state bourgeoisie used a mix of state and party mechanisms to acquire controlling interests in a range of financial, agricultural, mining and manufacturing enterprises. Besides personal enrichment, an elite vein of indigenous economic nationalism lay behind an endeavour to construct a transnational conglomerate that could play a lead role in the exploitation of resources within the country and region. By the late 1980s, given the scope of trading interests obtained, the promise of the SAP policy agenda to deliver investment opportunities through privatisation of SOEs, enhanced export-import stimulus, foreign exchange access and cheaper labour must have appeared irresistible. The party's holdings continued to grow that the state bourgeoisie positioned itself by the late 1990s to jointly engage offshore companies to take up opportunities unfolding in the Congo.

The economic nucleus emerged within ZANU-PF's original business arm, the M & S Syndicate, which soon after 1980 formed a joint venture with a UK-based firm, Unicorn Import/Export, to create ZIDCO Holdings.[23] These two companies, that is, M & S and ZIDCO Holdings, comprised the party's main investment vehicles, which by the late 1980s encompassed full or joint ownership of at least 12 companies and over 50 properties valued at Z$486 million [Mnangagwa, E., cited in ZimNews, 2001:6]. ZANU-PF gained leading stakes in Jongwe Printers; Ottawa [property management]; National Blankets [in partnership with Lonrho]; Catercraft [aircraft catering]; Zidlee Enterprises [duty free goods]; Woolworth Trading; Zidco motors; and Treger Holdings [building materials, hardware, machinery] [Curtin Knight, V., 1990:204]. With business and state intertwined, respective companies often received contracts to supply the SADC export market, local schools, airlines and the military. Through additional state avenues, such as the Zimbabwe Development Corporation, the Minerals Marketing Corporation and Zimbabwe Tourist Development Corporation, the Government mostly in partnership with foreign capital gained assets in tourist resorts, finance, electronics, food processing and mining.

Table 4.9 *Government Acquisitions during the 1980s*

Purchase of Existing Companies
62% share of Rhobank [now Zimbank]
47% share of Bank of Credit and Commerce International#
51% share of Zimbabwe Development Bank
Leading share of Fidelity Life Insurance
43% share of Zim Newspapers from Argus Group
42.6% share of Caps Holdings [pharmaceuticals]
49% joint venture with Heinz
40% joint venture with Anglo-American [Hwange colliery]
Leading share of MTD Mangula Group [copper]
51% joint venture with Rio Tinto [Empress Mine]
Leading share of Kingstons [retail]
85% share of Delta Corporation
85% share in Astra Corporation [engineering]
Joint venture with Siemens [Electro Technologies Corporation]

Source: Herbst, J., 1989:74 and various.

The state-based bourgeoisie, as orchestrated by ZANU-PF, had an arsenal of Rhodesian security legislation at its disposal to repress opposition.[24] In Matabeleland, according to Ronald Weitzer [1990:161], ZANU 'seized on genuine security problems' and 'transformed them into opportunities' to persecute ZAPU and establish a de facto one-party state. Only when ZAPU signed away its existence under the Unity Accord of 1987 was the Ndebele elite invited to enter the domain of accumulation. Soon after, Joshua Nkomo established the Development Trust of Zimbabwe, which subsequently acquired the country's biggest ranch [Nuanetsi] as well as a range of interests in tourism, horticulture, retail and manufacturing [Bond, P., 1998:205-206]. The Constitution Amendment Bill [no.7] of 1987 created the executive presidency, which removed Mr Mugabe from Parliament and granted

In the early 1990s, after near bankruptcy, the Government purchased the remaining 53% of shares and changed the name to the Commercial Bank of Zimbabwe.

him power to make war and peace, proclaim and terminate martial law and dissolve Parliament upon consultation with the Cabinet only [Mnangagwa, E.D., 1989:127-131; Sibanda, A.E., 1990:6].

Amongst the student and labour movement, protest often boiled over against what the Students Representative Council termed 'monopolistic politics of domination, corruption and petit-bourgeois primitive accumulation' [cited in Sachikonye, L.M., 1995b:191-192]. In late 1989, when the Government temporarily closed the UZ, the Secretary General of the ZCTU, Morgan Tsvangirai, declared the brutal tactics against the students no different from the apartheid era and persuaded the labour movement to cut formal ties with ZANU-PF. On charges of treason, he spent the next six weeks in jail—a detention the High Court subsequently ruled as unlawful [Ncube, W., 1991:169-170]. 'Over the past 12 years', Tsvangirai later said, 'senior party officials have accumulated wealth and with it, new friends: established local business, multinational corporations, commercial farmers. They are now in the process of merging politically. The SAP is the 'Social Contract' of this new, expanded ruling class' [cited in *African South*, August 1992].

The demise of democracy extended to within the party itself. To quote Dzikamai Mavhaire, a ZANU MP from Masvingo, on the adoption of the SAP:

> Our main concern is that this program was not mooted from within the framework of the party. It was mooted from the Government, that is, the Cabinet. It did not get enough publicity and discussion within the rank and file of the party. If that had been done we would have measured the pulse and taken the people along with us, that was not done. A document brought in by Government was explained to the Members of Parliament, as a general policy guideline. There were no indications on how the thing was going to be implemented [Parliamentary debates, 18, 44, 26/11/91:3137].

The state-based bourgeoisie competed with white capital but eventually shared the neo-liberal policy agenda. With half the Cabinet reputed to be members of the CFU [Dashwood, H., 1996:34] and harbouring extensive links with foreign capital, the annunciation of socialist goals had become a hindrance and an embarrassment. 'You don't talk about socialism', remarked Lazarus Nzareybani, a ZANU MP from Mutare [*Sunday Mail*, 10/12/89], 'in a party that is led by people who own large tracts of land and employ a lot of cheap labour'.

The failure of land reform in the 1980s to strengthen the communal economy and overhaul the large-scale sector damaged considerably the country's long-term prospects of prosperity and stability. The retention of the status quo underpinned economic stagnation, which international and national elites construed to justify the SAP. Once deregulated, the sustaining elements of the economy, namely, contained inflation and currency depreciation, welfare maintenance, fiscal stimulus, import protection and low interest rates, went in reverse. The resulting trend of deindustrialisation proved no short-term phenomenon as integration with the global economy in terms of export and investment stimulus failed to compensate. In a wilting mass-peasant economy, the withdrawal of subsidies on food, farming inputs, education and health effectively took away 'important palliatives for the land hungry' [Moyo, S., 1995:165-166]. The ensuing political turmoil soon overran any advantage gained from 'market equilibrium'.

Disintegration of the national political economy is the focus of the final chapter: the next three are devoted to the impact of the SAP on the local economy as a way to set the scene. Four household portraits are used to highlight how both structural economic realities and macroeconomic policy determine overall livelihood status. Under the SAP, as the two combined, a national crisis of livelihood surfaced, which forms the backdrop to the present state of chaos. For reasons of anonymity, households are called after an African totem[25], namely, Shumba [lion], Mukanya [monkey], Shiri [ostrich] and Mpofu [antelope], while each family member has been given a different first name. I begin with Shiri, which is a post-1980 resettled household.

5

Maize and Cotton: National Performance under the SAP and the Plight of Shiri Household at Muzvezve Resettlement

In Mashonaland West, the colonial state established a continuous line of large-scale farms along the tarred road heading northwest from Kadoma, via Patchway and Golden Valley mines, as far as the Sanyati communal lands. The war left most in tact but forced some white owners, particularly in remoter parts, to abandon their farms. After 1980, the Government mostly opened these lands for resettlement, such as at Muzvezve—located about 60 kilometres either way between Kadoma and Sanyati—which is where the Shiri family resides. Like other 'accelerated schemes' of the day, development commenced from scratch yet by the 1990s, Muzvezve comprised a total of 46 villages—dispersed in a horseshoe shape—each with an average of thirty-three households and serviced by three primary schools, one secondary, one medical clinic and reasonably adequate boreholes. Based on model 'A', villages were centralised in one place wherein each household obtained private access to arable land and public access to common grazing.

A symbiosis between state economic support and a family or patriarchal mode of production sustained the rise of smallholder capital regimes at Muzvezve, based mainly on cotton and maize. While the Agricultural and Technical Extension Service [AGRITEX], the AFC, GMB and CMB delivered the 'prime movers' of production and marketing support, women and children met the bulk of labour requirements. The resort to a family mode had repercussions on the long-term advancement of women and environmental sustainability particularly in a context of weak community governance and centralised land tenure. Nevertheless, within the state-regulated economy of the 1980s, Muzvezve residents managed to lift themselves out of destitution. Many households including the Shiri's oversaw the doubling of cattle herds, the construction of brick houses and the purchase of farming equipment such as ploughs, cultivators and in some cases, second-hand tractors. In the process, however, public sector losses forced a gradual reversal of the 'prime movers', evident in declining real producer prices and withdrawal of state economic services.

In broad terms, the SAP promised to stimulate a market-led recovery through state fiscal recovery [i.e. SOE reform, budget cuts, retrenchment and 'user fees'] and deregulation of prices, wages, foreign exchange allocation, imports, interest and exchange rates [Appendix 9]. Within this framework, reform of the agricultural SOEs [i.e. GMB, CMB, DMB and CSC] was at the forefront of agricultural market liberalisation, which directly related to the fortunes of smallholders, particularly as applied to the GMB and CMB. In a quest to remove the fiscal burden of price subsidies and create conditions for a lucrative private sale, the agricultural SOEs were to relinquish monopoly control over their respective markets, submit to the competition of private traders, rationalise operations and transform into profit-oriented or commercialised entities. In the lead adjustment document, *A Framework for Economic Reform* [GoZ, 1991a: 13-16, 21-22], the Government expressed reservations about grain market liberalisation but, nonetheless, maintained that the onset of competitive buying and selling, as in other commodity markets, would push producer prices up and consumer prices down to the benefit of smallholders and national food security.

As of the 1990s, if practice fulfilled market theory, Muzveze farmers were well positioned to capitalise because unlike most communal areas their land had yet to be enveloped by a demographic and environmental crisis. As would be expected of a former commercial area reserved for whites, the soil—being dark red—was high in nutrients generally characteristic of Natural Region III but did deteriorate in lower lying parts to the sandy clay loams typical of the

Sanyati communal. On the whole, given timely rain and adequate inputs, one hectare of the Muzvezve soil could yield up to five bales of cotton [i.e. 1.25 tonnes] or three to four tonnes of maize, which trebled, even quadrupled, the yields of communal areas generally [Takavarasha, T., 1994:165].

In the event, the implementation of the SAP accompanied the onset of a stagflation crisis, that is, a spiral of high inflation and a shrinking domestic economy [Appendix 11]. To begin with, widespread cost pressures immediately stemmed from the reduction or removal of price subsidies on essential goods and services [processed foods, clothing, health and education], productive inputs [fertiliser, seeds, fuel, credit] and infrastructure [rent, water and electricity]. Concurrently, ongoing currency depreciation following exchange rate deregulation fuelled rising import costs while the maintenance of positive interest rates sharply hiked the cost of servicing outstanding private and public debts. Meanwhile, amid excess labour conditions, the greater resort to enterprise bargaining saw a collapse of real wages, which damaged domestic markets and the peasantry's urban remittance base. Within this hostile macroeconomic environment, the extent and viability of liberalised markets significantly varied between maize and cotton.

Concerning the maize market, the Government liberalised in so far as private traders freely operated but after a trial period, finally stopped short of a fully commercialised GMB and continued to fix prices. Although well short of the ultimate aim to privatise the GMB, as the lead 'donor' involved, USAID claimed that as far as the reforms went, they succeeded in promoting food security [USAID, 1997:55]. The evidence cited points to the growth of private trade in grain and small-scale milling, which relative to the monopolistic nexus between the GMB and large-scale mills offered consumers a cheaper 'straight-run' maize meal. While not to denigrate this result as unwarranted, the full reality is that the national food economy markedly deteriorated under grain market reforms. In fact, the more the Government pursued the policy agenda, the more apparent that a freely operating market failed to offer prices high enough for producers to keep abreast of production costs or low enough for most consumers to maintain household food security. The Government's initial reservations proved correct: intervention was required to set an incentive price to ensure production and a consumer price to quell hunger and social unrest.

At a fundamental level, as part of the SAP, grain market liberalisation rendered the country's food economy more vulnerable to the shortcomings of the inequitable agrarian base. On the one hand, about 6,000 farmers upon Zimbabwe's fertile and irrigated lands were encouraged to primarily focus on export production while on the other, over half the country's population upon marginal and inadequate lands were increasingly relied on to feed an accelerating urban population when they struggled to feed themselves. The resort to market forces and rationalisation of the GMB network dangerously exposed a large part of national food requirements to the inherent structural weaknesses of smallholders, such as geographical remoteness, a dearth of land, irrigation, transport and, critically, market bargaining power. Choosing to work within the infeasible land structures, grain market theorists, such as Tom Jayne and USAID, underestimated the precarious position of national maize supplies and overestimated the capacity of private traders to offer fair and reasonable prices.

Fortunately, as a maize surplus household, the Shiri family, like others in Muzvezve, could increasingly turn to the cash crop cotton, which as a tradable export offered a comparatively lucrative market under the SAP. Liberalisation accorded more to plan in that several new trading companies entered the market; the CMB successfully commercialised; degrees of competition surfaced over producer prices, methods of payment and input contracts; and the CMB was eventually sold, re-emerging as the privatised—highly profitable—Cotton Company of Zimbabwe [i.e. COTTCO]. On the ground, however, by the late 1990s real advances in producer prices had yet to materialise. In the international sphere, like other raw commodity exports, the fortunes of cotton remained fragile while in the national, the rut of currency depreciation and imported inflation and the onset of a private trading cartel militated against real advances in producer prices.

Living standards universally slumped over the 1990s yet the depth of the descent varied from locale to locale and family to family. Although to a lesser extent than in land depleted communal areas, the fall in living standards among Muzvezve residents came at the worrying cost of accelerated environmental exploitation of the commons. In turn, land degradation brought the issues of tenure and local governance to the fore, the resolution of which may lead to positive local reforms. Yet, underneath, it is a serious indictment upon a development strategy hailed as the road to economic recovery that households, such as the Shiris', possessed with relatively fertile and adequate land could not make good in the deregulated economy. By way of contrast, as I now recount before elaborating on the rationale, impact and consequences of market liberalisation, the state-controlled system, in Muzvezve at least, propelled a 'rags to riches' scenario.

5.1 The Rise of Family Capital Regimes at Muzvezve

The Government's resettlement program of the early 1980s, according to Mr Mhishi, a former deputy director of the Department of Rural Development [DERUDE], was 'both by design and default first and foremost a political and social program' [1995:9]. The settler selection criteria actually targeted the poorest strata of Zimbabwean society: about 85% of those resettled came from communal areas while the remainder were either refugees or former commercial farm workers [Mhishi, S.G., 1995:6]. Mr Shiri and his two wives, for example, hailed originally from the drought stricken and overcrowded area of Chivi, south of Masvingo.

The land tenure system was based on three permits, issued and administered by Resettlement Officers from DERUDE, which sanctioned residence, cultivation and the depasturing of stock. About 98% of these permits were given to the male head of the household, which reflected traditional gender bias that the primary rights to arable land belonged to men [Chenaux-Repond, M., 1993 cited in Tshuma, L., 1997:82]. The tenure system has been regularly criticised for bestowing 'broad rights on the part of the state but remarkably few rights for the permit holder' [Bruce. J.W., 1990, cited in Tshuma, L., 1997:77]. Indeed, ultimate power over land vested in central Government, which involved an array of ministries.[1] Under the Rural Land Act, on the advice of Resettlement Officers, the Minister of Local Government, Rural and Urban Development could at any time revoke the permits in the event that the holder failed to comply with the rules. These included no employment outside the scheme or use of communal land;

evidence of ongoing agricultural productivity, adherence to subdivision restrictions; and maintenance of livestock, veterinary and environmental standards as prescribed under the Animal Health and Natural Resources Acts.

The Shiris resided in the Sanyati communal with relatives before they received 12 arable hectares plus a residential allocation in 1983 at Muzvezve. The Resettlement Officer in charge was persuaded, not without a 'special payment', to increase Mr Shiri's allocation from the usual five hectares to cater for his polygamy—his two wives had already given birth to 11 children by 1983. There was also the need of Mr and Mrs Gumbi to consider—first cousin relatives of Mr Shiri—and their five children, who were also landless and sought to join the household. Mr Shiri granted the Gumbis two hectares of his allocation, which although not a formal subdivision breached permit conditions in that any portion of land holding to anyone else beside the permit holder was forbidden. In any case, breaches of permit conditions were common particularly when it came to catering for destitute kin, releasing portions of land in Communal Areas[2] or abiding to grazing stock limits.

His need of land met, Mr Shiri required other factors of production, most importantly, cattle to provide draft power for the plough. He was fortunate that kinship networks provided him with four head to start his farming career at Muzvezve. Most settlers had fewer or none at all yet grazing was ample, over 100 hectares, and conditions were ripe to build up stock. Indeed, Mr Shiri was able to repay his kin as well as treble the amount of beasts to twelve by the late 1990s.

Other crucial elements in commencing the production and income cycle at Muzvezve included technical advice from AGRITEX, credit from the AFC and marketing support from the GMB and CMB. Until market liberalisation in the 1990s, the Grain and Cotton Marketing Acts granted the GMB and CMB a monopoly over domestic produce and the import and export of their respective commodities, which for the GMB encompassed a range of cereals besides maize. The law bound smallholders to deliver their output to the nearest GMB or CMB collection point or depot at fixed prices, which in the case of Muzvezve meant either Kadoma or Sanyati—each about 60 kilometres away. Once farmers registered with the marketing boards they received an identity card, which entitled them to obtain credit from the AFC to cover input and transportation costs. After harvest, the Stop Order Act bound the GMB and CMB to repay the farmer's debt to the AFC before issuing a cheque [Tshuma, L., 1997:112]. In model 'A' resettlement schemes, as marketing identity cards were normally issued to permit holders, the rights to receive credit and payment mostly accrued to men

Land, livestock, credit and productive surplus firmly under his control, Mr Shiri had only to look upon labour to launch an 'accumulatory spiral' [Cheater, A.P., 1986:100]. With the addition of a third wife in the 1980s, he strengthened his resort to polygamy to meet the heavy labour demands of cotton. Such practice accords to the national pattern, affirmed by Angela Cheater [1986:69] and Rudo Gaidzanwa [1988:4], that polygamy mostly occurs where household land may initially be beyond labour capacity, as has been the case in small-scale commercial areas and to a lesser extent, resettlement areas.[3] More so than monogamist households, the Shiri household presents a clear example of the symbiosis between the state agrarian bureaucracy and the patriarchal mode of production based, as it is, on the subjugation of women. The method, as the attached Shiri family tree indicates, coverts a labour deficit into a surplus yet over time fuels demographic and environmental pressure and raises ethical questions about the plight of women and children. Most polygamists rebut the criticism of squeezing family labour by the claim that 'every one is fed, clothed and schooled'.

Undoubtedly, the position of women remained highly vulnerable. A divorced, separated or widowed wife, for example, whose name was not on the permit had no legal right to reside on the scheme and could be left destitute. Many women, according to the Land Tenure Commission [GoZ/LTC, 1994 vol.1:60], sought the establishment of customary authorities because chiefs and headmen had traditionally defended women's rights to land [Gaidzanwa, R.B., 1988]. The Government, however, was against creating traditional 'power bases' in resettlement areas [GoZ, 1983:2]. Among the random gathering of lineages, the elevation of one family to a position of inherited authority or alternatively, to expand the jurisdiction of the nearest local chief, would not necessarily be seen as legitimate. The better option was probably to issue resettlement permits to each spouse and empower elected village authorities, such as the Village Development Committee [VIDCO]*, to uphold the property rights of women.

Unlike communal areas where local governance was often beset by a confusion of traditional and non-traditional actors, resettlement areas provided a clear domain for new village institutions to establish authority over such matters including, importantly, the conservation of common grazing. Unfortunately, however, in Muzvezve, as in most schemes, VIDCOs rarely moved beyond 'the level of intent' [Tshuma, L., 1997:71]. In Mr Shiri's village, most people regarded the VIDCO 'useless' and elected a 'headman' to look after affairs. The key problem appeared to be the absence of formally designated powers to the VIDCO and the exemption of representatives from the state payroll. The responsibility for land maintenance vested in the state, as mediated through Resettlement Officers, which proved institutionally inadequate—too remote and bureaucratic—to be effective on the ground. As a result, most residents in model 'A' schemes, the Land Tenure Commission stressed [GoZ/LTC, 1994 vol. 1:60], believed that the best way to secure conservation was to grant title deeds.

While issues of gender equality, local governance and tenure gathered pace, the Shiris attended to the business of farming. Besides the two hectares allocated to the Gumbis, Mr Shiri set aside another two hectares for his wives to grow food crops for household consumption, which left a total of eight hectares for commercial produce. Although cotton and maize prices fell in real terms over the 1980s—the latter by an average of 7% per annum between 1981 and 1988 [Takavarasha, T., 1994:171]—the reality was that by avoiding middlemen and agents the state-controlled system secured farmers higher prices than otherwise [Rukuni, M., 1994:33]. Maize prices did keep above export parity [Jayne, T.S., Chisvo, M., and Rukuni, M., 1994:290] and despite cotton prices to the contrary, there is little doubt that the Shiris, as with most Muzvezve families, established viable capital regimes over the 1980s. The construction of three primary schools and one secondary almost within a decade—in no small part pioneered by a financially

* A VIDCO is composed of six members—four elected from 100 households and two representing youth and women's organisations.

lubricant Parent-Teachers Association—points to the positive extent of community wealth generation.

By 1990, on a national scale, resettlement areas as a whole were contributing up to 7% of total maize and cotton sales respectively [GoZ, 1998c:7].[4] Crop yields were generally lower than in the large-scale sector but higher than in communal and small-scale commercial areas [GoZ/LTC, 1994 vol. 1:66]. This state of relative productivity was expected given most resettlement schemes were rain dependent, unlike the large-scale sector, and 56% were located in marginal regions yet possessed more virgin soils than the communal areas. Indeed, the impressive productivity of most schemes [GoZ/LTC, 1994 vol. 1:66] put them in good stead to reap the promise of higher producer prices under the SAP.

5.2 The Rationale of Grain and Cotton Market Liberalisation

In 1991, at the outset of the SAP, the Government aimed to halve the budget deficit in order to release liquidity to finance an expected surge in private investment following the deregulation of prices, wages, foreign exchange allocation, imports, interest and exchange rates [Appendix 9]. Within this overall adjustment rationale, agricultural market liberalisation—centred on the commercialisation and possible privatisation of the agricultural SOEs—formed a major part of fiscal deficit reduction. Debt liabilities of all the SOEs, to recall, comprised about 40% of the budget deficit. The Agricultural Marketing Authority was a prime culprit and therein, mostly the GMB and to a lesser extent, the CMB, CSC and DMB. Price subsidy payments, for instance, usurped 44% of expenditure on agriculture [GoZ, 1991b:25]. Under the SAP, to enable the phasing out of subsidies, the agricultural SOEs were to recover profits by rationalising operations and allowing market forces to determine prices.

Despite the overtones of 'economic rationalism', the proponents of agricultural market reform forwarded an altruistic rationale. The universal assumption was that state-controlled marketing undercut smallholder fortunes and liberalisation would achieve better buying and selling prices [WB, 1989:8]. In the Zimbabwean context, the specific objectives of reform as applied to cotton and maize markets were enhanced monetary gain and national food security respectively. As the main external protagonist to liberalise the maize market, USAID adopted wholly the outlook of the Jayne [1991] study. The argument assumed that rationalisation of the GMB network and the onset of private traders and millers would improve the availability and cheapen the costs of maize-meal, particularly in the drier Natural Regions. In respect of cotton, reform proponents argued that state-regulated pricing imposed an 'implicit tax' on Zimbabwe's 200,000-odd cotton producers and the resort to a market determined price would considerably enhance their profit margins.

Firstly, to take maize, between 1981 and 1991, output from the large-scale sector fell by 75,000 tonnes per year as the land area devoted to the crop shrank from 280,000 to 110,000 hectares in favour of export tradables [Mashingaidze, K., 1994: 214; Jayne, T.S., and Rukuni, M., 1994:377]. Until 1985, however, smallholder production boomed: a 50% rise in the producer price over 1980–1981 and release of the hybrid seed saw output increase by 147% and sales to the GMB triple [Mashingaidze, K., 1994: 214]. Then, and only then, did Zimbabwe qualify as the 'food basket' of Southern Africa. Continued surpluses required ongoing fiscal outlays to cover the GMB's deficit propelled by the imbalance between high buying prices [i.e. pan-territorial/seasonal] to stimulate production and low selling prices to promote food security, which fell below maintenance costs [i.e. staff, depots, collection points, transport, storage].[5] After 1985, under financial duress, the GMB reduced collection points from 135 to nine by 1991 while AFC credit to smallholders, as measured in fertiliser use, fell from 205,000 to 111,000 tonnes [Gibbon, P., 1995:12; Jayne, T.S., and Rukuni, M., 1994: 377]. Ever since, the fall in maize supplies from large-scale farmers has outweighed any increase from smallholders while national population growth outstripped supply altogether.

Accepting the structural problem of supply as given, reform proponents focused on food insecurity, which despite consumer price subsidies still affected, as mentioned earlier, over 30% of children under age five. Since 1983, just 18 out of 170 smallholder farming areas accounted for 75% of GMB purchases [Jayne, T.S., Chisvo, M., and Rukuni, M., 1994:294] while up to 80% of smallholders were normally net buyers of grain [USAID, 1997:50]. The key point made by Tom Jayne

[1991] and USAID [1997:9] was that centralised marketing siphoned grain out of deficit areas—at high cost—only for it to be returned, via a subsidised cartel of urban millers, as relatively expensive maize-meal. Toward the recovery of GMB deficits and improved food security, therefore, they recommended that the GMB withdraw food subsidies and rationalise operations so as to create space for private traders and millers to distribute and process grain more cheaply. Following the removal of subsidies, the 'inevitable price increases' would be offset, proponents assumed [USAID, 1997:10], by the improved availability of a cheaper and nutritious 'straight-run' maize-meal[6], which in turn would free smallholders to primarily focus on cash crops.

Turning to cotton, the argument for liberalisation emphasised that the state controlled trade regime 'implicitly' taxed smallholders through an overvalued exchange rate and absence of export parity, that is, an increasing gap between producer and export prices received. By the late 1980s, according to Doris Jansen and Kay Muir [1994:180], the Zimbabwe dollar was overvalued by about 50%, which meant that exported cotton realised far fewer Zimbabwe dollars than would otherwise be the case. To make matters worse, argued Kay Muir [1994: 48, 52], cotton producers were further penalised by a regulation that compelled the CMB to supply the local textile industry with subsidised cotton before it could export the balance. Over 1988–1989, for example, the CMB effectively incurred a loss of about Z$20 million because most cotton had to be sold locally at Z$1.64c/kg when the export price was Z$3.00/kg. Between 1980 and 1989, the local cotton subsidy averaged Z$5.2 million per year, which liberalisation proponents claimed comprised a direct loss to small farmers.

The reform agenda thus sought to remove the local cotton subsidy and adopt a depreciating market-determined exchange rate in a bid to boost export sales and foreign exchange levels. In turn, under liberalised domestic market conditions, proponents assumed that competition amongst an increasing number of traders to buy smallholder cotton would exert upward pressure on producer prices and improve marketing services. There were few qualms about the inflationary impact of currency devaluation or removing the cotton subsidy from the textile industry, which arguably suppressed the price of clothes to the benefit of smallholders. The beneficiaries of the subsidies and an overvalued dollar, Doris Jansen and Kay Muir [1994:181] stressed, were 'non-tradable', import-dependent and inefficient capital-intensive enterprises. If the trade regime were liberalised, the authors concluded, the depreciation of the Zimbabwe dollar would encourage a net redistribution of income to labour intensive ventures such as cotton production.

5.3 The Impact of Grain and Cotton Market Liberalisation

As it turned out, the pursuit of fiscal deficit reduction and economic deregulation under the SAP presided over a collapse of macroeconomic performance. During 1991–1996, compared to the late 1980s, the average real growth rate of GDP fell from 4% to 1.7% [CSO, 1997c:4] and formal employment creation contracted by one-third [GoZ, 1998a:9]. The average inflation rate rose from 15% to 25% [CSO, 1997c:4] while a counteractive monetary policy saw interest rates treble [Appendix 11]. Concurrently, the value of real wages fell by 35% [IMF, 1997:15] and the percentage of the population below the total poverty line rose from 52.8% to 75.6% [CSO, 1998a:35-36]. The stagflation crisis then hit hyper proportions in the late 1990s following collapses in the value of the currency—by 71.5% against the US dollar on 14 November 1997 [dubbed 'Black Friday'] and again by over 50% during October–November 1998.[7] Both inflation and interest rates reached over the 50% mark [Appendix 11] while an extra 10% of the population was reported to fall below the poverty line [UNDP cited in *The Zimbabwe Mirror*, 14-20/04/00].

The advent of macroeconomic instability wiped away the expected benefits of liberalising maize and cotton markets, which were—to recall—enhanced national food security and monetary gain respectively. Reform advocates, notably USAID [1997:44], tend to assume that market reforms had little to do with the outbreak of the economic crisis. The entire blame is put on the Government for financing a persistent budget deficit [Appendix 8], which upon monetarist assumptions fuelled a cycle of 'excessive demand', high inflation and interest rates [WB, 1995 vol.2:16-22; IMF, 1997: 8, 27-34]. As argued in the last chapter, however, the deficit was less an outcome of Government profligacy than a rising debt interest bill propelled by the tight monetary policy. In a mass-peasant and oligopolistic economy where state expenditure sustained welfare and up to 70% of productive inputs were imported [ZNCC cited in *The Zimbabwe Mirror*, 3-9/09/99], stagflation attributed far more to budget cutbacks and currency depreciation. Both prescriptions formed part of the rationale to liberalise agricultural markets and, therefore, must accept some responsibility that by mid-decade, the domestic market contracted by a reputed 40% [Sachikonye, L.M., 1995a:59].

5.3.1 The Inefficacy of Grain Market Reforms

At the outset of the SAP, the Government doubted the capacity of free market forces to satisfy national requirements of the food staple. The GMB was initially allocated a 'strategic role' in the maize market, which involved setting a floor and ceiling price to protect both production and consumption [GoZ, 1991b:32]. Yet, as outlined in the *Final Evaluation* report, USAID [1997:15-19, 12] sought to alleviate the GMB of this function so that grain market developments would be 'very much in line with the overall goals of the SAP'. Under its Grain Marketing Reform Support Program, the foreign NGO dangled US$25 million in balance of payments support—to be released in tranches of US$5 million—providing the Government fulfilled program conditionality toward, ultimately, a privatised GMB.

The enactment of the Grain Marketing Amendment Act [No.9] of 1991 and the Grain Marketing [Control] (Amendment) Order [No.1] of 1993 fulfilled the conditions of the first three tranches. The first amendment established a board of directors at the GMB—previously vested in the AMA—and offered greater autonomy over commercial operations with a view to eliminate subsidies [Tshuma, L., 1997:118]. Although management became technically free to determine prices, price setting in the words of USAID [1997:37] still remained 'highly political'. The second amendment formally sanctioned 'free and unfettered' grain sales among farmers, traders and millers in all parts of the country with exceptions that the GMB retained monopolies over sales to large-scale millers [Takavarasha, T., 1994:168] and the import and export of maize. A fatal 'impasse' resulted over the two remaining tranches, which entailed the 'full de jure privatisation of the GMB' [USAID, 1997:20]. In early 1997, at the behest of Parliament, the Minister of Agriculture informed USAID that in view of the country's food security, the GMB would not be privatised [USAID, 1997:20-23].

Two devastating droughts over 1991–1992 and 1994–1995 provided setbacks and strengthened the GMB's role as a national food distributor. The President declared the first a national disaster—maize output fell by 80% compared to previous years. Initially, however, shortages in the food staple stemmed from the inept decision—apparently upon World Bank advice and in the face of a drought warning by AGRITEX—to export 0.6 million tonnes of maize between March 1990 and December 1991 [Gibbon, P., 1995:14; Jayne, T.S., and Rukuni, M., 1994:381]. The GMB went on to import 2.3 million tonnes of maize, re-introduced price subsidies [until July 1993] to cover the difference between the imported and local price, restricted sales to private traders to 90 kilos per month as a measure against profiteering and introduced a Food for Work Scheme. Before the 1994–1995 drought, the Government wisely assigned the GMB the task of maintaining a Strategic Grain Reserve [SGR], which consisted of a 'two silos' policy, namely, a maize stock of 500,000 metric tonnes and a cash reserve to cover cereal imports. In May 1995, the Food for Work Scheme was replaced with the Grain Loan Scheme wherein people in need could borrow grain from the GMB and repay after subsequent harvests.

The GMB's deficit soared during the droughts, the continuation of which militated against the privatisation agenda. Selling the GMB as a loss maker to a private concern threatened rapid 'downsizing' in a bid to restore profitability—arguably at the expense of national food security. Annual GMB losses rose from Z$6.1 million in 1992 to $759 million in 1993 to $1,206.5 million in 1994, which then constituted 69% of all SOE losses [USAID, 1997:39; GoZ, 1994:7]. As the currency depreciated, the cost of the maize imports were enormous, over US$500 million [Laidler, M., 1993:49], which quadrupled what the GMB received from selling the grain at subsidised prices to industrial millers [Jayne, T.S., and Rukuni, M., 1994:383]. Under severe budget strain itself, the Government failed to finance the deficit, which forced the GMB to borrow increasing amounts at rising interest rates to cover debt servicing and operating costs. The total outstanding debt reached over Z$3.1 billion in 1994 with interest charges running at Z$90 million monthly [USAID, 1997:39]. After imposing a 5% drought income levy, the Government paid the

GMB Z$2.4 billion in 1996.

After the droughts, the Government and the GMB management board gained breathing space to pursue the agenda of commercialisation, which meant ongoing network rationalisation and adherence to market or subsidy-free prices. Between 1990 and 1997, the GMB halved employees to 2,600, reduced depots from 78 to 68 and planned thereon to halve both totals [FMB, 1997: 9; USAID, 1997:39-41; Gibbon, P., 1995:12]. As intended, the GMB increasingly focused on surplus areas, mainly in Natural Region III, and cutback operations in deficit areas so as not to siphon out grain and allow private trade to take root. Between 1994 and 1997, the Government refrained from fixing maize prices, which suggests that within this period, the pricing behaviour of a genuinely commercialised GMB was tested.

Deregulation of the grain market, according to USAID [1997:41,43], saw a reduction in the GMB's share of maize sales from 100% in 1991 to an estimated 10% in 1996 while that of the large millers decline from about 95% to 20%. The emergence in 1994 of the privately run Zimbabwe Agricultural Commodity Exchange [ZIMACE] and the national spread of individual traders and small-scale millers were believed to be making up the difference. The reforms were heralded as successful on grounds that they were perceived to break the monopoly of the GMB and the urban cartel over maize trading and milling [see also Chipika, S., 1995:20-22]. The final report of USAID optimistically concluded that such a development 'clearly had a long-term positive impact on food security status by freeing grain to move more readily into deficit areas and enabling hammer millers to expand the availability of less expensive straight-run meal' [1997:55].

A full picture of the national food economy under the SAP, however, reveals that the forgoing outlook is far fetched. According to the Nobel prize winning economist, Amartya Sen [1990:191], food security is best analysed in terms of entitlement relations, which is an outcome of the interplay between 'endowment' [i.e. land resources, labour capacity] and 'entitlement mapping' [i.e. producer prices, food prices, employment, wages]. In the final analysis, grain market liberalization offered nothing to address the 'endowment' problem and, as a contributor to the stagflationary impact of the SAP, failed to improve 'entitlement mapping', despite the apparent proliferation of traders and small-scale millers. The beneficial impact of improved availability of 'straight run' maize meal was dwarfed by the detrimental impact of removing food price subsidies and the onset of a more commercialised GMB. Nationally abundant and affordable supplies of the food staple proved increasingly elusive and unless the Government regressed, the reform agenda threatened a collapse in maize production and alarming social unrest.

To begin with, market deregulation exacerbated domestic shortfalls in maize supply. As of the 1990s, Zimbabwe required about 1.8 million tonnes of maize to feed itself [*The Financial Gazette*, 23/03/99] but throughout, output averaged about 1.5 million tonnes, which caused a regular resort to imports [*The Herald*, 7/05/99]. By the mid-1990s, the market share of large-scale farmers reached 10%, down from 90% in the early 1980s [USAID, 1997: 58]. Over the 1998–1999 season, according to the CFU President, Nick Swanopoel, the sector reaped a mere 60,000 tonnes—20% more than the previous season [cited in *The Herald*, 10/05/99].

Clearly, the better-endowed farmers with the advantages of infrastructure [irrigation, power, tarred roads, proximity to rail] responded well to the export stimulus of a depreciating exchange rate and enhanced exchange access, via Foreign Currency Accounts, evident in a stronger focus on tradables [tobacco, beef, pork, horticulture, game ranching, coffee etc]. Yet the deepening export bias dangerously magnified wealth disparities between whites and blacks and increasingly exposed maize production to a drought prone base, which contributed to food scarcity and inflation. During the 1991–1992 drought, for instance, as food inflation soared, tobacco remained well irrigated [Bond, P., 1998:322].

For the best part of the decade, according to a report authored by Professor Oni and sponsored by Friedrich-Ebert-Stiftung foundation, maize output from smallholders declined by 2.08% per annum [Oni, S.A., 1997: 37]. What emerged as a stimulus for externally oriented farmers turned out a curse for domestically oriented farmers. Largely propelled by persistent currency devaluation, formerly subsidised and heavily import-dependent industries critical to the fortunes of maize producers, such as agro-inputs, transport and processed foods [salt, flour, sugar etc], were thrown into a chronic inflation spiral. By 1995, the price of a 50 kg bag of fertiliser had risen by 300% and a packet of seeds by over 100% [Oni, S.A., 1997:43, 67,96; Chipika, S., and Chisvo, M., 1997:37].[8] The cost of fuel and transport regularly rose by margins of 60% while food inflation averaged above 20% until the late 1990s when it entered a hyper phase of up to and over 70% [*Business Herald*, 8/01/99; *The Sunday Mail*, 28/03/99]. The impact on the productive capacity of most smallholders was debilitating because market forces failed to deliver producer prices high enough to keep abreast of rising production costs.

Private traders, the USAID [1997:48] report observed, save farmers on transport costs and assume the risks of moisture and other infestations. Yet little evidence suggests that small farmers wanted to deal with private traders—rather they were compelled do so. About 98%, according to the late President of the Zimbabwe Farmers Union [ZFU], Mr Magadzire, offered prices 40% lower than the GMB [Magadzire, G.S.T 1994:7; see also Moyo, S., 1995: 153]. 'These buyers', he continued, 'have not brought competition but are mere middlemen.' In Hurungwe district, Brian MacGarry [1999:20] disclosed that in 1998 when the official price for Grade A maize stood at Z$2,400 per tonne, private traders offered $900.00 per tonne. The difference was at least five times the transport cost of the 40 to 50 kilometre distance to Karoi. The same behaviour was also evident at privately organised cattle auctions. 'These are nothing but arrangements to exploit farmers', observed a ZFU Memorandum of April 25 1996, 'by under weighing, under grading and under pricing their cattle'. 'The middleman', the Memorandum continued, 'can only make a profit when they under pay farmers and, therefore, must avoid properly organised sales where they must compete'.[9]

Similarly, a profit oriented GMB and bigger private traders, such as the ZIMACE, also tended to take advantage of the lack of market power among dispersed, remotely located and increasingly desperate smallholders. Between 1994 and 1997—a time when the GMB board of management held autonomy over pricing—the producer price stagnated and actually fell below the costs of maize production. Being confined to the major urban centres and limited to relatively small trading quantities, the ZIMACE provided no real competitive edge. In 1996, for instance, the volume of maize traded by the ZIMACE merely totalled 37,500 tonnes, which despite more than doubling by early 1998 remained too small to alter the dynamics of the market

[*The Financial Gazette*, 18/09/97; *The Herald*, 4/02/98]. In the final analysis, Government price intervention was critical not for reasons of 'political patrimony' but simply to avert a collapse in the production of the country's staple food.

In urgency to recover from the droughts, at the behest of the Government—not market forces—the producer price of maize rose from Z$275 per tonne in 1991–1992 to $550 per tonne in 1992–1993 to $900 per tonne in 1993–1994. Thereon, as mentioned, the price stagnated under a commercialised GMB until the Government in early 1997 ordered the Board to increase its producer price from Z$936 to $1200 per tonne [USAID, 1997:37]. These were only nominal increases, though, and in real terms, the 1997 producer price represented about 66% of the 1980 price value [MacGarry, B., 1999:21; Oni, S.A., 1997: 41-42]. In the face of soaring input costs, smallholders threatened not to grow the crop whereupon the Government ordered further rises to Z$2,400 in mid-1998 to $4,200 in early 1999 [See *The Financial Gazette*, 23/03/99, 01/04/99]. As the chief protagonist for higher producer prices, albeit via the Government, the GMB recovered the lion's share of the maize market, which reached 50% by December 1997, according to the GMB Managing Director, Martin Muchero [*The Herald*, 5/12/97].

As of 1999, even at Z$4,200 per tonne, problems of viability remained for maize farmers, particularly if reliant upon exhausted and low yielding soils as is the case for the majority. For just one hectare, at least Z$3,600 alone would have been required for adequate fertiliser [six 50 kg bags of compound A and D] and another Z$2,000 or so to cover transport, tillage, labour and the like. A yield of two tonnes per hectare may not have warranted this investment, particularly given a dependency on private buyers. In Muzvezve, the untypical high quality soils can yield four tonnes per hectare and transport options along the Kadoma-Sanyati tarred road helps farmers bypass private traders and sell directly to the GMB. Yet, despite an arguably viable price, most Muzvezve households including the Shiris, lacked ready cash to purchase the inputs for a major maize crop—a situation made worse by the cancellation of the stop order system in 1997 [*The Zimbabwe Farmer*, April 1997:7].[10] In contrast, as shortly discussed, COTTCO offered an input credit scheme, which largely explains the overwhelming dominance of cotton among Muzvezve farmers over the 1990s.

Meanwhile, as much as a lack of market competition applied over producer prices, it also applied over consumer prices. Besides the multiple cost-pressures released under the SAP, via currency depreciation, tight monetary policy [i.e. high interest rates] and the pursuit of cost recovery on public utilities, the high mark-ups sought by traders added an extra link in the chain of inflation that beset the food economy. From the trader to the miller to the retailer, food inflation ended up being passed on to the consumer. In Zimbabwe, the price of maize-meal intrinsically relates to 'social security', to quote the ZANU-PF secretary for Mashonaland Central, Andre Holland, 'and must be made cheap to keep the people fed and staple' [cited in *The Herald*, 19/03/99]. As the price soared, the Government ironically reacquainted itself with the imperative of stabilising the consumer price. Unlike the 1980s, however, the endeavour floundered amid high inflation, as a controlled end price meant either draining an already exhausted state budget, via price subsidies, or the profits of traders and millers.

The crunch came amid the hyper-inflationary aftermath of the currency crashes—the first on 'Black Friday' on 14 November 1997 and the second over late 1998. After the first, the GMB hiked the selling price of maize from Z$2,400 to $2,900 per tonne, which alongside other rising costs [fuel, packaging, power etc] forced millers and retailers to raise maize-meal prices by 24% in December 1997 and another 21% in January 1998 [*The Herald*, 17/01/98]. In conjunction with other price hikes of cooking oil, bread, soap and rent, the January price rise provoked nationwide riots: six people died and property worth Z$50 million was damaged in Harare and Chitungwiza alone [*The Herald*, 6/02/98]. Soon thereafter, ZANU-PF rank and file, the Zimbabwe Congress of Trade Unions [ZCTU] and the Confederation of Zimbabwe Industries [CZI] all demanded the reintroduction of price controls on maize [*The Herald*, 18/01/98 and *The Sunday Mail*, 25/01/98]. A price task force, headed by the Minister of Industry and Commerce, Nathan Shamuyarira, eventually pegged the GMB selling price at Z$3,000 per tonne and announced a 'gentleman's agreement' over prices with millers and retailers [*The Herald*, 13/02/98; *The Financial Gazette*, 25/03/99].

The turmoil continued. Due to domestic shortfalls, the GMB subsequently imported over 400,000 tonnes of maize at Z$5,000 per tonne—$2,000 above the official selling price. To avoid another riot, the Government subsidised the existing consumer price at a reported cost of Z$365 million per month [*The Financial Gazette*, 25/03/99]. When the producer price was raised to Z$4,200 per tonne, the GMB sought to increase its selling price from Z$3,000 to $4,900 in one hit [*The Financial Gazette*, 21/05/99]. The millers threatened a 62% hike in the price of maize-meal and would have been happy to deal with private traders had their prices been cheaper. The large-scale millers refused to absorb any increased costs and relinquish what some perceived as 'super profits'[11], which provoked the Government to announce a GMB-run milling venture [*The Herald*, 19/03/99, 06/04/99]. In the end, ahead of the land invasions in mid-2000, resolution of the maize price dilemma through the setting of an adequate producer and consumer price went beyond state fiscal capacity, which immediately uncovered the failure of market forces to perform the task.

The bread industry also suffered from a chain of cost inflation from wheat growers through to millers and bakers. From October 1998 onward, as the currency slumped, wheat production costs rose by 50% and the crop price doubled to Z$9,000 per tonne [*The Financial Gazette*, 27/05/99]. All at once, bakers faced a plethora of rising costs including a 103% increase for flour, 52% for oils, 75% for fats, 30% for yeast, 122% for salt, 25% for sugar, 20% for wages and 100% for transport [*The Financial Gazette*, 06/05/99; *The Herald*, 07/05/99]. The 'gentleman's agreement' arranged a year earlier crumbled as the price of bread rose by 70%, which was just one of many regular price hikes. The Government could only threaten to gazette the price of bread, as the finances to subsidise the price of wheat were simply not available [*The Financial Gazette*, 21/5/99]. Similarly, for want of finances, the pricing of other basic food commodities, such as rice, meat and milk, were handed over to market forces and as a result, these basics of life emerged as luxury items in the Zimbabwe of the 1990s.

The benefits of cheaper maize milling were predominantly confined to members of grain surplus households. Within Shiri household, for example, those employed and living elsewhere [i.e. the two sons of the late Joyce and the three sons of the Gumbis] were normally serviced with home grain all year round and were thus advantaged by improved access to small mills. Otherwise, for the majority of deficit households, maize from private traders remained expensive, especially given the lack of supply and competition. Many villagers in deficit areas, such as a Beitbridge West, lamented the withdrawal of the GMB network not so much to sell maize but to *buy* at better prices [*The Herald*, 22/11/97].[12] Rather than encourage households to diversify into cash crops, the reforms enforced a primary focus on food security [Masanzu, F., 1994:12]. Most urban counterparts of deficit households, on the other hand, still relied on industrially milled maize because the pricing of private traders had not been attractive enough to secure a sufficient market share to service urban centres.

At the macro level, grain market reforms aimed to commercialise the GMB and at the micro level, improve food security in the marginal Natural Regions through allowing private traders and millers to distribute and process grain. On both accounts, the situation markedly deteriorated. In 1998, a record 671,830 people countrywide had registered for emergency food aid of which over half were from Matabeleland South and Masvingo [*The Herald*, 2/03/98].[13] Simultaneously, at a rate of 50,000 tonnes of maize per month [*The Herald*, 28/04/99], the GMB diverted grain for food relief, particularly via the Grain Loan Scheme, which incurred an outstanding loss of Z$1 billion by mid-1999 [*The Herald*, 26/05/99]. The circle of depression between worsening food entitlement and rising GMB deficits points to the inefficacy of grain market reforms, which diverted from the root cause of food insecurity, namely, national land inequity and the peasantry's lack of land endowment therein. In April 1999, under fiscal stress, the Government scrapped the Grain Loan Scheme, which ignited among many the urgency of fertile land for survival.

5.3.2 The Elusive Benefits of Cotton Market Reforms

On the surface, the impact of cotton market reforms accorded more to the promise of generating greater export revenues and competition over producer prices as a way to benefit smallholders, who accounted for 70% to 80% of cotton output [RBZ, 1999:6]. In Zimbabwe dollar terms, at an annual average increase of 33.7%, the value of cotton exports rose from $275 million in 1990 to about $3 billion in 1999 [CSO, 1998b:viii; *The Financial Gazette*, 22/04/99]. In the meantime, the CMB successfully commercialised and privatised into COTTCO and beyond middlemen, new traders entered the market, such as COTTPRO Limited, owned by large-scale commercial farmers, and

Cargill Zimbabwe, an American multinational, which to some extent competed over producer prices, methods of payment and input contracts. Yet, paradoxically, real advances in material wealth continued to elude the majority of small cotton farmers. Even upon adequate land holdings, such as at Muzvezve, households at best only managed to reproduce.

In economies strongly dependent on commodity exports to finance an extensive range of imports, the external stimulus obtained from macroeconomic deregulation tends to be swamped by the damage of international trade constraints and an endless circle of currency depreciation, imported inflation and high—supposedly counteractive—interest rates.[14] In Zimbabwe, although currency devaluation stimulated commodity exports, accustomed price constraints in world markets militated against net foreign exchange gains. Meanwhile, the inflation spiral wrecked havoc on domestic purchasing power, which combined with the droughts and tight monetary policy drastically shrank the industrial base [Appendix 12]. For the best part, cotton exports performed strongly yet at the farm level, high inflation quickly absorbed the Zimbabwe dollar gains. In fact, against what emerged as a COTTCO dominated private trading cartel that tended more toward price collusion than meaningful competition, farmers struggled merely to obtain nominal price advances to keep abreast of production costs.

Within a relatively lucrative export market, in contrast to the GMB, the CMB transformed into a profit-oriented entity with ease. In 1991, the Government passed the Cotton Marketing and Control Act [No.8], which granted the CMB management autonomy over prices and allowed smallholders to sell to private traders [Takavarasha, T., 1994:169]. The CMB then became the Cotton Company of Zimbabwe [COTTCO] and by November 1994, the regulation requiring that cotton be sold to local spinners at subsidised prices expired [RBZ, 1994b:5]. Of enormous commercial advantage, COTTCO inherited standing CMB infrastructure, namely, nine transit depots for seed cotton and eight ginneries to process cotton into lint [Mariga, I.K., 1994:225]. In late 1997, the Government sold three-quarters of COTTCO's share equity, which generated Z$620 million [*The Financial Gazette*, 13/11/97; *The Herald*, 02/12/97]. The state retained a controlling stake of 25% while remaining shares were distributed among the public.[15] Thereafter, the company's turnover went on to experience a rise of over 120%, totalling about Z$6.5 billion in late 2000 [*The Zimbabwe Mirror*, 23-29/04/99, 8-14/09/00].

In the interim, however, the policy measures that accompanied this success—subsidy removal, import liberalisation, currency depreciation and positive interest rates—caused an industrial downturn, especially in conjunction with the droughts, not least within the textile industry itself [Appendix 12]. At the time of the SAP, as a result of a Z$1.5 billion investment surge in textiles over the late 1980s [Bond, P., 1998:170-171], many clothing companies carried outstanding debts. Amid the first drought, the doubling of interest rates [Appendix 11] escalated debt-servicing costs while state cost recovery on public utilities and the ongoing slide of the currency—especially given the import of 30,000 tonnes of cotton lint—added significantly to cost pressures. In turn, as the value of disposable incomes deteriorated under price inflation, the domestic market for clothes virtually collapsed—many companies recorded falls in local sales of over 50% [See Sachikonye, L.M., 1995a:57-63]. By 1994, unable to resolve the liquidity crisis, 87 out of 280 registered textile companies were reported closed and 45% of the sector's employees, that is, about 7,000 workers, lost their jobs [Sachikonye, L.M., 1995a:61; RBZ, 1994a:7]

In the textile sector, as in the economy generally, the resort to 'export-led' growth offered no panacea particularly in a country where over 70% of exports are commodity-based. Dr Bernard Chidzero—the Finance Minister responsible for the SAP—expressed early concern that Zimbabwean exports were fetching less foreign exchange than previously [*The Sunday Mail*, 28/04/91]. On the one hand, intense competition among producers and regular gluts dampened commodity prices while on the other, currency devaluation further cheapened the price without necessarily gaining an additional market share big enough to achieve a net foreign exchange gain. Over 1996–1997, for example, despite depreciation of the currency by 28% in real terms, a trade surplus of US$250 million converted into a deficit of US$230 million [Appendix 13], largely on account of rising import costs and falling commodity prices including gold, tobacco, nickel, copper and ferro-alloys [RBZ, 1998:23].

In the case of cotton, as the rising farm output volumes of Table 5.0 indicate, exports performed well. Over the foregoing period, for example, export earnings from cotton lint, as distinct from raw cotton, rose from US$96 million to US$174 million [RBZ, 1998:23]. Yet lint comprised only 30% of Zimbabwe's cotton exports—the remaining 70% was exported in raw form [*The Herald*, 01/05/99], the market fortunes of which are fickle. Over 1998–1999, the world cotton price fell by 25% [RBZ, 1999:6], which together with the collapse of the Zimbabwean currency seriously dented export performance in real US dollar terms. Meanwhile, the hyper-inflationary impact undermined prospects for the textile industry to add value to raw cotton and absorbed the Zimbabwe dollar export gains—farm input costs, such as seeds, fertilisers and chemicals, jumped 120% [RBZ, 1999:6]. By September 1999, according to CSO calculus, 'the Zimbabwe dollar only commanded what 9.1 cents did in 1990, meaning that the purchasing power was reduced by 90.9% … [and] … what the 1990 dollar bought would now be purchased by $109.60' [CSO, *Prices*, 11/10/99].

Table 5.0 *Volumes of Cotton Sales through Marketing Authorities, 1990–2000*

Year	Tonnes
1990-91	183,347
1991-92	200,168
1992-93	59,893
1993-94	204,951
1994-95	178,920
1995-96	84,286
1996-97	297,168
1997-98	313,106
1998-99	288,078
1999-00	271,873

Source: CSO, 1998c: 31; 2000b: 31.

In the context, contrary to promises of advancing real producer prices, the key issue under cotton market reforms merely concerned the extent of nominal price increases to keep cotton producers afloat. In fact, the evidence suggests that real producer prices in the 1990s remained below the values obtained during the 1980s [Oni, S.A., 1997: 41-42]. For clean Grade A cotton, producer prices increased from Z$1.17/kg in 1990 to Z$7.22/kg by 1998, which at that point represented about 80% of the 1980 price value [MacGarry, B., 1999:21]. Subsequently, out of a record turnover of Z$3.9 billion, COTTCO offered client growers an extra $256 million as a seasonal price adjustment, which brought the price up to $8.92/kg [*The Financial Gazette*, 18/03/99; *The Zimbabwe Mirror*, 23-29/04/99].[16] Yet, amid the rut of imported inflation and currency depreciation, genuine export parity pricing really entailed paying growers in US dollars [RBZ, 1997a: 8], which despite discussions never eventuated.

A profit oriented trading cartel proved to be an equal an obstacle in delivering real advances in producer prices as the former state monopoly. As of the late 1990s, any meaningful price war between the three main trading boards had yet to occur. From the perspective of Muzvezve and Sanyati farmers, prices offered by COTTCO, COTTPRO and Cargill always appeared in unison, varying only by a few cents. With an 80% market share [*The Financial Gazette*, 01/04/99], COTTCO usually set the lead price while the other two tended to follow suit [*The Herald*, 10/03/98]. As time progressed, the market became more concentrated: in April 2000, for example, COTTCO bought a 60% controlling stake in COTTPRO [*The Zimbabwe Mirror*, 8-14/9/00].

The chief market protagonist on behalf of smallholder cotton growers has been the Zimbabwe Farmers Union [ZFU], which on an annual basis campaigned vigorously for a rise in producer prices. In 1999, to cover cost inflation, the ZFU demanded a 180% price increase to Z$21.00/kg and advised growers to boycott depots until this was obtained. At one point, cotton bales belonging to farmers who broke the boycott were publicly burnt in Sanyati whereupon COTTCO, COTTPRO and Cargill increased their prices to $13.30, $13.25 and $13.55 per kilogram respectively [*The Herald*, 27/04/99]. COTTCO finally offered $14.50/kg, which though a 100% producer price increase since the previous year still remained below inflation parity [*The Herald*, 20/05/99]. In the interim, a comment by a COTTCO regional manager, who was subsequently disciplined, revealed the perennial structural predicament of smallholders whatever the market policy:

> They will sell it to us whether they like it or not [*The Sunday Mail*, 02/05/99].

On a more positive note, some competition between the trading companies surfaced over service provision. In 1998, for example, to the frustration of Muzvezve farmers, payment from COTTCO took a full month, which motivated Cargill to offer instant payment on crop delivery. The following year, to match Cargill, COTTCO offered payment after one day while COTTPRO offered 90% instant payment, 10% in two weeks time plus free transport of bales. COTTCO then answered with free transport as well, which effectively broke the ZFU boycott. Yet the key initiative launched by COTTCO in 1998, which largely accounts for its dominant market share, was the input credit scheme. Similar to the former stop order system, COTTCO provides farmers with a full kit of inputs—seeds, fertilisers and chemicals—on credit and recovers the debt on crop delivery. In the advent of crop failure, the debt is passed over interest free until the next season.

As of 1999, the increase in the producer price went some way toward restoring viability of the crop at Muzvezve but not enough to eliminate the close threat of poverty. In the case of Shiri household, 39 cotton bales were reaped in that season, which was about an average harvest. At approximately 250 kilograms each, 39 bales represented 9.75 tonnes. At Z$14.50/kg offered by COTTCO, the output would have realised about Z$141,375,00. Out of this sum, the Gumbis obtained two tonnes off two hectares [$29,000], Rodwell and Ester one and a quarter tonnes off one hectare [$18,125], Stewart one tonne off one hectare [$14,500] and the remaining 22 bales went to Mr Shiri off five hectares [$79,750]. Each income was to last a year and at least Z$3000 per hectare or tonne went on inputs [seeds, fertiliser, chemicals]. There was no cost of labour but the children and women who worked many days in the field would be paid indirectly in the form of clothes, shoes, medical and school fees.[17]

As per the family tree, dividing Mr Shiri's annual income for 1999 among his sixteen dependants [excluding the eldest sons Rodwell and Stewart and the Gumbis] realises about Z$4000 for each person. Although more than double the rural poverty datum line of $1,817.23 per person per year for Mashonaland West set by the Government's Poverty Assessment Study Survey [PASS] in 1996 [GoZ/MPSLASW 1996:25], over the late 1990s inflation ran at 70% and money lost value by the day. The Shiri family probably made ends

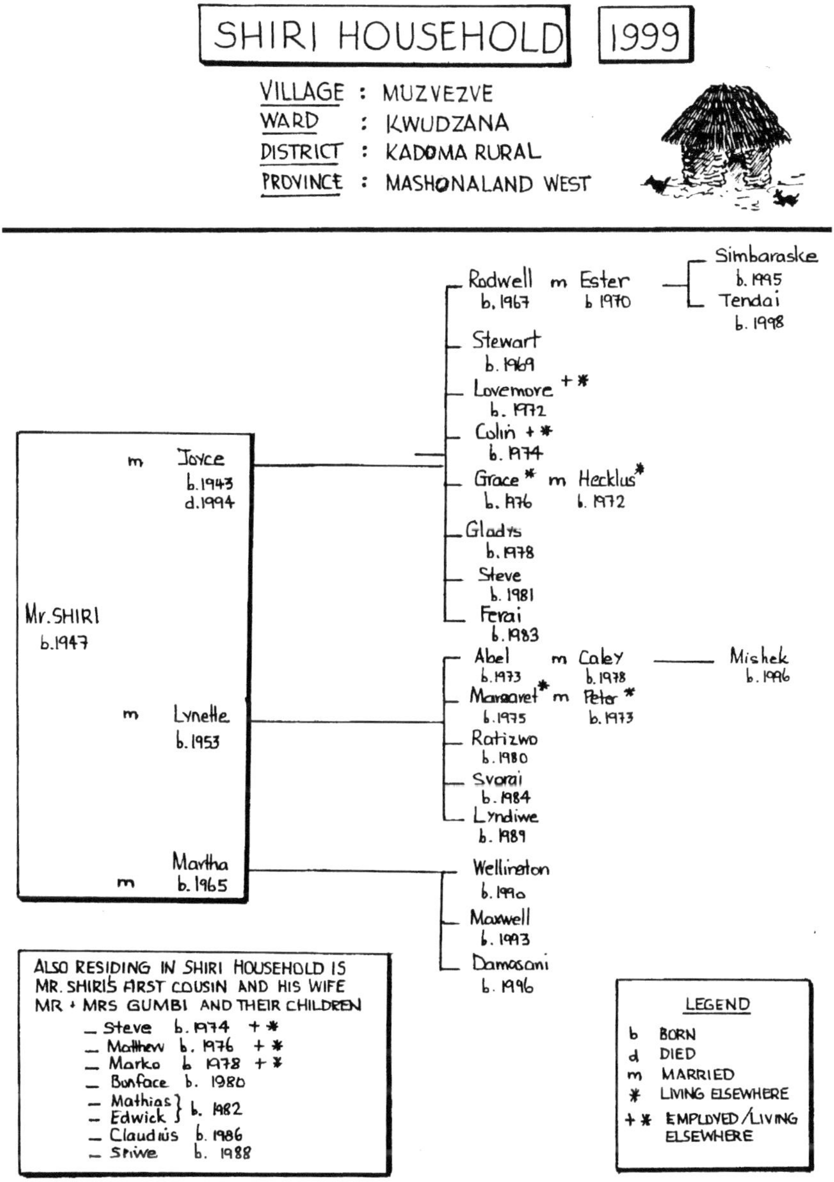
SHIRI HOUSEHOLD
1999
VILLAGE : MUZVEZVE
WARD : KWUDZANA
DISTRICT : KADOMA RURAL
PROVINCE : MASHONALAND WEST
Mr. SHIRI b. 1947
m Joyce b. 1943 d. 1994
Rodwell b. 1967 m Ester b. 1970
Simbaraske b. 1995
Tendai b. 1998
Stewart b. 1969
Lovemore +* b. 1972
Colin +* b. 1974
Grace* b. 1976 m Hecklus* b. 1972
Gladys b. 1978
Steve b. 1981
Ferai b. 1983
m Lynette b. 1953
Abel b. 1973 m Caley b. 1978
Mishek b. 1996
Margaret* b. 1975 m Peter* b. 1973
Ratizwo b. 1980
Svorai b. 1984
Lyndiwe b. 1989
m Martha b. 1965
Wellington b. 1990
Maxwell b. 1993
Damasani b. 1996
ALSO RESIDING IN SHIRI HOUSEHOLD IS MR. SHIRI'S FIRST COUSIN AND HIS WIFE MR + MRS GUMBI AND THEIR CHILDREN
Steve b. 1974 +*
Matthew b. 1976 +*
Marko b. 1978 +*
Boniface b. 1980
Mathias, Edwick b. 1982
Claudius b. 1986
Shiwe b. 1988
LEGEND
b BORN
d DIED
m MARRIED
* LIVING ELSEWHERE
+* EMPLOYED/LIVING ELSEWHERE

meet in 1999 but barely. At about Z$2,285 per year, the individual income for Mr Gumbi's six dependants [i.e. Mrs Gumbi plus five resident sons] would be below the poverty line but the depth was countered by the fortune of three other sons employed and the two household hectares reserved for food production. With ready labour available, the Gumbi's plight for an adequate livelihood was clearly constrained by access to land.

Wealth disparities among Muzvezve households appeared to deepen during the 1990s. Out of the 210 students at the local secondary school, for instance, over half experienced chronic difficulty paying the Z$305.00 total fee per term [Interview with the Principal, 14/05/99]. Despite the uniformity of good soil, the livelihood plight of each household is unique. The number of household dependants in relation to the size of the land holding and the amount of remittances from employed members are equally critical in determining poverty status as macroeconomic policy. Better off households are distinguished by lower dependency ratios, more employed members and more land available per person [CSO, 1998a:56-57].

The enhanced export stimulus obtained under the SAP came at the cost of macroeconomic instability, the socioeconomic damage of which outweighed any conceivable gain. Within this paradox, given a reasonably adequate landholding, cotton at least offered small farmers a means to reproduce and that is about all. For the most part, as people struggled to make a living, cotton remained one of only two crops, the other being sunflower, which experienced a positive annual growth rate among smallholders, albeit small at 1.56%. Yet, at the same time, cotton yields declined at an annual rate of 2.37%, which points to the inability of many growers to afford sufficient inputs [All data taken from Oni, S.A., 1997: 37-38]. The increased output mainly stemmed from an expansion in the area planted, which carried ramifications on long-tern environmental stability. In Muzvezve, as elsewhere, issues of local governance and land tenure came to the forefront, which I briefly recount before concluding.

5.4 Issues of Future Sustainability

The Land Tenure Commission [GoZ/LTC, 1994 vol. 1:86-87] expressed grave concern about growing land pressure in resettlement areas, which gives credence to the word among Sanyati communal residents that Muzvezve is 30 years behind the demographic and environmental crisis they themselves now experience. Shiri household, for instance, along with many others, seems on the brink where there are too many people in relation to the land available. The two eldest sons Rodwell and Stewart have applied for resettlement, indicating that after 17 years, there is need to resettle the offspring of those resettled. At the community level, demographic pressure spilled over when a group of youth in early 1999 illegally occupied a portion of common pastureland and sowed crops. By mid-year, despite the serious environmental ramifications, most authorities, whether the Minister, the Rural District Council or the VIDCO, seemed in a state of paralysis to remove these people. Further resettlement can relieve the congestion yet the scenario is liable to repeat itself in the new area, as the temptation to enter polygamous relations to resolve the labour problem remains as strong as ever.

In resettlement areas like Muzvezve, given the strong commercial orientation among households, the Government is appropriately moving to apply freehold tenure, which promises to secure the property rights of women and much needed collateral rights to obtain credit [GoZ, 1998c:13].[18] Freehold tenure alone, however, does not necessarily guarantee sustainable commercial farming, particularly in a context of household productive relations and other structural constraints such as remoteness. The inherent danger is that resettlement areas may emulate the small-scale commercial sector, which absorbs a lot of child and female labour but generates little wage employment amid declining yields and returns.[19] If, as expected, the common grazing is retained, then there is no doubt that an imperative is to empower the elected authority on the ground, namely, the VIDCO, to manage this vital resource.

In the final analysis, the most effective means to counter the self-destructive cycle of family population outgrowing available land resources is to engender a far more prosperous rural-urban dynamic and rate of gainful employment absorption than what the SAP presently delivers. With 'A' level passes, Stewart Shiri, for instance, would much rather find employment than work the land. As has been outlined earlier, toward the goal of a thriving indigenous agrarian bourgeoisie, national food economy and embracive rural-urban dynamic, a thoroughly broken up large-scale sector offers the greatest possibilities. Put simply, more people need to share in the country's prime resources to enlarge the wealth base and generate employment.

The key lesson is that liberalised markets do not work in countries where colonial structures have given rise to agrarian export enclaves, a heavily import-dependent industrial base and a land-deprived mass-peasantry that lacks the wherewithal to keep abreast of true market value. In regard to maize, the scenario was one of stagnant producer prices, reduced productive capacity among smallholders, declining national stocks, rising grain imports, higher GMB deficits, rising consumer prices, worsening food insecurity and finally social unrest. Linked to an export market, deregulation of the cotton market fared better yet, as mentioned, the sought after export stimulus came at the cost of a rut between imported inflation and endless currency depreciation, which quickly absorbed the Zimbabwe dollar gains at the farm level. Overall smallholders emerged as losers while the winners were a minority of exporting enterprises that qualified to receive Foreign Currency Accounts.

In Zimbabwe, the provision of price subsidies on basic necessities remained fundamentally linked to social stability yet foreign donors, such as USAID and the IFIs, armed with US dollars and free market ideology, encouraged the Government to lose sight of this important reality. In Muzvezve, upon feasible land holdings, the story told is one of survival. To where I turn next, namely, the communal areas of Sanyati and Wedza, the impact of the SAP threatened and in certain circumstances spawned a real crisis of survival. Over the last half-century, the structural determinants of livelihood, specifically, demographic and environmental pressures, had become entrenched in such places that the advent of macroeconomic hostility in the 1990s pushed many households over the edge.

6

Exposure, Defence and Fate: the Case of Shumba and Mukanya

What follows are real life accounts of two families over the last fifty years, which takes in three economic epochs: the late colonial period [1950–1980], the state-led period of independence [1980–1990]; and the market-led period [1990–2000]. The Shumbas and Mukanyas reside in the Sanyati and Hwedza communals of Mashonaland West and Mashonaland East provinces respectively. Although the Natural Region and endowed land quality differs markedly in both areas, the strength of local institutions and macroeconomic performance to counter the demographic and environmental constraints induced by colonial land apportionment seems to hold equal, if not greater, sway over livelihood status. In other words, irrespective of the geographical location, land management, conservation, employment opportunity and affordable essentials [i.e. food, clothing, farming inputs, health care and education] are key determinants of household capacity to reproduce and cope with the number as well as gender of dependants.

Historically, in the face of declining soil fertility and rising population, these realms of environmental and macroeconomic management only increased in importance. Within racially skewed economic structures, the Rhodesian state attempted to enforce communal land conservation; maximise employment growth through state-directed industrialisation; ensure the availability of cheap food; and shift the main burden of African health and education delivery onto the Church. After independence, the Government retained the state-directed economy, expanded welfare services and encouraged the commercialisation of communal areas through production and marketing services. While living standards improved—within an inadequate space—the commercial push hastened environmental decay, especially where reformed local institutions were ineffective. Then, during the 1990s, economic deregulation under the SAP witnessed the collapse of macroeconomic performance, which alongside environmental decline caused a generalised fall in communal living standards.

Over the time frame reviewed, that is, from late colonisation through to liberation and the present, both the national and the household economy underwent a rise and fall scenario. Being an outcome of contending national and international ruling class interests and economic structural realities, macroeconomic policy and performance are beyond any household's control. Under a given cost of living, rate of economic growth and state welfare regime, therefore, the livelihood plight of a household depends on a coincidence of local and family-specific factors. Pre-eminently, as touched on, these include the effectiveness of local institutions toward the preservation of the community's natural resource base and family population relative to arable land allocated and, more crucially, employed wage earners and associated remittances.

In these respects, the Mukanyas of Hwedza have fared much better than the Shumbas of Sanyati. With the advent of macroeconomic hostility in the 1990s, apart from better fortune in regard to the marital fate of daughters and employment of sons, the Mukanyas had a far healthier subsistence economy to fall back on than did the Shumbas. Over the years, a strong kin-based chiefship and allied village bodies acquired a pro-active reputation in land management and resistance to relocating displaced people in the village. The Sanyati chiefship and village institutions, on the other hand, appears to have been overwhelmed not only by an ever rising influx of settlers but also, being a middle to lowveld area, a more powerful commercial assault spearheaded through cotton.

6.1 The Tragedy of the Shumbas

Located in Mashonaland West, Sanyati Communal Lands are about 120 kilometres north west of Kadoma. Along the tarred road coming from Kadoma, via Golden Valley, passing Muzvezve, about opposite the Sanyati Baptist mission but three or so kilometres inland, lies Shumba household. The village I call Baobab is located in Lozane ward of Kadoma Rural District Council. The mission, established in 1952, is run by American Baptists and consists of a hospital and boarding school up to 'A' level. The growth point Arda is located in the southwest corner of the communal area. To the west of Arda within several kilometres flows the Manyati River and across the other side is Gokwe district in Midlands province. The designation of a standard map that Sanyati is within Natural Region III is probably valid when referring to existing or former large-scale commercial areas but within the communal itself the land is sandy and dry and more characteristic of Natural Region IV or V.

6.1.1 The Late Colonial Period, 1952–1980

The rise of commercially oriented smallholder agriculture, which now dominates the Sanyati economy, dates back to the late 1950s. For a long time before, Sanyati belonged to the animal kingdom and served as a hunting ground for the chiefdoms residing in the Gokwe area. The Rhodesian state through its agricultural bureaucracy sponsored the eradication of the tsetse fly and encouraged settled agriculture. Thousands of African immigrants poured into the communal area including chief Who'chele's and headman Lozane's band in 1952 of which Mr and Mrs Shumba were a part.[1] Many like them were victims of the 'belated enforcement of colonial laws restricting black tenancies in areas designated for white occupation' [Worby, E., 1995:9]. Commercial agriculture took off with the introduction of cotton in the mid-1960s and the hybrid maize seed in 1980. According to Eric Worby [1995:8], who completed anthropological work in Gokwe, cotton had a revolutionary impact on African society through monetising the local economy, accentuating wealth disparities and altering cultural norms such as *humwe*.[2]

In the early 1950s, within virgin country, the Shumbas practised shifting cultivation otherwise referred to as 'slash and burn'. After bush was cleared, burnt and the soil ploughed, crops were sown in the ash for a few years and then the family moved on to a fresh area, leaving the fields to fallow. From an African perspective, being low in cost and based on returns to labour rather than to the land, the method was neither irrational or ecologically unsustainable [Kramer, E., 1998:87]. To the Rhodesian Native Affairs Department [NAD], however, conditioned on European agricultural methods and pressed to squeeze more dislocated black people into the reserves, shifting cultivation was low yielding and wasteful.[3] The Native Land Husbandry Act of 1951 required communal residents to settle in one place, fence and contour ridge their arable plots, improve soil productivity, demarcate grazing land and keep a minimum of livestock. Land Development Officers, according to the Shumbas, were 'very strict' and failure to comply usually meant a fine.

Regardless of the Native Land Husbandry Act's additional intention to abolish the power of traditional authorities [i.e. chiefs, headmen and kraalheads] to allocate land, the earliest settlers in Sanyati soon established their lineage as the source of hereditary authority at the village level. Mr Shumba's first cousin acquired the position of Baobab kraalhead, which carried some weight over land allocation because the headman and chief usually acted on advice from below. In a permanent site of their choosing, the Shumbas gained at least seven hectares of arable land and more would be allocated to their sons and a widowed daughter when the time came.

At this stage, the virgin soil bore good harvests of maize, sorghum and millet, the primary purpose of which was to make *sadza*[*] and ward off hunger. Small farming had yet to attain commercial viability in the Sanyati communal and transport was scarce and expensive. The nearest market place was Kadoma, over 100 kilometres away, and to transport a bag of maize apparently cost £4, which destroyed profitability. Within such structural limitations, the Master Farming Certificate[4] awarded by the authorities to Mr Shumba seemed somewhat superfluous. The livestock the Shumbas owned proved a more promising source of income, which included cattle, goats, a few pigs and chickens. At one point, during the 1950s, Mr and Mrs Shumba owned 30 head of cattle, obtained through reproduction, which by selling one or two beasts provided ready cash.

As can be seen from the family tree, Mr and Mrs Shumba went on to have ten children, five daughters and five sons, the first born in 1947 and the last in 1975. A sole dependency on rain-fed

---

[*] *Sadza* is maize-meal cooked as porridge or dough, which along with relish [i.e. meat and vegetables] is a standard meal in Zimbabwe.

agriculture combined with such a high birth rate was potentially a one-way ticket to poverty. The natural fertility of the soil would not last forever and with the steady flow of settlers into the Sanyati communal, the size of the common grazing was diminishing. The Shumba cattle herd had already peaked at 30 head and would halve in size by the end of the 1970s. And the chance of supplementing the menu with wild game such as impala, gudu or guinea fowl was fast disappearing. The neighbouring commercial farm owned by a white man nicknamed *Nyoka* served as a sanctuary but this remained strictly out of bounds. Fortunately, Mr Shumba found a job in 1960 at the nearby Sanyati Baptist Mission as a cook, which provided the expanding family with a lifeline and still does. Besides the wages, the position brought other rewards such as leftover stew and occasional bags of rice, salt, sugar, biscuits, flour and the like.

Mr Shumba's employment foreshadowed a time of relative prosperity in colonial Rhodesia, which lasted until the mid-1970s when the war of liberation greatly intensified. This was, to recall, the UDI period named after Prime Minister Ian Smith's Unilateral Declaration of Independence [UDI] in 1965. Contrary to today's orthodoxy, a highly protected economy averaged a 9% growth rate until 1974 led largely by an explosion in local manufactures from some 600 products to 6,000 [Mlambo, A.S., 1997:29; Bond, P., 1998:117]. Inevitably, as discussed, racially skewed structures curtailed the dynamic, not least by provoking war, but nonetheless, communal areas still received stimulus. In Sanyati, the expansion of transport improved the commercial viability of agriculture while households with a regular wage income like the Shumbas could hire workers at harvest time. Importantly, the soil produced good harvests without applying compound fertiliser, which boosted savings capacity. The Shumba household, for instance, managed to purchase farming equipment and consumer goods over the UDI period, such as a plough, scotch cart, sewing machine and radio.

Mr and Mrs Shumba considered the children's education another worthy investment. In this respect, as opposed to the four sons born in the 1960s, the four daughters born in the 1950s were more exposed to the inequities of colonial rule and gender. The Rhodesian Government blatantly discriminated against the provision of African secondary education while a patriarchal culture generally conditioned females to be mothers and field hands rather than careerists.[5] The four daughters completed primary education at the local state school but none attended secondary. Places were rare and too expensive, such as at the Sanyati Baptist Mission. As the family tree indicates, the two eldest, Mandy and Chipiwa, were mothers by the 1970s and the younger two, Tecla and Kuda, also had children by the 1980s. Time and gender, on the other hand, favoured more the four Shumba sons, all of whom benefited from the explosion in African education after independence in 1980. Although the burning of the primary school by ZANLA guerrillas disrupted their primary education, the four went on to attend boarding schools and successfully complete 'O' levels.

The title of kraalhead in the family put Mr Shumba in a precarious position with the guerrillas. An alliance between African traditional authorities and the Rhodesian regime openly surfaced in the late 1960s when Ian Smith officially restored the powers of chiefs and headmen and included them on the state payroll in a bid to bolster African support [Kriger, N., 1992:74].[6] Although kraalheads were left out, as the war heated up, the guerrillas considered all traditional authorities hostile unless they acted against the Rhodesian regime. Mr Shumba disassociated his family from the chief and headman's counsel and actively supported the guerrillas. Like most rural families, the household became an appendage of a 'People's Committee', which helped organise guerrilla logistics. The provision of food had to be shared amongst households: roasted chickens, for example, were often demanded by the guerrillas, which gave the official symbol of ZANU-PF—*jongwe* [i.e. rooster]—a lasting resonance amongst the peasantry.

Adolescents were also demanded by the 'freedom fighters' to act as *chimwidos* and *mujibas*[7], which involved spying on Rhodesian forces, detecting 'sell outs' and transporting food, blankets and ammunition. Mr and Mrs Shumba managed to send most of their eldest children to stay with relatives in Bulawayo except for Richard and Tecla. These two served the nationalist cause carrying food for the guerrillas, repairing their clothes on the sewing machine and the like. At one point Richard was almost bashed to death by Rhodesian forces, while at another sexual favours were demanded of Tecla by one of the guerrillas. Mr

Shumba sent her away, which almost cost him his life but definitely his radio and watch. A kraalhead in a nearby village and several Baptist missionaries were less fortunate receiving execution for being 'sell outs'. In 1978, the word is that one hundred Rhodesian soldiers were killed in an ambush not far from Arda—the Sanyati growth point. The relationship between ZANU and the Sanyati peasantry was thus forged in bloodshed.

6.1.2 The 1980s

The first decade of independence brought mixed fortunes to the Sanyati communal. While expansion of health and education services offered clear rewards, the promotion of commercial agriculture through the state marketing boards, despite being of some financial benefit, hastened a 'tragedy of the commons'. Otherwise called thc 'law of diminishing returns', the term refers to the demise of community livelihood as a result of environmental decline brought on by too many people and livestock within a fixed land area.[8] In Sanyati, as elsewhere, this demographic predicament was primarily an outcome of colonial land policy and an enclave economic base that offered few off-farm employment opportunities. Even so, given the overall resort to a family mode of production, that is, a reliance on wives and children to meet labour requirements, an intensified commercial exploitation only added to population pressure and environmental decay, especially in desert-prone areas like Sanyati.

From the perspective of Shumba household, the 'tragedy' manifested by way of deforestation and cultivation of unsuitable land, such as water catchments, both of which contributed to erosion, soil depletion, reduced common grazing and, therefore, greater vulnerability to drought. Indeed, the very opposite of what needs to happen in a congested resource-dependent community that remained mainly unrelieved by land redistribution and resettlement. Some relief though was provided by Nyoka's abandoned farm—the fences were pulled down and communal dwellers gained crucial access to wood fuel, grazing and building materials.

Another contributing dimension was ineffective local governance. Generally speaking, the Government did not effectively replace the colonial alliance between Rhodesian district officials and African traditional authorities, which previously enforced conservation, albeit to squeeze in more people. New legislation sent confusing signals as to the position of traditional vis-à-vis state authorities over land responsibility. The District Council Act of 1980 replaced the 220 former African Councils with 55 elected District Councils, which the Communal Lands Act of 1982 empowered to administer communal land upon consultation with traditional authorities. Meanwhile, as mentioned earlier, the wartime 'Peoples Committees' were demobilised and replaced with elected VIDCOs and WARDCOs, which other than a consulting role lacked real power [Makumbe, J.Mw., 1996:45]. As a further complication, local ruling party cells of ZANU-PF also sought to assert authority. 'This profusion of overlapping and incongruent local organisational structures', the Land Tenure Commission noted, 'each with its own boundaries and drawing on different sources of legitimacy, has thus created weak and disparate local institutions' [GoZ/LTC, 1994 vol.1:26].

While the District Council lacked an on-the-ground presence and the VIDCOs and WARDCOs had no secure line of authority, most communal residents, to again quote the Land Tenure Commission [GoZ/LTC, 1994 vol.1:24], 'gravitated' towards traditional authorities to resolve land issues. In the Sanyati communal, however, the rapid influx of settlers between 1950 and 1980 went beyond the ability of the chief Who'chele and headman Lozane to properly service the community in this respect. Indeed, these two remained hard-pressed to protect the interests of their own direct clan let alone give attentive counsel to numerous 'stranger' clans outside the royal lineage. To some extent then, the breakdown of environmental management in Sanyati over the 1980s reflected the inability of traditional authorities to cope with rising numbers.

In the early 1980s, optimism ruled the day and the economy boomed for a couple of years recording growth rates of 11% and 15%. Arda is living testimony of the phenomenal stimulus given to smallholder agriculture over the 1980s. The major state-owned agricultural traders, the GMB, CSC and CMB established depots there and the latter, a ginnery. The state-owned credit facility, the AFC, and AGRITEX—the Ministry of Agriculture's Agricultural and Technical Extension Service—also established offices. The most popular African bank, the POSB, opened a branch, as did the second most popular, CABs. The primary school was rebuilt and secondary schools were opened at Arda and nearby Nueso.

Mr Shumba's wages were not adequate to support four sons away at boarding school as well as the family, which included Mandy, who lived at home with five children without a husband. Maize and cotton farming would help meet basic food and cash needs. By now the sandy soil was depleted in nutrients and the yield of both crops depended on the application of fertiliser. Given timely rain, adequate labour, use of pesticide for cotton and *maximum* application of fertiliser, two tonnes of maize or one tonne of cotton [about four bales] could be expected off one hectare. From seven hectares, therefore, given three for maize and four for cotton, at the very best, the Shumbas could obtain for cash sale two to three tonnes of maize, which excludes the three tonnes they required to feed themselves for the year[9], and up to twelve bales of cotton. Such yields would be 'farmers kingdom' and in reality, the input costs, labour constraints and drought would halve or quarter these totals.

Nevertheless, the Shumbas became part of Zimbabwe's so-called agrarian revolution, which saw the smallholder share of national maize and cotton output increase from less than 15% in 1980 to over 50% by decade end [Rukuni, M., 1994:33; Mudimu, G., 1994:26]. The 'prime movers', that is, production and marketing support, enabled the household to capitalise in the good seasons but not in the drought years of 1983–1984 and 1986–1987. In the early 1980s, the family made use of AGRITEX, AFC credit and, most of all, state marketing channels, which bypassed middlemen who always sought to buy below official prices. Initially, the GMB and CMB offered reasonable prices and the Shumbas invested in a cultivator and planting machine and opened an account at Standard Chartered Bank in Kadoma. As time wore on, however, in parallel with rising deficits, the 'prime movers' subsided: AGRITEX became selective; AFC credit more expensive; and real producer prices began to fall. The key rationale of the SAP, to recall, aimed to restore the viability of State-Owned Enterprises [SOEs] and producer prices.

Mr and Mrs Shumba; their two youngest children, Askina and Barnabus; Mandy and her offspring; and the four sons during school vacations met household labour requirements. Kuda contributed as well after she returned home with two children—also as a single mother. By pulling the plough, the cattle stock, numbering fifteen in the early 1980s, shared the labour burden and remained vital to productive capacity. Although the opening of Nyoka's farm provided extra grazing, being thickly wooded, the area fell short of requirements particularly when considering the collective need of the Sanyati communal and recently established nearby resettlement schemes. Of some interest on Nyoka's farm was the discovery of a spectacular cave by a few Shumba 'herd boys'. The entrance looked dark but opened into a gloriously lighted area best described as a natural Greek theatre. A white beach lay at the bottom and to the side were ancient clay pots signifying that at one time the place had been used for ancestral worship through spirit mediums.

The unsuccessful marital fate of two daughters, despite the extra labour gained, was a misfortune for the Shumbas not least because the household missed out on *lobola*, that is, bride price paid in cash or cattle. Unsupported mothers, as John Iliffe [1987:238] writes, constitute a chronically poor group in African society—before, during and after colonisation. In Shona culture, land is usually distributed on a patrilineal basis and rarely given to single mothers, especially in land scarce communal areas. The parents decided to fragment their holding for Mandy, giving her three hectares, and incorporate Kuda on their remaining four hectares.

The Government's welfare-oriented macroeconomic approach, which controlled inflation at an average of 15% for the decade and most significantly, offered affordable health and education services, remained a crucial link in household livelihood. Although barefoot, the offspring of Mandy and Kuda were at least well fed, healthy and being educated. Under the Government's Primary Health Care strategy, which families earning less than Z$150.00 per month received free [Renfrew, Dr. A., 1992:26-27], the children were treated for malaria at the Mission hospital as well as immunised against measles, whooping cough, polio, tetanus, tuberculosis and diphtheria. This helped Mandy and Kuda finance their children's primary schooling, which included uniform and building fees. Secondary education, as Mr and Mrs Shumba discovered, attracted higher expenses: 'O' level exam fees, for instance, were part of the Cambridge Examination Syndicate and pegged to British pounds. Fortunately, apart from a sudden 20% devaluation in 1983, the Government's managed float generally kept the Zimbabwe dollar fairly stable.

The family hoped that Mr and Mrs Shumba's investment in the education of the four sons would pay off in the form of their gainful employment and assistance toward the secondary education of their nieces and nephews. By decade end, the employment prospects of the two eldest, Wilson and Richard, looked promising while the two youngest, Elias and Manuel, had yet to finish their 'O' levels. Wilson gained a temporary position as a primary school teacher and sought a place at a Teachers College. Richard had a certificate of expertise in agriculture and found temporary employment as a secondary school teacher. Although by now both were married and had their own children, they still managed to send remittances by way of groceries and clothes, which helped relieve Mr Shumba's pressured pay packet. Between them they accommodated and funded the secondary education of Mathias and Stedford.

Yet, despite the promise of their employment and the fact that the household had remained overall self-sufficient in grain, Mr and Mrs Shumba were exceedingly worried. By the 1990s, their cattle herd had dwindled to just seven head. A few beasts went as *lobola* payment for their sons, a few were sold to the CSC but several because of disease and death. Lack of feed appeared to be the main problem, which apart from drought reflected a degraded common grazing area. From inside and outside, people had settled there and cleared land for their fields, even along stream banks. Some said that 'strangers' had 'bought their way in' by illegally bribing traditional authorities, the VIDCO or the Council itself. The indiscriminate cutting of trees and persistent encroachment of animals into fields was of further concern. The cost of independence, Mr Shumba lamented, seemed to be the 'relaxation of discipline' as most of this went 'unpunished'.

6.1.3 The 1990s

In terms of better health, education and farming services, however, the Shumbas admitted that the 1980s delivered some improvement in livelihood. They were perplexed then as to why the Government launched the SAP officially in 1991 to 'improve living conditions, especially for the poorest groups' [GoZ, 1991a:4]. In a liberalised market, the savings derived from rationalising the state bureaucracy were supposed to finance a private investment surge. Households were expected to benefit from increased employment opportunities and higher producer prices following the commercialisation/privatisation of SOEs and their submission to the market competition. The world of *praxis*, however, belied the abstract policy model presented. Soon after the launch, inflation soared; the value of wages and the currency fell; and employment opportunities contracted. Besides macroeconomic hostility, two other factors secured the Shumbas' descent into abject poverty: the advent of more single mothers and environmental decay partly propelled by drought.

Tecla returned home in the early 1990s as a single mother with four children and Chipiwa followed her as a widowed destitute with five children. The youngest daughter Askina also became a single mother and resided at home with two children. In 1999, she moved to the house of her new betrothed but the two children, Sebastion and Immaculate, remained. As a divorcee, Wilson remarried into another household but a child from his first, Fortunate, also stayed at the Shumba home. This time Mr and Mrs Shumba allocated one hectare to Tecla and incorporated Askina, like Kuda, on their own holding—now reduced to three hectares. For Chipiwa, as a widow, traditional authorities showed more flexibility [not least because of the family link to the kraalhead] and granted her a vacant stand of two hectares.

What forces conspired against the Shumba daughters for all of them to end up as unsupported single mothers? Apart from Chipiwa, their plight seems to reflect the misfortune of being assigned to men without economic wherewithal or integrity. Such a problem reflects generally the dangers of a poverty-stricken economy but specifically, the vulnerability of women within a patriarchal gender culture that relative to men sidelines female education and employment opportunity. In worst case scenarios, disempowered women end up the victims of men. The Shumba sisters had little choice other than return to the bosom of the family and share amongst siblings—often the first defence against poverty [Iliffe, J., 1987: 245]. The realistic employment options available were in domestic service, local retail or horribly, prostitution. The latter position invited an early death from AIDs while the two former positions earned scant, if not slave, wages.

In Chipiwa's case, the law plainly failed to protect her. After her husband died, the in-laws repossessed the Bulawayo town house and simply cast her and the children out. Although the Legal Age of Majority Act [1982] and the Matrimonial Causes Act [1985] gave African women the same legal capacity and maintenance rights previously granted to white women, neither technically recognised traditional and unregistered marriages like Chipiwa's. Thus, as aff irmed by the Land Tenure Commission [GoZ/LTC, 1994 vol.1: 64] and recent Supreme Court rulings [See, for instance, *The Herald*, 13/03/99], divorced or widowed women from an unregistered traditional marriage, though enacted through the process of *lobola*, do not necessarily receive maintenance rights. Chipiwa had no certain legal recourse and in any case, lacked the finances to put up a legal fight.

The population of the Shumba household increased from 12 to 34 during the 1990s. Besides the three daughters and twelve children already mentioned, the total includes the return of Manuel, his wife and two children; the two children of Mandy's eldest daughter, Sarah [another single mother]; and the wife of Andrew, Chipiwa's second born. Manuel, like Chipiwa, received a stand of two hectares, which increased the household's land holding to eleven hectares. Yet, regardless, the extra numbers probably assured that the household crossed the threshold when a large family becomes a burden rather than a labour bonus [Iliffe, J., 1987:6, 273]. Annually, seven tonnes of maize plus the relish would be required just to feed everyone. At best, such a quantity could be obtained off three to four hectares, which would leave six hectares or so available for cotton production to meet cash needs. But such assumes timely rain, the availability of cattle and sufficient possession of inputs—seeds, fertiliser and insecticides—without which gainful production was not possible.

In any case, the entire death of the Shumba cattle herd by the mid-1990s crushed optimistic forecasts. The droughts of 1991 and 19 and again in 1994 and 1995 played a decisive role but prolonged dries have always been an accustomed feature of the landscape. At a deeper level, the death of all seven beasts from lack of feed and disease raises serious issues about environmental management of -

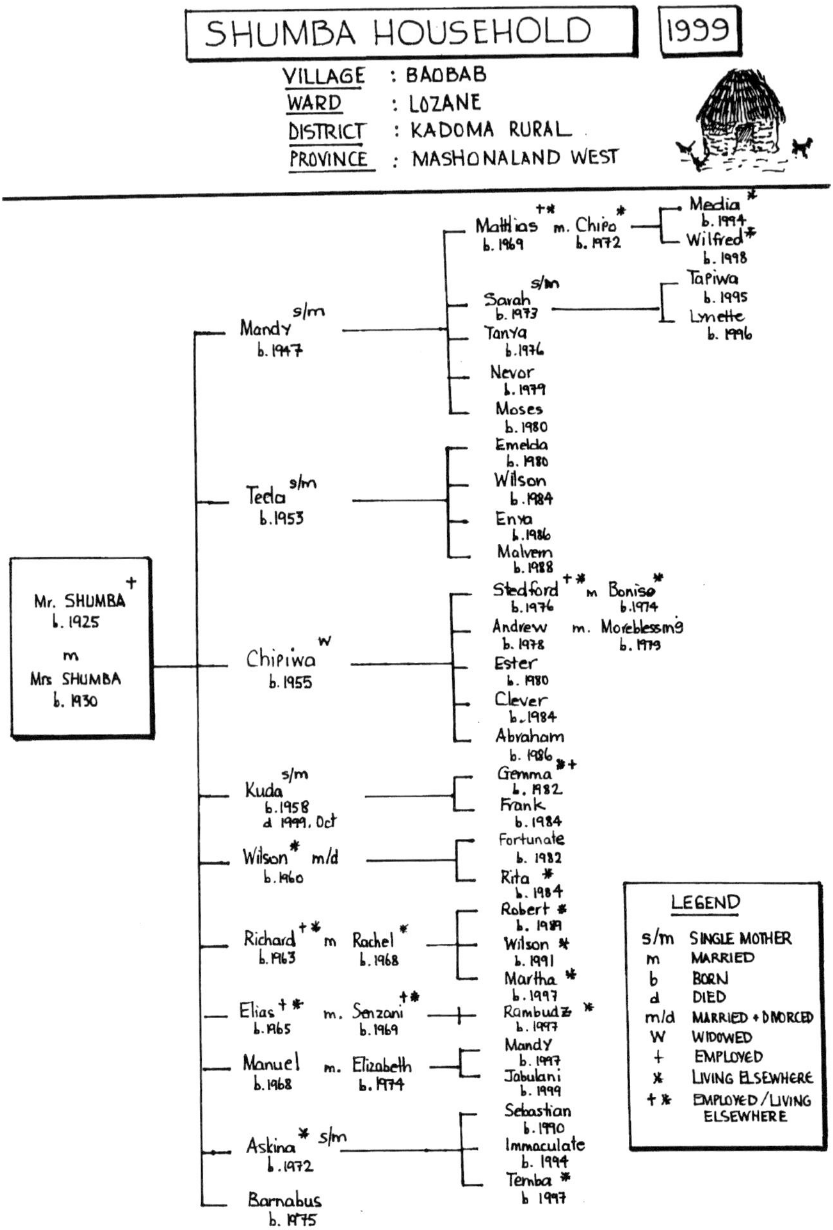
SHUMBA HOUSEHOLD
1999
VILLAGE : BAOBAB
WARD : LOZANE
DISTRICT : KADOMA RURAL
PROVINCE : MASHONALAND WEST
Mr. SHUMBA + b. 1925
m
Mrs SHUMBA b. 1930
Mandy s/m b. 1947
Matthias +* b. 1969 m. Chipo * b. 1972
Media * b. 1994
Wilfred * b. 1998
Sarah s/m b. 1973
Tapiwa b. 1995
Lynette b. 1996
Tanya b. 1976
Nevor b. 1979
Moses b. 1980
Teda s/m b. 1953
Emelda b. 1980
Wilson b. 1984
Enya b. 1986
Malvern b. 1988
Chipiwa W b. 1955
Stedford +* b. 1976 m Boniso * b. 1974
Andrew b. 1978 m. Moreblessing b. 1979
Ester b. 1980
Clever b. 1984
Abraham b. 1986
Kuda s/m b. 1958 d 1999, Oct
Gemma *+ b. 1982
Frank b. 1984
Wilson * m/d b. 1960
Fortunate b. 1982
Rita * b. 1984
Richard +* b. 1963 m Rachel * b. 1968
Robert * b. 1989
Wilson * b. 1991
Martha * b. 1997
Elias +* b. 1965 m. Senzani +* b. 1969
Rambudzo * b. 1997
Manuel b. 1968 m. Elizabeth b. 1974
Mandy b. 1997
Jabulani b. 1999
Askina * s/m b. 1972
Sebastian b. 1990
Immaculate b. 1994
Temba * b 1997
Barnabus b. 1975
LEGEND
s/m SINGLE MOTHER
m MARRIED
b BORN
d DIED
m/d MARRIED + DIVORCED
W WIDOWED
+ EMPLOYED
* LIVING ELSEWHERE
+* EMPLOYED/LIVING ELSEWHERE

the Sanyati commons and the appropriateness of an unbridled commercialism in such a congested and fragile area. The loss of draught power for cropping, manure for the vegetable garden and nutrition from the milk spelt disaster for the Shumbas. The herds of most households were similarly decimated, which destroyed the chance of borrowing beasts from kin and pushed the price of hiring out of the family's reach. The hand-held hoe offered the only course, which meant a predominant focus on maize production for subsistence, perhaps supplemented with a few bales of cotton to meet urgent cash needs.

Table 6.0 *Year on Year Inflation of Basic Necessities, December 1996 – May 2001*

Item	**% Change Dec96/ Dec97**	**% Change Dec97/ Dec98**	**% Change Oct98/ Oct99**	**% Change Dec99/ Dec00**	**% Change May00/ May01**
Food	18.9	62.9	86.4	42.9	38.5
Bread and Cereals	24.3	56.1	85.5	48.2	57.4
Meat	21.3	58.5	81.7	33.1	45.2
Fish	12.2	77.3	88.1	48.4	79.6
Milk, Cheese, Eggs	23.6	54.2	96.2	30.7	93.9
Fruits and Vegetables	20.0	85.7	91.8	50.7	19.5
Non-Food		37.0	59.7	63.9	70.4
Clothing	8.7	23.7	66.0	50.1	61.5
Footwear	12.6	41.4	66.3	59.1	71.7
Medicines	10.4	60.2	55.6	51.8	122.7
Medical Fees	8.6	11.0	19.0	53.4	46.0
School Fees	50.8	19.4	33.7	44.4	66.1
School uniforms	19.7	35.7	44.4	45.7	49.6
Public Transport	26.5	46.3	93.1	105.4	100.8
Rent, Rates, fuel and Power	23.8	18.0	35.9	60.4	82.8

Source: CSO, *Prices*.

Even on the subsistence front, however, the household could not make ends meet because the cost of the minimal inputs and basic necessities under the SAP went beyond the family's purchasing power. The outbreak of inflation was no doubt the most debilitating aspect of the reform program. Over the late 1990s, as the currency collapsed on and after 'Black Friday' [14 November 1997], Table 6.0 records the devastating hyper-inflationary impact on the cost of basic necessities. Fundamentally, the source of inflation related to supply rather than demand, more specifically, a profoundly concentrated and heavily import-dependent production base. The state macroeconomic regime previously kept the menace in check through price, exchange and interest rate controls but once dismantled, whether propelled by rising import or debt-servicing costs, state cost recovery or 'profit-push', inflation took on a life of its own in a spiral of price reaction.

Meanwhile, the Shumba household remained powerless—without the means, whether via credit, employment wages or remittances, to keep abreast of such rising costs. Mr Shumba's meagre wages were being fully absorbed simply purchasing the nitty-gritty essentials for the family. The Baptist hospital cancelled his accustomed bonus of occasional kitchen leftovers because of budget cutbacks and pressure to recover costs from 'user fees'. The household menu became very sparse: tea without sugar or milk; bread without margarine, sadza without meat; and relish without tomatoes. Chipiwa, for instance, qualified to register for a 'food for work' programme at the mission.

Credit also remained out of reach. Without cattle or any significant collateral, the family encountered difficulties registering for the input credit scheme from COTTCO, let alone securing a loan from private or public sources. In fact, Standard Chartered Bank in Kadoma closed the Shumba account for a lack of regular deposits. In any case, recourse to credit offered no lasting salvation. Interest rates on AFC loans, for instance, rose from 13% in 1991 to over 31% by 1998, which combined with inflation effectively absorbed the mark up most communal farmers could obtain from real producer prices [Chipika, S., and Chisvo, M., 1997:36; *The Herald*, 31/01/98].

In a high-inflation economy that created less employment than the numbers retrenched[10], the hope of the household gaining a return from its investment in the education of the four sons failed to materialise. Only Richard and Elias managed to secure permanent formal employment as a Zimbabwe Farmers' Union [ZFU] extension officer and Anglican Church trainee pastor respectively. Yet, as average real wages fell by one-third between 1990 and 1997 [UNDP/PRF, 1998:37], the capacity of these two to send even minor cash remittances, let alone sponsor the education of their cousins, was severely undermined. With average O level passes, both Wilson and

Manuel could not find a place at Teachers College and returned to the land. When the Government announced land resettlement 'phase' two in late 1997, Manuel applied in the hope that virgin soil would guarantee him a better livelihood. Mathias, Stedford and Gemma managed to find employment in the informal sector but largely this is a cul de sac of survival activities, which I review next through Mpofu household.

In contrast to the 1980s, the educational and health prospects of this third Shumba generation, that is, the offspring of the four sisters, deteriorated markedly in the 1990s. Few could complete their secondary education due to a lack of cash to cover the exam fees alone, which skyrocketed in proportion to the fall of the Zimbabwe dollar.[11] Likewise, without the cash, they could not obtain proper health care. Although in theory free medical treatment remained for families below the income threshold, which rose to Z$400.00 in 1992, dire financial straits forced hospitals to charge fees [*The Zimbabwe Mirror*, 26-31/03/99; *The Herald*, 6/05/99]. In terms of adequate drug supplies, staff, equipment, beds and buildings, mission hospitals including the Sanyati Baptist were among the worst hit [*The Herald*, 3/05/99]. The Government set up the Social Dimension Fund [SDF] in 1992 to assist people pay health and school fees but none of the Shumbas has been a recipient so far. Many of the children appear gaunt and suffer from recurrent malaria. Kuda herself died in late 1999, most probably from malaria—she just got weaker and weaker.

The Shumbas could not engage the new cotton traders of the 1990s because the family was out of the production game. The impact of the SAP formed an integral part of their descent into absolute poverty; the cost of living increased too suddenly while employment opportunities contracted, particularly for the educated sons. Other factors, of course, were at work in their downfall: national land inequality, environmental decline, ineffective local governance and gender inequity. Yet, within the structural context, the SAP as a development strategy offered little to halt the crisis of livelihood. Life only got worse for the unsupported mothers and their children while the exploitation of the environment accelerated. According to the Baobab kraalhead, during the SAP years, people came in droves looking for stands to help them escape poverty. Even the white soil in the cave on Nyoka's farm, despite being a sacred place of spiritual worship, was upturned in a futile attempt digging for gold.

6.2 The Greater Strength of Clanship: The Mukanyas in Hwedza

In Mashonaland East province, to the heartland of the Zimbabwean plateau, Hwedza Communal Lands are situated south east of Harare, about half way heading toward the Chimanimani Mountains on the Mozambican border. This is the territory of the *mbire* people—the name of the hand played xylophone-type instrument—who traditionally belong to the *Svosve* royal dynasty. The country is highveld, above 1200 metres, and declared unsuitable for cotton. In the valleys, the soil is fertile and the area borders on being in Natural Region IIb and III. Jesuit priests, linked to Silveira House in Harare, established a mission called St Mary's, which consisted of a secondary school and hospital, not far from the Hwedza growth point. A tarred road built after independence runs from the growth point to Murinbinda in the southeast corner of the communal.

The Mukanya family, like most in the Hwedza communal, originally hailed from around Marondera to the north. The colonists progressively possessed the prime farming land there and pushed the people into a small communal area called *Svosve*. Soon after the Land Apportionment Act of 1930, land scarcity and a proposed relocation caused a split in the chiefdom. The then Chief Svosve refused to move south to the present-day Hwedza communal area while about half the community left including the forebears of our Mukanya family. Thereon, the Svosve chiefship was rotated between the two communities in the north and south until 1943 when the Government sanctioned the right of the Hwedza communal to have its own chief Svosve. Mukanya kin meanwhile permeated the southern corner of the Hwedza communal such that the village carried their namesake. The current chief and the village kraalhead are the siblings of Mr Mukanya and his first son Oliver is a contender to inherit the chiefship. Mukanya village is thus of royal lineage—all inhabitants are related through blood and marriage.

The move southward paid off in the long run. In June 1998, a group of Svosve villagers from the northern communal made the front page of *The Herald* when they squatted on four Marondera large-scale commercial farms designated by the Government for resettlement [*The Herald*, 23/06/98, 28/06/98]. After five days, the squatters left but only after assurances by the northern chief Svosve and Vice-President Muzenda that they would definitely be resettled. In Mukanya village, however, land desperation has not reached boiling point. Although by no means a commercial farmer's paradise and more oriented to subsistence, there seems a greater contentment. In contrast to Sanyati, the history reveals less of a commercial theme and one more concerned with village governance and land management for quality of life's sake. The state of the physical environment is far healthier with tracts of forest, grazing areas and mountain streams that almost last the year round. The source of the better management has not come from the state but from the accountability inherent in kinship and an authoritative chiefship.

6.2.1 The Late Colonial Period

Mukanya village comprises about forty-five hectares of arable land and fifteen main households—each with about three arable hectares and access to communal grazing. From its inception, agriculture took on a subsistence character, which has continued to the present. According to Mr Mukanya, the orientation is largely a consequence of land shortage and a lack of transport to local grain depot centres. In the early 1960s when Mr and Mrs Mukanya were newly-weds, the unfertilised soil produced a diversity of crops including maize, ground nuts, round nuts, sunflower, millet, rapoko, pumpkins, beans and green vegetables, which could be supplemented with game meat like impala. In fact, food was so in abundance that the Mukanyas claim many people were 'not interested in Western civilisation'. Minor cash needs such as for clothing could be meet by selling to private traders who annually roved the area at harvest time.

Unlike others, the Mukanyas realised early that wage employment and labour migration had replaced agriculture as the economic basis of life. Mr Mukanya obtained a building certificate in Marondera and his consequent employment on building sites served as the main source of family income. Although distance and transport militated against the commercial viability of agriculture, Hwedza is conveniently located to the major employment centres of Harare and Mutare—within a three-hour bus ride each way. From the late 1950s throughout the UDI period, according to Mr Mukanya, building jobs were plenty. The casual nature of employment suited him as he could return home to attend to farming during the agricultural season. The straddling of town and country proved an effective way to support the family, which as the tree indicates totalled nine children—three daughters and six sons—the first born in 1963 and the last in 1983.

The household during the 1950s and 1960s managed 20 head of cattle on well-maintained grazing land. Apart from endowed land quality, the healthy commons reflected Chief Svosve's defiance of the white administration's desire to settle more people. He also willingly imposed punishments on anyone who let stock transgress, cultivated a stream bank or cut down trees, regardless of what the Rhodesian state said about the status of customary law. In a similar vein of conservation but not of colonial resistance, along with the headman and kraalhead, he cooperated with the Rhodesian land development officers in implementing the requirements of the Native Land Husbandry Act through the building of contour ridges and storm drains. Unlike in dry, flat areas where measures of water and erosion control encountered most resistance [Elliot, J., 1991], the Mukanya elders could see some sense, especially given the high land gradient.

ZAPU party cadres made the first visit to the village in the mid-1960s. They apparently tried in vein to get the villagers to flout conservation measures and other rural regulations such as cattle dipping and payment of cattle and dog taxes. The Mukanyas claim that people feared the Rhodesians more and in any case, were basically content and accordingly not politicised. Minor cash needs, as mentioned, could be met by selling produce to private traders; consumer prices remained stable; and there seemed to be wage employment for those who wanted it. St Mary's Mission provided basic health care and although no secondary school yet existed, a state primary school offered a 'high standard' education, which all nine Mukanya children attended. The slumber of the village soon changed, however, when the nationalists returned in the mid-1970s as armed ZANLA guerrillas.

The royal lineage of the family made Mr Mukanya a suspected enemy and he was required to prove his allegiance from the beginning. The guerrillas chose him to be the coordinator of the village committee and his son Oliver as a *mujibah*. The village became a 'hot spot' as the guerrillas set up permanent operations and the Rhodesians sought to destroy them. Caught in the tug of war, villagers at one point were forced by Rhodesian forces to dip their cattle and many including Mr Mukanya had to invariably flee for their lives after either side suspected or observed affiliation with the enemy.

The highlight was a famous battle in 1977 called *Mukanya ma jet*. Before dawn, helicopters dropped a couple of Rhodesian squadrons on a mountaintop. They descended and encircled a *kopje* where a band of seven guerrillas were still conducting a *pungwe*.[12] There was panic. Two young *chimwidos* were shot dead as they ran into a line of advancing Rhodesians and Oliver received a spray of bullets from a jet that miraculously skimmed his legs and arm. But the guerrillas soberly took up positions and proceeded to inflict heavy damage. One of them up a tree managed to down two jets. By mid-morning the Rhodesians refrained from attack, content to surround the *kopje* yet, as legend has it, all seven guerrillas walked away amid dense fog brought on by spirit mediums. Thus, through fear, bloodshed and myth, Mukanya village like that of Baobab and many others became firmly tied to the rise of ZANU. To quote Mrs Mukanya: 'we were born with this thing and we shall die with it'.

6.2.2 The 1980s

In contrast to Sanyati, the seeds of demographic and environmental crisis in Mukanya village had not been fully sowed. Tight kinship-based authority, the pinnacle being the chiefship, had so far managed to protect the village and the grazing area from settler invasions. Over the 1980s, in the light of the new Government's commercial agrarian policy and reforms to local governance, the Svosve chiefship emerged strong enough to regulate the environmental impact of the former and incorporate the new institutions of the latter, namely, VIDCOs and WARDCOs, within the overall kinship structure. In turn, the strength of village authority seemed to pay off in the form of foreign NGO and central Government interest to conduct environmental development projects. Hwedza's convenient proximity to the major cities of Harare and Mutare, though, certainly helped ease environmental pressure.

Not only is the location conducive to attract the visits of outsiders but also improves people's employment options beyond land exploitation and grain market dependency.

The Mukanyas reduced their cattle herd from twenty to eight over the 1980s due to the natural expansion of village population and the allocation of additional stands to male heirs. The fertility of the soil had also declined over four decades of settlement and for the first time fertiliser had to be applied to obtain the maximum maize yield of two tonnes per hectare. Sunflowers and groundnuts were additional commercial options but as these crops were land extensive and labour intensive, the Mukanyas mainly focused on maize production. Contrary to the 1980s norm, the nearest GMB depot was really beyond a 'scotch cart ride' being located at Hwedza growth point some 40 kilometres away. St Mary's Mission, however, provided villagers with transport to ferry their surplus maize to the GMB depot and also operated a fertiliser credit scheme, which could be repaid after the harvest.

The Mukanyas earned reasonable money from maize in the early 1980s but like the Shumbas found the profit margin decreased as time progressed. Even so, the cost of essential commodities such as soap and cooking oil, the parents maintain, were kept within reach during the decade. Tangible benefits of independence included the building of a village medical clinic and state secondary school. Yet income from maize farming plus Mr Mukanya's employment enabled the first four children to attend the recently opened secondary school at St Mary's Mission. The advantages of the latter included a lower teacher/pupil ratio and better English tuition from qualified teachers from overseas.

In regard to local governance, the same introduced legal framework, which in Sanyati appeared to be unworkable, seemed to operate fairly successfully in Hwedza and Mukanya village in particular. Like elsewhere, the *Realpolitik* of village management lay between District Councils, the VIDCO and traditional authorities while the WARDCO seemed somewhat superfluous. The key point of difference with Sanyati appeared to be the pervasive kinship structure and an authoritative chiefship, which effectively protected the community against the misappropriation or misuse of common land. Put simply, members of the community, Council, the

VIDCO or traditional authorities were and continue to be deterred from acts of environmental transgression, such as cutting down trees or illegal land transactions, lest they risk being shunned or even punished. The dynamic Mrs Mukanya, as elected village representative on the VIDCO, and Chief Svosve himself continue to keep a watchful eye.

In fact, according to the Chief [Interview, 14/04/99], he, the Council or the VIDCO could not act unilaterally over land matters as each effectively had a veto, which put the brakes on corruption. The District Council has the final say over the allocation and use of land, the Chief pointed out, but traditional authorities must be consulted lest the Council violates customary law and the rights of the people under it. Indeed, the working relationship between the Hwedza chiefship and the District Council probably accords to the Government's original vision of how reformed local governance should operate. The net and vital outcome is a relatively well-preserved common grazing area and wood lots.

This is not to say the system of local governance in Hwedza was without problems. The key issue of whether the chief, headman and kraalhead should be made ex-officio members of the Council and paid for their services applies to Hwedza as it does nationally. The kraalhead of Mukanya village, for instance, resented the unpleasant task of collecting cattle and household levy for the Council [Z$3.00 per beast and $10.00 per household respectively in 1999] when people complained that the veterinary, health and road services were poor. Chief Svosve received an 'allowance' for his duties from the Council mainly to cover transport yet was against the idea of putting traditional authorities on the state payroll—'we are not employees of the Government nor should we be'.

Nevertheless, the governing arrangement between the Council, VIDCO and traditional authorities has borne some fruit in Hwedza and Mukanya village. Departments of central Government concerned with rural development—financed to a large extent by NGOs—have harnessed all three participants to implement projects. AGRITEX, for example, pioneered communal conservation projects in the area while the Forestry Commission conducted several tree planting projects in eucalyptus, indigenous and citrus [Elliot, J., 1991:83; personal research, 1998, 1999]. The allocation of land and labour by the VIDCO and traditional authorities has been central to the success of both projects. Other NGOs embarked on *tso tso* stove campaigns and beehive feasibility studies.[13]

In a relatively stable macroeconomy, the decade of the 1980s for the Mukanya household was a comfortable one. The mission education of the first two sons, Oliver and Doubt, proved a worthy investment. Oliver obtained a place at Teachers College while Doubt became a trainee manager at Hunyani Paper and Packaging Company in Mutare. With two sons permanently employed, the education and employment prospects of other siblings improved considerably. Employment indeed was fundamental, as the basis of the household's livelihood had not been from agriculture but from the cash wages of Mr Mukanya's building contracts. On three hectares of land with limited labour and declining producer prices, household agriculture was best suited to subsistent food production. The efforts of village governing bodies to conserve the communal resource base would be a critical factor in the hard times ahead under the SAP.

6.2.3 The 1990s

As elsewhere, the SAP greeted the village with soaring inflation and a shrinking national economy, which combined with the droughts, amounted to a severe attack on the community's livelihood base. Mr Mukanya's building contracts completely dried up and along with many others, the household tried to derive a main income from small farming. Yet, as Mr Mukanya discovered, the impact of cost inflation discouraged a commercial orientation and only affirmed the subsistence role of agriculture. A spiral of poverty threatened to engulf the family but they avoided the depth of the slump the Shumbas experienced. In terms of village environmental management and the marital and employment success of their daughters and sons respectively, the Mukanyas were much more fortunate.

The decisive blow to a commercial agricultural orientation came immediately after the SAP commenced: St Mary's Mission had to cancel its transport and credit-fertiliser services due to 'unsustainable cost pressure'. Being quite isolated from the GMB depot, the action exposed villagers to transport hawkers. Lest they paid the exorbitant cost, most would have to resume their pre-independence dealings with private traders, who received a new lease of life under grain market liberalisation. In circumstances of minimal competition and high inflation, as was the case, they would no doubt drive a hard bargain, even below the costs of reproduction.

For the time being, however, the drought of 1991–1992 put production completely on hold. Several of the village wells ran dry and the Mukanyas lost three beasts, which reduced their herd to five head. If not for the Government's drought relief scheme involving direct food relief, food for work programs, child supplementary feeding programs, farm debt rescheduling and livestock purchase, people would surely have starved. The VIDCO played an active role in implementing the drought relief and in 1993 launched an Under Five-Feeding Project, which consisted of a vegetable garden and crèche. The Ministry of Health took an interest in the project and provided the funds for a fence around the garden.

The 1992–1993 season had to be one of recovery in both maize supply and hopefully cash. Like most, the Mukanyas sought to sell their surplus maize and had to negotiate with the private traders. Yet the price offered—in the range of Z$220.00 to $300.00 per tonne—barely covered the cost of production. The amount of fertiliser required to produce that tonne, that is, about five 50 kg bags, cost about $250.00 alone. The GMB offered $550.00 per tonne but the problem, as mentioned, remained transport. In the end, Mr Mukanya begrudgingly sold to the traders.

The following season in 1993–1994 the household tried a new strategy and joined a group-lending scheme run by the AFC. The credit came in kind—seed packs and fertiliser—and on condition that the maize was sold to the GMB minus the debt. All in the group fulfilled their part of the contract but after the sale members went away saying 'never again'. After the costs of transport, inputs and the interest had been deducted, there was nothing left but petty cash. The SAP hailed as the framework of economic recovery seemed to deliver little incentive to produce on a commercial level.

Meanwhile, the Mukanyas tried to keep abreast of accelerating secondary education and health costs, the former rising by 150% in 1992 alone [Mlambo, 1997: 89]. The last six children still lived at home at the beginning of the decade. As of the mid-1990s, annual fees at the

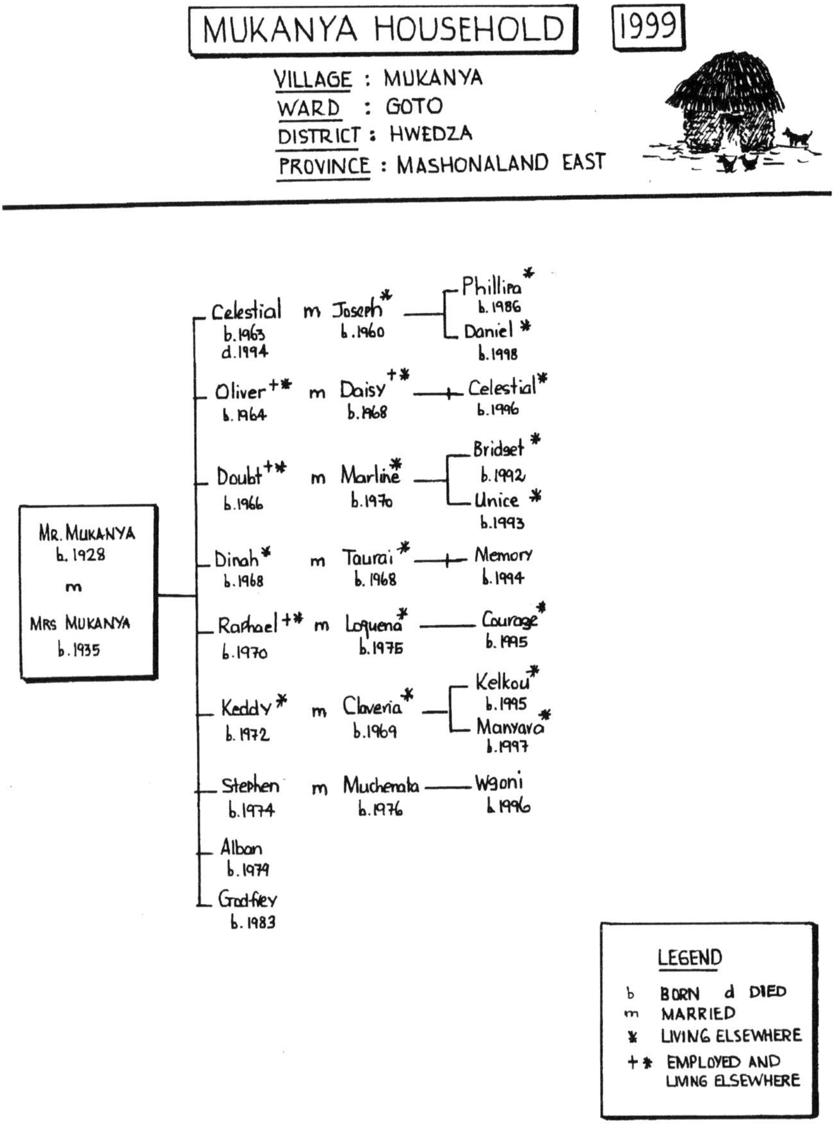
MUKANYA HOUSEHOLD
1999
VILLAGE : MUKANYA
WARD : GOTO
DISTRICT : HWEDZA
PROVINCE : MASHONALAND EAST
MR. MUKANYA b. 1928
m
MRS MUKANYA b. 1935
Celestial b. 1963 d. 1994 m Joseph* b. 1960
Phillipa* b. 1986
Daniel* b. 1998
Oliver+* b. 1964 m Daisy+* b. 1968
Celestial* b. 1996
Doubt+* b. 1966 m Marline* b. 1970
Bridget* b. 1992
Unice* b. 1993
Dinah* b. 1968 m Taurai* b. 1968
Memory b. 1994
Raphael+* b. 1970 m Loquena* b. 1975
Courage* b. 1995
Keddy* b. 1972 m Claveria* b. 1969
Kelkou* b. 1995
Manyara* b. 1997
Stephen b. 1974 m Muchenata b. 1976
Wgoni b. 1996
Alban b. 1979
Godfrey b. 1983
LEGEND
b BORN d DIED
m MARRIED
* LIVING ELSEWHERE
+* EMPLOYED AND LIVING ELSEWHERE

mission and state secondary schools amounted to Z$6,000 and $485.00 respectively plus uniform and exam costs. Fortunately, financial pressures of this kind eased on Mr and Mrs Mukanya. The two employed sons, Oliver and Doubt, accommodated and sponsored the secondary education of Raphael and Stephen respectively. Doubt even found Raphael employment at a Mutare packaging factory. After completing 'O' levels, the two daughters, Dinah and Keddy, married into other households. This left the last two sons, Alban and Godfrey, on the parents' hands. Unlike the others, these two had to attend the Government school and even then, lest he sell one or two beasts, Mr Mukanya was forced to ask his sons to help out.

The first-born Celestial died from an illness in 1994. The two surviving daughters did not pursue careers and ended up working in agriculture, which is the case with the majority of Zimbabwean women. The same forces of patriarchy and cultural conditioning that give women relatively less choice over their lives were at work on both the Shumba and Mukanya daughters. The coincidental but critical difference is that the latter seemed to strike better fortune with the men they married, which in the harsh economic calculus of the SAP relieved the household of extra burden and replenished it to a degree via *lobola* and occasional casual labour.

As with most, the livelihood of the Mukanya household during the SAP years deteriorated into pretty much a hand to mouth existence. Inflation and reduced employment opportunity eroded the household income base while cash cropping offered no viable recourse. If not for the two formally employed sons and stable marriages of the daughters, the household could well have fallen below the food poverty line. Although deprived of education, health care and a full diet, the question as to whether poverty in Hwedza would reach crisis proportions of malnutrition, disease and death, as is encompassing households in Sanyati, remains of some doubt. The capacity to survive without cash through subsistence livelihood is greater thanks to the governing bodies of the village of which the clan-based chiefship of Svosve has been instrumental. The household's retention of five head of cattle through a terrible drought attests to this, as does the expanding village wood lots. Oliver and Doubt recently received a stand of two hectares each in the village and the prospect of resettlement does not entice them.

Nor does it the women's group who maintain the Under Five-Feeding Project—'life is best in Hwedza', they said.

6.3 Future Implications

As to whether the SAP caused damage in communal areas is beyond dispute—the key issue concerns the extent. The withdrawal of subsidies on food items, productive inputs, education and health immediately heightened the exposure of household livelihood to factors of family-specific fortune and the condition of the local natural resource base. Individual families have limited influence over the amount of land allocated to the household, the marital status of daughters or employment remittances but put together as a community, greater influence can be asserted over village land management. From a historical perspective, as per the case studies, the effectiveness of village institutions in managing the demographic and environmental pressures courted under colonial land distribution emerges as a crucial defence against SAP-induced macroeconomic hostility. If the Sanyati commons, for example, had been better maintained and the Shumbas still possessed a few beasts to pull a plough, then despite all, their poverty descent would not have reached such depths. Livelihood fates under the SAP tend to be most severe in places where village institutions are weak and depletion of the community's land resource base is great.

True, the country is geographically diverse: differences in soil fertility and rainfall across Natural Regions tend to correlate with varying extents and depths of poverty. Even so, different landscapes and soils pose alternative options. Whatever the endowed land quality, the universal challenge is to ensure that land exploitation is sustainable and geared around the community's long-run interest. In Sanyati, the greater severity of poverty experienced in the 1990s seems to attribute less to geographical location than the constant influx of 'stranger' clans over the years and the associated commercial onslaught through cotton, which respectively de-legitimised and overwhelmed the authority of the chiefship to control land exploitation. The ambivalent reforms to local administration in the early 1980s fell short of formally empowering the non-traditional and potentially legitimate authority, namely, the elected VIDCO, which may have been better able to maintain the commons. Less subject to settler invasions and commercialism, on the other hand, the clan-based chiefship in Hwedza managed to retain authority over the environment and, in the 1980s, effectively harness the VIDCO to further improve the subsistence economy.

In Sanyati at least, within the context of land scarcity, household productive relations and ineffective local governance, agrarian commercialism appears to have done more harm over the longer term than good. Should not the emphasis be on sustainable subsistence production? Future prosperity would seem to depend far more on increased community boreholes, water catchments, vegetable gardens, orchards, wood lots, chicken runs and protected pastureland than clearing and cultivating more fields for cotton. Nothing less than a social agricultural revolution is warranted to realign land use around local needs, which probably entails a shift toward organic technologies proposed by the likes of Kropotkin [1899] and Schumacher [1993]. Both authors denounce the commercialised scientific approach to agriculture in peasant societies and advocate cost-effective agro-forestry techniques of soil creation to produce a 'luxurious vegetable and animal food' for the end purpose of local consumption [Kropotkin, P., 1974 {ed}:69]. Agriculture in Mukanya village has been more akin to this direction, which partly explains the community's stronger defence against the impact of the SAP.

By no coincidence, the same village displays strong leadership and community participation, which is a result of an undisturbed clan-based chiefship. Where the chefship has lost its centrifugal status, such as in Sanyati, an apparent imperative would be to empower village authorities to better maintain the commons and community welfare. The National Symposium on Agrarian Reform in 1987 rightly recommended devolving authority over all land use to VIDCOs wherein traditional authorities would be made ex-officio members [Roth, M., and Bruce, J., 1994:48; Ranger, T., 1993:381]. State supervision would only be required to uphold VIDCO decisions and the law generally. The 'qualified success' of the Communal Area Resource Management Program for Indigenous Resources [CAMPFIRE] demonstrated to the Land Tenure Commission that 'rural communities can own and utilise resources effectively and sustainably provided there are clear benefits to the community and that the community is empowered through local level institutions' [GoZ/LTC, 1994 vol.1:44].[14]

Even if local governance and land management is got right national land redistribution and macroeconomic performance remain outstanding realms of crucial importance to family livelihood. In any event, if communal areas are to regain a subsistence capacity, let alone a sustainable commercial orientation, there is an unequivocal need to attach more land. 'The people do not want resettlement', according to a Senator Chief Ndiweni [cited in Ranger, T., 1993:364], 'all they want is an extension of the communal lands'. The other dimension is to realign macroeconomic management around the provision of affordable health and education services, which can make all the difference to livelihoods, especially those of single mothers. I now put the poverty impact of the SAP in national perspective, partly through the life of Chiti Mpofu, which links us to the tribulations of a Blind Peoples' cooperative in Chitungwiza—Zimbabwe's third largest city.

7

The National Poverty Struggle, the SAP and the Tribulations of Chiti and the Chitungwiza Blind

The understandable inclination of free market advocates is to argue 'adjustment has not worsened poverty' [Kiguel, M., and Jones, C., 1995:12]. In response to deteriorating formal wage incomes, health indicators and wealth inequality in Zimbabwe under the SAP, one World Bank report 'inferred' poverty increased but could not 'attribute causality' [WB, 1996:67-68]. As is often the case, a methodological haze tends to be invoked about the difficulty of distinguishing between the effects of the macroeconomic policies from the entrenched structural causes [Zuckerman, E., 1991:249]. 'Declining health outcomes', the same report notes, 'are not the result of the program but of a complex interaction of economic, social, epidemiological, and environmental factors' [WB, 1996:49]. Otherwise, defensive arguments either resort to the 'no alternative' line or the hypothetical scenario—'the crisis would be worse without adjustment'—or blame forces outside the logic of reforms [Bond, P., 1998:382], such as the drought, fiscal overruns, past economic policies and AIDS [see WB, 1996:IV; Kapoor, K., 1994:4].

Make no mistake, poverty in Zimbabwe is firmly rooted in a class structure that conceivably enables only 4% of the population to control up to 90% of national wealth [Mwanza, A., 1992:204]. Out of a total active workforce[1] of 4,921,031 people in 1997, for instance, only 1,820,000 [37%] derived an income from regularly paid formal employment while the rest, that is, some 3,101,031 [63%] workers, relied on family agriculture or informal enterprise [CSO, 1997a:96].

Whether in rural or urban areas, the bulk of the country's workforce and associated dependants were literally engaged in hand-to-mouth survival activities. Over half the national population resided in barren communal areas beset generally by a 'threefold' crisis of demography, environment and local governance [Wolf, E.R., 1969:285]. Therein, most families could not meet subsistence requirements; the extent of household poverty hinged crucially on the number of dependants relative to land quality, land size and urban remittances; and gender relations tended to conspire against female livelihood.

In Matabeleland South, directly south of Filabusi, the people of Insiza communal lands struggle daily against poverty. From flat and drought prone land—very characteristic of Natural Region V—no livelihood whatsoever could be secured from rain-fed agriculture. Since colonisation, the survival imperative has been to escape into some alternative vocation, which applied generally to the sons and daughters of a village I call Shava, as it did to those of Mpofu household in particular. In the 1980s, the three sons, namely, Chiti, Kezious and Elton, along with thousands of others, went to Chitungwiza in search of a living—a satellite township of Harare, about 30 kilometres southeast. Unable to afford the higher education necessary to find permanent wage employment, the three turned to informal business ventures.

A major focus of this chapter is on Chiti and his wife Sibongile, both blind, and their attachment to a Blind Peoples' Cooperative called Shungu Dzedu [i.e. 'our keenness']. Within the overall structural predicament of African poverty, compared to the able-bodied, the physically disabled are extra vulnerable to the social evils inherent, such as begging, disease and homelessness. The formation of Shungu Dzedu in the mid-1980s, however, offered much hope to the blind of Chitungwiza, particularly as the Government, and local and foreign NGOs showed a willingness to support its business activities. In fact, the Cooperative acquired the title deeds of a fine building in Makoni Shopping Centre as well as a lease off the Chitungwiza Town Council to an agricultural plot located within the industrial estate known as Tilco. At the outset of the 1990s and the SAP, on behalf of 21 other blind members, Shungu embarked upon several small enterprises, which encompassed chicken raising and the production of chalk, pillows, mattresses and candles.

What promise then did the SAP hold for local urban markets and the tens of thousands of informal and small-scale entrepreneurs engaged therein? 'The overall social impact of the SAP for this group', the lead adjustment document theoretically predicted, 'will be positive' [GoZ, 1991a, annex III:16]. Ultimately, as the state rationalised itself, and liberalised market forces made the formal sector more export oriented, indigenous enterprise—informal and small-scale—was expected to feed off the external dynamic through increased subcontracts, credit access and an easing of inherited by-laws, such as licensing, zoning and building specifications [GoZ, 1991a:19-20]. There was a strong resort to supposition in that labour-intensive export dynamism would simply overrun the stagflationary effects of exchange rate depreciation, price decontrol, higher user fees, state retrenchment and increased import competition. 'Greater competition' would apparently bring down inflation [GoZ, 1991a, annex III:2] while 'modest' retrenchments—'maybe 20,000 formal sector workers, 10,000 civil servants and perhaps 2,000 parastatal employees' [GoZ, 1991a, annex III:10]—would prove 'frictional'.

In the event, the domestic damage of state fiscal contraction, currency depreciation, import liberalisation and tight monetary policy went beyond what an export charge centred mainly on raw or semi-processed commodities and subject to accustomed world trade constraints could ever offset. A stagflation crisis gripped the economy, which forced people of all classes to flood informal markets peddling wares and services. Between 1991 and 1993, for instance, new entrants into the informal sector grew at a rate of 14% per year [WB, 1996:57]. With the atrophy of family agriculture and urban livelihood at the root, any attempt to draw positives out of informal sector growth really seeks to transform a 'curse into a virtue' [Mhone, G., 1995:70]. Most micro enterprises—over 70% of which are headed by women [WB, 1996:45]—could barely survive in an economy that squeezed turnover between cost inflation of productive inputs [i.e. transport, power, rent etc] and deflation of the selling price [due to gluts, intense competition and weak demand].

Many of the 1.6 million people [excluding dependants] found by the USAID-commissioned Gemini Survey [1991] to be *solely* reliant upon informal enterprise in the late 1980s had fallen below the poverty threshold by the late 1990s [Gemini cited in Ndoro, H., 1996:32; *The Herald*, 12/04/99].[2] Despite Chiti's efforts, the small-scale ventures of Shungu Dzedu progressively collapsed and after the year 2000, overcome by debt, the entire asset base of the Cooperative had to be liquidated. Unable to receive adequate support from an under-resourced and overwhelmed welfare system, many of the blind members returned to begging and probably this day can be witnessed along First Street, central Harare, outside the Standard Chartered Bank.

The point is, as Keynes would argue, whatever the structural predicament, macroeconomic policy retains a vital bearing on poverty levels through influencing the cost of living, the provision of welfare, employment opportunity and wealth concentration. True, the outbreak of stagflation related comprehensively to structural deficiencies on the demand and supply side but dismantlement of the state-directed macroeconomic regime let the spiral loose. Contrary the protestations of free market theorists, the SAP had a terrible impact on poverty levels. The next chapter discusses the disintegrating effects on the national political economy; here my main focus is on local urban socioeconomic fabric. I elaborate on the structural aspects of poverty so as to highlight the national poverty struggle and the importance of macroeconomic policy. The life of Chiti Mpofu and the rise of Shungu Dzedu are then recounted before turning to the outbreak of socioeconomic stress in the 1990s and the plight of local enterprise and livelihood therein.

7.1 The Structural Determinants of Household Poverty

In the mid-1990s, two national poverty surveys were conducted—the Poverty Assessment Study Survey [PASS] by the Ministry of Public Service, Labour and Social Welfare [MPSLSW] and the Income and Consumption Expenditure Survey [ICES] by the Central Statistical Office [CSO].[3] The PASS specified the per capita income and the ICES the per capita consumption expenditure necessary for a household or a person to keep above the Total Poverty Line [TPL] [basic nutrition plus non-food needs such as clothing, education, health] or just the Food Poverty Line [FPL] [basic nutrition]. The number of households or people below the poverty lines divided by the total population of people or households gave the prevalence of poverty, that is, the percentage of households or people below the poverty lines as a proportion of the total population.

Table 7.0 *Prevalence of Household Poverty in the mid-1990s*

SECTOR	MPSLASW/PASS		CSO/ICES	
	TPL	FPL	TPL	FPL
	Z$817	Z$494	Z$1,200	Z$570
	Prevalence of Poverty % of			
	Poor	Very Poor	Poor	Very Poor
Rural	75	60	76.2	50.4
Urban	39	21	41.1	10.2
All Zimbabwe	61	45	63.3	35.7

Source: GoZ/MPSLASW, 1998b; CSO, 1998a.

Table 7.0 indicates the approximate national average amount of Zimbabwe dollars per month determined by each survey at the time for a family of four to five people to keep abreast of the FPL or TPL. As can be seen, both surveys found that around 40% of urban households and over 70% of rural households could not afford a basic standard of living and of the latter, over half could not afford a basic food basket. Because poor households tend to have more members than non-poor households, the prevalence of poor people becomes higher: about 75.6% of all Zimbabweans are poor, concluded the CSO [1998a:30], and 47.2% are extremely poor.

Table 7.1 *Prevalence of Rural Poverty by Land Use Areas*

Land Use Area	Prevalence		Depth
	Poor	Very Poor	Poverty Gap Index
Resettlement Areas	88.1	56.6	50.7
Communal Areas	81.7	57.4	52.7
Small-scale Commercial	66.4	32.8	40.7
Large-scale Commercial	56.0	26.8	41.4

Source: CSO, 1998a: 52.

Up to 77% of poor people/households and 89% of the extremely poor lived in rural areas [CSO, 1998a:29], which reflected the fact that about 68% of the total population were engaged in the four agricultural subsectors, namely, the small-scale commercial, large-scale commercial, resettlement and communal areas [Appendix 2]. The CSO report, as per Table 7.1, uncovered a high prevalence of poverty throughout each sector. Yet, as measured by the poverty gap index, which records the mean shortfall of consumption expenditures below the Total Poverty Line, the depth of poverty varied. Although resettlement households registered the highest prevalence, more communal households fell below the poverty line to a greater extent, especially when compared to commercial farm worker households.

Table 7.2 *Distribution of Communal Land Population ['00s] by Natural Regions*

Natural Region	I	II	III	V	V	Total
Province						
Manicaland	807	1812	1551	2138	1398	7706
Mash. Central		1796	390	1148		3334
Mash. East		2739	519	1619		4877
Mash West		995	1461	271	87	2814
Mat. North			116	2671	621	3408
Mat. South				2033	1998	4031
Midlands		31	3224	3449	907	7611
Masvingo			1221	4285	2640	8146
Total Pop	807	7373	8482	1 7614	7651	4 1927
Pop density#	80.5	51.3	31.6	22.6	17.7	25.6 [av]
Area as a % of total	0.6	8.8	16.5	47.7	26.4	100
Pop as a % of total	1.92	17.59	20.23	42.01	18.25	100

Source: Thomas [1992] cited in Moyo, S., [1995]: 130.

In a mostly rain-dependent and congested agrarian economy, geographic location and demographic pressure have an immediate bearing on poverty levels. Such a predicament, however, continues to emanate from an inequitable class order. Settler colonists and multinational companies enclosed the prime cropping areas and vast tracts of ranching land, which deprived the African peasantry and

Number of people per square kilometre.

entrepreneurs of an adequate resource base. Inevitably, upon generally fragile and remotely located soils, the resort to a family mode of production courted, to varying extents, a demographic, environmental and livelihood crisis, which most authorities and tenurial regimes, whether state, traditional or individual, proved powerless to stop. Concurrently, privileged and extensive use of large-scale commercial land, as has been argued, denied the economy maximum agrarian drive, more so that the capital-labour regime applied showed rare dispensation to share wealth equitably.

Over half the country's population live in communal areas [Appendix 2]. Table 7.2 based on the 1982 census reveals that about 74% of communal land is located within the poorest Natural Regions of IV and V and supports slightly over 60% of the total communal population. In the better Natural Regions, although the total population progressively declines, population density sharply increases because colonial authorities allocated significantly less communal land.

Table 7.3 *Household Poverty Prevalence by Province*

PROVINCE	**% Households**		**Prevalence % of**	
	Urban	In NRs I & II	Poor	Very Poor
Harare			36.4	6.8
Bulawayo			16.9	9.3
Midlands	29	0.6	63.9	40.2
Mashonaland West	24	71	66.7	40.4
Mashonaland East	6	56	67.5	34.4
Manicaland	13	42	69.4	43.4
Matabeleland South	10	0	75.8	51.6
Mashonaland Central	11	74	80.4	46.1
Masvingo	13	0	75.8	52.4
Matabeleland North	22	0	81.1	67.2

Source: CSO, 1998a: 33-34.

The assumption that the extent of rural poverty corresponds with land quality and proximity to urban markets seems to generally hold but should not be seen as automatic. As shown in Table 7.3, the CSO report found that the severest poverty was in the three driest and least urbanised provinces, namely, Masvingo and Matabeleland South and North.[4] With access to either better land, developed urban centres or both, comparably less poverty was found in Mashonaland West and East, Manicaland and Midlands. Mashonaland Central, however, presented an 'enigma' in that the province recorded the second highest poverty prevalence, even though 74% of households were located within prime regions with fairly close proximity to Harare.

The 'enigma' is further substantiated when using the Human Poverty Index [HPI], which is a broad poverty measure based on *longevity* [the percentage of people who die before 40 years], *knowledge* [the percentage of adult illiteracy] and *decent standard of living* [access to health services, safe water and child malnutrition under age five]. As can be seen from Table 7.4, on the basis of this composite measure, the UNDP-sponsored *Human Development Report* [1998] ranked the four most fertile provinces, namely, the three Mashonalands and Manicaland within the first five.

Table 7.4 *Ranking of Provinces by the Human Poverty Index*

PROVINCE	Non-survival 40 years %	Illiteracy %	Under Weight Children %	No access# %		HPI Rank
				Safe Water	Health Care	
Mash. Central	20.65	33.00	16.9	28.38	9.6	1
Manicaland	21.95	24.78	11.7	29.98	9.3	2
Masvingo	19.37	24.15	23.2	31.77	3.1	3
Mash. West	18.10	24.58	17.6	22.64	11.2	4
Mash. East	16.85	20.12	16.3	41.42	7.0	5
Mat. North	11.96	26.28	9.1	23.88	8.8	6
Midlands	16.85	18.48	11.0	31.42	9.9	7
Mat. South	10.78	22.00	6.8	28.76	6.3	8
Harare	13.6	5.96	10.7	1.54	7.3	9
Bulawayo	9.70	6.36	4.0	0.07	14.0	10

Source: UNDP/PRF/IDS, 1998: 68, 86

Geographical location and proximity to urban centres do not fully account for the main determinants of poverty. Of equal importance to land quality is the number of dependants per household relative to the size of the land holding. Non-poor

No access to health care is defined as being unable to visit a medical clinic either because of distance or non-affordability. No access to safe water means an absence of piped water inside or outside the house or from a nearby communal tap, protected well or borehole.

households, for instance, have 50% more land per person than poor households [CSO, 1998a:56]. Any sudden addition of mouths to feed can cause a fall below the poverty line unless family lineage status allows the household increased but relatively disproportionate land access. Generally though the overall dearth of land, high household/land dependency ratios and skewed land access explains why the Mashona and Manica peasantry produce a grain surplus in the aggregate when the majority of households are grain deficit [Rukuni, M., and Jayne, T.S., 1995 cited in UNDP/PRF/IDS, 1998:76]. The regular sale of crops comes from a *kulak* stratum probably comprising about 10% of the communal population while the rest appears to be split almost equally between grain self-sufficiency and outright deficit [GoZ, 1991a:6,98; Cousins, B., Weiner, D., and Amin, N., 1992:7; World Bank, 1996; 12; Chipika, S., and Chisvo, M., 1997:42].

Irrespective of the Natural Region, family agriculture for most is not commercially viable and should not be seen as such. Indeed, as Table 7.5 points out, households with a sole income dependency on agriculture experienced the highest and deepest poverty. Those with a main reliance on 'own business' and 'gifts and transfers', otherwise referred to as informal enterprise and income remittances respectively, fared better but still mostly failed to provide a minimum family livelihood. The main escape route appeared to be formal wage employment of the family head: households so placed experienced significantly less poverty.

Table 7.5 *Household Poverty by Main Source of Income*

Main sources of income	**Prevalence [%] of**	
	Poor	Very Poor
Salary and Wages	52.4	24.9
Own Business	75.9	42.5
Gifts and Transfers	78.4	48.4
Family Farming	86.8	62.9

Source: CSO, 1998a:45.

The foregoing sheds some light why poverty is so high in Zimbabwe. In 1997, only 37% of the active labour force, as mentioned, had regularly paid formal employment and out of all positions, men occupied 71.6% [CSO, 1997a:101]. On this basis, women disproportionately bear the brunt of poverty; none more so than single, separated or divorced mothers [see Kanji, N., and Jazdowska, 1993: 22-35; Brand, V., Mupedziswa, R., and Gumbo, P., 1995:210]. The broader reality is that largely for a lack of formally paid employment, two-thirds of the Zimbabwean population struggle daily to meet the basic needs of life whether through family agriculture, informal business or a mix of both.

The national predicament of poverty is synonymous to a mass-peasantry in profound crisis, which of itself is fundamentally an outcome of exclusive production and wealth structures established under colonialism. First and foremost, any victory over poverty necessitates comprehensive agrarian structural reform based on land redistribution, which should proceed, as has been proposed, along dualist lines to serve both subsistent and commercial/capitalist needs. Until then, the *only* weapons available to alleviate poverty amongst the peasantry have always fallen under the purview of macroeconomic policy; the chief planks being, low inflation, employment opportunity, health care and education.

7.2 The Background of Chiti and the Rise of Shungu Dzedu

In so far as Chiti struggles to overcome impoverished rural roots, his lifetime quest is akin to most Zimbabweans but, unlike most, he became blind as a child, which has made the task all the more difficult. Contrary to the norm, during his formative years, charity and specialised welfare services played a crucial role in his wellbeing and future prospects. By the late 1980s, as an educated adult, Chiti appeared to gain a winning edge in the poverty struggle, particularly with the advent of formal employment. In addition, the formation of Shungu Dzedu Blind Peoples' Cooperative, although short of a certain future, offered him as well as other blind people great hope for a better future. Two main forces of underlying benevolence toward Chiti's upward rather than downward path emanated from the Church and a relatively stable macroeconomic environment.

Several years before his birth in 1962, Chiti's grandparents offered his young mother as a fourth wife to a Mr Ngwenya in return for food. At the time, amid an accustomed drought stricken Matabeleland, the transaction was an act of survival to avoid 'definite hunger'. People in the Filabusi area tried desperately to avert reliance on rain-fed farming in favour of an autonomous livelihood but relatively few could find formal employment in the big cities and the wages drawn from the local scheelite, chrome and asbestos mines around Mberengwa and Zvishavane were too meagre. Mr Ngwenya was at least employed by Rhodesian rail as a stationmaster and he owned cattle; however, Chiti's mother faced a harsh life—a dusty field of one hectare and a mud hut awaited her with little support to be expected from a polygamous husband. Nevertheless, she would bear him seven children, as the attached family tree records.

The baby Chiti was born with sight and his earliest visual memories are of herding cattle in 'thick forests'. When he was four an attack of measles made him partially blind and he recalls 'losing friends' as a result. Like many children, his labour was required on the land and school was forsaken. The light continued to fade, however, and by 1975 he was confirmed blind. His mother heard that the boy could learn braille at the Lutheran mission school near West Nicholson called Masase Primary. She went there to plead his case and her prayers were answered as a Lutheran nun named Sister Birgetta took mercy upon Chiti. She became his guardian for the next nine years until he completed O levels in 1985.

In 1977, as the war raged, ZIPRA guerrillas burned Masase Primary School whereupon Sister Birgetta and Chiti transferred to Mnene Mission, which was also in Mberengwa district and run by Lutherans. The same year, Chiti's father, Mr Ngwenya, died 'from an illness'. As the fourth wife, the inheritance rights of Chiti's mother were virtually non-existent and in effect, she was left to the mercy of the eldest son of the first wife. She and the children faced utter destitution had it not been for Mr Mpofu's hand in marriage. He was a good-natured bachelor and out of genuine love, it seems, wanted the entire family to stay with him in Shava village, Insiza communal lands. Being the brother of the village kraalhead, Mr Mpofu had five hectares including goats and cattle and, as an itinerant worker, often derived a casual wage from nearby mines and building sites.

Chiti recalls enjoying his primary schooling as he was integrated into the classes of able-bodied students and 'treated like any other child'. He proved a gifted student in English and regularly

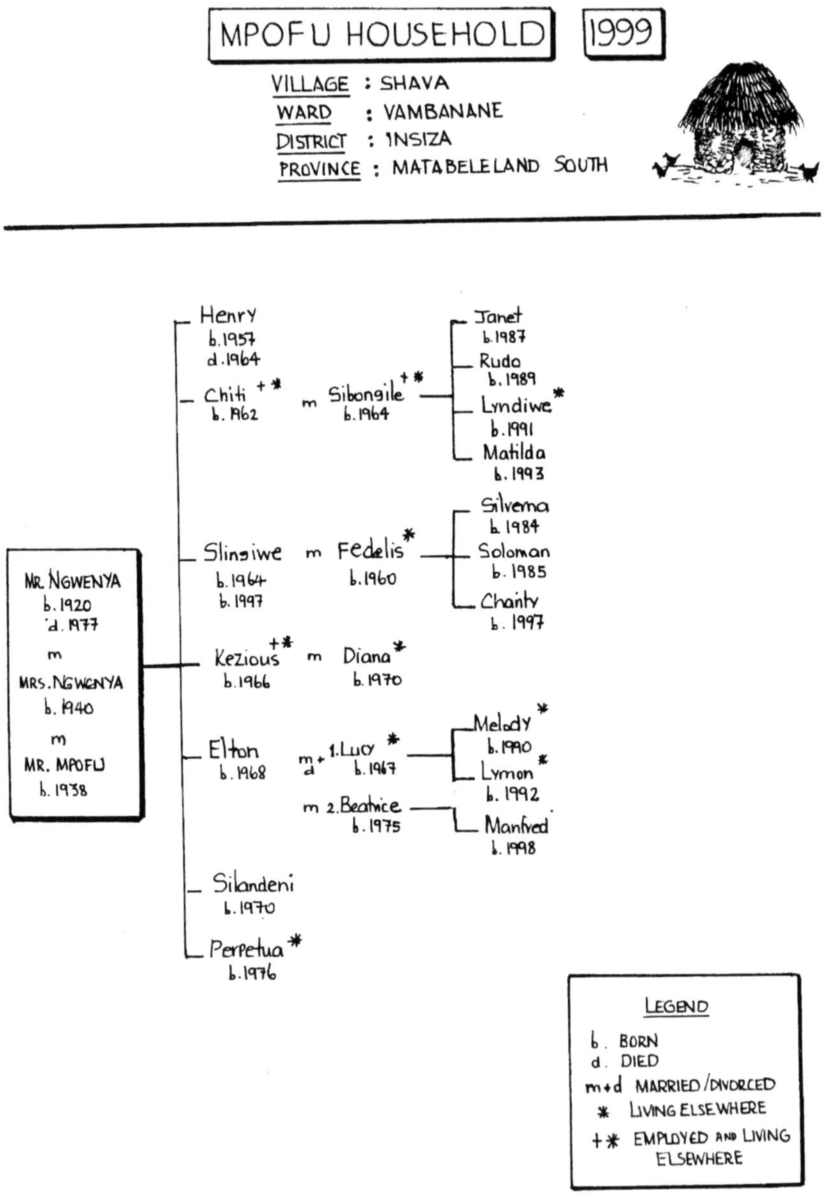
MPOFU HOUSEHOLD
1999
VILLAGE : SHAVA
WARD : VAMBANANE
DISTRICT : INSIZA
PROVINCE : MATABELELAND SOUTH
MR. NGWENYA b. 1920 d. 1977 m MRS. NGWENYA b. 1940 m MR. MPOFU b. 1938
Henry b. 1957 d. 1964
Chiti +* b. 1962 m Sibongile +* b. 1964
Janet b. 1987
Rudo b. 1989
Lyndiwe* b. 1991
Matilda b. 1993
Slinsiwe b. 1964 b. 1997 m Fedelis* b. 1960
Silvema b. 1984
Soloman b. 1985
Charity b. 1997
Kezious +* b. 1966 m Diana* b. 1970
Elton b. 1968 m+d 1. Lucy* b. 1967
Melody* b. 1990
Lymon* b. 1992
m 2. Beatrice b. 1975
Manfred b. 1998
Silandeni b. 1970
Perpetua* b. 1976
LEGEND
b. BORN
d. DIED
m+d MARRIED/DIVORCED
* LIVING ELSEWHERE
+* EMPLOYED AND LIVING ELSEWHERE

obtained first grade. During vacations, he stayed on the mission with Sister Birgetta and his blind friend, Best Nyoni. By then, Shava village had become a 'hotspot' as the Rhodesians occupied a fort at the nearby growth point, Avoca. Chiti now looks back on the sanctuary of the mission as a kind of paradise: his need of food, clothing and shelter met, education was the only immediate stress, which for him was a blessing. During Rhodesia, he recalls, the missions were well resourced from strong international links and he presently laments their gradual withdrawal from the forefront of African welfare since the late 1970s.

In 1982, with the financial help of Sister Birgetta, Chiti commenced his secondary schooling at Copota Mission near Masvingo, which was run by the Dutch Reformed Church. The school was for the disabled only but he resented being separated from able-bodied students, which he claims 'does a lot of damage to the confidence of blind people'. His friend Best Nyoni was sent to the Jairos Jiri disabled centre. Any loneliness soon ended, however, as his future wife, Sibongile, also blind, was enrolled at Copota. Despite chronic shortages of braille literature and stationary, Chiti passed all five O level subjects. Yet, fatally, his results were too low to qualify for a Teachers College and without the financial support to go on to A level, his education suddenly ceased.

Even if the rains succeeded at Shava village, without use of fertiliser, the yield was below subsistence needs. The wages Mr Mpofu earned from the mines were barely enough to support him, let alone a family of stepchildren and their fertiliser needs. As the pre-colonial Ndebele knew, the soil was best suited for grazing and could support vast herds. Yet such required finances and an extensive land holding, both of which were unavailable. The grazing scheme the VIDCO tried to implement in the late 1980s collapsed because people persistently 'cut the barb wire' to allow their stock to feed. Most of the cattle sold to the CSC at West Nicholson were from the surrounding commercial farms wherein land appeared to be too plentiful.

For Chiti, the situation was what he could do for the household rather than what it could do for him. There was really no choice but to follow his brothers, Kezious and Elton, who had gone to Chitungwiza in search of a crust. Since the late 1970s, conveniently located to the main employment centre of Harare, Chitungwiza had experienced phenomenal growth.[5] In 1986 Chiti was temporarily diverted from reaching this destination because the Lutheran Church secured him a place at Vashandiri Study Centre in Gweru. The following year, after being transferred to the Catholic affiliated Dorothy Duncan Centre outside Harare, Chiti linked up with his brothers to share a one-room accommodation. Both the foregoing centres were geared to imparting job skills to the blind such as chalk making, switch board operating, accounting, knitting and so on.

A white man belonging to the Rotary network met Chiti at the Dorothy Duncan Centre and offered him a job in 1987 as a switch board operator in his Harare based manufacturing company. Chiti and Sibogile married in the same year and the first of their four daughters was born. But the good fortune of formal employment did not last. Toward the end of 1988, the white man sold the factory and the new managers retrenched Chiti, whereupon he joined the ranks of the unemployed along with Sibongile, Elton and Kezious.

Both Chiti and Sibongile qualified to receive a welfare payment of Z$90.00 each per month. Considering the needs of the infant and the two brothers, the family's welfare income would have been well below the official Total Poverty Line recorded at Z$356.00 per month for a family of four in 1991 [Rakodi, C., 1995:450, footnote 17]. Yet five single Zimbabwe dollars represented about US$2.50 in the late 1980s [Appendix 7], which under the state price regime was enough to purchase a very healthy meal to feed four or five. Although basic food may have been affordable, other needs and wants such as adequate clothing, footwear, furniture, bedding, entertainment, transport and dark glasses were generally beyond them.

The family managed to find very cheap rent at Z$15.00 per month for one room but the drawback was that the living conditions were unsanitary and barely tolerable. Chitungwiza was at the forefront of the national housing crisis: four families usually shared a four-roomed house and, if upmarket, a single home toilet instead of a public one. Over the 1980s, as has been mentioned, in line with World Bank and USAID recommendations, the Government shed involvement in public housing to create space for private finance to lead the charge [Bond, P, 1998:265-298]. But the housing crisis only got worse: over the late 1980s, on a national scale, less than 19,000 housing units on average were built annually while the population of Harare alone increased by 30% [Auret, D., 1995:24-25]. Concurrently, ongoing scarcity saw the doubling of house prices and rents rise proportionately.

Only employment could secure the livelihood of Chiti's family and avert the need to beg, as was the case for many Chitungwiza blind. The very promise of employment was what attracted Chiti and Sibongile to Shungu Dzedu. The aim of the Cooperative, to quote from the constitution, was 'to provide employment and a source of income to blind people who would otherwise depend on inadequate subsistence allowances from the Department of Social Welfare and degrading street begging'. Silveira House, the Jesuit Catholic training centre based at Tafara on the western outskirts of the city, played a leading role in forming Shungu Dzedu and promoting its quest to emancipate blind people. By late 1986, 23 people, 21 of whom were blind, had joined, which included Chiti and Sibongile. In 1989, Sibongile was elected to the executive committee, which was a paid position, albeit below a subsistence wage. From a residential home, Shungu started with a chicken-raising project, which went well but was closed by the Chitungwiza Town Council because the number of chickens went beyond the allowance for an urban household.

Meanwhile, Silveira House secured a lease from the Town Council to a plot of land in the surrounding and lonely industrial area called Tilco. The plan was for Shungu to develop a market garden to serve Chitungwiza and adjacent Seke Communal Land. The cost of installing a bore, pump, pipes and durawall, however, went beyond the available budget. It was decided to sublease the agricultural plot to the Zimbabwe Association for Crime Prevention and Rehabilitation of the Offender [ZACRO]. In 1992, ZACRO received a grant of Z$400,000 from the Australian High Commission to install the above with the exception that a cyclone fence instead of a concrete durawall was erected, which later proved a fatal flaw.

Shungu and Silveira agreed that mattress, pillow, chalk and candle making would be suitable alternative projects for the Cooperative. Silveira purchased a stand at Makoni Shopping Centre, one of Chitungwiza's main transport and commercial hubs.

European donors, namely, Bilance and Miserior, provided funds to construct a building. The German and later South African Embassy supplied three sewing machines, a blowing machine, moulds and a drying stand for pillows, mattress and chalk production. Another Australian based NGO called Chiedza Light Foundation, to whom the author belonged, shipped a renovated candle-making machine to Shungu.

In 1989, Chiti found employment again as a film roller at a photo-processing outlet in Harare. His wage was Z$500 per month, which for the time being covered the basic needs of his family including the birth of three more daughters by 1993. At the close of the 1980s, the emergence of Shungu Dzedu and the advent of employment seemed to bode well for the future. Shungu had been doubly fortunate: they retained the lease to the agricultural plot and by 1992, acquired the title deeds of a superb building in Makoni, which contained three spacious work areas, two offices and three toilets. It would prove tragic, however, that at the very time the building was complete and the chalk, pillow, mattress and candle projects were ready to go, the SAP descended and all—including the hope of the blind members—would be enveloped in a whirlwind of economic and social chaos.

7.3 The Outbreak of Socioeconomic Stress in the 1990s: Selected Evidence from Chitungwiza

Without comprehensive land reform as a centrepiece, the SAP aimed to counteract the structural features of poverty through eliminating the bias against job creation and stimulating export-led growth [WB, 1996:47-48]. In the structural context, however, the measures deemed necessary—state cost recovery on public utilities/services, currency devaluation, positive interest rates, deregulated import flows, liberalised price and wage setting—caused a deep domestic contraction, wherein the prospect of an export-led recovery diminished. By 1995, from the formal economy alone, over 50,000 people lost their jobs—26,000 from the public and 25,510 from the private sector [ZCTU, 1996:15; GoZ, 1998a:4; UNDP/PRF/IDS, 1998:11]. The depression encompassed inward-oriented enterprise—mostly within the parastatal, manufacturing, informal and smallholder sectors—which unfortunately engaged the overwhelming majority. The worst strategic casualty of all was the central budget, which carried dire ramifications on the provision of health and education and, therefore, the country's social fabric.

7.3.1 Falling Living Standards

No general cap applied on price rises while the greater resort to enterprise bargaining [Appendix 9]—amid excess labour conditions—virtually guaranteed that wage rates would not keep pace. Thus, over 1990–1994, as prices of all goods rose by an average of 173%, the value of real wages declined by between 10% to 15% per year [*The Daily Gazette*, 2/06/94]. The Consumer Council of Zimbabwe [CCZ] then claimed an average urban family of five required about Z$1500 per month to meet basic necessities yet about 80% of the formally employed earned below Z$900 [cited in *The Sunday Times*, 10/02/94]. Between 1989 and 1996, the share of gross operating profits in GDP rose from 40.5% to 54.8% while that of wages and salaries declined from 57.3% to 45.0%, which in effect meant workers were 44% worse off than 1990 [CSO data cited in UNDP/PRF/IDS, 1998:22; ZCTU, 1996:68]. Thereon, after 'Black Friday', between January and April 1998 alone, as the minimum wage stood at Z$1,500 per month, the cost of a food basket for an average family increased by 57% from Z$3,469 to $6,067 [see Table 6.0; CCZ cited in *The Financial Gazette*, 27/05/99].

A Scandinavian study undertaken over 1993–1995, which selected Chitungwiza as an urban locale, reported that one-third of households surveyed experienced a decline in income while virtually all recorded dramatically reduced expenditure on furniture, electrical appliances and clothing [Bijlmakers, L.A., Basset, M.T., and Sanders, D.M., 1998:101]. Indeed, the average household budget became fully absorbed meeting the basics of life such as food, rent, transport, school and medical fees. The PASS found that 54% of the Chitungwiza population were not meeting basic needs—30% 'very poor' plus 24% 'poor'—which was well above the national average for urban areas [PASS cited in Bijlmakers, L.A., Basset, M.T., and Sanders, D.M., 1998:99-100]. The retrenchment of 6,000 workers by June 1995 from the locally based company, Cone Textiles, due to liquidity problems, certainly added to these statistics [Sachikonye, L.M., 1995a:59].

The housing industry slumped and rents soared. By mid-1993, following a 100% rise in interest rates, 'negative equity' beset high-density areas whereby a borrower owed more for the house than what it could be sold for [Bond, P., 1998:295]. Mortgagees were squeezed between high interest rates and falling house prices and rent continually rose reaching Z$300.00 per month for a single room by early 1999. Building societies experienced difficulty issuing new mortgage bonds due to problems of affordability, partly reinforced by the Government's withdrawal of a 3% loan subsidy. In Chitungwiza, provision of low-cost housing crawled: over 1993–1994, for example, against an official waiting list of 32,388, the Town Council managed to construct 376 houses [Auret, D., 1995:40].[6] Housing finance from USAID and World Bank mostly bypassed the satellite city, probably deterred by the Town Council deficit and the high arrears among tenants and landlords [Bond, P, 1998: 290, 293, footnote 10]. Amid reports of 30 people to a stand, overcrowding and unsanitary conditions got horribly worse.

Meanwhile, retrenchment, high inflation and falling real wages forced almost everyone to compete in urban informal markets including the spouses of the professionally employed [Gibbon, P., 1995:32]. For most small-scale businesses, the macroeconomic environment proved virtually impossible. On the demand side, the flood of suppliers and shrinking disposable incomes forced price deflation while on the supply side, rising production costs occurred 'at a pace which could not correspond to end product prices' [Chipika, S., 1995: 1; see also Silveira House 1998:3-21]. In a select range of activities, however, such as—amongst others—money lending, some entrepreneurs managed to do well. A director of one prosperous firm commented:

> Money lending is unique because it flourishes when everybody else is suffering. I don't see the sector crumbling. In fact, as people become poorer and poorer, the more they need to borrow. But we make sure we lend to those who can repay [cited in *The Zimbabwe Mirror*, 6-12/04/01].

7.3.2 Social Decay and Social Reaction

People reacted to the crisis of living in various ways: some turned to crime, others to vice and many to religion, all of which gained ascendancy during the 1990s. On the first dimension, the *Quarterly*

Digest of Statistics by the CSO includes a section 'reported crimes by type'—a glance at house break-ins and thefts seems to indicate a marked increase [Table 7.6]. In Chitungwiza, the growth of a kleptocratic economy was reflected in the increased prevalence of conmen, thugs, thieves and countering industries such as debt collection, security, locksmiths and real estate[7] agencies. A related occurrence—indicative of great social distress—was the three days of rioting and looting in mid-January 1998 sparked, to recall, by a round of price hikes. 'Vandalism rules supreme in Chitungwiza' reported *The Herald* [20/01/98] and, indeed, the President called in the army to quell the situation and recover property. Riots, to quote Martin Luther King, are the 'voice of the unheard'.

Another headline 'Vice is Rife at Makoni' in *The Sunday Mail* on 23 May 1999 captured an additional dimension of social decay—increased high-risk sexual activity as reflected in the booming growth of beer outlets at the shopping centre where Shungu operated and the accompanying element of prostitution. Put plainly, single unemployed women, often mothers, engaged simply to gain money, while employed men, in a position of power, succumbed to temptation.

Table 7.6 *House Break-ins and Theft in the 1990s*

Year	House Break-ins & Theft
1988	34 009
1989	34 255
1990	36 750
1991	39 657
1992	47 893
1993	50 465
1994	57 943
1995	49 755
1996	53 496
1997	47 189
1998	49 925
1999	57 263
2000	61 314

Source: CSO, 1997b:8: 2000b:7.

Conversely, the other side of the poverty coin was reflected in the great waves of Christian revivalism that swept over many in the

Zimbabwe of the 1990s. From visual observance, the 'white-robed apostles' of Chitungwiza belonging to African Apostolic Churches increased in such numbers that they came to dominate the landscape on weekends. These Churches are a support to the poor, to quote John Iliffe [1987: 264], 'their puritanism encourages wise use of limited funds, they offer cheap healing, they relieve the boredom of poverty, and they provide collective aid'. ' "If they do not overcome poverty" ', he quoted an observer, ' "at least poverty does not overcome them" '.

7.3.3 The Fiscal Crisis and the Ramifications on Health and Education

While the spiral of cost inflation, falling domestic demand and higher—supposedly counteractive—interest rates pushed households and many companies to or over the brink, the entire state fiscus including most SOEs followed suit. Over 1991–1996, state operational expenditures, that is, the revenue left over after debt service, wages/salaries and SOE transfers, fell by 30% in real terms [GoZ, 1998a:3, 12]. In the 1980s, the Government managed to mediate welfare amongst an impoverished peasantry through fiscal deficits sustained by a range of controls but notably negative interest rates. In the deregulated economy, upon positive interest rates, a shrinking revenue base and a devaluing currency, the exigencies of deficit financing [not least propelled by drought and poverty] courted the budget in a debt spiral. Therein, despite ongoing retrenchment, higher 'user fees', cutbacks and commercialisation of SOEs, the fiscal deficit persisted mainly because the Government increasingly borrowed to service outstanding debt, which then fed into the deficit and debt.[8]

As the spiral deepened and ate into funds, most SOEs and state departments including those concerned with welfare provision were continually compelled to increase fees and rationalise staff and services. As argued in the next chapter, at least before the outbreak of political chaos in the year 2000, the fiscal crisis should be seen less a consequence of Government profligacy or mismanagement than an ill-conceived development strategy that in the structural context reaped a circle of economic decline. In a great paradox, the very pursuit of deficit reduction only added fuel to the stagflation crisis, which ultimately fed back into undermining the state fiscal position. The more the Government sought to recover fiscal balance, whether through further retrenchment, deeper cutbacks, higher 'user fees' or taxes, the more depressed and impoverished the economy.

In parallel to that of the central Government or for that matter, any domestically focused business entity, the liquidity position of Zimbabwe's 24 urban councils became equally appalling. Most urban council revenue was derived from rates and charges yet, due to the economic crisis, resistance against increases and defaults among residents including state departments became widespread. By the late 1990s, for example, defaulting ratepayers owed Harare City Council Z$400 million; residents owed Gweru City Council $110 million for health services; and the national Government owed all city councils $1.7 billion in unpaid accounts [*The Financial Gazette*, 20/04/99; *The Zimbabwe Mirror*, 13-19/10/00]. Inevitably, city infrastructure disintegrated: 'roads in most towns and cities are badly pot holed', commented the mayor of Gweru [cited *in The Zimbabwe Mirror*, 13-19/10/00], 'effluent from sewage plants spills into the streets while refuse continues to pile up'.

Although the health ministry except for Home Affairs received the least cutback, health expenditure, as a proportion of the total budget, declined by over 30% from 6.4% in 1990–1991 to 4.3% in 1995–1996 [WB, 1996:62]. In real terms, the health budget per head of the population fell by 40%; on wages and salaries of hospital staff by over 30%; and on medical supplies and services by 20% [PRF, 1997:18]. At one point in November 1995, pharmaceutical companies stopped supplying the Ministry of Health because of unpaid debts [Bijlmakers, L.A., Basset, M.T., and Sanders, D.M., 1998: 96]. Yet, the health system still had to provide the majority with free treatment as about 75% of rural and over 25% of urban households earned incomes below the Z$400 per month threshold [UNDP/PRF/IDS, 1998:47]. An under-funded Social Dimensions Fund [SDF] set up to cover the cost of fee exemptions only managed to pay 20% of accounts [UNDP/PRF/IDS, 1998:47].[9] Thus, as these comments from a Harare nurse imply, hospitals over time had to discriminate to distribute scarce resources:

> It is not logical to give a dying person medication when we can give it to someone else. We also consider if one can afford to buy but generally

> we don't give for free. We discharge the patients not because they are fit to go home but because we have nothing to offer them [cited in *The Zimbabwe Mirror*, 29/09-5/10/00].

Meanwhile, revenue generated by higher user fees comprised no more than 2% of total health expenditure [PRF, 1999:11]. Most ill-stricken families above the threshold either avoided hospital or sacrificed necessities to pay health expenses. Between 1989 and 1995, national outpatient attendance fell from 7,037,344 to 3,977,104 [Mandebvu, M., 1997:11] while antenatal attendance dropped by 40% [PRF, 1999:11] and the maternal death rate doubled.[10]

In Chitungwiza, although the PASS declared 30% of people 'very poor', according to the cited Scandinavian study, only 7% to 8% of residents over 1993–1995 were officially entitled to free health while one in six ill could not afford treatment [Bijlmakers, L.A., Basset, M.T., and Sanders, D.M., 1998: 104]. Even if entitled, there was no guarantee that the clinic had the appropriate drugs in stock, as Chiti who suffered from a recurrent skin infection often discovered. Private doctors provided an option but, as of 1999, Z$200.00 was required just for the examination fee. By the late 1990s, higher than elsewhere, Chitungwiza experienced alarming increased rates of tuberculosis, malaria, dysentery, acute respiratory ailments and venereal infections.[11] The 19,114 new cases of tuberculosis recorded in 1997, compared to Harare's 2,500, was claimed HIV-AIDS related, which medical experts believed affected 40% of the Chitungwiza population [*The Herald*, 19/01/98].

On a national scale, health data indicates that the country returned to a state on a par with the colonial era or probably worse. Between 1990 and 1997, infant mortality before the age of one year, per 1,000 births, rose from 60 to 80 compared to 85 in 1978 while child mortality before the age of five rose from 26 to 36 just below the 1978 figure of 37 [Ministry of Health cited in *The Herald*, 7/04/99]. The average proportion of children underweight [i.e. wasting], which reflects acute malnutrition, rose from 11% to 17% while overall life expectancy fell from 61 to 49 years compared to age 56 in 1978 [UNDP/PRF/IDS, 1998:41,46]. Presently, up to 30% of the sexually active population are believed HIV positive [WB, 1996:38; UNDP/PRF/IDS, 1998:46]. And the general 'resurgence of old diseases' [UNDP/PRF/IDS, 1998:47], as listed above, was accompanied by an outbreak of cholera, which first surfaced in January 1999 and by April, infected 2,148 people countrywide—over 200 in Harare [*The Herald*, 13/05/99].

To a real extent, the plight of the education system paralleled that of health. Allocations fell from 18% of the total budget to 15%, which in real per capita terms represented a 33% drop [PRF, 1997:18; WB, 1996:65]. Although rural students remained exempt from tuition fees, other costs soared, such as uniforms, books and paper, sport, building and exam fees, which were reputed to account for the bulk of expenditure in communal areas [Mudimu, G., 1994:27]. While the SDF assisted only 20% of applicants, countless students were sent home unable to pay these expenses.[12] Officially, compared to the early 1980s, by the mid-1990s there were 10% fewer children completing primary school in urban areas where tuition fees applied and 25% countrywide writing 'O' levels [MacGarry sj, B., 1993:23; Mandebvu, M., 1997:11]. Ironically, after being at the forefront of persuading Governments to introduce user fees in the 1980s [Watkins, K, 1994b:134], the World Bank subsequently lamented:

> The current policy of charging fees [i.e. for tuition] while over half the students in high-density urban areas are eligible for fee payment by the SDF generates enormous costs for households, school administrators, the ministry of education and the SDF itself ... Doing away with fees in these areas might generate overall savings to society [1995 Vol.2:53].

7.4 The Plight of Shungu Dzedu, Chiti and Other Small-Scale Businesses

In mid-1994, Chiti himself was retrenched from the film processing company whereupon, as elected business director of Shungu, he fought gallantly to save the Cooperative but to no avail. All of Shungu's micro enterprises progressively collapsed under the SAP policy regime and the indebted Cooperative had to be liquidated by the year 2000. Unable to derive adequate support from the Department of Social Welfare, many of the Chitungwiza blind, as *The Herald* [22/05/99] observed, resumed begging in central Harare. A lack of management expertise and discipline among members, particularly concerning payment of allowances, contributed to the downfall. Yet, without doubt, most damage emanated from a hostile macroeconomic environment and increased impoverishment of surrounding markets and of the members themselves. In a desperate situation, business rationality gave way to survival, even though this meant consuming the Cooperative's working capital.

In the early 1990s, Shungu refined their production technique in the Makoni building. Silveira House supplied initial rounds of raw materials for the production of chalk [i.e. super fine white powder, unipaste] and pillows/mattresses [i.e. cloth and cotton waste] and the Australian NGO—*Chiedza*—supplied materials for candle making [i.e. wax, wick and steric acid]. Early on, Shungu employed some 30 people, 75% of them blind, which was not wise, as a reliable market had not been secured. The quest of the heart to emancipate the blind, however, was in control. Both the above organisations paid temporary allowances of Z$300 per month to enterprise employees: Chiedza for about 12 months; and Silveira for about 18 months plus the electricity bill. The final products lived up to the motto of Shungu—'Quality Production is Our Survival'. Indeed, production was not a problem but securing the market emerged as the real challenge.

Meanwhile, the tenants who subleased the agricultural plot from Shungu, to recall, the Zimbabwe Association for Crime Prevention and Rehabilitation of the Offender [ZACRO], fell four months behind rent payments in late 1993. From the Z$400,000 obtained from the Australian High Commission, ZACRO installed a bore, pump, irrigation pipes and a cyclone fence but not all monies had been adequately accounted for. In 1994, the High Commission terminated relations with ZACRO, which included an agreement to pay two security guards. Shungu took over the plot and discovered that the pump was too weak to sustain a market garden. Nonetheless, the Cooperative could resume the chicken business while members gained access to individual plots to grow maize.

Although blaming a lack of security as the main deterrent for a further grant, the Australian High Commission refused to re-employ the security guards or erect a durawall. To the chagrin of members, most of their chickens were stolen before they could be sold. The scattered feathers among a nearby squatter camp along the Manyame River seemed to point to the source of the thieves. As with the street children of Harare [Ndoro, H., 1996: 45], the squatters of Tilco suddenly surfaced in the 1990s. Shungu employed two pathetically paid security guards but the thefts continued. In 1997, an armed gang of six overwhelmed the two guards, dismantled the irrigation pipes, damaged the pump in their attempt to remove it, loaded everything on to a truck and drove off, never to be heard of again.

Turning now to Shungu's micro enterprises, reproduction vitally hinged on a market that bought in bulk and paid instant cash, otherwise inflation would erode the revenue base. For chalks, an inelastic demand base among schools, interest for a bulk buy and relatively few competitors enabled the enterprise to turnover. The pillows/mattresses and candle enterprises, on the other hand, faced the competition of formal large-scale suppliers with established economies of scale. Further, in a country where most people struggled to afford food, these products emerged as luxuries, even though to the favour of candles over 90% of rural households and 16% of urban existed without electricity [CSO. 1997a: 118]. The panacea of an export market was unattainable, as the additional product requirements, such as packaging, imposed huge extra costs. As it was, the transport costs accrued in search of a domestic bulk buyer for these items threatened to absorb the mark up of the quantity sold.

Nonetheless, Chiti worked hard to overcome the capital and marketing constraints. In response, Chiedza supplied another round of raw materials and Shungu reduced employees from 30 to 20. He then mobilised the blind community to attend a street protest about the plight of the disabled, which received press coverage. Soon after, the Central Purchasing Authority in the Ministry of Finance, which supplied Government Stores, allocated Shungu a tender for pillows and mattresses. This was followed by a Z$65,000 low-interest loan from the Ministry of National Affairs, Employment Creation and Co-operative Development and a Z$65,000 grant from the Social Dimensions Fund, due in part to the advocacy of Silveira House. Tragically, though, cost inflation, delayed payments from the Central Purchasing Authority, marketing constraints and rising poverty among members all seemed to conspire against success. Once Silveira and Chiedza terminated the allowances, survival imperatives progressively and inevitably took precedence over the working capital.

In respect of pillows and mattresses, as payment from the Central Purchasing Authority usually took three months, by the time

Shungu got paid for an order, input costs had risen that the money fell short to fulfill the next order, more so if workers were to receive an allowance that covered the cost of living. Over one period, for example, the price for one metre of cloth rose from Z$14.65 in November 1994 to $15.16 by January 1995 to $21.76 by April. Upon an elastic demand and narrow selling base, Shungu's enterprise lacked the pricing power to keep ahead of cost inflation. In the end, the Central Purchasing Authority refused to deal further with the Cooperative, due to the partial fulfillment of orders. The Authority itself was later closed—a decision consistent with the ideology of the SAP but also brought about by suspected corruption.

Similarly, cost inflation damaged the candle enterprise. The deathblow came during the currency collapses over 1998–1999 when, as an imported petroleum extract, the price of wax rose from Z$19.00 per kg to $36.00 per kg—almost a 100% increase. The logic of inflation demands instant price rises to match the cost of inputs but given, as argued, a weak demand base, rising costs could not easily be passed on. The price of the 25 centimetre candle was increased to Z$3.00 while the established opposition candle, of less wax content but neatly packed, cost between Z$2.60 to $3.50. Wholesalers expressed interest in the Shungu product providing it was wrapped and boxed but such required an initial outlay of Z$20,000 to packaging manufacturers, which was beyond budget. Increasingly, the profit margin became insufficient to maintain stocks as well as pay adequate wages. The three workers employed drew a subsistence wage yet in so doing, the working capital diminished.

As from 1996, Shungu rented out space in the Makoni building, which led to a parade of business tenants, which encompassed security, debt collection, real estate, computer services, photocopying and even a foundry. The increased prevalence of the kleptocratic economy explains the appearance of the first three. Ironically, most were plagued by kleptocratic scandals themselves and the police shut several of them down. Local security firms experienced difficulty breaking into the lucrative domain of the CBD and relied on local businesses around Makoni such as that provided by Shungu itself, car yards and grocery stores. As of 1999, most local guards were paid a poverty wage of less than Z$600.00 per month. One of the guards at Shungu—again ironically—was suspected of stealing two sewing machines. Computer services and photocopying, however, seemed to thrive—charging 80 cents per copy, both businesses turned over $300.00 to $400.00 per day.

Located out the back, the foundry, owned by a Mr Mutasa, mainly produced battery terminals, employed 10 men on wages worth Z$1,000 each per month and turned over about $40,000 per month of which $5,000 was surplus. Under the SAP, withdrawal of subsidies to ZISCO saw the price of steel rise by 218% within 18 months while import liberalisation saw a flood of cheap imports [Chipika, S., 1995:15]. The experience and contacts Mr Mutasa gained during the UDI period served him well in the 1990s. Although imported battery terminals are cheaper, he maintained, only the loyalty of his formal sector contacts, such as Glynn's Bolts, Stancefield and Consolidated Motors, saved his business. He also stressed that international competition and currency depreciation constrained his capacity to pay higher wages and invest in advanced technology such as dye moulds and a lathe.

Although most of the blind members were entitled to support from welfare, as of April 1997, monthly payments at Z$50.00 and Z$20.00 per adult and child respectively plus rent assistance were hopelessly inadequate [Kaseke, E., Dhemba, J., and Gumbo, P., 1997:18].[13] Chiti's family, for example, accrued Z$180.00 per month excluding rent assistance yet the Total Consumption Poverty Line in urban areas as set by the PASS for a family of six was Z$1,227.44 per month [GoZ/MPSLASW, 1996:23]. In response, Chiti and Sibongile sent three daughters to Shava village to take advantage of the cheaper cost of living, particularly in their primary education. Yet building and sporting fees [about Z$100.00 per child per year in early 1999], uniforms, stationary and pens still had to be paid for. As of 1999, the SDF had not forwarded assistance and often the children were sent home, due to non-payment of fees or no uniform.

But besides education, malnutrition undoubtedly threatened the three daughters in Shava village. The droughts had decimated Mr Mpofu's five remaining head of cattle and thus the household's productive power in the good seasons. Too old to work in the mines, Mr Mpofu now relied on shepherding other people's goats between seasons. Otherwise, he maintained, the advent of rain made all the difference from being totally dependent on Government relief, such as the GMB's Grain Loan Scheme [scrapped, to recall, in April 1999] to 'having something'. His widowed neighbour, Mrs Mhou, was busy planting trees and digging massive holes to catch water, which were life saving measures. The fate of the three daughters vitally depended on the capacity of Chiti and Sibongile to send remittances.

Meanwhile, Kezious, the brother of Chiti, had set up a retail business in hardware, which appeared to tap into a middle-class niche market. In 1997, he was lucky enough to sublet a table at Highfield market in Harare for Z$200.00 per month. With only Z$200.00 left in his pocket, Kezious bought stock wholesale, such as bulb plugs, window levers [from Mr Mutasa's foundry] and plumbing joints, and sold it retail. By 1999, he rented another table at Makoni Shopping Centre and employed his sister-in-law at Z$750.00 per month. Both tables combined turned over $25,000 per month: the one at Highfield generated $700 to $1,500 per day compared to $300 to $500 from the Makoni table. The main constraint, he stressed, was not having the stock diversity to meet the demand, particularly door locks. His marriage childless, Kezious accommodated and financed the education of his sister, Perpetua, and regularly sent remittances to Shava village.

While income drawn from the welfare system and proceeds from building rent failed to alleviate poverty, the Shungu members put pressure on the working capital of the Cooperative's only successful enterprise—that of chalks. As of the mid-1990s, with the advent of a contract from Kingstons—a national chain of school suppliers—the chalk business was doing reasonably well. Nevertheless, members demanded disproportionate outlays of dividends, which should be seen as desperation to avoid begging—the very ethos of the Cooperative after all. Hungry people, as a true saying goes, know no reason. Staff at Silveira House claimed they lacked the expertise to arrest the demise of the Cooperative, which was understandable because such would involve, among other factors, restoring macroeconomic stability particularly low inflation [Interview, 23/03/99]. In turn, beyond adhoc measures of price subsidies and controls, lasting resolution of inflation required attendance to the structural problem of supply through comprehensive land reform and strategic import substitution.

Chiti kept persevering. In late 1997, to replenish the capital base of the chalk enterprise, he approached the state-owned Commercial Bank of Zimbabwe [CBZ] at Makoni for a loan. Predictably, the manager refused whereupon Chiti wrote to President Mugabe himself who eventually redirected the matter to the Governor of Mashonaland East and the Mayor of Chitungwiza [See *The Herald*, 17/09/98]. In the end, despite the fanfare, Shungu received a loan from the CBZ, which totalled Z$50,000 at a 50% rate of interest. In exchange, the bank received the title deeds of the Makoni building, which cast the death net over Shungu. As the Cooperative failed to repay this loan, the CBZ finally switched on the machinery of debt collection and liquidation.

By the late 1990s, new entrants into the chalk business created marketing constraints and pressure on producers to deflate prices. Kingstons, for example, refused to purchase Shungu's chalk at Z$11.00 for a box of white and $12.50 for assorted coloured, citing cheaper alternative sources. Instead, the retail chain offered $7.10 and $9.00 respectively, which was below the cost of production, despite the fact, according to Chiti, that Kingstons sold the same box for $25.00. Other marketing outlets, such as the Ministry of Education and the Town Council, were behaving in like manner. Inevitably, once again, the working capital dissipated and hence, most members of Shungu succumbed to the fate already mentioned. Of course, the collapse carried ramifications on innocents. The four daughters of Chiti and Sibongile, for example, three of whom topped the class at their school in Shava village, seemed to have been deprived of a future.

Since the SAP commenced, 'there has been', concluded the CSO report [1998a:35-36], 'an unambiguous increase in poverty'. From 1990/1991 to 1995/1996, between the times of conducted surveys, the prevalence of household poverty increased from 40.4% to 63.3% while that of people from 52.8% to 75.6%. Therein, households unable to afford a basic food basket more than doubled from 16.7% to 35.7%, which included families like the Shumbas and the Mpofus. Within the structural constraints of poverty, the *increase* has a lot to do with the failure of the economic reform strategy recommended and conditionally sponsored by the world's leading development institutions, namely, the IMF and World Bank.

One casualty was the country's health, the indicators of which, as cited above, went into reverse. Apart from the omnipresent charge of Government fiscal mismanagement, which I deal with next, the tendency among SAP proponents is to blame AIDS. To quote the World Bank report on Zimbabwean poverty:

> The controversy [over adjustment] has shifted the focus of the debate away from a major factor behind declines in some key health indicators—the spread of HIV/AIDS ... Rapid growth in acute malnutrition and tuberculosis are both associated with AIDS ... The epidemic poses enormous problems not only for the health system but also for the economy as a whole ... [1996:49, 64].

Such a view is not candid. While no doubt AIDS relates to many cases of ill health and household poverty, the question ignored is why poor countries have the highest prevalence. Underneath the spread, as Thabo Mbeki inferred at the 13th world conference on AIDS in Durban, there is a greater evil than the disease itself:

> The world's biggest killer and the greatest cause of ill health and suffering across the globe, including South Africa, is extreme poverty ... it seems to me that we could not blame everything on a single virus ... [cited in *The Age*, 11/07/00].

Not unlike the state fiscal deficit, HIV/AIDS is an outcome of economic decline and poverty, not the primary cause. Single women and unsupported mothers, as has been pointed out, are at the forefront of poverty, which causes among many a resort to prostitution. Further, as state, hospital and patient budgets are under enormous strain, the likelihood increases that venereal diseases—often forerunners to contracting HIV—remain untreated [MacGarry sj, B., 2000:26]. Very simply, development programs that fail to maintain economic growth and welfare must assume responsibility for the spread of HIV and other diseases.

Besides those of Shungu Dzedu outlined, the number of small-scale enterprises nationwide, according to official statistics [cited in *The Financial Gazette*, 6/05/99], fell from just under 500,000 in 1991 to 227,000 by 1998. Under the SAP, subject to rising costs and gluts of suppliers, increasingly impoverished local markets undermined the pricing power of many enterprises to keep abreast of inflation. Clearly, most Zimbabweans fared better under the regulated macroeconomic environment before the SAP. Indeed, relatively stable prices, employment levels and exchange rates would have gone a long way toward helping Shungu Dzedu sustain their enterprises and prevent the slump into present misery.

Meanwhile, as living standards fell, the measures implemented—state cost recovery, currency devaluation, positive interest rates, deregulated import flows, liberalised price and wage setting—did not bring about the export-led recovery promised. Instead, as the socioeconomic crisis deepened, the country descended into political chaos. In the late 1990s, the Government revisited the land issue and the IMF refused to release credit, both of which contributed to the 'Black Friday' currency crash. The devastating effects bolstered a political opposition that encompassed urban working and middle classes including white farmers and established business. A now frustrated and aggressive state bourgeoisie virtually gave up on the SAP and turned to alter prevailing structural conditions under the banner 'the land is the economy and the economy is the land'.

8

Zimbabwe Ruptures under the SAP

As the crisis of economic survival took hold, the Zimbabwean polity began to fall apart. On one side, a stratum of militant nationalists—war veterans, peasants and ZANU-PF leaders—blamed the crisis on inequitable production structures while on another, a transnational liberal coalition—Western states, the IFIs, development NGOs, multinationals, organised labour, white farmers and civil groups—blamed fiscal mismanagement and poor governance. Divisions culminated on 14 November 1997—'Black Friday'—when in the midst of an IMF-led global credit boycott and external deficits, the announcement of unbudgeted war veteran gratuities and land acquisition plans sparked a deep currency crash. Thereon, as the stagflation spiral hit hyper proportions, liberal forces mobilised behind the Movement for Democratic Change [MDC], which promised constitutional democracy and economic stabilisation. The Government meanwhile sought to broaden investment horizons, via the DRC war, and resolve the constitutional and land question diplomatically. Yet, as the June 2000 elections approached, faced with a defiant but credible opposition, the ruling party sanctioned land invasions and violence in a bid to save itself.

Presently, ZANU-PF no longer plays within the rules of international society and economic rationality: judicial rulings have been disobeyed and political opponents persecuted—costing over a hundred lives so far—in what appears an orchestrated attack on private property rights and foreign interests. As I write in 2002, within the large-scale commercial sector, over 2,000 farms out of about 6,000 have been invaded while some 10.3 million hectares [93%] out of about 11 million has been designated for state expropriation and fast track resettlement without compensation for the soil [*The New York Times*, 29/06/01; *The Guardian*, 16/05/02]. Aggressive indigenisation, President Mugabe warned, may not stop there:

> The land will be settled but who owns our mines? We are gold, copper, asbestos and iron producers, but most of the benefits are enjoyed by the former colonialists [Interview with the *Independent* [UK] cited *in The Age*, 17/06/00; *The Zimbabwe Mirror*, 16-22/06/00].

Nor has the manufacturing sector escaped political harassment: over April and May 2001 about 20 companies, mostly foreign-owned, were visited by war veterans demanding reinstatement of retrenched workers or payment of redundancy packages [*The Zimbabwe Mirror*, 04-10/05/01].

Since the advent of political turmoil, to quote the *Economist* [February 2001], 'Zimbabwe has the worlds fastest collapsing economy'. All foreign exchange earning sectors are registering negative growth and with the rise of a parallel market offering treble the official rate of exchange, state reserves are fast drying up. The country cannot import adequate supplies of fuel and electricity, let alone meet external debt repayments, which reached accumulated arrears of US$488 million [Makoni, S., 2000:1]. In the year 2000, 400 factories and 14 mines closed shedding a reputed 64,000 jobs [*The Zimbabwe Mirror*, 12-19/04/01; Makoni, S., 2000: 1] while foreign investment and resultant employment creation fell by 80% and 70% respectively [ZIC cited in *The Zimbabwe Mirror*, 15-19/10/00]. The tourist industry has collapsed: visitors fell from a record of 2.4 million in 1998 to about 619,200 in 2000 resulting in the loss of 100 operators and at least 5,000 jobs [*The Zimbabwe Mirror*, 5-11/11/99, 11-17/05/01; Makoni, S., 2000:3]. AGRITEX predicts that over the 2000–2001 season commercial farmers reduced areas planted in all crops by between 15% to 50% and the country faces a serious shortage in the food staples wheat and maize unless large-scale imports are undertaken [*The Zimbabwe Independent*, 22/06/01].

The fiscal position of the state remains in dire straits: public debt, both external and domestic, stands at well over Z$200 billion and almost one-quarter is owed by SOEs. Interest repayments—about 80% apply to domestic sources—have grown from 15% of total state expenditure in 1990 to an estimated 48% in 2001, which converts to about US$3.2 million per day [Makoni, S., 2000:1; *The Zimbabwe Independent*, 22/12/00]. If wages and salaries [about 35%] and transfer payments to loss-making SOEs [about 10-12%] are added, over 80% of fiscal outlays are accounted for, which leaves very little for education, health and capital infrastructure. In recent years, due the DRC war, defence has received the lion's share of discretionary revenue while the health system has become a shadow of the past. With a sharp escalation of poverty-related diseases caused by inadequate nutrition, sanitation and income, the Government admits hospitals are under funded, staffed and equipped to cope [GoZ, 2001:1].

In December 2001, the US Congress and the Presidency finally passed the Zimbabwe Democracy and Economic Recovery Act, which aims to extend the freeze on non-humanitarian aid, debt relief, investment and trade until the rule of law is restored.[1] Specific conditions entail a return to civilian control of state security forces, a free judiciary, press and democratic elections, withdrawal from the DRC and lawful land reform based on a return of 'title to property held prior to January 1, 2000' [Bill S 494 IS from ZimNews despatch, 15/03/01]. The Bill compels US representatives to the IFIs to continue the block on aid, loans and debt relief until these conditions are met. Other weapons include travel bans on high up Zimbabwean officials and suspension of their reputed international accounts and assets.

The rationale of the Bill rests on several assumptions, shared amongst Western states, the MDC opposition and resident NGOs, which are aptly captured in the article by Robert Rotberg [2000] already referred to in the introduction. The first is that the state of lawlessness is the work of a tyrant—President Mugabe; the second, that past economic policies recommended by external creditors are right and decline reflects gross mismanagement; and finally, that the ownership structure bequeathed by settler colonialism is for the time being good enough to sustain embracive growth and liberal democracy. From this perspective, recovery depends on economic strangulation to bring down the Mugabe regime in order to allow a more democratic order to emerge, which abides by the conditions of external credit including lawful land reform.

All three assumptions are dubious, however, and arguably form part of the problem than the answer. No person, whether Mugabe or the late war veterans leader, Chenjerai Hunzvi, can single-handedly instigate a national upheaval. The unresolved contradictions in the political economy, namely, land inequity, scant local markets and skewed wealth distribution came to an unprecedented head during the 1990s. Economic deregulation under the SAP—a core condition of Western credit—provided the catalyst by releasing a spiral of *stagflation*, which undermined majority livelihood and Government capacity to meet fiscal targets as well as stabilise the peasant–capitalist order. Thereon, the global community's unreliable support for the economy and lawful land reform only fuelled nationalist sentiment to aggressively redistribute the land and assert strategic interests in the DRC. The more the country was isolated, the more ZANU-PF perceived the emergent opposition as a foreign—even *neo*-Rhodesian—obstruction to genuine economic emancipation. Relative to this goal, liberal democracy and the rule of law, according to the President [*The Mail & Guardian* (SA), 11/06/01], are 'extraneous'.

The SAP then, initially viewed with optimism by the country's elites completely backfired. The fault, according to proponents, lies with the 'reform design and implementation ... not the concept [i.e. of economic deregulation] itself' [UNDP/PRF/IDS, 1998:32]. Such a position, however, really clutches at straws—in reality, as has been outlined, implementation of the concept impoverished the population, which in turn exposed the imperative of real structural reform. Once the Government committed itself on the land front, the economy went into a tailspin and the country returned to the politics of liberation. Zimbabwe's development crisis is the harvest of economic failure and poverty, which of itself *primarily* attributes to colonial production and wealth structures, not governance as such. The SAP cannot be held to account for the structural base of the economy but it can for amplifying the inherent capacity to spawn economic and social imbalances and related political turmoil.

The opening section overviews the political economy behind the SAP and, therein, the mounting contradiction between economic liberalisation and the need of structural reform toward which the international aid community, as led by the IMF, lacked empathy and constructive engagement. To then expose the inadequacy of the orthodox view of Zimbabwe's macroeconomic crisis, various aspects of economic decline are substantiated—deindustrialisation, the damage of trade liberalisation, stagnant investment and the demise of the state fiscal position. I then turn to the national land issue, which in the early 1990s—consistent with the export thrust of the SAP—assumed a backseat but in so doing, became a 'time bomb'. The concluding section focuses on political outcomes and the mechanics of disintegration—entry into the DRC, the explosion of the land issue, Western, IMF and MDC intransigence, national polarisation over a new constitution and the outbreak of land invasions.

8.1 The Flawed Political Economy of the SAP and Irresolute External Support

Like any other the world over, the Zimbabwean SAP aims to meet the conditions of external credit and as a result, the policies are no different. All three official documents, namely, *A Framework for Economic Reform 1991–1995*, the *Zimbabwe Program of Economic and Social Transformation* [ZIMPREST] [1996–2000] and the current *Millennium Economic Recovery Program* [MERP], abide by the core policy components. Essentially, rationalisation of the public sector, via fiscal and monetary restraint, combined with maintenance of a free market regime over trade, capital flows, finance, wages, prices and investment is expected to stimulate a sustained rise in export-oriented investment that will boost employment, bring down inflation and poverty. Pointedly though, official thinking increasingly emphasised the need to accompany the SAP with a greater focus on indigenous empowerment. In contrast to the free market idealism of *Frameworks* [January 1991], both *ZIMPREST* [February 1998] and the *MERP* [November 1999] devoted more space to socio-political imperatives such as land redistribution and affirmative action in indigenous business.

Zimbabwe's experience of the SAP falls into two periods: the first from 1990 to late 1997 distinguished by comprehensive policy implementation but mounting socioeconomic distress; and the second, from late 1997 to the present marked by political instability, policy reversals and disintegration. An important fact is that by 1997 the state-regulated regime no longer existed and the economy operated on the basis of free market forces. The turning point came in August when militant war veterans prompted the Government to act on indigenous imperatives, which included gratuity payments but more significantly, land redistribution. The latter meant assaulting the property rights of the very agrarian sector the SAP declared a 'pillar of growth' [GoZ, 1991a:17]. Combined with external imbalances, this political paradox underpinned 'Black Friday' when the local dollar depreciated 71.5% against the US dollar [*The Financial Gazette*, 19/02/98]. Thereafter, as captured in Appendix 9, amid an invigorated stagflation spiral, the SAP was thrown totally off-track; signs of policy regression surfaced on all fronts bar wage and investment policy.

In an earlier report, the World Bank [1995 vol.2: 95] briefly referred to the political dilemma that beset the Zimbabwean case of economic liberalisation:

> If not accompanied by other measures, the liberalisation of markets … will not contribute to broad based agricultural growth. Without further structural changes – related especially to access to productive resources … future agricultural growth in Zimbabwe is likely to remain slow and concentrated among narrow socio-economic segments of the population …

Yet, a liberalised predominately white and foreign-owned economy is not easily reconciled with an agenda of structural reform through land redistribution. In a real sense, Black Friday revealed free market hostility toward indigenous imperatives, which shattered the Government's faith in the liberalisation strategy. The following statement from the MERP belies the official position of embracing the free market:

> The national economic crisis mirrors deleterious effects of neo-imperial machinations aimed at limiting national sovereignty over the redistribution of national assets such as land in favour of indigenous Zimbabweans [GoZ, November 1999 cited in *The Zimbabwe Mirror*, 21-27/01/00].

In the aftermath of 'Black Friday', the economy became a 'victim of politics' [*The Zimbabwe Independent*, 12/12/97] wherein the SAP agenda became more or less void. In a complete circle of development failure: economic, social and political crises tumbled into one another.

Such depths may not have been reached had Zimbabwe received consistent balance of payments support from the IMF upon which the release of additional credit from other multilateral, bilateral and NGO sources including the EU, the World Bank, the ADB and USAID also depended. Throughout though, as indicated in Appendix 10, IMF support has been irresolute: less than half of the funds promised were released over 1991–1995; a complete suspension prevailed between September 1995 until June 1998; and thereafter, the two stand-by arrangements negotiated were suspended after release of initial tranches. Project lending from the World Bank, however, continued until recently but in parallel with the IMF, no balance of payments support eventuated beyond the adjustment credits in the early 1990s [i.e. IBRD and IDA 3313, IBRD 3322].[2]

As much as the foreign currency was needed to sustain import flows, protect the national currency, bolster investor confidence and discourage state domestic borrowing the impasse with the IMF accentuated the extent of economic failure and, therefore, contributed to the outbreak of the development crisis. The plethora of loan conditionalities asserted, whether economic [deficit reduction] or political [good governance], became progressively unrealistic and less able to salvage the prevailing order, let alone the SAP.

8.2 The Features of Economic Decline

Yet, fundamentally, if the recommended policies had worked in the early 1990s there would not have been such need for external finance to rescue the economy from political chaos in the late 1990s. From the beginning, as already noted, a crisis of *stagflation* took hold: the real growth rate of GDP fell from an average of 4% over 1985–1990 to just 1.7% over 1991–1996 while the inflation rate averaged 25%, up from 15% [CSO, 1997c:4]. Appendix 11 outlines the related macroeconomic trends of falling per capita income and employment growth, currency depreciation, exorbitant interest rates and a rising burden of external debt relative to GDP. The value of real wages, to recall, fell by 35% over 1991-96 [IMF, 1997:15] while formal employment creation since the 1985–1990 period also declined by a third to average about 8,300 net new jobs per year [GoZ, 1998a:9]. Conversely, over the same period, relative to a population increase of 14.8%, non-agricultural employment opportunities contracted from an average growth rate of 16.2% to a mere 1.5% [Mandebvu, M., 1997:13].

8.2.1 Deindustrialisation: The Inadequacy of the Orthodox View

The defenders of the SAP blame stagflation on a *solitary* but core implementation shortfall, that is, the failure to reduce the state fiscal deficit, which as a percentage of GDP averaged about twice the target before doubling again in the year 2000 [Appendix 11]. In a classical monetarist framework, SAPs are said to offer a package deal on stabilisation providing the implementation of core policy components is synchronised. 'There was a logical inconsistency', to quote Peter Robinson [1998:13], 'in pursuing various dimensions of liberalisation with vigour'—especially price and interest rate decontrol—'while not taking measures to reduce the budget deficit to levels where its financing did not pose a threat to macroeconomic stability'. The reliance on bank liquidity and Reserve Bank accommodation to fund the deficit fuelled monetary growth, which upon monetarist assumptions caused excess demand and high inflation and, therefore, necessitated a restrictive monetary policy to counter inflation and protect savings [WB, 1994a:49-50; vol. 2, 1995:19-22].[3]

Although orthodox economists admit that the higher interest rates of tight monetary policy carried serious repercussions on both private investment and public debt service, they maintain that the root cause of the problem is Government failure to reduce the fiscal deficit through adequate recurrent expenditure cutbacks, user fees, state retrenchment and sales of SOEs. The analysis concords with the rational choice school in that poor governance is invoked as the underlying reason for fiscal mismanagement and consequent deficits. In other words, the key problem is a profligate ruling elite, which refuses to relinquish the channels of state largesse for political or rent-seeking gain. The persistent budget deficit—a symbol of poor governance in the orthodox view—lies at the heart of the impasse between the Government and the IFIs, which in turn has caused a chain reaction of irresolute support for the Zimbabwean SAP among the Western aid community generally.

In reality, however, orthodox prescriptions of state rationalisation and restrictive monetary policy caused far more damage than Government mismanagement. Inflation was less an outcome of monetary growth than the liberalised pricing power of an oligopolistic base faced with increasing charges for imports and public utilities [power, fuel, water, transport etc]. As *cost* inflation entrenched itself and effective demand collapsed, higher interest rates tended to only add fuel to the stagflation spiral. Therein, the budget emerged as a casualty of a shrinking revenue base and an ever rising debt interest bill to such an extent that the serious pursuit of cost recovery measures including significant state retrenchment [Appendix 9] failed to correct the deficit. Unlike in theory, the Government faced a real dilemma whether more expenditure cuts and public asset sales actually offered an escape route or a means to further emasculate and impoverish the national economy. The core issue was not fiscal laxity *per se* but how the SAP policies in general impacted on the structural conditions *below* the state, which is an area classical analysis tends to overlook.

Prior to the SAP, the economy's class and production structures offered limited scope to generate the broad-based national wealth needed to overcome adverse external terms of trade as well as stagnant and inflation-prone markets. In the early 1990s, for instance, according to a study by Gun Stenflo [1993], some 3% of the population accounted for 30% of total consumption while 50% were responsible for 15% [cited in WB, 1996:35]. Nearly 70% of the country's exports remained linked to commodity markets while the industrial sector imported about 70% of productive inputs and relied on domestic consumption for over 66% of output [National Merchant Bank, cited in *Business Herald*, 12/02/98; ZNCC, cited in *The Zimbabwe Mirror*, 3-9/9/99]. As outlined earlier, although short of an agrarian and industrial strategy to alter the structural predicament, the state-regulated regime managed to counter inherent tendencies toward external imbalances and shrinking domestic markets. But once dismantled in favour of export-led growth, upon its own structural base, the liberalised economy succumbed to these distortions.

The process was paradoxical though in that the SAP, as intended, stimulated the tradable sectors but in so doing, weakened the national market and eventually the balance of payments. While deregulation of the exchange rate, exchange allocation, import and capital flows, under trade liberalisation, encouraged foreign inflow and export activity, these measures also reinforced the precarious reliance on primary exports and opened sources of imported inflation, elite wealth acquisition, foreign competition, speculation and capital flight. The pursuit of fiscal rationalisation and tight monetary policy, at least to an initial extent, released liquidity and encouraged savings for private investment but also fuelled cost inflation and the slump in aggregate demand. In another two-edged vein, as liberalised price and wage regimes transferred a bigger investment surplus to capital, the depreciation of real wages inherent, according to an IMF study by Botchwey, Collier, and Gunning [1998], saw per capita consumption fall by 37% over 1991–1996 [cited in UNDP/PRF/IDS, 1998:31].

The cumulative impact on the industrial sector was the exact reverse of the intention:

> It is expected to achieve rapid growth and diversification of exports and to provide equipment, machinery and intermediate inputs to various sectors of the economy and to meet a large percentage of demand for manufactured consumer products, thereby reducing the economy's import dependence [GoZ, 1991b:38].

The downturn enveloped the leading inward-oriented sectors, such as peasant agriculture, parastatals and manufacturing, which two severe droughts [1991–1992, 1994–1995] facilitated but good rains between and after never offset. Appendix 12 captures the extent of deindustrialisation: in real terms, the manufacturing sector contracted by over a fifth during the 1990s, which as a share of GDP represented a decline from about 25% to under 15% [FMB, December 1998:4]. As can be seen from Appendix 12, the droughts had a severe impact on production but even after the reasonable seasons of 1995–1996 and 1996–1997 performance still remained about 20% below the 1991 level. In fact, by 1997 the deepest slumps had occurred in the subsectors of strategic significance to employment creation, import-substitution and value-added exports, namely, textiles, clothing, metals and to a lesser extent, chemicals. The sales volumes of many companies, notably ZISCO, collapsed by half simply because of inflation and falling demand [Sachikonye, L.M., 1995a:59,74].

8.2.2 Trade Liberalisation as a Two-Edged Sword

World market integration proved a two-edged sword: growth in the tradable sectors came at the expense of an enhanced wealth divide and poorer national market. As with other heavily import-dependent economies, the attempt to gain an export edge through a market exchange rate invoked a circle of currency depreciation, imported inflation, consequent currency appreciation, further depreciation and so on. The official rate underwent regular downward adjustments—19% in 1991, 15% in 1993 and 17% in 1994 [WB, vol.2 1995:9]—to unify with market value, which fostered external demand but also stagflation and endless exchange rate instability. Meanwhile, Foreign Currency Accounts [FCAs] granted to exporters and foreign investors promoted export activity and capital inflow but also speculation and capital flight. Import liberalisation, while stimulating investment through easier access to inputs and capital goods, also enticed unwarranted luxuries and cheap foreign goods that undercut the market share of local companies. Overall, the obtained external orientation wrought more damage than benefit and ironically exposed constraints on the balance of payments.

In nominal terms, total trade, that is, the sum of exports and imports, rose nearly eight-fold between 1990 and 1997 while trade and current account deficits, as a percentage of GDP, increased from 1.4% and 3.8% respectively to 6.4% and 9.2% [IMF, 1997:7; CSO, 1998b:iii]. After the 1991–1992 drought until mid-decade, as shown in Appendix 13, the net reserve balance recorded a surplus: favourable movements in export commodity prices, high unrequited transfers and strong capital inflow offset the rising burden of import, investment and service payments abroad. Thereafter, as trends in export commodity prices and capital inflow reversed, continued import, service and investment payments drained foreign reserves to less than a months import cover at the time of the Black Friday currency crash [RBZ, 1998:24]. The Government–IMF impasse from late 1995 over the budget deficit had serious repercussions on the capital account—directly through suspended official flows and indirectly through affecting investor confidence. Yet, at a deeper level, deterioration reflected a shrinking domestic economy increasingly exposed to commodity export prices and erratic capital movements.

Over 1990–1997, as imports rose faster than exports annually at 35% against 32% respectively, the trade deficit [excluding gold sales] increased at a rate of 43% per year. On the import side, machinery and transport equipment [39%], manufactures [22%], chemicals [14%], fuel [11%] and miscellaneous items [8%] comprised the average account while on the export side, tobacco [29%], manufactures [33%], food products [16%] and crude materials [14%] shared the receipts [All data cite in CSO, 1998b:iii-ix]. An enlarged trade deficit is not necessarily a bad sign if import consumption propels the value-added export growth needed to overcome adverse terms of trade. In Zimbabwe, however, import pressure accorded more to exchange rate instability, foreign competition and luxury consumption than a sustained productive investment push. As a result, the export charge facilitated by trade liberalisation, whether in agriculture [tobacco, cotton, sugar, cereals, coffee], mining [gold, nickel, asbestos, copper, chrome] or manufacturing [textiles, ferro-alloys, cotton lint], *predominantly* focused on non-dynamic world markets [CZI, cited in *The Zimbabwe Mirror*, 1-8/10/99].[4]

According to James Jowa, the chief economist of the ZNCC, currency devaluation 'is only beneficial when the cost to the country of the high import bill is offset by the benefits derived from increased export proceeds' [cited in *The Zimbabwe Mirror*, 12-19/04/01]. Despite notable exchange earning successes, such as tourism and horticulture[5], on the whole, concludes John Makamure, another ZNCC economist, devaluation 'pushes up input costs, leading to a fall in output and a contraction in exports' [cited in *The Zimbabwe Mirror*, 3-9/09/99]. 'In real terms', agreed the head of ZimTrade, Freddy Chawasarira [cited in *The Zimbabwe Mirror*, 3-9/12/99], 'nothing is being achieved': the value of exports in US dollars falls while the Zimbabwe dollars gains are eroded by inflation. Indeed, as the Zimbabwe dollar lost 120% of its value over 1997–1998, inflation hit record highs while export volumes fell by 20% and the value in US dollars by over 70% [*The Herald*, 10/05/99; *The Zimbabwe Mirror*, 24-30/09/99]. In the process, expectations of devaluation exacerbate the trade imbalance; by logic, export orders are delayed while imports are hoarded and orders rushed [Bond, P., 1998:248].

Meanwhile, import liberalisation opened the door for trade competitors, such as South Africa, to usurp a greater share of the domestic market. In 1992, as Zimbabwe opened its trade regime,

South Africa 'drastically' reduced preferential export margins under the bilateral trade agreement and raised import duties to protect its industries [*The Financial Gazette*, 22/4/99; *The Herald*, 28/04/99].[6] Thus, between 1990 and 1998, South African goods increased their share of the local market from 20% to 38% while Zimbabwe's trade deficit with South Africa nominally rose by 2,400% [from Z$579 million to $14.5 billion] [CSO data cited in *The Financial Gazette*, 29/04/99]. The potential to correct the imbalance seemed undercut: an EU-South Africa trade pact announced in March 1999 aims within 12 years to open up South Africa's market to 86% of EU goods in return for EU market access for 95% of South African goods [*The Zimbabwe Mirror*, 9-15/07/99].[7] Nonetheless, Government remained committed to open trade: not until mid-decade did a few industries, namely, clothing and textiles, electronics, luggageware and selected agricultural products receive tariff protection above the norm [RBZ, 1997c:20].

'The hedonistic tendencies of Zimbabwe's elites', wrote Patrick Bond [1998:390], 'were given free reign'. As workers and peasants surrendered a third of their standard of living, central shops replenished stocks of imported luxury goods [cars, jewellery, exotic fruits, cell phones, videos, suits etc] to serve enriched niche markets. Such minority pursuits caused enough stress on the external account that in September 1998 the Government imposed a 15% surcharge on non-essential imports and 100% on such goods that can be sourced locally [*The Financial Gazette*, 1/10/98]. At a subsequent conference on national debt at Nyanga, Michael Mataure, an MP from Chimanimani, responded to the charge from business leaders that Government luxury consumption was a key cause:

> Don't separate yourselves from ordinary Zimbabweans. The Pajeros, the second Merc, the boat in Kariba, all these are part of the problem. If you lead by example, then the Government will also follow and want to be like you [cited in *The Financial Gazette*, 13/05/99].

8.2.3 Stagnant Investment

'Small markets and low purchasing power amongst Africans', Masata Fujita, a Japanese official from UNCTAD commented, 'is the main deterrent to Japanese foreign direct investment on the continent' [cited in *The Sunday Mail*, 30/11/97]. In this respect, whether from a foreign or indigenous perspective, Zimbabwe under the SAP appeared most unattractive. The World Banks private sector investment arm, the International Finance Corporation, for example, attributed its declining loan portfolio to poor local markets and a 'free-falling Zimbabwe dollar', both of which crushed the capacity of domestic-oriented firms to service hard currency loans [*The Financial Gazette*, 18/03/99]. For similar reasons, after contemplating an investment project for several years, McDonalds—a symbol of global capitalism—eventually shelved the idea [*The Financial Gazette*, 25/03/99]. The biggest productive foreign investment project over the 1990s— the Hartley Platinum Mine by BHP—collapsed by decade end on account of geological, financial and commodity-price constraints [*The Zimbabwe Mirror*, 11-17/06/99].

Initially, companies took advantage of open access to imports, foreign exchange and importantly, subsidised offshore finance[8] to upgrade equipment. Over 1991–1995, fixed investment reached levels 57% higher than the 1986–1990 period and averaged 22% of GDP compared to 17% [GoZ, 1998a:57]. Contrary theoretical forecasts, however, heavily capital-intensive, the investment surge created less employment than the 50,000 workers retrenched. Nor could it be sustained: by 1993, according to the World Bank [1995 vol.2:129], most manufacturing firms harboured enormous excess productive capacity in the range of 80%. On internal and external fronts, the economy lacked dynamic outlets and, as a result, levels of fixed investment declined to 13% by 1999 [RBZ, 1997b:30; Makoni, S., 2000:10]. From mid-decade, the Government appealed to the private sector, via a build-own-operate-transfer [BOOT] scheme, to invest in local infrastructure [i.e. roads, bridges, dams etc] but only one project eventuated [*The Financial, Gazette*, 11/03/99].[9]

There was no aversion to speculative financial activity, however, which emerged as a main preoccupation of foreign as well as indigenous capital. Indeed, while the economy averaged a 0.8% annual growth rate over 1991–1995, the finance industry expanded at 5.4% [Robinson, P.B., 1998:18]. Three new commercial and six merchant banks emerged between 1990 and 1997 and, according to estimates, the net asset base of the industry rose from Z$11 billion to $82.1 billion [Moyo, T., 1998:9]. Rather than investment in real production, financial growth mainly accorded to speculative dealings on share, money, property and currency markets.

Total market capitalisation on the Zimbabwe Stock Exchange, for example, soared from a low of US$1.5 billion in 1992 to US$6.1 billion by 1997 [RBZ, 1997b:24]. Otherwise, as was the case with 77.7% of foreign FCA deposits in 1994 [ZCTU, 1996:7, 86; Bond, P., 1998:255], high-interest bearing short-term maturities absorbed capital, the sums of which like the above were unavailable for long-term investment and, as evident in 1996 [Appendix 13], could quickly exit the country. By simply holding US dollars and then selling as they appreciate, currency dealing offered another lucrative opportunity. Indeed, the difference converted into windfall gains for Banks at the time of the 'Black Friday' currency crisis [*The Herald*, 23/12/97]. Inevitably though, the disjuncture between finance and a viable productive base fatally exposed several new players to non-performing loans and large fluctuations in real estate and share prices.[10]

8.2.4 Monetary Policy and the Fiscal Crisis

Through virtual 'ultimatums', according to Patrick Bond [1998:247,293,387], the IFIs insisted upon positive interest rates to encourage savings and investment as well as fight 'demand' inflation. With two-thirds of population either below the poverty line or heading there, high interest rates remained irrelevant and seemed to only engage non-productive capital. Indeed, against a target of 25% of GDP, domestic savings [i.e. excluding foreign] averaged below 15% until 1997 and then fell to 9% by 2000 [RBZ, 1997b:30; Makoni, S., 2000:10]. In a letter to *The Herald*, a member of the public pinpointed the apparent inconsistencies of monetary policy:

> The monetary policy adopted by the Reserve Bank of Zimbabwe to arrest inflation is, in fact, fuelling it. What has to be appreciated is that Zimbabwean inflation is cost-push rather than demand-pull. In fact, companies are closing down due to dwindling demand as a result of low disposable incomes. Our inflation is the result of the fall of the Zimbabwe dollar and the monetary policy. The main propellers being petroleum products and electricity costs, both of which are substantially imported. So, to further dampen demand by stifling money supply is rather insane.

> Recent increases in commercial bank lending rates will raise the cost of borrowing for companies. High interest rates will impact negatively on private sector investment plans and on efforts to reduce the Government budget deficit since high interest rates mean the Government has to spend more on interest payments on its domestic debt. What we need are policies that stimulate demand and increase investment in the economy ... [Letter to *The Herald*, 24/05/99].

In respect of fuel and power, to meet the import bill for 100% and 40% of national supplies respectively, the responsible SOEs, NOCZIM and ZESA, required about US$300 million per year [*Business Herald*, 29/04/99], which alone points to the comprehensive impact of currency devaluation on national inflation.

Table 8.0 *Summary of Central Government Accounts, 1990–2000 [Z$ millions]*

Year	Revenue & Grants	Expenditure & Net Lending	Budget Deficit	Source of Deficit Financing		Accumulated Domestic Debt#
				Domestic	Foreign	
1990/91	6 758,8	8 355,5	-1 596,7	1 502,4	+94,5	7 849,0
1991/92	9 363,8	11 073,1	-1 709,3	1 320,9	+388,4	7 992,8
1992/93	10 763,9	13 408,3	-2 644,4	1 278,2	+1 366,2	9 070,9
1993/94	13 675,0	15 810,8	-2 135,8	1 777,3	+358,5	12 874,6
1994/95	16 514,3	22 829,6	-6 315,3	6 115,4	+199,9	24 671,4
1995/96	20 876,6	26 024,0	-5 147,4	3 972,5	+1 174,9	33 154,8
1996/97	27 289,5	32 396,7	-5 107,2	5 107,2	-	31 408,9
1997/98*	59 095,4	69 716,5	-10 621,1	10 621,1	-	38 471,3
1999	60 707,0	79 638,4	-18 930,9	18 930,9	-	73 904.6
2000^	76 971,0	132 151,1	-55 180,0	55 180,0	-	153 070,1

Source: RBZ [various years].

Nevertheless, the fight against inflation rested entirely on tight monetary policy, which the World Bank [vol.1&2 1995:9,20] admitted adversely affected 'the profitability of firms' and led to a 'rise in bankruptcy and default problems' but claimed it necessary 'without supporting fiscal deficit reduction'. Yet, under circumstances of

Totals include borrowings for domestic and external debt repayments

* July 1997 to December 1998 [18 month period].

^ As at December 2000. For the latest update visit the RBZ web site: www.ibz.co.zw

continued domestic borrowing, the high interest rates increased the debt burden to such an extent that fiscal rationalisation failed to reduce the deficit. Over 1991–1996, although non-interest expenditure, as a percentage of GDP, declined from 37.1% to 29.8%, total recurrent expenditure persisted at a 1980s average of 40.6% largely because interest charges on every revenue dollar collected increased from 17 cents to 37 cents [GoZ, 1996:2, annex 1:ii]. Meanwhile, as the economy contracted, state revenue declined from 36% of GDP in 1991–1992 to 28% by 1994–1995 [IMF, 1997:30].[11]

Table 8.0 illustrates the debt spiral wherein the Government progressively borrowed just to service debt, which then perpetuated the deficit and borrowing requirements. In 1999, for example, the Government set aside Z$7.4 billion to service the debt but, as interest rates rose, $11.4 billion was needed in the first quarter alone [*The Financial Gazette*, 20/05/99].

The other source of public debt is external, which accounted for about 41% of Government borrowings [CSO, 1997b:103]. Between 1990 and 1997, the total stock of external debt rose from US$2.9 billion to $4.9 billion of which, according to Appendix 14, about 80% accrued to the public sector via Government [about 70%] and SOEs [about 12%]. With the inflow of adjustment credits, the share of public debt owed to the multilateral institutions [i.e. the IMF, World Bank and ADB] increased from over 20% in 1991 to over 50% by 1997. Debt service [principal and interest] averaged well over US$500 million per year during the 1990s of which the Government paid about 65%, SOEs 15% and the private sector 20% [RBZ, 1997a:15]. For the first time since 1980, debt repayments were delayed in 1999 amid the currency collapses of 1997–1998, which as Appendix 14 indicates, escalated the cost of debt service in Zimbabwe dollar terms [*The Financial Gazette*, 27/05/99].

'Provided proceeds from state asset sales are used to reduce the stock of domestic debt', advised the World Bank [cited in *The Financial Gazette*, 11/12/97], 'budgetary interest payments would fall substantially, which would allow the Government to increase resources for the social sectors while lowering the overall fiscal deficit'. Where market conditions were conducive, such as in finance, tourism and agricultural tradables, the Government sold five enterprises for about Z$3 billion, namely, the Commercial Bank of Zimbabwe [CBZ],

Zimbabwe Reinsurance Group [Zimre], Rainbow Tourism Group, the CMB and DMB. Otherwise though, fiscal salvation could not be expected from selling chronically indebted SOEs. As of the mid-1990s, subtracting total liabilities of state assets [i.e. Z$20 billion] from the total book value [i.e.$22.5 billion] offered a net value of only Z$2.5 billion [GoZ, 1996:vi].

The Government genuinely feared indebted enterprises would be sold cheaply to foreign proprietors and then in a quest for commercial viability lead to a severe depletion of national infrastructure. With the descent into political chaos after 1997, market conditions only got worse: 'no investor', to quote Andrew Bvumbe, the Director of the Privatisation Agency of Zimbabwe, 'wants to put money in an unstable and unpredictable environment' [cited in *The Zimbabwe Mirror*, 28/07-3/08/00].

Perennial loss makers included the GMB, ZISCO, NOCZIM, ZESA, CSC, NRZ, AFC and Air Zimbabwe. While high interest rates and currency devaluation generally undermined debt-servicing capacity, some more than others remained seriously undercapitalised [i.e. ZISCO[12], Air Zimbabwe] or particularly susceptible to drought [CSC, GMB, AFC], devaluation [NOCZIM, ZESA, Air Zimbabwe], political pricing [NOCZIM, ZESA, GMB] and shrinking domestic markets [ZISCO, NRZ, AFC]. Initially, combined losses of these eight subsided from Z$1.3 billion in 1993–1994 to $1.2 billion by December 1996 but then rose to $3 billion a year later [RBZ, 1995:13; 1997c:13; 1998:17]. As the currency crash took its toll, combined losses reached $10.7 billion in 1998 and 1999 and total liabilities amounted to $45 billion by 2000 [*The Zimbabwe Mirror*, 21-27/05/99, 28/07-03/08/00]. NOCZIM recorded a staggering loss of Z$5.5 billion over 1997–1998, which partly reflected looting by managers [for at least $1.4 billion] but more so, politically induced disparities between fuel procurement prices and selling prices [RBZ, 1998:17] in an effort to curb the inflation spiral.

The economic crisis fundamentally stemmed from a deficient structural base but attributed to the SAP in so far as the policies removed the controls that to a vital extent protected the economy against stagflation and state fiscal failure. In the depressed context, whether a blanket sell-off of public assets, deeper cutbacks or a greater resort to foreign borrowing would resolve or escalate the crisis remained far from crystal clear. As it was, the SAP had already undermined Government capacity to mediate welfare amongst an impoverished peasantry and protect urban living standards, which apart from the program itself threatened the political order. In mid-1997, the World Bank had yet to comprehend:

> ... a substantial degree of structural adjustment has taken place, which has created a greatly improved business climate for domestic and foreign investors. Outward-oriented sectors such as commercial agriculture and horticulture, tourism and mining responded well to the new policy environment ... Zimbabwe's labour costs are now very competitive in international terms [May, 1997b:3].

An earlier Bank report concurred:

> The economy does appear to be healthier as a result of the policy changes, which means that implementing a poverty reduction strategy that promotes growth and simultaneously invests in the poor should be feasible and should yield positive results in the second half of the decade [1996:77].

8.3 The 'Time Bomb' of Land, 1990–1997

With the industrial and service sectors failing to provide alternative opportunities, most households urgently sought extra land to sustain basic survival. In a structural and macroeconomic context wherein private companies owned 61% of prime commercial land and the exchange rate floated, however, comprehensive land redistribution to improve welfare could not easily be integrated without undermining investor confidence and the national currency. From the outset, therefore, the SAP proved a fillip for agrarian capitalist classes—established white and aspirant black—to ensure land reform remained sensitive to foreign exchange earning capacity and geared toward capital accumulation. The 1990 National Land Policy explicitly aimed to promote capitalist agriculture through a settler selection process and tenure application, which emphasised economic rather than social equity criteria.[13]

Ironically though, the restrained rationale coincided when the state gained more power to resolve the national land question. For ten years Section 16 of the Lancaster House Constitution restricted land redistribution to market transactions at market value and allowed the state to expropriate land upon payment in foreign currency. After the relevant clauses expired in 1990, the

Constitutional Amendment [No. 11] empowered the state to compulsorily acquire *any* land for the public good and determine the amount payable in local currency. The procedure of appropriation, as per the amendment, specified that the state must give due notice to all parties, justify the acquisition and declare the basis of fair compensation. The owner received the right to contest in which case the state had to apply for a confirmation order from an Administrative court or withdraw the notice [GoZ/LTC, 1994 vol. 2.:145].

The Land Acquisition Act of 1992 gave effect to the amendment and further enabled the state to designate *rural* land for compulsory purchase at set prices [Moyo, S., 1995:247]. In the case of designation, after due notice and justification[14], the property owner could still object but the Minister of Lands gained complete discretion whether or not to revoke the notice [GoZ/LTC, 1994 vol. 2:146]. As to compensation paid, the Act provided for an appointed committee of six persons plus an evaluation officer to decide the amount with reference to a First Schedule, that is, a set of principles laid down by the Legislature and additional though not contrary guidelines offered by the Minister. Examples include farm size, type of soil, extent of cultivation, crop variety, yield, fixed assets, improvements and land price histories [Tshuma, L., 1997: 130-131; Moyo, S., 1995:245]. In the event of a dispute, the Act allowed the owner recourse to the courts, which can refute the assessment if, and only if, there is proof that the state or committee failed to follow correct procedures or abide by the set principles [Tshuma, L., 1997:131-132].

The white agrarian bourgeoisie, multinational companies and the UK and US all raised objections that state power to determine land prices violated the rule of law and human rights. The then Chief Justice of the High Court, Anthony Gubbay, even questioned the sovereignty of an elected Government to amend a constitution that had originated from outside an elected Parliament:

> It must not ... be assumed ... that an affirmative vote of one hundred members will enable Parliament to pass a constitutional Bill which goes to the extent of damaging or destroying the very foundation or structure of the Constitution [Gubbay, 1991, cited in Tshuma, L., 1997:126].

In amending the constitution, noted Lawrence Tshuma [1997:127]—a Program Legal Counsel at the International Development Law

Institute in Rome—the Parliament never violated prescribed procedures and, therefore, the Court had no jurisdiction over the matter. Given that the amendment allowed property owners recourse to the courts, the Government thought the comments by the Chief Justice indicated zeal to defend established property rights.

In any case, within the goal of five million hectares, the Government aimed not to cause an agrarian upheaval but fairly limit individuals and companies to one farm unit. Land sought was to be unused, derelict, near communal areas or held by foreign/absentee landlords for speculative reasons [GoZ cited in Tshuma, L., 1997: 124-125, 130]. True to this approach, only 24% of the 200,000 hectares or so designated by mid-decade lay within the best ecological zones while the rest spread over Natural Regions III, IV and V—over 58% in the latter two. In the fertile Mashonalands, out of the 60% of net arable land reported uncropped only 6% was designated. The Government protected the tobacco region around Marondera and the high-value estates of Lomagundi, Mazowe, Harare and Chegutu districts. Instead, ranching land received the main focus—mostly adjacent to communal areas and owned by people with multiple farms [All data cited in Moyo, S., 1995:249, 251-252].

Between 1990 and 1997, against a target of 110,000 families, only 19,000 families were resettled on approximately 200,000 hectares compared to 52,000 families on about 3.3 million hectares during the 1980s [GoZ, 1998c:6]. The common view amongst the Western press, diplomatic and NGO community is that land redistribution is a preserve of ZANU-PF cronyism driven by political imperatives to reward allies with large farms. The charge, however, tends to be exaggerated: as of April 2000, only 423,000 hectares—less than 10% of total land redistributed since 1980—had been granted to 400 black lessees mostly through the Tenant Farmer Scheme of the late 1980s mentioned previously [*The Zimbabwe Mirror*, 21-27/04/00]. The media uncovered the on-going scheme in 1994 whereupon the President cancelled 72 leaseholds recently awarded to high officials [See *Daily Gazette*, 26/03/94; *The Herald*, 4/05/94]. Apart from white farmers, land redistribution accorded more to the interests of *kulak* peasants: the ZFU, for instance, lobbied persistently that only farmers with a 'proven productive record' should benefit from resettlement [The late G. Magadzire, ex-ZFU President, cited in *The Sunday Mail*, 19/03/95].

But more to the point, the free market framework of the SAP served as an overwhelming constraint on the broad-based and dualistic land reform, as argued in an earlier chapter, Zimbabwe so urgently required. Put simply, lest the Government incited panic and deterred foreign investment, a thorough overhaul of commercial property rights could not be countenanced. Yet, simultaneously, from highly skewed structures of wealth, the SAP also failed to deliver the low inflation growth promised and, therefore, intensified the need for land. At least half the rural population by the mid-1990s could not properly feed themselves, which apart from an absence of employment and income opportunities indicated access to either insufficient, degraded or no land at all. The land issue thus evolved as a political time bomb under the SAP more so that the Government lost the fiscal capacity to enact an adequate land transfer within the law.

8.4 The Descent into Chaos, 1997–2000

The year 1997, to quote the chief editor of *The Zimbabwe Mirror* [1-7/12/99], Ibbo Mandaza, 'represented the final thaw in post-independence politics, laying bare the unresolved and bottled-up contradictions between the former colonies and the new ruling class and between the latter and the various social forces within'. The coalition of elites responsible for the SAP now irretrievably fractured over a question of national salvation. In essence, the ZANU-PF hierarchy realigned itself with the peasantry over the land issue while white farmers and established business joined the urban civil alliance in a push for liberal democracy through constitutional reform. Meanwhile, IMF and allied creditors refused to replenish the external account or unequivocally support land reform, which no doubt contributed to the 'Black Friday' crash. Then, as the economy collapsed, militant nationalists sought redemption from war in the DRC and land delivery on the domestic front, which the transnational opposition, as spearheaded by the MDC, threatened to halt.

8.4.1 Entry into the DRC

While domestic stagnation conditioned the state bourgeoisie to look outward, South Africa's growing dominance and the impasse with the IFIs strengthened nationalist resolve to assert regional economic interests. The implosion of Zaire presented the ruling party with an opportunity to carve out an economic domain in Africa's third-largest country and forge the sought after transnational conglomerate able to challenge foreign capital. In 1996, President Mugabe provided Laurent Kabila's forces with US$5 million and military intelligence to help overthrow the Mabuto regime [ZimNews, 2001: 18]. Once accomplished in May 1997, the state-controlled Zimbabwe Defence Industries soon announced a Z$2 billion export deal to supply the Democratic Republic of Congo [DRC] with foodstuffs and military hardware [*The Herald*, 1/12/97]. More lucrative opportunities to enter the world's diamond, cobalt and timber markets came with the deployment in August 1998 of 12,000 Zimbabwean troops in the resource-rich Kasai-Oriental and Katanga provinces.

Zimbabwe obtained mining, forestry and agricultural concessions as barter payment for helping defend the Kabila regime against the Ugandan and Rwandan backed Rally for Congolese Democracy.[15] From the hierarchy of ZANU-PF and the Zimbabwe Defence Force [ZDF], after initial attempts, a corporate structure eventually emerged called Operation Sovereign Legitimacy or Osleg (Pvt.) Limited.[16] This company then formed a joint venture with Comiex—owned by the Kabilas—to create Cosleg, which received two rich mineral concessions transferred from the Congolese mining parastatal—Miba, namely, the Kimberlite and Senga Senga river deposits, as well as a logging concession 1.5 times the size of the UK. To supplement Cosleg's military muscle with the offshore expertise needed to develop the claims, the Zimbabwean Government and Oryx Natural Resources, an Oman-based company, formed Oryx-Zimcon (Pvt), which then combined with Cosleg to create Sengamines—the core management entity of Zimbabwe's business operations in the DRC [All data taken from ZimNews, 2001: 20-24; *The Zimbabwe Independent*, 20/04/01; *The Observer* (UK), 28/08/01].

In a context of huge disparities in global wealth, Zimbabwe's quest to acquire an indigenous transnational capacity from the Congo's resources is no more illegitimate than deferring to the dominance of European, American, British or South African multinationals. As one of the world's last frontiers, the Congo is of enormous significance to African development: two DRC minerals, for example, namely, cobalt and col-tan, were for sometime deemed 'wonder ores'.[17] Tragically though, as displayed by European powers over past centuries, the process of primitive capital accumulation often entails war, which in the Congo has usurped near three million lives so far as well as the commercial benefits derived by *all* parties [*The Guardian Weekly*, 10-15/05/01]. By late 2000, according to the Finance Minister, Mr Makoni [cited in *The Mail & Guardian* (SA), 01/09/00], the war had cost Zimbabwe US$200 million for which the public at large could see no benefit.

8.4.2 The Explosion of the Land Issue and Belated Western Engagement

In April 1997 suspension of the War Veteran's Compensation Fund after revelations of looting by high officials provoked a virtual uprising. 'The ex-combatant factor in Zimbabwe', to quote Ibbo Mandaza [1997:6], 'has, unlike in other post-colonial situations in Africa, provided the cutting edge to politics, demonstrating the unusual and rare capacity to raise the great class question in general, and thereby shaking the post-colonial state at its very roots'. With firm links to the peasantry and the ruling party's historical ethos, the country's 60,000 odd war veterans have the capacity to keep the *telos* of the state in check. The action taken on 11 August 1997 to blockade Heroes Day ceremonies nationwide and drown out the President's speech with *Chimurenga* songs profoundly embarrassed the regime. In a subsequent *tête-à-tête* on 21 August, veteran leaders warned the President that he would find himself on the run lest he forget the essence of the struggle [Deve, T., 1997:8-9]. The Z$4 billion worth of gratuities[18] then offered gained the state bourgeoisie a temporary lease of life but long-term survival hinged on unfettered land redistribution.

'We have reached a stage in our history where the land issue has to be redressed', the Minister of Lands, Kumbirai Kangai, summed up the mood [cited in *The Herald*, 02/12/97], 'The living conditions of our peasant farmers are deplorable'. By November 1997, some 1,775 farms covering over 5 million hectares across 45 districts had been identified for designation, which fell to 1,471 farms when the official notice was released on 28 November [see *The Herald*, 28/11/97]. The 1990 land criteria prevailed. Within the best three Natural Regions designated land, comprising 37% of the total, was mostly under-utilised; 34% of the designated land bordered communal areas; 32% applied to owners with multiple farms; and 40% was foreign-owned [mostly by companies and UK citizens] [Moyo, S., IDS seminar, 25/02/98].[19] Significantly, the Government now adopted a dual framework, which aimed to allocate 80% of acquired land to the impoverished including retrenched farm workers, via A1 non-commercial schemes, and the remaining 20% to capitalist farmers, via A2 commercial schemes [GoZ, 1998c:11-12].[20]

The President declared that owners would be compensated for assets but not for the soil because 'it was never bought from us' [*The Herald*, 27/11/97]. Of course, the fiscal position could not permit otherwise so inevitably expectations for assistance focused on the former colonial power. In early November, however, the UK refused outright to fund the program [see *The Financial Gazette*, 13/11/97] and denied any moral obligation. 'Colonisation is not something that people of my generation benefited from', a visiting UK Minister of State, Anthony Lloyd, commented [cited in *The Financial Gazette*, 8/01/98], 'We are willing to help but on the basis that land should first of all be geared towards poor people'.

The British outlook caused dismay on the Zimbabwean side. The assumptions implicit are that multinational landholdings do not currently benefit the UK; that acquired land only goes to ZANU-PF cronies; and that the state should not promote black commercial farming on the same status and scale of whites. Like the IMF, Britain treated the Government not the economy as the patient, which had serious ramifications on economic stability. The day before 'Black Friday', for instance, 'anxiety' amongst commercial farmers was reported 'at its peak' [*The Financial Gazette*, 13/11/97].

Thereon, as inflation soared, time was running out; sporadic land invasions were becoming difficult to contain [see *The Herald*, 7/05/99; *The Financial Gazette*, 27/05/99]. But progress remained frustratingly slow—too slow. Out of the 1,471 farms designated in November 1997 only 170 owners did not object while the rest pursued the issue through the courts 'at each and every stage' [*The Herald*, 27/03/99, 7/05/99]. Belatedly, the Western aid community engaged itself at the September 1998 Donor Land Conference in Harare yet really misread the depth of the socioeconomic crisis and urgency of land. Stakeholders pressured the Government to pay for the soil and commit to a limited inception phase. At a predicted cost of US$189 million of which the Government and donors were to pay 40% each and the beneficiaries 20%, the plan aimed to resettle 18,200 families over 2 years on 1 million hectares, then 150,000 families on 5 million hectares over 5 years [*The Financial Gazette*, 8/04/99].

8.4.3 IMF Intransigence

Figure Three *Mpofu's view of IMF Deliberations*

Taken from *The Herald*, 24/03/99.

Still, the IMF 'indulged in the political game of delays and uncertainties rendering whatever shortcomings there were on the part of Zimbabwe ever more serious and life threatening to the economic and socio-political fabric of the country' [*The Zimbabwe Mirror* , 11-17/02/00]. Allied donors, as noted, followed suit that over the second half of 1998 aid inflows fell by 45% [*The Zimbabwe Mirror*, 1-7/09/00]. Under the umbrella of poor governance—the DRC war[21], price controls on basic foods, tariffs on luxury imports, directives to liquidate FCAs, the unofficial exchange rate peg and fiscal overruns all surfaced as obstacles at one point or another. The cartoonist Mpofu captured the damaging circularity of IMF negotiations.

President Mugabe became more exasperated

> I don't like the IMF, we should do without it. The IMF is just a tool used by the Americans and British to get at us … Because the IMF has turned political, we have also become political towards it. They want to manipulate us and turn us into puppet regimes [*The Financial Gazette*, 13/05/99].

And threatening:

> We are the sufferers, but are expected to respect our oppressor's rights. Revolutions are not fought that way. IMF money is not more important than our land … The Americans and British are blaming us for everything but their companies are taking away billions of dollars … While we are struggling to give our people seeds and fertilisers to increase production, some whites are keeping what they grow to create shortages so that they can sell at higher prices … Take care! Our country should not fall into the hands of foreigners or those stooges and puppets of foreigners [*The Herald*, 29/05/99].

Seeing the writing on the wall, Nick Swanepoel, the CFU President, wrote to the then IMF Managing Director, Michael Camdessus:

> Every step regarding the purchase of farms from our members by the government has been conducted according to the laws of Zimbabwe … Every farmer so far, has been treated in a fair way in terms of compensation paid for his farm. Is there any possibility that the IMF stand-by facility can now be released?

Lazurus Dhlakama of the Employers Confederation also sent a letter:

> The current economic and social situation is bad. Rapid movement by the IMF and the WB on the stand-by agreement and structural adjustment credit is critical.

As did Silas Hungwe, the ZFU President:

> We would like to urge you to move swiftly to provide the much-required support in order to guarantee social and economic development of the country. Further delays in providing the support can only hurt much more the poor of the Zimbabwean population [All quotes cited in *The Financial Gazette*, 22/04/99].

Finally, albeit too late, IMF wavering prompted the World Bank President, James Wolfensohn, to warn Michel Camdessus:

> There is a strong sense that the IMF has been shifting the goal posts, has no intention of ever going forward with the stand-by facility because it wants to see a change in government and the IMF executive directors are angry that President Mugabe did not meet them during their visit last year ... Without balance of payments support, government may try to prevent the fall of the Zimbabwe dollar by fixing the exchange rate and imposing import and price controls... Social unrest will be hard to contain. If the land reform program does not deliver visible results during 1999 political pressure will mount to openly tolerate farm invasions. To deliver the program needs donor support. Transition within the ruling party ZANU-PF towards a new generation of liberal leaders will be severely handicapped [cited in *The Financial Gazette*, 20/05/99].

Indeed, he predicted the outbreak of land invasions and accompanying oppression of civil society, the private sector and the judiciary.

8.4.4 The Emergence of the MDC Agenda

In 1997, industrial action exploded: 233 strikes surfaced including national stoppages by farm workers in October and by *all* workers on December 9 [Sachikonye, L.M., 1997:9-10; 1998:8-9]. The latter was provoked by Government hikes in indirect taxes and introduction of a 5% income levy to finance the war veteran gratuities.[22] Led by the ZCTU, supported by established business, white farmers, urban middle and working classes, the national strike captured the intersection of domestic opposition and external forces over the governance question. Besides the tax rises, any aspect of the development crisis, whether the fiscal deficit, inflation, poverty, wealth inequity, the DRC war or land invasions is interpreted as an outcome of autocratic and corrupt mismanagement. Thus, in the words of the then ZCTU Secretary General and current MDC leader, Morgan Tsvangirayi, the quest to achieve human-centered development entailed a new constitution:

> ... that provides clearly for basic social, economic and civil rights; for the clear separation of powers between the executive, judiciary and legislature; for the limitation of the powers of the executive; for such powers of parliament and the judiciary that they are not subordinated to the executive;

> and for such powers of the electorate as to make parliament fully accountable to the people [May Day address, 1999].

Toward this end, the ZCTU, civil groups and aid associations, notably from the Netherlands and Scandinavia, had established the National Constitution Assembly [NCA] in May 1997, which simultaneously served as a nucleus of the MDC. By straddling the leadership of both the ZCTU and NCA, Morgan Tsvangirayi and Gibson Sibanda [the then ZCTU President] channelled interest groups into a National Working Peoples Convention in February 1999 from which the MDC launched [*The Financial Gazette*, 20/05/99; *The Zimbabwe Mirror*, 28/05-3/06/99]. As the champion of the liberal democratic path, the party promises to stabilise the economy within the confines of the SAP through constitutional reform that should ensure responsible government and, therefore, disciplined fiscal management and, most importantly, a resumption of global financial support.

In regard to the land issue, the MDC adheres to the Western position of a market-friendly program that will probably exclude majority need. Morgan Tsvangirayi:

> You can never distribute land to everyone. There is no country in the world that has developed on the basis of putting people on the land [cited in *The Zimbabwe Mirror*, 24-30/09/99].

Thus, within prevailing land structures, the MDC Secretary for Lands, Tendai Biti, spoke of a non-dualist commercial orientation, which as has been outlined proved disastrous in the 1980s:

> Any MDC land reform programme must be aimed at totally destroying the dual economy that exists in this country. At least 19 million hectares of land representing at least 48% of the land in this country is communal land that is being used at sub standard and sub scientific levels. The challenge of land reform should be to transform the 19 million hectares and capture them into the formal economy through a series of public sector investments [cited in *The Zimbabwe Standard*, 20/08/00].

8.4.5 National Polarisation and the Constitutional Debate

Since 'Black Friday', as the economy floundered and the polity polarised, the chance to reach a national consensus over any future direction slipped away. In late 1998, for example, a Tripartite Negotiation Forum [TNF] composed of labour, business and Government—an outcome of the National Economic Consultative Forum [NECF][23] set up in mid-1997—proposed a potentially nation-saving 'social contract' but this too ended up a 'victim of politics'. Within the overall context of a managed exchange rate float, all three parties agreed in theory to a freeze on wages, prices and taxes [Business Herald, 18/03/99]. The ZCTU, however, boycotted negotiations due initially to a temporary Presidential decree banning strikes and stayaways [The Herald, 24/05/99] but thereafter, to the leadership's affiliation with the MDC and apparent intention not to give ZANU-PF political mileage [The Zimbabwe Mirror, 7/01-13/01/00, 23/02-01/03/01].

Inflation continued unchecked while the enterprise bargaining system continued to short-change employed labour over the living wage and, in many cases, retrenched labour over redundancy payments.[24] In response to calls from party ranks, not to forget the food riots of mid-January 1998, the Government unofficially revised the SAP agenda evident in attempts to curb market sovereignty over the prices of basic goods and services, foreign exchange allocation and the exchange rate. Yet, as the saying goes, once the SAP train is boarded, it is fatal to jump off [The Zimbabwe Mirror, 11-17/02/00]. Controls on end prices without controlling input costs threatened firms with bankruptcy while directives to liquidate FCAs encouraged capital flight and any disjuncture between official and market rates of exchange spawned a black market. Land delivery represented the Government's solitary weapon of political survival.

As a last gasp to reconcile the country, in April 1999 the Government invited the National Constitution Assembly [NCA] to join a 395 member Presidential appointed Constitutional Commission [CC] to produce a draft constitution for a national referendum to be held in mid-February 2000. Although handpicked, the CC represented a diverse range of interests and significantly, accorded to the reasonable proposition that 'the Government of the day must lead the campaign to review the constitution' [**E. Zvobgo, National Legal Secretary, cited in *The Financial Gazette*, 5/02/98**].[25] The NCA refused to join, however, claiming a state-directed process would be exclusive, non-transparent and subject to political interference [***The Financial Gazette*, 01/04/99**]. The missed opportunity to work from within fractured NCA ranks:

the National Council of Churches, for instance, resigned claiming a political agenda had surfaced [*The Financial Gazette*, 06/05/99]. Thus, instead of being a nation-building process, the debate tore the country apart: until referendum day, the NCA and CC constantly sought to delegitimise one another as playthings of foreign donors and the President respectively.

One of the key issues within the CC and between the latter and the NCA concerned whether to replace the current Executive President with a Ceremonial President and introduce an Executive Prime Minister answerable to the Parliament. In the end, the draft constitution retained the Executive President yet created an appointed Prime Minister to which the President had to concur.[26] Of direct relevance though to the land question, section 57 [paragraph 2]—condemned by the Western media as means to a land grab—seemed to capture a realistic ethical basis upon which the national issue could be resolved:

> ... where agricultural land is acquired compulsorily for the resettlement of people in accordance with a program of land reform, any compensation payable must reflect an equitable balance between the public interest and the interests of those whom the land is acquired ...

Albeit short of the liberal democratic model sought by the opposition, many critics including Professor Julius Ihonvebere believed the draft superior to the present constitution [See *The Zimbabwe Mirror*, 14-20/07/00]. In any case, it was rejected—54% to 46%—in a poorly attended referendum: only 10% of the population voted. The draft actually passed in 63 out of 120 constituencies: most people in rural areas voted yes but more in urban areas voted no. In all likelihood, the majority voted against the economic management of ZANU-PF rather than the draft constitution. Irrespective, the result fired the cause of militant nationalists to immediately redistribute the land, lest an MDC victory in the coming June elections denied them the chance.

'Before independence, when the white colonialists grabbed farms', President Najoma of Namibia told reporters at a regional summit in Victoria Falls [cited in *The Zimbabwe Mirror*, 28/04-4/05/00], 'where was the rule of law and the so-called good governance?' The remark captures the sentiment of militant African nationalism, which in parallel to the liberal opposition grew by the day in Zimbabwe over the late 1990s. It may not encompass the majority but where the vein runs through the peasantry, war veterans and the state bourgeoisie, there is a violent disregard of political opposition, election protocol, property rights, the rule of law and the plight of farm workers. Adherents have no interest in economic rationality *per se*; the structural predicament, specifically, the extent of foreign ownership and African marginalisation, necessitates immediate acquisition of African economic power in both the national and international arenas. As one source from the ZANU-PF caucus commented:

> Macroeconomic stabilisation is half the answer or no answer at all. We have been down that hopeless route since 1991 when structural adjustment was adopted. What the parliamentarians and the people now want are real projects which benefit real people not just abstract concepts [cited in *The Zimbabwe Mirror*, 27/10-2/11/00].

According to Government sources [cited in *The Zimbabwe Mirror*, 4-10/05/01], 63,000 families were resettled under the fast track scheme between July and December 2000 compared to 74,000 over the previous 20 years.

Alternatively, the MDC embraces the Western agenda of good governance, which seeks to restore liberal democracy as well as the SAP. In regard to land reform, the apparent policy is to evict illegal settlers [*The Zimbabwe Mirror*, 23-29/03/01] and, as mentioned, not allocate land for subsistence reasons. As the June 2000 election results indicate, the MDC encounters problems among the Mashona peasantry where the dialogue of market-oriented land reform, the rule of law, civil rights and judicial independence is of little relevance to hungry people in need of land. But beyond established capitalist classes, the MDC has broad electoral appeal in Matabeleland where many seek to avenge the *Gukurahundi* of the 1980s as well as in *all* urban areas. The key drawcard is the promise to stabilise the economy through a resumption of IMF balance of payments support, withdrawal from the DRC, a depoliticised land program and a resurrected social contract.

In the event of election, just how an MDC government will reconcile the inherent contradictions between free market prescriptions and the nationalist cause to redress past inequities is unknown. The dubious consolation is that IMF loans will actually be granted to prop up what still remains an impoverished and non-viable national economy. In any case, as I write, an MDC electoral victory could conceivably mean civil war. Militant nationalist elements have no toleration for an opposition perceived as a Western agent with a mission to return the country to appendage status. Too much is at stake: land redistribution and the DRC war are considered the only real means to economic salvation.

In large part, the SAP reaped this turmoil: the policies exposed the imperative of real structural reform and the more the global community disengaged itself through unrealistic conditionalities, the more determined the Government to follow through on the nationalist agenda. Unfortunately, as a result, Zimbabwe lost white farmers instead of retaining their expertise in a thoroughly land reformed, stronger and more democratic agrarian order. A slight hope is that out of the current agrarian mess, an indigenous anchor class emerges, that is, the propeller of a thriving African private sector, which is a necessary foundation to build a workable democracy whether its MDC or ZANU-PF.

Conclusion

Zimbabwe, as I write, confronts a profound development crisis of interrelated economic, social and political dimensions. African and Western states are as much divided over the causes as the Zimbabwean public, which obstructs a resolution. From foregoing evidence, the root cause is economic in that a program of market liberalisation exposed the incapacity of a highly skewed production base to meet majority basic needs. The IFIs and Western states, however, refused to concede market failure and sought to resolve the governance question before the economic, which only fed into political turmoil and total economic collapse. A constructive approach now requires engagement to help the country first resolve the economic problem through agrarian reform whereupon the advent of a free market and democratic governance regime becomes a more realistic proposition. In impoverished Africa, Western-propelled globalisation needs to take a backward step to gain at least a semblance of credibility and Zimbabwe is the place to start.

In the final analysis, most aspects of the development crisis, whether political [authoritarianism, corruption] or economic [internal and external deficits, low investment, inflation, food insecurity], have derived from a non-dynamic domestic economy, which has been underpinned by an agrarian sector wherein only a privileged few could generate wealth. The dismantlement of state protection under the SAP comprised no structural remedy: rather, as the sought after export panacea proved elusive, if not unattainable, the program only amplified the shortcomings of the existing order. Crucially, the national food economy seriously deteriorated—in the skewed agrarian context, market liberalisation presided over a deepening crisis of food production and entitlement. Unlike in other liberalised mass-peasant economies of the world, because of the more brutal form of colonialism experienced, the Zimbabwean peasantry mostly lacked a subsistence base to fall back on. This predicament formed the crux upon which the country revisited liberation politics.

The experience of ZANU-PF under the SAP proved cathartic. As the alliance with foreign capital backfired and the MDC assumed the role of Western patron, the state bourgeoisie reacquainted itself with the liberation agenda. True, crude power ambition underlined the left-wing move but then, radical land reform actually promises to better serve the country in the long run. Indeed, as has always been argued, a dynamic linkage between agrarian change and industrial growth offers the best prospect to overcome the real source of economic and political ills, namely, the skewed wealth base. As per the outlined state-led scenario, a dual land reform—upon a healthier food economy alone—could form the nucleus of a positive domestic multiplier that strengthens forces of supply and demand toward overcoming the stagflation crisis. Therein, democratic development emanates from an autonomous indigenous economic base, which creates the material opportunities for the emergence of a more 'rational' state—one that is less prone to corruption, patrimonial rule or the imperatives of foreign capital.

Of course, the present situation of fast-track resettlement appears to be falling well short of the ideal. According to Western papers, ZANU-PF rewards high-up officials with farms while peasant militias are clearing and ploughing acquired land at will. If so, this is contrary the strategic approach advocated, which should retain productive white farmers, allow the market to allocate subdivided freehold land and ensure that land annexed for communal purposes be subject to elected and truly empowered village bodies that will help ensure sustainable subsistence exploitation. Of more immediate and alarming concern, however, are reports that amid the effects of drought and the collapse of the large-scale sector, ZANU-PF is monopolising food for political purposes. If so, such reveals the critical depth of the crisis wherein a desperate state bourgeoisie will give no quarter to an opposition labelled a Western obstruction of African emancipation.

Zimbabwe is in urgent need of a legitimate political solution to forever settle the land question. Until then, there is no foreseeable hope of restoring the rule of law and democratic electoral processes, let alone attaining an upward development path. Toward a legitimate resolution, acceptance by the Western development community of immediate and comprehensive land redistribution as the number one priority and practical assistance in the form of a land fund and project expertise would go a long way. In turn, constructive engagement requires a sympathetic understanding of the structural origins of the crisis and the infeasibility—at least over the short term—of imposing free market and good governance aid conditions on an impoverished country in turmoil. In all likelihood, if the US and UK offered ZANU-PF a carrot to secure historical recognition through permanent resolution of the national question, Zimbabwe would gain a consensual political base to hold a free and fair election and, over the longer term, greater discretion to liberalise the economy.

Instead, however, Western states continue to demonise Mr Mugabe, which the Organisation of African Unity and African members of the British Commonwealth have criticised for destabilising the country [see *The Age*, 15/03/02, 18/03/02]. Clearly, the approach seeks to encourage the MDC, which promises to restore past property rights as well as the planks of neo-liberalism—'good governance' and 'sensible economic policy'. But what, though, is really on offer for the majority of Zimbabweans? In all likelihood, a truncated democracy in which another authoritarian government again centres the macroeconomic regime on a minority of tradable enterprises to secure international credit and debt repayments.

Meanwhile, propelled by an endless cycle of currency depreciation, imported inflation, tight monetary policy and state fiscal rationalisation, an unresolved stagflation crisis will continue to impoverish majority livelihood. Without thorough agrarian reform, tinkering with fiscal and monetary policy offers no lasting escape—only affirmation of a severe under-consumption and under-employment equilibrium. The aforementioned 'social contract' holds more promise to arrest the inflation spiral but again, without a legitimate political resolution of the agrarian question, there is no chance of implementing it.

The African writer, Chinua Achebe, who calls himself a 'missionary in reverse', once reprimanded a group of Western bankers in Paris:

> You talk about structural adjustment as if Africa was some kind of

> laboratory... But Africa is people! [cited *The Guardian Weekly*, 3/01/01]

The remark is a reaction to the present separation of economics from social reality. This dangerous disparity stems from the dominance of a free market ideological paradigm, which in effect treats the world as a domain of Western capital. Although claiming otherwise, the policies undermine the social wage in many developing countries. For the time being, globalisation is delivering benefits to the West but ultimately, increased world impoverishment threatens the survival of capitalism and democracy. There is much to fear from indebted countries in misery—hostile political movements, war, unwanted refugees and disease. Conversely, there is little to fear and much to gain from more dynamic economies, even if based on state protection.

To reverse the unfolding tragedy between North and South, a key priority is to allow each nation to choose its own path to economic growth and development. In turn, as a petition circulated by a group of French university students recently recognised, such a step entails rescuing 'economics from its autistic and socially irresponsible state' [cited in *The Age*, 22/12/00; *The Australian*, 6-7/01/01]. In other words, the ideological hold of neo-liberalism on economics must cease—after all, the subject is about the history of ideas. No single school of thought, whether classical, Marxist or Keynesian, has a universal monopoly over what is right. The Rhodesian economist, John Handford, got one point right:

> Pragmatism—that is the key to it all—a philosophy based on the concept that the wisdom of an approach is to be judged by its practical consequences [1976:6].

Zimbabwe presents an opportunity for the West to rethink African development policy and improve relations with the continent. The overriding imperative is to resolve the land issue, which will set the political and economic conditions for an upward development path. As the crisis stands, the clock will never be turned back. The Rhodesian legacy of a commercially secluded and underutilised agrarian base is gone and gone forever. Western states could help ensure that the upheaval is for the sake of basic needs, industrial growth and democracy, which will be to the benefit of Africa and ultimately, their own societies.

Notes

1 – Rhodesian Political Economy, 1890–1962

[1] 'A fight to the finish' is not an exaggerated expression if applied to the Australian Aborigines or the Indians of North, Central or South America.

[2] As a modernisation theorist, Robert Brenner argues that a country's domestic class structure carries a more critical influence than global market forces on the extent of balanced development. Global market forces tend only to entrench the existing domestic class structure, which of itself impacts decisively on the extent of investment capitalisation and equality in resource distribution and, therefore, the overall potential for endogenous economic development. He writes referring to the plantation economies of the Caribbean:

> This is not to deny that there was a long-term transfer of surplus away from the periphery, it is to root this in a different dynamic. Thus it was the characteristic feature of the forced labour systems that their difficulties in developing the productivity of labour through the application of fixed capital were more than 'counterbalanced' by their success in reducing the costs of labour through reducing the subsistence of the workforce. As a result, the market for capital goods was limited and the market for consumer goods was similarly cut down, while there arose significant demand for luxuries by the ruling class [1977:84-85].

[3] The Column was composed of 500 mounted soldiers and 200 settlers each of whom Rhodes promised 3000 acres of land and up to 15 gold claims in Mashonaland. From the growing trading centre of Bulawayo, the Column established Fort Victoria [Masvingo], Fort Charter [Chivhu] and further north Fort Salisbury [Harare]—a route that followed the central watershed area of the Zimbabwean plateau, containing the prime natural regions. The term 'colonial belt' refers to the main economic artery of the country developed in the wake of the pioneer column—the farms, towns, rail, roads and telegraph that soon linked Rhodesia to the world economy via the Beira Corridor to the Mozambican coast, and via Beitbridge and Plumtree to South Africa.

[4] Lippert had managed to persuade Lobengula to sign this concession, which gave him sole rights to issue European land titles within BSAC territory [Rasmussen, R.K., and Rubert, S.C., 1990:167]. He betrayed Lobengula by selling the concession to the BSAC.
[5] Introduced in 1894, the hut tax amounted to 10 shillings per household and 10 shillings for each extra wife beyond the first.
[6] The white population was estimated at 1,500 in 1891 [Rasmussen, R.K., and Rubert, S.C., 1990:93], which rose to 11,000 by 1901 [Appendix One].
[7] According to Elizabeth Schmidt [1996:67] although maize was grown as a cash crop, millet continued as the staple food because the labour demands upon women of grinding millet were a lot less than maize. Maize became the staple food with the advent of grinding mills in the 1930s. Giovanni Arrighi [1973a:203-204] records that in the period 1905–21 African cattle increased from 114,560 to 854,000 head while the number of ploughs rose from 440 to 16,900.
[8] Charles van Onselen [1976:106-114] outlines the strategies of *chibaro*, meaning forced labour, used by the Rhodesian Native Labour Board. All preyed upon less fortunate people by getting them in debt through paying their tax, providing food, clothing or transport in exchange for labour. The Rhodesian Pass Laws were also important as they sought to stop the drain of local labour heading to South Africa for higher wages. Rhodesia though continued to remain a poor labour-recruiting field for the mining industry and settler agriculture until the mid-1920s. 'Even in the best year for local labour, 1911,' Charles van Onselen [1976:101] notes, 'local labour only accounted for 14,000 relatively short-term workers of the [mining] industry's 38,000 black workers'. After 1922, however, Giovanni Arrighi observes [1973a:191], local African labour was increasingly available 'irrespective of whether real wages were falling, rising or remaining constant'.
[9] A land bank was established in 1912, which provided loans of up to £2,000.
[10] Examples include the doubling of hut tax [1904], Private Locations Ordinance [1908], African Beer Ordinance [1912], Dog tax [1912], land rent, cattle dipping and grazing fees.
[11] Giovanni Arrighi [1973a:204] notes '30% of the land assigned to Africans—as against 75% of that alienated to Europeans—was within 25 miles of a railway line', which seriously undermined the profitability of African agriculture.
[12] As early as the mid-1890s, partly as a result of Rhodes's own personal friendships, the two British owned international banks, Standard Chartered and Barclays, were established in Rhodesia [Bond, P., 1998:43,53].
[13] By the time of the Land Apportionment Act, Africans had purchased 43,000 acres compared to the 31,000,000 acres by Europeans [Arrighi, G., 1973b:338] yet regardless, if located on designated white land, black freehold farmers would be moved to the more marginal African Purchase Areas.
[14] Patrick Bond [1998:63] informs that in 1936 [the first year when data was recorded] Standard and Barclays held just 50% of their assets in local loans—the rest were held in external balances. Local loans from these foreign banks were generally of a short term and low risk nature not for fixed capital formation.
[15] Total mineral exports increased from a low of £3.1 million in 1931, to £3.9 million in 1932, and to £6.5 million by 1935. Gold accounted for 80% of mining

exports and 66% of total exports in 1933 and about 37% of production, at this stage, was foreign owned [Bond P., 1998:51].

[16] To the acrimony of economic nationalists in opposition, Moffat chose to purchase the country's mineral rights off the BSAC for £2 million in June 1933.

[17] The colonial board system forced Rhodesia to maintain 100% foreign exchange cover for its local currency in London through Standard and Barclays. The linking of money supply growth to the amount of foreign exchange, according to Patrick Bond [1998–80], 'unnecessarily transmitted and amplified global financial fluctuations to the local markets'. Unregulated capital flows were causing economic instability in the early and late 1950s, which prompted the state to assert controls.

[18] The Farmers Debt Adjustment Act sought to relieve the debt burden of white farmers through interest rate subsidies, cancellation of fees and deferred loan repayment.

[19] The substitution of maize for the traditional crops of millet and sweet potatoes was more land extensive as was the plough's replacement of the hoe.

[20] In 1926 the African population was recorded at 936,000 living off a land area estimated to be capable of carrying 940,000 people under the traditional shifting system of agriculture [Government of Southern Rhodesia, 1955:1]. Over the 1930–45 period, the reserve population is estimated to have increased from about 1 million to about 1.4 million [Rasmussen, R.K., and Rubert, S.C., 1990:282]. In 1944 the reserve cattle herd totalled 927,000 yet the area's carrying capacity was estimated to be 645,000 head [Government of Southern Rhodesia, 1955:2].

[21] The World Bank lent the Rhodesian Government US$80 million in the mid-1950s to construct the Kariba dam, which had a total cost of £114 million. The hydro scheme served the power needs of both Northern and Southern Rhodesia but tragically, 56,000 people from the Batonka community who lived on the Zambezi River lost their land [Bond, P., 1998:73].

[22] In 1952, according to John Handford [1976:131], there were 725 manufacturing enterprises in Rhodesia employing 68,000 people. Manufacturing employment rose to 75,000 by 1960 and the value of net output reached about £60 million per annum. The total number of manufacturing employees was under the 240,000 recorded in agriculture and the 94,000 in domestic service but over the 52,000 employed in mining [Handford, J., 1976:133; Astrow, A., 1983:49].

[23] The number of mining employees peaked at 93,700 in 1937 and gradually declined to 73,600 in 1945 to stabilise at around the 50,000 mark of today [Clarke, D.G., 1980:23].

[24] One of the earliest reports on food security in African areas [Nutrition Council Report of 1957/58] noted 'widespread malnutrition' [cited in Moyo, S., Moyo, N.P. and Lowenson, R., 1985:11-13].

[25] The Central African Federation incorporated both Northern and Southern Rhodesia and Nyasaland. Largely at the behest of Southern Rhodesia, the motives behind its emergence were primarily economic—an expanded national market, a share in the wealth of the Zambian Copperbelt and an improved investment climate. The Federal Government had no authority over the constitutional

advances within its constituent territories. Once Britain granted independence to Northern Rhodesia and Nyasaland in late 1962 the Federation dissolved—officially on 31 December 1963 [Rasmussen, R.K., and Rubert, S.C., 1990:95-97].

[26] The state-run Native Development Fund provided loans, which rose from £5,000 in 1958–1959 to £40,000 by1961–1962. In 1961, some 26 companies including banks and agro-chemical concerns founded the African Loan and Development Company with a capital base of £250,000 [Bond, P., 1998:95].

[27] Despite the passing of two bank acts in 1956 and 1959, which empowered the Federation's central bank, the Bank of Rhodesia and Nyasaland, to impose formal credit controls, the Government still remained reluctant.

[28] William Duggan [1980:231] points out, however, that the Native Development Fund established in 1948, which received revenue from a 10% tax on all goods marketed by African farmers, accounted for nearly 50% of expenditure on African agriculture. In large part, according to Martin and Johnson [1981:59], Africans also funded their own education through a £1 annual tax on every black male and the fundraising of parents.

2 – The Skewed Fortune of the UDI Economy

[1] A key factor underlying the ZAPU split was disenchantment over Joshua Nkomo's leadership, particularly his preference to establish a government in exile. Ndabaningi Sithole, Robert Mugabe and Leopold Takawire, among the leading founders of ZANU, promised a strategy of internal organisation and political action within the country. ZAPU continued to have a strong Shona base after the split until ZANU's military tactics in the 1970s came to dominate the northeast of the country, the Shona heartland, which left ZAPU its Ndebele stronghold in the southwest. According to Astrow [1983:127-144,168], ethnic tensions began to emerge over the war burden, which ZANU predominately carried. As power loomed closer, 'petty bourgeois' rivalry amongst political leaders increasingly fuelled tensions especially between military wings. Once ZANU resumed power in 1980 Robert Mugabe offered an 'olive branch' to the ZAPU hierarchy. In the context of South African 'destabilisation', however, the Ndebele dissident outbreak soon resulted in an ethnic war in which many Ndebele innocents were massacred.

[2] After dissolution of the Federation on December 31 1963, the Reserve Bank came into existence on May 22 1964. In 1970 the Government decimalised the currency, making the new dollar equivalent to one-half a former Rhodesian pound. The Rhodesian Government ironically forced Britain to service the debt to the World Bank [Handford, J., 1976:50]. Corporate private debt continued to be serviced by the companies concerned. The default on public debt carried a long-term cost in increased liabilities, which the independent Government of Zimbabwe inherited.

[3] The Byrd Amendment, passed by US Congress in November 1971, prevented the US from banning the imports of strategic minerals from any non-communist

country providing such materials were being imported from communist countries. Thus, irrespective of UN sanctions, the US could import chrome from Rhodesia because such was already being imported from the USSR. Apart from chrome, the amendment legalised other Rhodesian exports such as nickel, asbestos and, at least, 20 other minerals. After intense lobbying the Carter administration in 1977 managed to persuade Congress to repeal the amendment.

[4] In 1973, for example, there were no fewer than 68 Trade Union leaders in detention [Sachikonye, L., 1986, cited in Bond, P., 1998:124].

[5] The main actors in food and beverages included Lyons [UK], Liebigs [UK], Delta Corporation [UK-SA], National Canners [UK], Heinz [USA], Cadbury-Schweppes [UK], OK bazaars [SA], Pick 'n' Pay [SA] and Anglo-American Corporation [SA]. In regard to cement, tiles, glass, timber, paper and matches, Salisbury Portland Cement Co [SA], Ceramic Holdings [SA], IPCORN [UK-SA], Tanganyika Concessions Ltd [UK], the Rhodesian Pulp and Paper Co [SA], Umtali Board and Paper Mills Ltd [UK] and the Lion Match Co. [UK] dominated. In metals, chemicals and pharmaceuticals big multinationals include Johnson and Johnson [USA], International Harvester [USA], Massey Ferguson [Canada], Goodyear Tyre and Rubber Co. [USA], Hochst [Germany], Kodak [USA] and Union Carbide American Metal Climax [USA] [All data here is cited in Tandon, Y., 1990:83-87 and Stoneman, C., 1978:70-71].

[6] The 1969 republican constitution, which established a House of Assembly, Senate and office of President, granted Africans 16 seats out of a total of 66 in the Lower House. A further increase in African representation would only be granted when the African tax contribution exceeded 24% of income tax revenue. At just 0.6% in 1968–1969 the attainment of Parliamentary democracy in Rhodesia was put off indefinitely. The African contribution through indirect tax [i.e. sales tax, custom duties, excise duties] and education and health fees—estimated at 15% of total revenue in 1969—was not taken into account [Handford, J., 1976:54-55].

[7] The purpose of TILCOR was to locate growth points in African rural areas and stimulate the development of secondary industry. Successful enterprises included the Katiyo Tea Estates in the Honde Valley, Seke industrial estates near Chitungwiza and agricultural estates at Sanyati, Chisumbanje and Jotsholo [Handford, J., 1976:60-61; Rukuni, M., 1994:29].

[8] The SR 52 won first prize in 1971 at the Royal Agricultural Fair in Toronto, Canada. The seed was not suitable for the drier African areas but the triple hybrid seed R201 had an impact in these areas from the late 1960s [Rukuni, M., 1994:28-29]. Other agricultural breakthroughs during the UDI included higher yielding groundnut seeds, improved winter wheat varieties and rust resistant wheat.

[9] For many white farmers, particularly those upon light sandy soils such as around Karoi and Centenary, tobacco was considered the only worthwhile crop. It could take four hectares of cotton and maize, for instance, to generate the same revenue as one hectare of tobacco [Handford, J.,1976:100].

[10] Rhodesia's oil bill trebled between 1973 and 1977 [Riddell, R., 1990:352]. Petrol rationing was introduced under the slogan 'Don't drive Rhodesia dry' [See Godwin, P., and Hancock, I., 1993:136]. In the late 1970s, Ian Smith commissioned the construction of

an ethanol plant at the Triangle Estate to produce fuel from sugar cane. The oil import bill was subsequently reduced from 29% of total import value in 1979 back to 22% in 1981 [Mlambo, A., 1997:42].

[11] African school places increased by about 116,000 per year between 1970 and 1974 and the financial years 1973–74 and 1974–75 saw a 25 percent increase in revenue [Handford, J., 1976:183,184]. Vocational or Technical schools, known as F2, which were non-academic and seen as sub-standard by Africans, were introduced in 1966 and numbered 56 by 1975.

[12] When the South African Rand devalued in December 1971 and again in October 1972, the pressure to follow suit was intense. The parity of the Rhodesian dollar to the Rand [Rh$1.00 = R1.19] and to the US dollar [Rh$1.00 = US1.73c] remained fixed, however. Handford [1976:33-34] notes that the June 1973 edition of the *Rhodesian Journal of Economics* outlines the pros and cons of the issue. Following further devaluation of the Rand in 1975 and deterioration in the terms of trade, the Rhodesian currency was eventually devalued by about 18% over the second half of the 1970s [Table 2.4].

[13] Patrick Bond [1998:130] comments on the disarticulation between production and consumption:

> UDI-era manufacturers placed exorbitant emphasis on luxury goods production for the domestic white market, rather than expanding into extensive low-cost basic consumer goods which might have helped generate increased buying power in the process and which would have had greater export potential into independent Africa.

[14] About 2,000 farms, over several million acres, had been abandoned by 1979 and cattle rustling reached alarming proportions as did cattle disease in the reserves due to the breakdown in dipping services. Between April and November of 1979 total net livestock losses on commercial farms were in the region of 47,118 - 64,796 [Godwin, P., and Hancock, I., 1993:251]. In April 1978, the Chamber of Mines terminated all mining exploration.

[15] Assistant Secretary of State, Dean Acheson, when testifying before a Congressional committee on post-war economic policy in November 1944, spoke candidly:

> If you wish to control the entire trade and income of the US, which means the life of the people, you could probably fix it so that everything produced here would be consumed here, but that would completely change our Constitution, our relations to property, human liberty, our very conception of law. And nobody contemplates that. Therefore, you find you must look to other markets and those markets are abroad... .we cannot have full employment and prosperity in the US without foreign markets. That is point one [cited in Williams, W.A., 1972:237].

[16] The two other 'internal' nationalist parties, which formed part of the executive council and contested the April 1979 election, were the African National Council

[Sithole], led by Ndabaningi Sithole, and the Zimbabwe United People's Organisation [ZUPO], led by Chief Jeremiah Chirau. About 64.5% of the eligible electorate voted in the election. Abel Muzorewa's UANC won 68% of the vote and a majority of 51 seats out of 100 while the ANC [Sithole] fell a distant second and ZUPO did not win a seat. Whites were guaranteed 28 seats and, as mentioned, the key strategic portfolios [All data from Rasmussen, R.K., and Rubert, S.C., 1990:137-138].

3 – The African Experience of SAPs and the Global Debate

[1] The aim of social protection, according to Polanyi [1944:132], is 'the conservation of man and nature as well as productive organisation' while that of economic liberalism 'a self-regulating market'. Tradable goods refers to export items while non-tradable goods refers to non-export items consumed locally.

[2] The Report also noted that US$40 billion from the personal fortune of the world's richest man, Bill Gates, the Director of Microsoft, which totaled about $50 billion, would be enough to achieve and maintain universal access to basic education, health care, safe water and sanitation [cited in *The Age*, 12/09/98].

[3] The Africa Policy Information Center [APIC] is an educational affiliate of the Washington Office on Africa and seeks to 'widen the policy debate in the US on African issues'. Data is gathered from a range of sources worldwide and sent, via email, to all subscribers. For more information about APIC, either visit the web site - http://www.africapolicy.org – or send an auto response email to apic-info@igc.org

[4] Both scholars were among the group who founded the Mont Pelerin Society in April 1947, which had a declared mission to counteract Keynesian style ISI policies and install monetarist principles in economic management. Sponsored by banks and financiers, later by the US and UK, the society was responsible for setting up, by 1991, 78 free market 'think tanks' worldwide, such as the Adam Smith Institute, The Heritage Foundation, and forging relationships with 81 institutes in 51 countries [Wheelwright, T., 1995:41-44; see also Cockett, P., 1994].

[5] An all-African initiative, the ADB Group was established in 1963 with the aim of promoting African self-reliance through the provision of non-concessional loans. Although keen to retain an 'African identity', the weak capacity of African members to pay financial subscriptions forced the ADB to court members and capital from the industrialised world. The resort to 'policy-based' adjustment lending in 1986 reflected this dependency, which in turn has invoked criticism that the ADB is a small replica of the World Bank. For a history and full discussion of these issues see E. Philip English and Harris M. Mule, *The African Development Bank* [1996].

[6] Conversely, Asian, Latin American and East European countries increased their share of world commodity markets. For example, South East Asia increasingly

dominated markets for cocoa beans, coffee and timber while Latin America and Eastern Europe that of iron ore and cotton respectively.

[7] Graham Bird [1996:494] also notes that between 1988 and 1990 out of the 39 IMF SAPs negotiated, 72% broke down.

[8] The World Bank's World Development Report for 1986, according to Colin Leys [1996:80], adopted the thought of Robert Bates 'wholly, summarising it word for word on page 92'.

[9] The Structural Adjustment Review Initiative [SAPRI] is funded by the World Bank with the aim of generating a grassroots review of SAPs in the eight countries selected. These are Ghana, Mali, Uganda, Zimbabwe, El Salvador, Ecuador, Bangladesh and Hungary. In each country, the ultimate goal is to reach a consensus between civil society, the Government and the World Bank about SAPs. The Development Group for Alternative Policies [Development GAP] in Washington functions as the secretariat of the Structural Adjustment Participatory Review International Network [SAPRIN]. For more information about the procedures and protocol of SAPRI as well as in-country progress visit the Development GAP's web site [http://www.igc.org/dgap] or that of the World Bank [http://www.worldbank.org/research/sapri/index.htm] or the SAPRIN site itself [http://www.saprin.org].

[10] The extent of US involvement in Chile is revealed in recently released CIA documents [See *The Guardian Weekly*, 23/11/00; and *The Age*, 15/11/00].

[11] In the late 1970s, the Zambian Government commenced a turbulent relationship with the IMF. Several SAPs were initially implemented and then abandoned in a context of great socioeconomic stress. In mid-1991, as part of a renewed attempt to fulfil IFI conditionalities, the Kaunda Government phased out maize subsidies and doubled the price of maize meal. In subsequent riots 27 people lost their lives. The Movement for Multi-Party Democracy, led by Trade Union leader Frederick Chiluba, on a platform of economic mismanagement, was elected to power in October 1991. The aid freeze was lifted by the IFIs and the Chiluba Government went on to pursue the same policies of civil service retrenchment and economic liberalisation that finished Kaunda's reign [Chakaodza, A.M., 1993:35-42]. Currently, one quarter of the national annual budget is spent on debt repayments and the manufacturing sector is reported to have collapsed [See *The Guardian Weekly*, 18/01/01].

[12] Under IFI adjustment, Ecuador's economy failed to stabilise. Out of a population of twelve million people, seven million are classified poor and of these about four million are native Indians. In early January 2000, President Mahuad announced a plan to 'dollarise' the sucre as a way to end the devastating cycle of devaluation and inflation— the rate of the latter was running at 60%. Two weeks later, in fear that their savings would be made worthless, thousands of Indians were allowed to break through military barricades and seize congress. A three-man junta, led by Colonel Gutierrez, Chief Justice Solorzano and Indian activist Vargas, ruled Ecuador for the next five hours during which President Mahaud resigned. In response to threats by US officials to isolate the country and sensing division in the military, a General by the name of Mendoza dissolved the

junta. Vice-president Noboa became Ecuador's sixth President in four years. He immediately announced that the dollarisation of the currency would go ahead [*The Australian*, 24/01/00; *The Age*, 24/01/00; *The Guardian Weekly*, 27/01/00].

[13] For example, property rights comprised major themes of the 1987 and 1996 World Development Report[s]. Frederick Cooper [1993:199, footnote 5] observes that the arguments of rational choice are often left 'dangling'. He cites the example of Goran Hyden's No Shortcuts to Progress [1983], which identifies an 'economy of affection' and a lack of property rights as major economic constraints but fails to advocate a capitalist reorganisation of the peasantry even though this is the logical implication.

[14] The 10 African countries selected in the Sahn, Dorosh, and Younger study were Cameroon, Gambia, Ghana, Guinea, Madagascar, Malawi, Mozambique, Niger, Tanzania and the Democratic Republic of Congo. The fact that the research was funded by USAID questions the academic integrity of the work. The free market ideological position of USAID and its willingness to use loan conditionality to enforce it is well known [See Moore, D., 1995:19-20]. Most likely the authors may not have had the research autonomy to bite the hand that feeds them.

[15] Indeed, as from 2001, the US is required by a provision in the Foreign Appropriations Bill, passed by Congress in late October 2000, to oppose any loan from either the IMF or World Bank that makes the imposition of 'user fees' on basic health and education services conditional. This is a significant and long overdue concession that such measures worsen poverty. For more information, contact the Washington based Globalisation Challenge Initiative by email: global.challenge@juno.com or visit the web site:www.challengeglobalization.org

[16] Official guidelines identified 'labourers, cleaners, charwomen, drivers, stewards, cooks, porters, sweepers, messengers and security personnel' as the dispensable employees [Jonah, K., cited in Logan, B.I., and Mengisteab, K., 1993:20].

[17] In a belated admission, President Clinton made this departing comment: 'If the wealthiest countries ended our agricultural subsidies, leveling the playing field for the world's farmers, that alone would increase the income of developing countries by $20 billion a year' [cited in *The Guardian Weekly*, 18/01/01].

[18] The Congressional Record referred to in Ould-Mey's article originated from US Senator, Larry Pressler, and is titled 'Opening Markets for US Wheat' [29/04/93, p.S5100]. He observed that 'in 1991, total US agricultural exports to Africa totalled $1.9 billion. In 1992 that total had risen to $2.6 billion—a 35% increase'.

[19] The 1992 World Investment Report, released by the UN, revealed that during the 1980s over 80% of foreign direct investment went to industrialised countries. Asia's share remained steady at about 10%, Latin America's share declined from 14% to 5% while Africa's share declined from 3% to barely 1% [cited in George, S., and Sabelli, F., 1994:90-91].

[20] A Danish Government study in the late 1990s [the exact year is unknown] on the Rwandan tragedy titled 'The International Response to Conflict and Genocide: lessons from the Rwanda experience' agreed with this statement by

Colin Leys. Mohameden Ould-Mey [1995:147] also comments on the SAP in Rwanda that preceded the tragedy.

[21] Under the changes, foreigners had to obtain approval to convert the Malaysian ringgit into foreign exchange and all assets in shares were subject to a 12-month freeze. The controls were considered temporary and would be lifted once the market stabilised. A year later, the 12-month freeze on foreign share assets was replaced by a flat exit tax of 10% but the currency peg and the ban on international trading remained [*The Australian*, 29.09/99].

[22] In contrast to Thailand and the Philippines, which experienced sharp rises of foreign direct investment in 1998 of 80% and 40% respectively, flows to Malaysia fell by 40% and remained flat in 1999 [The Australian, 15/06/00].

[23] Malaysia is South Africa's second largest foreign investor, for example, and the state-owned petroleum company, Petronas, is the single largest investor in the country. Other major Malaysian investment destinations are Chile, Indonesia and West Africa.

[24] In 1991, when Chief Economist of the World Bank, Larry Summers wrote the famous toxic memo, reading—'the economic logic behind dumping a load of toxic waste in the lowest wage country is impeccable' [cited in George, S., and Sabelli, F., 1994:99].

4 – The Demise of a Macroeconomic Compromise

[1] In addition, the Employment Act of 1980 vested the right to fire workers in the Minister of Labour and set the rate of remuneration for casual labour double that of permanent employees.

[2] I derive this figure by adding the 2.7 million hectares actually redistributed from the commercial sector during the 1980s and the 3.5 million hectares the World Bank [1991] claimed were underutilised in 1990. Sam Moyo [1995:92-95] points out that commercial output was not adversely affected by land redistribution in the 1980s and the World Bank's 1990 figure was very sensitive to this possibility.

[3] The Land Tenure Commission [GoZ/LTC, 1994:70, 85] noted that the small-scale commercial sector consistently failed during the 1980s to out yield communal and resettlement areas. Poor crop management, remoteness and the limited farming experience of heirs were cited as the main constraints. The relatively high incidence of polygamy within the sector, [See Cheater, A.P., 1986:69; Gaidzanwa, R.B., 1988:4] by discouraging the use of wage labour, should also be considered an obstacle toward the development of capitalist productive forces.

[4] In his most widely read work—*Progress and Poverty*—Henry George [1839-1897] argued for a 'single tax' to capture the market appreciation of land value, sometimes referred to as the *produit net* [Galbraith, J.K., 1987:53-54, 166-169]. Because rises in land value attributed largely to population increases and public investment in infrastructure, George argued that the public through the state had a bigger right to any speculative gain than individual owners.

[5] With assistance from the World Bank, an ex-staff member of the World Bank established the Whitsun Foundation in 1974 as a policy think-tank. In response to the Government's announcement to resettle 162,000 families, the Foundation wrote in a 1983 report that 'this would strike at the productive core of commercial agriculture ...' [cited in Weiner, D., Moyo, S., Munslow, B., and O'Keefe, P., 1984:19].

[6] The speculative boom eventually crashed and the SAP proved the catalyst. Once interest rates were hiked in February 1991 and again in September, within the next nine months, share prices fell by 65% and city land values by 45%. 'Many billions of Zimbabwe dollars', Bond writes [1998:225], ' paper investments, but nevertheless representing the life savings of many hundreds of thousands of people—essentially went up in flames'. These included pension funds that had been invested on the ZSE, which left many retrenched workers in the early 1990s without redundancy packages.

[7] During demobilisation and the formation of the Zimbabwe Defence Force, dissident elements within ZIPRA remained at large. In November 1980 and February 1981, 'the last major actions of the war' were fought between Ndebele and Shona soldiers at Entumbane camp near Bulawayo [Beach, D.,1994:183]. In December 1981, a bomb meant for the Central Committee went off at ZANU headquarters in Harare and by February, arms caches were found on ZAPU property. Former ZIPRA commanders were then arrested and ZAPU members of Cabinet including Joshua Nkomo were sacked.

[8] Model A resettlement schemes refer to family holdings comprised of five arable hectares, a small residential plot and access to common grazing—usually about 10 to 30 hectares per household depending on the natural region. Model B schemes were collectivised large-scale farms mainly reserved for ex-combatants and ex-farm workers wherein members were suppose to farm cooperatively and share profits. By the late 1980s, hampered by community feuds, high turnover and lack of productive resources [GoZ/LTC, 1994:61], model B schemes were being de-collectivised through subdivision [Moyo, S., 1995:265]. Model C refers to household out grower schemes on state farms run by the Agricultural Development Authority [ADA], which involved no more than 847 settlers [GoZ/LTC, 1994 vol.1:58]. Model D refers to extensive ranching schemes, located mainly in Matabeleland South, which were attached to communal areas and used on a rotational basis. Implementation was hampered by the dissident outbreak in the early 1980s and did not move much beyond the experimental stage.

[9] The Ministry of Land, Resettlement and Rural Development was dissolved in 1983 and merged with Agriculture to become the Ministry of Lands, Agriculture and Rural Resettlement. The key body in implementing resettlement—the Department of Rural Development [DERUDE]—was then transferred in 1984 to the Ministry of Local Government, Rural and Urban Development and in 1995 merged with the District Development Fund [DDF]—the construction wing of District Councils [Mhishi, S.G., 1995:7; GoZ/LTC, vol.1 1994:59-60; Masuko, L. and Nyoni, D., 1993:5].

[10] VIDCOs and WARDCOs resulted from a 1984 Prime Ministerial directive entitled 'Structures of Village Development Committees, Ward Development Committees and Extension Services', otherwise referred to as 'Prime Minister's

Second Directive on Decentralisation'. VIDCOs compose six members, four elected from 100 households, and two representing youth and women's organisations. The Chairman and Secretary from six VIDCOs and two women and youth representatives make up a WARDCO.

[11] To make labour amenable to a corporatist solution, the Government centralised the union movement in 1980 under the Zimbabwe Congress of Trade Unions [ZCTU], which in 1990 recorded a membership of 250,000 [Raftopoulous, B., 1992 No. 55:58-59]. The Labour Relations Act of 1985 banned strikes in 'essential services' but retained restrictions on labour dismissal. It also set up a collective bargaining system at three levels: the national level [Wage and Salaries Advisory Boards]; the industry level [employment boards and councils]; and the shop floor/firm level. During the 1980s, most negotiations occurred at the industry level while into the 1990s under the SAP, the main negotiating arena shifted down to the shop floor level [Kanyenze, G., 1996:55; Sachikonye, L.M., 1995a:64; UNDP/PRF/IDS, 1998:27].

[12] Food subsidies over 1982–1983 were reduced from 7.7% of total state spending to the 5.3%, which immediately translated into a 100% hike in the price of maize-meal, 30% for bread and 25% for cooking oil [Davis, R., and Sanders, D., 1987:9, cited in Bond, P., 1998:346]. In line with IMF and World Bank demands for SOEs to reduce their deficits, the costs of fuel, electricity, steel and transport went up simultaneously.

[13] After 1983 the Government adopted a two-tier exchange rate, which applied an official rate on the import of goods and more of market rate on the export of goods. According to Riddell [1990:377], the policy was to the benefit of the manufacturing sector: internally, a higher exchange rate minimised import costs and inflationary pressures, thus stimulating domestic demand, while externally, a lower exchange rate stimulated export demand. From mid-decade, import consumption fell by at least 35% [Lehman, H., 1990:59] and shortages of imported inputs forced several companies, such as Hunyani Paper and Packaging, Circle Cement and Leyland Zimbabwe, to close temporarily [Kadenge, P., Ndoro, H., and Zwizwai, B., 1992:172]. Others were forced into a dangerous reliance on worn out equipment: use of old tyres, for example, caused a number of tragic bus accidents. Such calamities probably reflected less an acute exchange shortage than a political problem of allocation. For city property development, for example, there seemed no shortage of foreign exchange—over 75% of applications were granted [Bond, P., 1998:241]. In 1986, the Government eased the restrictions on capital repatriation: companies were allowed to remit up to 50% of after-tax profit on investments made prior to 1979. In May 1987, however, this margin was reduced to 25% but for investments made after 1980 the margin remained 50% [Chakaodza, A.M.,1993:61].

[14] Over 1982–1983, as input costs rose following currency devaluation and subsidy removals on public utilities, the Government tightened price control and awarded increases below what was required to accommodate rising costs. Declining real wages after 1982 eased the resulting profit squeeze: by 1990, as shown in Table 4.6, real wages in all sectors were below their 1982 peak and remained above 1980 levels only in agriculture, mining and manufacturing. To reduce costs and improve profit levels, many enterprises re-organised production

lines, invested in staff training, increased their product range and more vigorously pursued export markets [Riddell, R.C., 1990:355].

[15] In regard to the World Bank's loan to replenish Zimbabwe's rail network [IBRD 3277], local companies received only 7% of contracts [Bond, P., 1998:358] while a similar bias was evident in the loan [IBRD 3274] to upgrade the Hwange thermal power plant. Foreign consultants with a track record are often employed to write Bank reports. The event highlighted by Bond [1998:301, footnote 12, 364-65] was the Government's refusal to spend US$7.5 million of the Bank's housing loan [IBRD 3278] on such a purpose.

[16] The loan to expand the Hwange power plant [IBRD 3274] called upon ZESA to raise retail prices by 60%. 'The result', writes Bond [1998:355], 'was a flat energy consumption growth rate for 1981–1984, by comparison with a 9% annual growth for 1971–1981'.

[17] The Small Enterprise Development Corporation [SEDCO] was established in the early 1980s as a credit agency to assist African entrepreneurs. Through a US$10 million loan [IBRD 3279] , the World Bank successfully demanded that SEDCO lift interest rates from 14.3% to 18% and de-emphasise lending to cooperatives in order for them to 'rationalise their operations' and meet the demands of 'fair competition' [Bond, P., 1990:11].

[18] To assess a country's comparative advantage, the DRC method measures the cost in domestic resources of earning or saving a unit of foreign exchange by the local production of a good. The world market, therefore, is the ultimate reference for the way a country's internal economy should be structured [George, S., and Sabelli, F., 1994:62-65]. A DRC value of less than unity indicates that a firm, industry or subsector is operating efficiently in that the cost of production in a unit of local currency [i.e. Z$1.00] is below the value of a unit of foreign exchange [i.e.US$1.00]. The Jansen Report awarded Zimbabwean manufacturing as a whole the figure of 1.27, which was the lowest in sub-Saharan Africa and compared very favourably with developed economies. The Report was reluctant to suggest that the currency was overvalued by 20% because, if so, this would have given Zimbabwe's protected economy a near perfect score of efficiency and debunked the Bank's ideological stance [See George, S., and Sabelli, F., 1994:258, endnote 10]. In the ZISCO-led subsectors of iron, steel and non-ferrous metals, however, with DRC figures of over 3, Jansen recommended de-industrialisation to save foreign exchange. 'The ensuing massive lay-offs of workers would be undesirable', the Report noted [1983, cited in Bond, P., 1998:345], 'but a study of alternative product lines and more efficient use of existing plant and machinery should be undertaken'.

[19] In the mid-1980s, antagonism between Zimbabwe and the US over Grenada, Angola and the shooting down of a South Korean airliner by the USSR for suspected espionage, cost the country trade and aid opportunities [Sibanda, A., 1988:259].

[20] Although the ceiling on profit remittance—set at 25% for pre-1979 and 50% for post-1980 investments—remained until October 1990, the new code eased borrowing, lending and share trading restrictions on foreign investors. It also led to the establishment of the Zimbabwe Investment Centre [ZIC], as a 'single window clearance agency', and the signing of the Overseas Private Investment

Corporation [OPIC] agreement with the US and the World Bank's Multi-lateral Investment Guarantee Agency Convention. Both the latter are designed to protect and insure foreign investors against 'political risks' such as war/riot damage or state expropriation.

[21] As has been noted elsewhere, ownership in the manufacturing sector was heavily concentrated in foreign hands, namely, Britain [54%], South Africa [18%], the Netherlands [10%] and the United States [7%]. In 1982–1983, out of 1,344 manufacturing enterprises only 7.8% were responsible for 41% of total net output [Ndlela, D.B., 1986:144]. Well over half of all manufactured products were produced by a few firms [Riddell, R.C., 1990:389]. Zimbabwe's industrial base was a prime example of imperfect competition, which invoked a need for price controls to prevent super-profiteering.

[22] The case for structural racism rests on the reluctance of the mainly white-controlled banking sector to lend to blacks. According to Tony Hawkins, a conservative economist based at the UZ, only 3% of private bank lending went to black Zimbabweans over the 1980s [Hawkins, T., cited in Bond, P., 1998:187]. If racism was not the reason, then, the key obstacle, as the banks argued, was the lack of black collateral.

[23] The Director of Unicorn Import/Export, Chandra Patel, was a relative of the Malawian Asian family, the Joshis, which acquired business and political links with ZANU during the liberation struggle. Chatal originally put up most of the equity capital for ZIDCO but the M & S gained a controlling share of 55% during the 1980s. The Joshi brothers, Jayant and Manharial, along with Emmerson Mnangagwa [former Minister of Justice and current Speaker of Parliament] and Sydney Sekeramayi [former Minister for State Security and currently Minister for Mines] formed the ZIDCO board of directors. Jayant is the managing director.

[24] Security powers are prescribed under the Emergency Powers Act, the Subversive Activities Act [1950], the Unlawful Organisations Act [1959], the Preventative Detentions Act [1959] and the Law and Order Maintenance Act [1960]. The Ministers of Justice and Home Affairs could detain indefinitely any one deemed a public enemy while the Central Intelligence Organisation and the police could detain people without formal charges for up to 30 days [Ncube, W., 1991:165].

[25] Totems are usually named after an animal and serve to indicate a hereditary line or clan. In both Shona and Matabele culture, people of the same totem seem to rarely marry.

5 – Maize and Cotton: National Performance under the SAP and the Plight of Shiri Household at Muzvezve Resettlement

[1] The Agricultural Land Settlement Act and Rural Land Act, passed in the latter years of the colonial state, prescribed state powers in resettlement areas. The

principal Ministries involved include Agriculture, Local Government, Health, Transport, Education, Construction and Social Welfare.

[2] The minority of those resettled who did have communal land usually transferred it to relatives to safe keep. Yet the fact that most people resettled were landless assured that resettlement over the 1980s failed to relieve pressure in communal areas [Mhishi, S.G., 1995:10].

[3] The prevalence of polygamy in the small-scale commercial sector can be anywhere between 15 and 43% [Gaidzanwa, R.B., 1988:4]. The research by Chenaux-Respond [1993] into three resettlement areas claimed that up to 14% of male permit holders who had settled as monogamists and 13% of polygamists had married one or more additional wives since their arrival [cited in Tshuma, L., 1997:82].

[4] Other crops as a percentage of national sales include sunflower [3%], groundnuts [4%] and sorghum [8%].

[5] On the surface, pan-territorial and pan-seasonal pricing appeared irrational: under the former a uniform country-wide depot price was paid to all farmers irrespective of their location while under the latter, an annual pre-planting price encouraged farmers to deliver produce to the GMB at the same time, thus enhancing storage costs. Yet in so doing, the GMB attended to one side of the country's food price dilemma, that is, the need for reasonably high producer prices to stimulate production from smallholders. The other side was the need for low consumer prices to help promote national food security. Endeavouring to balance both, the GMB's buying and selling prices were often out of kilter, which automatically fed into the deficit. Over 1988–1989, for example, the difference incurred a net loss of Z$20 million [All data taken from Takavarasha, T., 1994:156-161].

[6] Small-scale hammer millers process a whole grained maize-meal with more protein, iron, calcium and B-vitamins than the more refined maize-meal from large-scale industrial millers.

[7] On Black Friday the Zimbabwe dollar fell from Z$12.00/US$ to Z$26.00/US$ until the Reserve Bank injected US$15 million bringing the rate back to Z$18.00/US$ [*The Herald*, 15/11/97].

[8] The price of compound A and D fertiliser per tonne rose from Z$463.8 and $416.6 in 1990 to $1,604.0 and $1,970.0 respectively in 1996—over a 300% cost increase within five years [Oni, S.A., 1997: 43].

[9] Similar to the GMB, the CSC underwent commercialisation and became the Cold Storage Company Limited in 1994. The Company soon relinquished the unprofitable function of organising public cattle sales in smallholder areas. Although beef off take from communal areas is tiny—accounting for less than 2% during the 1980s [GoZ, 1991b:24]—the multitude of farmers makes them a significant source all the same. The ZFU sought to establish a Trust Fund to regulate cattle sales according to the law.

[10] Since it was no longer compulsory for farmers to market their crops through the GMB, at the behest of the World Bank, the stop order system was cancelled [Tshuma, L., 1997:116-117]. This meant that the AFC could no longer recover debt from the proceeds of the debtor's output at the time of sale to the marketing boards.

The cancellation of the stop order system emerged as a key factor behind the smallholder credit squeeze under the SAP.

[11] According to Nicholas Siziba, a commentator for *The Zimbabwe Mirror* [2-8/07/99], even at Z$4,900 per tonne, the large-scale industrial millers could still realise a profit of about Z$800 per tonne.

[12] The GMB subsequently opened a depot at Beitbridge to counter looming hunger among the 110,000 inhabitants of the district [*The Herald*, 19/02/98].

[13] The numbers registered for food aid in each province were as follows: Matabeleland South 313,839; Masvingo102, 515; Midlands 88,824; Mashonaland Central 60,619; Matabeleland North 42,421; Manicaland 39,041; Mashonaland West 17,430; and Mashonaland East 7,430. Out of the total, 350,375 registered for free food and 321,455 requested aid under the Government/GMB Grain Loan Scheme.

[14] As evident in Appendix 11, to the US dollar, the value of the Zimbabwe dollar fell from about US$1/Z$2.45 in 1990 to US$1/Z$5.11 in 1992 to US$1/10.02 in 1996 to US$1/Z$38.00 by 1999. In nominal terms, the currency depreciated by over 400% during the 1990s but in real terms, due to the circle of imported inflation and consequent currency appreciation, actual depreciation is less.

[15] Apart from the Government's 25% share, major share holders included the National Social Security Authority [18.87%], Old Mutual [11.16%], the Post Office Savings Bank [10%] and Saxa Investments [10%]. Otherwise remaining shares were widely dispersed among smallholders, commercial farmers, COTTCO employees, the National Investment Trust and indigenous business groups.

[16] In addition, COTTCO paid the Government $500 million in dividends and tax.

[17] It takes about five people two days to pick a 250 kg bale for instance.

[18] When phase two of the land resettlement program announced in late 1997, the Government had accepted the recommendations of the Land Tenure Commission to provide security of tenure and inheritance in resettlement areas. After a 99-year leasehold title, the Government plans to grant freehold title to all households. 'Title will be registered in the name of the household head or the names of both spouses. Where the sale of the freehold interest is to be effected, the consent of both spouses must be sought before ownership is transferred' [GoZ, 1998c:13].

[19] In 1992 resettlement areas provided only 5,950 non-family members with either permanent or casual employment [Mhishi, S.G., 1995:10; ILO/SAMAT, 1995:69].

6 – Exposure, Defence and Fate: The Case of Shumba and Mukanya

[1] The group hailed from Roseday near Mvuma between Harare—Masvingo, which had been designated a European area. The then headman Lozane never made it to Sanyati—he was murdered by bandits who stole 60 head of cattle when

crossing the Manyati river. Between the 1962 and 1969 censuses, African settlers in the Gokwe area rose from 49,000 to 133,490 [Hanford, J., 1976:69].

[2] The term *Humwe* refers to a reciprocal household labour system [i.e. the exchange of field hands]. Before cotton, labourers would usually receive beer during work hours but after the introduction of cotton, heavier labour demands, such as regular weeding, spraying and the necessity to keep the cotton bolls clean [on which grading and price depends], did not mix well with beer consumption. Thus, by the 1970s, in Worby's words, the *humwe* evolved from 'beer party to tea party'. Yet, workers could not exist on tea alone—the counterparts of sugar, bread, margarine, jam and usually a slaughtered goat came also to be expected. Over time, then, the humwe became increasingly an expensive operation and the preserve of the richer, often polygamous, church-going households. Eric Worby's major work is his PhD dissertation completed at McGill University, entitled *Remaking Labour, Reshaping Identity: Cotton, Commoditisation and the Culture of Modernity in Northwestern Zimbabwe* [1992].

[3] A 'general impasse', to use the term of E. Kramer [1998:88], beset European and African relations over agriculture. The agricultural and industrial revolutions in Europe convinced NAD officials of the 'superiority of Western civilisation'. The resulting attitude of 'all to teach and nothing to learn' led to the application of misguided policies. For example, the age-old African method of planting a mix of crops in the one field was discouraged when, in fact, the practice introduced nitrogen to the soil while tree felling was encouraged, which had a disastrous impact on sandy African soils.

[4] Master farmer certificates were awarded to African farmers who passed Government standards on soil conservation, cattle dipping and crop rotation.

[5] The 1962 census revealed, for example, that 58% of African females born after 1947 had never attended school compared to 46% of males and that less than 6% of African primary school enrolments obtained a place in secondary school [Martin, D., and Johnson, P., 1981: 58].

[6] The two relevant legislative acts were the Tribal Trust Land Authority Act of 1967 and the African Law and Tribal Courts Act of 1969.

[7] *Chimwidow* and *mujibah* are the feminine and masculine Shona terms respectively for guerrilla spy or helper Norma Kriger's book *Zimbabwe's Guerilla War* [1992] records many of their 'voices'.

[8] The concept originates from T.R. Malthus's *Essay on the Principle of Population* [1798]. In theory, the process of decline can be countered by technology that replenishes soil fertility and arrests falling yields. On the whole though, besides compound fertilisers, not much was on offer to compensate for the devastating impact of clear felling, particularly in marginal dry areas like Sanyati.

[9] According to various studies a family of six requires about 1,425 kilograms of grain per year to ensure a sufficient supply of the food staple [Jayne, T.S., Chisvo, M., and Rukuni, M., 1994:297]. The Shumba household in total comprised about 13 people for the most part of the 1980s.

[10] Over 1991-1995, according to state sources [GoZ, 1998a:9], employment creation amounted to '8,300 net new jobs per annum [i.e. 41,500] ... one-third less than average formal job creation during the 1980s'. Over the same period, 51,510 workers were retrenched: 26,000 and 25,510 from the public and private sector respectively [GoZ, 1998a:4; ZCTU, 1996:15].
[11] The elder Wilson and Manuel, for instance, could improve their chances of obtaining tertiary education and employment by sitting the A level exam. But they simply did not have the Z$5,700 per subject to pay the exam fee for a minimum of three subjects, not to mention tuition costs. As of the late 1990s, the Government endeavoured to indigenise the syllabus, that is, to delink from the Cambridge system so as to remove the import content and susceptibility to imported inflation.
[12] For reasons of anonymity, the real name of the village and battle has been withheld. A *kopje* is like a rocky-forested hill while a *pungwe* was an all-night 'get-to-together' with the guerrillas. Sometimes they were jovial affairs with singing and dancing while at other times they could turn horrible with the execution of 'sell-outs'. Again Norma Kriger's book is insightful.
[13] The *tso tso* is a slow combustion stove—the mass adoption of which would conserve wood fuel and reduce demand. Most households in the village, however, could not afford the building costs and the government did not fulfill its promise to provide the iron grills.
[14] CAMPFIRE was introduced by the Department of National Parks in 1984 and aimed to give communities full control over the exploitation of wildlife. On their behalf, Rural District Councils have engaged safari operators and invested proceeds back into the relevant community. Conflicts have arisen when animals damage the crops of villages not benefiting, which have been resolved by compensation payments.

7 – The National Poverty Struggle, the SAP and the Tribulations of Chiti and the Chitungwiza Blind

[1] The active labour force includes everyone above age 15 excluding the sick, retirees, students and homemakers, who totalled 1,807,620 people in 1997[CSO, 1997a:96].
[2] The figure of 1.6 million people recorded by the Gemini survey amounts to about 27% of the adult labour force involved in 845,000 micro or small-scale businesses nationwide encompassing arts and crafts, dressmaking, hairdressing, furniture, metallurgy, electrical repair, security, and general retail [foods, second-hand clothes, sweets, cigarettes etc] [cited in Ndoro, H., 1996:32].
[3] The Ministry surveyed 19,173 households among 671 communities during August–November 1995 while the CSO surveyed 17,555 households among 395 communities over July 1995 to June 1996.

[4] The relatively high percentage of urbanization in Matabeleland North is deceptive, as most of the urban centres are small, poor and isolated from the major markets.

[5] In fact, Chitungwiza was originally part of Seke communal lands and became a catchment of the exodus in rural population during the final years of the war, which saw the population of Salisbury alone double [cited in Iliffe, J., 1987:240]. In 1977, the Government by proclamation established Chitungwiza as a separate urban area and subsequently as a Town Council in 1981 By then, according to the 1982 CSO Census, the population was 172,556, which increased to 274,912 by the 1992 CSO Census. Presently, the population of Chitungwiza is reported at 500,000 [*The Herald*, 19/01/98].

[6] Nationalwide the urban housing backlog [excluding unregistered lodgers and squatters] rose from 240,000 in 1985 to well over 1 million by 2000 [*The Zimbabwe Mirror*, 13-19/10/00].

[7] The trustworthy real estate firm was required to avoid the high incidence of the notorious double house sale to two different people at one time.

[8] As referred to in Appendix 9, over 1991–1996, the quantitative targets of the civil service retrenchment were basically fulfilled in that 94% of selected posts were abolished [GoZ, 1998a:4]. The program to commercialise SOEs, according to the IMF [1997:33], was also 'quite successful' in so far as non-tax revenues [i.e. cost recovery] rose from 2.9% of GDP to 4.3% and combined losses of the ten leading SOEs were reduced from about 3% of GDP to 1%. At the same time, however, as interest rates rose and the Government borrowed to service outstanding debt, the interest bill grew by an average of 12.2% per year in real terms [Robinson, P.B., 1998:6-7].

[9] The SDF was also designated to assist the poor pay school fees, buy a basic food basket and re-train people retrenched but was without adequate finance. From an initial allocation of Z$20 million in 1992, funding increased to $100 million by 1994–1995 but then declined to $50 million in 1995–1996 [PRF, 1997:19]. By 1997–1998 the SDF's outstanding deficit for school and health fees totalled $71.9 million [*The Herald*, 2/02/98]. Meanwhile, the food money program reached only 4% of the target population [WB, 1996:51].

[10] Officially, the maternal death rate rose from 73.6/100,000 in the late 1980s to 159.5/100,000 by the mid-1990s [UNDP/PRF/IDS, 1998:46]. Other sources, such as the Demographic Health survey and the health minister, Dr Timothy Stamps, estimated the rate at 283/100,000 and 350/100,000 respectively [cited in Mlambo, A.S., 1997:87].

[11] A sharp escalation of TB, malaria, dysentery and venereal disease was also reported in Mbare—the most crowded of Harare's suburbs [*The Herald*, 8/01/98].

[12] In 1996–1997, for instance, about 235,238 pupils applied for assistance with school fees [*The Herald*, 2/02/98].

[13] Further, according to Sibongile, every 12 months welfare recipients had to reapply to the Department and the process could take up to six months without back pay.

8 – Zimbabwe Ruptures under the SAP

[1] A full text of the Bill may still be available from the ZimNews web site: www.zwnews.com An earlier version of the Bill actually passed the Senate in 2000 but the House of Representatives ran out of time before the Gore-Bush Presidential election. The Bill was co-sponsored by senators Bill Frist, a Republican, and Russell Feingold, a Democrat, and supported by the US State Department as well as influential interest groups such as the Heritage Foundation and the World Peace Foundation.

[2] The World Bank froze its loan portfolio on 2 October 2000 because of outstanding arrears amounting to US$45 million [WB news release 03/10/00, www.worldbank.org/developmentnews].

[3] Over the 1990s, out of the main sources of monetary growth, namely, foreign inflow, foreign borrowing and state deficit financing, the latter emerged as the main culprit although both the former were of significant assistance early on [*The Herald*, 4/05/99]. The Government increasingly resorted to short-term instruments to meet requirements, which set a path of rapid monetary growth, according to the Reserve Bank [*Economic Highlights*, 13/10/00], 'unrelated to economic activity' [See also WB, vol.2 1995:17]. Of the total domestic debt, short-term treasury bills accounted for 3.9% in 1990, progressively rising to 53.4% in 1995, 88.1% in 1999 and 94.5% by December 2000 [RBZ, *Economic Highlights*, 16/03/01]. The restrictive monetary policy invoked to counteract money supply growth largely relied on the rediscount rate, that is, the interest rate at which banks borrow from the Reserve Bank. Since all other rates move in line with the rediscount rate, the higher the rate the tighter the credit squeeze.

[4] Although pure export manufactures [i.e excluding ferrochrome, iron and steel, cotton lint] averaged a 14.7% growth rate in US dollar terms over 1991–1995 [GoZ, 1998a:64], according to a CZI Study—*The Manufacturing Sector in Zimbabwe* [1999]—about 80% of *total* export manufactures continued to be resource-based and experienced declining shares in world markets. Only about 20% were gaining a rising share and of these few were science-based products [i.e. electronics, pharmaceuticals] capable of offsetting decline. As from 1996, the downturn in commodity prices, particularly tobacco, gold, copper, nickel and ferro-alloys, carried dire ramifications on external performance [RBZ, 1997c:21; 1998:23]. Tobacco prices, for example, virtually collapsed over the late 1990s—by 38% in 1998 alone [*The Financial Gazette*, 1/04/99].

[5] Over 1990–1996, in US dollar terms, tourism grew fourfold [RBZ, 1997b:24] while large-scale commercial agriculture emerged as the second largest exporter of cut flowers to the European Union [*The Herald*, 9/03/98].

[6] In July 1999, however, South Africa reinstated some of the trade preferences on Zimbabwean goods, notably clothing and textiles, footwear and leather products [*The Zimbabwe Mirror*, 17-23/03/00].

[7] The EU-South Africa trade deal invoked grave fears among SADC members that the regional free trade protocol would give the EU a clear avenue to dump

subsidised agricultural produce and manufactures [Hawkins, T., cited in *The Zimbabwe Mirror*, 9-15/04/99]. The EU responded that the trade concessions obtained in the South African market would automatically extend to all SADC members [*The Zimbabwe Mirror*, 24-30/03/00].

8 Until 1995, the Reserve Bank provided forward cover, which protected the service of offshore debts accrued by domestic banks from currency devaluation [i.e. the difference between the nominal interest rate on foreign loans and the real rate at which loans had to be repaid in hard currency] [Bond, P., 1998:383]. In so doing, as the Zimbabwe dollar depreciated, the Reserve Bank spent Z$2 billion in 1991 and an estimated $600 million in 1994 [WB, vol.2 1995:21].

9 The one successful BOOT project was the Limpopo River Bridge—a joint venture between Joshua Nkomos Development Trust of Zimbabwe and Gusv Company of Bulgaria. Lack of incentives and 'insecurity about ownership of property', according to the Zimbabwe Economics Society Vice-President, Ternard Kwashirai, was the key investment deterrent. Yet, the BOOT scheme guaranteed ownership until companies fully recovered costs and also offered a range of tax incentives.

10 In 1998, the United Merchant Bank, headed by Roger Boka, collapsed; another— the Zimbabwe Building Society— after being exposed to the former, had to be bailed out by the Reserve Bank; and yet another—Solid Insurance—was reported insolvent [*The Financial Gazette*, 25/03/99; *Business Herald*, 27/05/99]. The Government passed the Reserve Bank of Zimbabwe Bill in 1999 to strengthen regulation of the banking industry [*The Sunday Mail*, 9/05/99].

11 Apart from the primary cause of low growth, the trend of declining revenue was assisted by reductions in corporate, income and capital gains taxes as well as, ironically, a significant loss of expertise from the Tax Department. Under the voluntary retrenchment program the most skilled accountants departed enticed by more lucrative opportunities in the private sector [Robinson, P.B., 1998:15]. Subsequent efforts to recover revenue through indirect tax increases and income levies, such as the 5% drought levy [renamed development levy] and 10% levy on tobacco auctions, tended to exacerbate the crisis of stagflation.

12 As market reforms got underway, according to *The Herald* [11/03/99], ZISCO relied on 'obsolete plant and equipment that had outlived its usefulness by over 30 years'. In 1993 Blast Furnace Number four collapsed, which accounted for 70% of manufacturing capacity. A Government guaranteed 10-year bond issue sought to attract Z$500 million to help the parastatal meet debt obligations and upgrade equipment but only raised $34 million. 'Investors preferred short-term money market investments', the CBZ claimed, 'as opposed to locking in their funds in the 10-year bond issue due to the uncertainty in the direction if interest rates and inflation'. A report from the World Economic Forum cast a bleak future for ZISCO: 'At international prices, this enterprise is a major loser and no amount of restructuring will allow it to compete, yet the Government regularly finds some reason to continue its budget support' [cited in *Zimbabwe Independent*, 20/02/98]. Subsequently, however, a Chinese [Shougang] and German Company [Ferostaal] invested in the

rehabilitation of ZISCO with the promise of a $2.9 billion export deal on completion [*The Herald*, 20/05/99].

[13] In respect of settler selection, DERUDE adopted a points system based on need and suitability. Out of a maximum of 40 points, only10 accorded to need [i.e. size of family and current land holding] while the remaining 30 related to suitability [ie. agricultural skill, education, age, health and livestock owned] [Tshuma, L., 1997:137].

[14] By convention, the designation process is carried out by a provincial Land Identification Committee made up of an AGRITEX officer, Government officials and representatives of the CFU, ZFU and District Council [Tshuma, L., 1997:133].

[15] The Agricultural and Rural Development Authority [ARDA] directly received 531,000 hectares of farmland while the NRZ immediately began transporting raw materials out of the DRC for processing [*The Zimbabwe Mirror*, 5-11/11/99].

[16] The Osleg board of directors consists of army supremo General Vitalis Zvinavashe; the former permanent secretary of defence, Job Whabira; the director of the Minerals Marketing Corporation of Zimbabwe, Onesimo Moyo; the general manager of the Zimbabwe Mining Development Corporation, Isiah Ruzengwe; and several other officers from the ZDF.

[17] Col-tan is short for columbite-tantalite and is used in any item that needs a capacitor to maintain the electric charge of a computer microchip [e.g. mobile phones]. From US$30.00 a pound the price soared to $210 over 1999 but has since declined back to about $40.00 [*The Independent* (UK), 21/03/01, 03/08/01]. Cobalt is used to make alloys for jet engines and rechargeable batteries—the price reached $35.00 a pound in 1999 and is now around $15.00 [*The Chicago Tribune*, 25/11/00]. The SADC forces [i.e. Zimbabwe, Angola, Namibia] control access to the latter while Uganda and Rwanda the former.

[18] Each registered war veteran—about 60,000 of them— received entitlement to a Z$50,000 lump sum payment, a $2,000 monthly pension for life, free education and health and preferential access to land [*The Herald*, 18/11/97, *The Financial Gazette*, 11/12/97].

[19] Just 300 farms of the designated total accounted for 2.5 million hectares, which included 10 of the 18 farms— comprising 300,000 hectares—owned by the Oppenheimer family—the proprietors of Anglo American Corporation [*The Financial Gazette*, 19/02/98]. Other designated company land included 80,000 hectares held by Lonrho and farms owned by Cambells Pty Ltd, Texas Land and Cattle Company and Meickles Ltd [*The Herald*, 28/11/97].

[20] Under A1 schemes settler households are to be allocated 3 to 6 hectares for residential and cropping use and between 24 to 180 hectares—depending on the Natural Region—of communal grazing land. A2 schemes are private holdings of varying size geared toward specialised farming, which selected beneficiaries will have opportunity to buy outright [Dr Ignatius Chombo, chairmen of the inter-ministerial committee on resettlement, cited in *The Zimbabwe Mirror*, 4-10/05/01].

[21] When Zimbabwe entered the DRC war in August 1998, the IMF cancelled the stand-by agreement negotiated the previous June [Appendix 10] yet shortly after in October, arranged with Uganda—another DRC participant, a US$2.2 billion loan [*The Zimbabwe Mirror*, 26-31/03/99]. The outgoing IMF director, Michael Camdessus, commented: 'Zimbabwe needs to reduce to the minimum its spending on defence.

We know for certain war is the worst enemy of development. The country just needs to reduce its spending on military affairs' [cited *The Zimbabwe Mirror*, 21-27/01/00].
[22] Bizarrely, as riot police dispersed peaceful demonstrations in the cities and thugs assaulted the ZCTU Secretary General, Morgan Tsvangirayi [See *The Zimbabwe Independent*, 12/12/97], the President scrapped the despised levy at the ZANU-PF annual conference held in Mutare the next day. Delegates unanimously shouted '*Hatidi* [We do not want]' [*The Financial Gazette*, 11/12/97].
[23] The aim of the National Economic Consultative Forum, as the title implies, was to provide an arena for leading economic stake holders to debate and resolve issues. Apart from the TNF, other task forces set up by the NECF were suppose to deal with land reform, taxation and expenditure, corruption [both private and public], indigenisation and industrial policy. To some extent, lack of funds inhibited progress—partly alleviated by grants from the World Bank and UNDP—but overall, the outbreak of the political crisis paralysed the NECF as much as the country.
[24] 'There are indications that some firms can afford 100% pay increments', the relevant Minister, Florence Chitauro, eventually commented [cited in The Herald 21/05/99], 'but they hide behind National Employment Council level agreements'. In 1999, an understaffed Labour Relations Tribunal had a backlog in the thousands of cases dating from1993 wherein laid off workers still awaited entitlements [*The Zimbabwe Mirror*, 30/07-05/08/99, 27/04-03/05/01].
[25] The 395 member Constitutional Commission included all Members of Parliament and 241 representatives from opposition parties, business and farming groups, professional associations, church clergy, media personnel and other civic groups [*The Herald*, 29/04/99]. Conservative analysts such as Eric Bloch and Tony Hawkins were members as was Edgar Tekere [from Zimbabwe Unity Movement] and Nick Swanpoel [CFU President]. Eddison Zvobgo further clarified the Governments outlook: 'Our position is that we are going to consider no other document except the one that is going to be produced by the commission. We will not take notice of the draft constitution produced by the NCA or any other such group. Such drafts are just political essays and they are useful to get good grades at universities and not for national constitution making' [cited in *The Financial Gazette*, 6/05/99; *The Zimbabwe Mirror*, 5-11/99].
[26] According to the Commission, 6 out of 10 provinces preferred a non-executive President yet all provinces wanted the head of state to be popularly elected and to exercise some executive powers with the approval of Parliament [*The Zimbabwe Mirror*, 10-16/12/99]. Pro-draft critics insisted that the position of Prime Minister, as the day to day supervisor of Government business, assured that the President could not act unilaterally while pro-NCA critics maintained that what came out is a Prime Minister accountable to the President not Parliament. Debates about the draft constitution pervaded the Zimbabwean media during the lead up to the referendum.

APPENDICES

1) Population of Rhodesia/Zimbabwe by Ethnic Group 1901–1997

Year	Africans	Europeans	Asian	Mixed	Total[#]
1901	700,000	11,100	-	-	711,100
1921	1,110,000	23,700	1,300	2,000	1,137,000
1931	1,410,000	50,100	1,700	2,400	1,464,200
1941	1,930,000	69,300	2,600	4,000	2,005,900
1951	2,680,000	138,000	4,400	6,000	2,828,400
1960	3,610,000	218,000	6,700	9,900	3,844,600
1962	3,860,000	222,000	7,400	10,900	4,100,300
1965	4,260,000	210,000	8,000	12,600	4,490,600
1969	4,880,000	230,000	9,000	15,300	5,134,300
1972	5,400,000	262,000	9,600	17,700	5,689,300
1975	6,000,000	277,000	10,000	20,400	6,307,400
1982	7 297,000	147,000	10,800	21,600	7,476,400
1992	10,284,000	82,800	13,400	30,100	10,410,300
1997	11,655,770	93,792	4,926	33,789	11,788,277

Source: Based on CSO data [various years].

2) Total Population by Land Use Sector as of 1992 and 1997

SECTOR	POPULATION		% of TOTAL	
	1992	1997	1992	1997
Communal Lands	5 352 304	6 269 464	51.40	53.2
Large-scale Commercial	1 176 586	1 108 894	11.30	9.4
Small-scale Commercial	170 167	289 184	1.63	2.5
Resettlement	426 687	295 152	4.10	2.5
Harare	1 464 015	1 871 943	14.27	15.9
Bulawayo	621 742	671 024	5.97	5.7
Other Urban Councils & Admin areas	1 158 301	1 221 375	10.92	10.3
Rural Growth Points	42 746	62 238	0.41	0.5
ZIMBABWE	10 412 548	11 789 274	100	100

Source: CSO, 1994:28; 1997[a]: 36.

[#] Totals may exclude other groups

3) Zimbabwean Agriculture in Natural Regions

NATURAL REGION	DESCRIPTION, LOCATION and % of TOTAL AGRICULTURAL AREA
I	Specialised and Diversified farming region. Rainfall is high, above 1000mm per year, temperatures comparatively low, permitting a range of agricultural activities: fruit, coffee, tea, forestry, intensive livestock and 'European' vegetables - potatoes, cauliflower, green peas and beans, broccoli etc Location: predominately highveld [1200-1700m] in the Eastern tips of Manicaland. % of total agricultural area: 1.8%
II a & b	Intensive Farming Region [IIa] Rainfall is confined to summer and is moderately high [750 - 1000mm]. The region is suitable for intensive cropping [tobacco, cotton, maize, wheat, soyabeans, tea, coffee] and livestock [dairy, pork, poultry, sheep, beef]. Location: middleveld [900 -1200m] to highveld; predominately the Mashonaland Provinces - East, West and Central. [IIb] Less reliable rainfall but still good farming land for a diverse range of agriculture and includes the sugar producing area of Triangle and the Hippo Valley. Location: lowveld [0 - 900m] in Masvingo [around Chiredzi] and Mashonaland East Province. % of total agricultural land area: 15.4% [a & b].
III	Semi-Intensive Farming Region Rainfall is 650-800mm but is erratic and often falls in heavy bursts after severe mid-season dry spells. Output of cotton, tobacco and maize often varies depending on local climate. Other popular crops include groundnuts, millet, rapoko and sunflower. Location: highveld, predominately Midlands province. % of total agricultural land area: 18.5%
IV	Semi-Extensive Farming Region Subject to fairly low rainfall [450-650mm] and periodic droughts. Land is best suited for livestock production, namely, cattle and goats. From season to season output of maize, cotton, millet, rapoko, ground nuts and sunflower is irregular. Location: middleveld to lowveld, predominately Matabeleland North Province, the western reaches of Midlands and Masvingo Provinces and the northern reaches of Mashonaland. % of total agricultural land area: 37.4%
V	Extensive Farming Regions Rainfall is too low and erratic for any reliable crop production without irrigation. Extensive cattle and game ranching are the recommended agricultural activities. Location: lowveld, predominately located in Matabeleland South Province, the eastern part of Masvingo and the north western reach of the Zambezi basin. % of total agricultural land area: 26.9%

Source: Chavunduka, G.L., 1982: 22.

4)

Balance of Payments 1968–1977
[Rh$ millions]

Year	1965	1969	1970	1971	1972	1973	1974	1975	1976	1977
Merchandise, net	-22	32..0	27.9	3.1	62.5	89.6	55.2	33.0	156.8	130.8
Invisible transactions, net:										
Services	-11.2	-5.3	-16..8	-24.8	-21.8	-58.5	-81.3	-89.5	-77.4	-91.7
Investment income	-14.9	-17.8	-21.0	-30.4	-35.1	-38.5	-39.8	-37.5	-48.6	-43.5
Transfers	-1.0	-4.3	-2.6	-3.3	-2.8	-6.9	-18.8	-26.5	-23.2	-15.3
Balance on Current account	-49.1	4.6	-12.5	-55.4	2.7	-14.4	-84.7	-120.5	7.4	-19.7
Balance on Capital account	39.5	9.9	26.3	30.5	-2.3	51.6	62.6	101.7	25.7	-22.2
Net Balance	-9.6	14.5	13.8	-24.9	0.4	37.2	-22.1	-18.8	33.1	-41.9

Source: CSO, 1977 cited in Clarke, D.G., 1980:156.

5) Macroeconomic Indicators 1970–1979

Year	Real GDP at 1965 Prices % Change	Annual Inflation Rate	Employment as a % of the Population	Average Interest Rate	Total External Debt Z$ m	Debt Service Ratio	External Debt as a % of GDP	Exchange Rate US$/Z$*
1970	3.8	3.5	16.1				13.4	
1971	12.0	3.2	16.2				11.1	
1972	9.6	4.0	16.7				9.5	
1973	3.2	6.0	16.9				8.5	
1974	9.3	9.8	17.1				5.1	
1975	-1.1	9.5	16.7	6.5	190.0	1.0	4.9	1.76
1976	-1.6	9.5	15.9	6.5	145.0	1.0	3.8	1.60
1977	-7.3	9.5	15.1	7.6	154.0	1.0	4.3	1.59
1978	-3.0	9.0	14.3	8.8	418.0	1.0	9.9	1.48
1979	-0.9	11.0	13.8	8.8	524.0	1.0	13.3	1.47

Source: RBZ, CSO and IMF data [various years] as cited in GoZ/LTC, 1994:423–426.

* Rates reflect units of foreign currency per Zimbabwe dollar

6)

Balance of Payments 1981–1989
[Z$ millions]

Year	1981	1982	1983	1984	1985	1986	1987	1988	1989
Merchandise, net	-57	-116	87	246.6	325.6	520.3	634.1	905.1	779.1
Invisible transactions, net:									
Services>	-263	-193	-262	-243.7	-297.5	-253.4	-263.9	-357.3	-451.8
Investment income^	-96	-162	-221	-156.6	-203.6	-308.0	-353.8	-432.0	-451.6
Unrequited transfers*	-24	-62	-58	51.8	16.3	53.7	113.5	94.7	123.8
Balance on Current account	-440	-533	-454	-101.9	-159.2	12.6	129.9	210.5	-0.5
Balance on Capital account	134	343	286	232.6	279.7	137.5	115.3	89.9	99.8
Unrecorded flow	86	66	10	33.6	83	-201.7	-11.5	-120.5	-219.1
Net Balance	-220	-124	-158	164.3	203.5	-51.6	233.7	179.9	-119.8

Source: RBZ and CSO data [various years].

> Service payments largely refers to the external costs accrued by Government and through the transport of goods.
^ Investment income mainly refers to the repatriation of interest, profits and other remittances.
* Unrequited transfer payments included foreign currency pensions paid to expatriate Zimbabweans—a requirement of Lancaster House.

7) Zimbabwean Macroeconomic Indicators, 1980–1990

Year	Real GDP at factor cost % Change	Real GDP per capita % Change	Annual Inflation Rate	Budget Deficit as a % of GDP	Average Interest Rate on loans	Total External Debt in US $ m	External Debt as a % of GDP	Debt service ratio	Exchange Rate US$/Z$*	% of Population formally employed
1980	10.7	7.5	9.9	8.2	7.50	785.6	12.9	3.0	1.55	13.7
1981	9.7	6.6	14.5	7.5	7.50	1,259.2	12.7	9.5	1.45	13.7
1982	1.5	-1.4	13.3	9.4	13.00	1,871.0	18.1	16.3	1.32	13.7
1983	-3.6	-6.2	21.0	11.3	13.00	2,191.1	18.2	24.6	0.99	13.2
1984	2.3	-0.5	1.7	12.2	13.00	2,179.7	25.5	27.0	0.80	12.8
1985	7.3	4.3	2.7	10.6	13.00	2,414.7	28.1	29.4	0.62	12.6
1986	2.2	-0.6	15.5	13.3	13.00	2,626.0	29.9	29.4	0.60	12.9
1987	-1.1	-3.8	8.9	10.8	13.00	2,853.3	32.5	33.3	0.60	12.6
1988	6.5	3.7	11.9	11.6	13.00	2,667.7	32.1	27.5	0.56	12.7
1989	4.9	2.1	12.4	8.6	11.50	2,790.9	31.5	21.3	0.47	12.8
1990	2.1		15.5	10	12.00	2,946.5	35.4	24.5	0.41	12.7

Source: RBZ, CSO, World Bank, IMF and GoZ data [various years]

* Rates reflect units of foreign currency per Zimbabwe dollar.

8) World Bank and IMF Loan Portfolios in Zimbabwe, 1980–1989

World Bank[*]				
Project ID number	Date Approved	Date Expired	Project Type	Amount US$m
IDA 1291	17.11.82	N/A	Small farm credit	30.4
IDA 3270	17.05.83	31.03.89	Rural afforestation	7.3
IBRD 3276	07.07.83	30.09.91	Agricultural extension and research	13.1
IBRD 3305	18.05.89	31.12.97	Agricultural credit and export promotion	36.3
IBRD 3268 IDA 3268	26.03.81	N/A	Manufacturing Rehabilitation	50.0 15.0
IBRD 3272	15.02.83	30.07.87	Manufacturing export promotion	70.6
IDA 3273	29.09.82	30.06.86	Fuel supply	1.2
IBRD 3274	14.12.82	30.06.90	Power 1	105.0
IBRD 3282	12.01.88	30.06.94	Power 2	44.0
IBRD 3269	19.05.81	30.06.86	Transport Rehabilitation	42.0
IBRD 3277	02.08.83	30.06.90	Railways development	40.0
IBRD 3275	17.05.83	30.06.86	Highways 1	26.4
IBRD 3291	10.05.88	N/A	Highways 2	38.6
IBRD 3278	19.06.84	30.09.93	Housing development	43.0
IBRD 3294	01.06.89	31.12.99	Urban sector and regional development	80.0
IBRD 3279	09.05.85	30.06.94	Small scale enterprises promotion	10.0
IBRD 3281	22.07.86	30.09.93	Family health 1	10.0

IMF				
Facility	Date Approved	Amount approved	Date Expired	Amount Drawn
Stand-By[#]	08.04.81	37.5	07.04.82	37.5
Stand-By	23.03.83	300	22.09.84	175.0

Source: World Bank and IMF web site

[*] The International Bank for Reconstruction and Development [IBRD] forms the core of the World Bank operations. IBRD loans usually include a 5-year grace period and a 15 to 20 year repayment period at market rates of interest. The International Development Association [IDA] is an affiliate, established in 1960, which provides softer loans at much lower rates of interest and a grace and repayment period of up to 10 and 40 years respectively.

[#] Stand-by credits consist of 4 tranches, usually equivalent to 25% of the quota, and repayments are expected within 5 years.

9) A Concise Policy Matrix of the Structural Adjustment Program [SAP], 1990–2000

Policy Area	Aim	Rationale	Progress in Implementation
[I] Wages	To reduce the role of the state in wage determination and employment security in favour of a market system of collective bargaining.	State interference in the labour market is perceived to have fostered an anti-employment and capital-intensive bias amongst employers. Greater employer autonomy in respect of wage negotiations and hiring and firing procedures is expected to encourage labour-intensive investment and help fulfil the original ESAP target of 100,000 new formal sector jobs per year [**GoZ, 1991a, annex III:10**]	In 1991 an amendment to the Labour Relations Act of 1985 granted employers the power to retrench without ministerial approval and enabled collective bargaining agreements at the plant level 'to supersede the authority of those formulated by unions and employer organisations at the national employment council level' [**Sachikonye, L.M., 1995a:64**]. The IMF [**1997:11**] observed: 'greater flexibility in wage negotiation and improved labour mobility achieved'
[11] Prices	To allow market forces to determine prices rather than the state.	Administered cost-plus pricing of goods and services is believed to discourage investment in production efficiency and leads to high cost output with an anti-export bias. Market freedom to determine prices is considered a precondition for efficient and pro-export investment. As the production base expands and competition amongst producers grows, the reasons underlying price control, namely, to ensure an affordable cost of living and ameliorate restrictive trade practices, are expected to disappear [**GoZ, 1991a, 13-14**]. The higher inflation rate following price de-control is expected to subside to 10% by 1994.	By mid-decade all price controls including subsidies had been phased out [**WB, 1997b:3; IMF, 1997:11**]. In response to high inflation during the latter half of the decade—sparked by the 'Black Friday' [14/11/97] currency crisis—the Government overrode the price autonomy of several parastatals, notably, NOCZIM, ZESA and the GMB, in a bid to control the end price of fuel, electricity and maize respectively. Otherwise, despite the threats, the price autonomy of the private sector and most parastatals has remained in tact. Various attempts to forge a 'social contract' between labour, business and the state to arrest the inflation spiral have so far been unsuccessful.

[III] Investment	Attract and facilitate greater foreign and indigenous investment. As a percentage of GDP total investment is predicted to rise from an average of 20% during the 1980s to 25%.	Restrictions on capital repatriation, domestic borrowing, share equity holdings and foreign exchange access as well as complicated licensing procedures on import and export flows and the granting of visas are identified as major deterrents of foreign investment during the 1980s. In respect of indigenous investment, perceived obstacles include access to finance, land and basic facilities as well as inherited colonial by-laws enforced by local councils that impose numerous licensing, zoning and building specifications on entrepreneurs in the informal sector. An easing and simplification of red tape as well as attendance to indigenous constraints comprise vital components to stimulate investment under the SAP.	For foreign investors, liberalisation measures included introduction of Foreign Currency Accounts [FCAs]; abolishment of licensing for projects under US$40 million; removal of restrictions on domestic borrowing; a rise in the equity margin to 40% for any company listed on the ZSE; lifting of controls on dividend remittance; full capital repatriation for post-1993 investors; and generous tax concessions in Export Processing Zones. For indigenous investors, the Government reserved certain sectors [eg. agriculture, transport, retail/wholesale] and established the Indigenous Business Development Centre in 1990 as well as the National Investment Trust in 1997. Progress on the land front was very slow, however, and informal vendors complained heavily of Council/police harassment in enforcing by-laws during the 1990s.
[IV] Fiscal Rationalisation	To halve the state budget deficit from 10% of GDP to 5% through a reduction in the civil service wage bill [from 16.5% of GDP to 12.9%], elimination of subsidies to SOEs, increased cost recovery for public services and general expenditure restraint.	State fiscal restraint is at the core of the SAP rationale to ease pressure on domestic liquidity and release funds for productive investment. The key components of public sector reform are a reduction in the civil service excluding education by 25% [i.e. about 26,000 posts]; commercialisation and, if possible, privatisation of SOEs; and a general policy of 'user pays' for public services. Although higher unemployment is considered frictional, the Government intends to assist the retrenched with re-training and protect vulnerable groups through targeted subsidies and continued free health. The cut in recurrent expenditures is to be accompanied by an expanded Public Sector Investment Programme, that is, the maintenance of capital expenditures to 'crowd-in' private investment.	By 1997, the Government had introduced cost recovery measures; eliminated 23,000 posts in the civil service and 12,000 from the military [the civil wage bill equaled 12% of GDP in 1995]; and successfully commercialised the parastatal sector in so far as a consolidated loss [1.7% of GDP in 1993/94] of the 20 largest enterprises had been converted into a profit [0.6% of GDP in 1996/97] [WB, 1997b:3]. The primary deficit, that is, the total deficit minus interest payments, was brought down from over 5% of GDP to 3% by mid-decade and reached a surplus by 1999. But the burden of public debt service, especially since the currency crash of late 1997, largely underlined the persistent high deficit and low capital expenditures. Peace in the DRC and privatisation of SOEs are posed as solutions - of the latter only 5 have been sold.

[V] Finance	To shift from the administered system of interest rates and monetary aggregates toward a market regime based on open market operations and freedom of entry.	In Bernard Chidzero's view [**1994:286**], tight controls on the financial sector bred complacency and a captive market that rarely extended beyond established businesses. A liberalised sector—open to global market forces—is expected to engender a greater vibrancy and transform the capital and stock market into a vehicle to broaden the productive base. Theoretically, the onset of positive interest rates should raise the pool of loanable funds through increased capital inflow and savings [the SAP target is 25% of GDP] as well as lead to improved investment efficiency with a greater labour intensity.	'Targets achieved' according to the IMF [**1997:11**]. Since 1991 interest rates have been market-determined and monetary aggregates rest on open market operations – RBZ bills, the rediscount rate and reserve requirements. Entry regulations were also relaxed that the number of commercial and merchant banks increased from 4 to 7 and 4 to 10 respectively. While the upswings in savings and capital inflow have not translated into sustained productive investment, tight monetary conditions and related high interest rates intensified the Government's burden of domestic debt. In early 2001, to release state revenue and stimulate the economy, the RBZ restructured domestic debt by artificially reducing interest rates below the inflation rate.
[VI] Trade	To replace the state-controlled trade regime with a market based system in accord with Article VIII of the IMF Charter [i.e. full current account convertibility].	The adoption of an export-led strategy is a fundamental plank of the SAP, which is expected to realise an average GDP growth rate of 5% per annum. The key components are a fully convertible market-determined exchange rate; import de-control; tariff reform; and export incentives. Trade liberalisation is the means by which the hitherto inward-oriented Zimbabwean economy is to integrate with the global economy and receive greater export, import and foreign investment stimulus. All other policy measures outlined above are intended to complement this essential thrust.	By mid-1997, the foreign exchange allocation system had been dismantled and 'current account transactions and most capital account transactions freed from control' [**WB, 1997b:3**]. The Zimbabwe dollar was thus made fully convertible; all exporters had direct access to foreign exchange, via FCAs; import licenses, except for a few items, were abolished; and the average tariff declined from 25% to 16%. Serious foreign exchange shortages in the aftermath of Black Friday, however, led to policy reversals evident in a pegged exchange rate, intermittent RBZ directives to liquidate FCAs and import compression

10) World Bank and IMF Loan Portfolios in Zimbabwe, 1990–2001.

World Bank				
Project ID number	Date Approved	Date Expired	Project Type	Amount US$ m
IBRD 3287	23.03.90	30.06.98	Forest resources	14.5
IDA 3318	02.06.98	30.09.05	Park Rehabilitation and Conservation	62.5
IDA 3331	29.05.98	31.07.01	Agricultural services and marketing	8.8
IDA 2399	24.06.92	31.03.95	Drought Recovery	150.0
IDA 63096	16.09.99	31.12.01	Land Reform Support Project	5.0
IBRD 3309	18.01.94	31.12.99	Power 3	90.0
IBRD 3286	04.12.90	30.06.99	Railways 2	38.6
IDA 45029	29.05.97	30.06.00	RDC Pilot Capital Development Project	12.25
IDA 45031	19.05.98	31.12.03	Community Action Project	60.0
IDA 35628	25.4.96	31.12.02	Enterprise Development Project	70.0
IBRD 3302	04.06.91	31.12.98	Family Health 2	25.0
IDA 3333	17.06.93	31.12.00	Sexually Transmitted Diseases Prevention and Care	64.5
IBRD 3313 IDA 3313	21.01.92	31.12.93	Structural Adjustment Credit1	125.0 50.0
IDA 3322	29.06.93	31.12.97	Structural Adjustment Credit 2	125.0

IMF				
Facility	Date Approved	Amount approved	Date Expired	Amount Drawn
EFF*	24.01.92	268.8	11.09.92	95.4
EFF	11.09.92	154.5	10.09.95	116.4
ESAF#	11.09.92	460.6	10.09.95	203.5
Stand-By	01.06.98	175.0	03.06.99	52.0
Stand-By	02.08.99	193.0	01.10.00	33.7

Source: World Bank and IMF web site

* Extended Fund Facility – renown for wide ranging policy conditionalities and allows recipient to borrow up to 140% of their quota.

Enhanced Structural Adjustment Facility – offers longer term loans on more concessionary terms

11) Macroeconomic Indicators, 1991–2000

Year	Real GDP at factor cost % Change	Real GDP per capita % Change	Annual Inflation Rate	Budget Deficit as a % of GDP	Average Commercial Interest Rate*	Total External Debt in US $m	Debt service ratio	Average Exchange Rate Z$/US$^	External Debt as a % of GDP	% of Population formally employed
1991	3.2	2.3	23.3	9.2	12.00 – 17.25	3 136	23.5	3.73	59	12.32
1992	-5.5	-11.8	42.1	6.4	21.75 – 47.50	3 798	30.0	5.11	56	11.87
1993	2.0	-2.1	27.6	10.4	28.30 – 47.50	3 991	30.0	6.52	62	10.77
1994	5.3	3.3	22.3	7.6	32.77 – 40.00	4 290	25.0	8.12	63	11.33
1995	-1.1	-3.2	22.6	12.6	31.56 – 38.49	4 419	19.8	8.66	62	10.75
1996	7.0	3.9	21.4	10.7	30.10 – 37.07	4 694	17.6	10.02	55	10.69
1997	2.0	-0.1	18.8	6.2	31.59 – 37.86	4 966	18.0	12.23	59	10.69
1998	1.5	-9.3	31.7	6.7	40.50 – 58.00	4 510	21.0	24.37	78	10.61
1999	-0.1	-0.9	58.5	9.8	56.00 – 76.00	4 508	21.0	38.25	82	10.09
2000	-5.0		55.9	23.0	76.00			55.00 [Oct]		

Source: RBZ and CSO data [various years]

* These figures cover the range of rates charged: the lower end of the range reflects the base lending rate
^ Rates reflect Zimbabwe dollars per unit of foreign currency.

12)

Volume of Manufacturing Output, 1990–1999
[1980 = 100]

Year	Food-stuffs	Drink & Tobacco	Textiles & Ginning	Clothes & Footwear	Wood & Furniture	Paper, printing & publishing	Chemical & Petroleum products	Non-metallic mineral products	Metals & metal products	Transport equipment	Other Manu-factures	All Manu-factures
Weight	13.5	10.4	10.1	7.2	4.4	6.1	12.5	3.7	28.8	2.1	1.2	100.0
1990	144	130	217	145	90	137	159	161	111	147	49	139
1991	147	134	226	149	101	144	159	171	114	143	48	143
1992	150	134	177	125	106	143	138	158	101	141	39	130
1993	123	127	192	128	95	150	130	130	82	82	95	119
1994	130	127	206	125	106	169	149	170	92	133	85	131
1995	142	119	81	100	115	156	134	157	88	139	53	113
1996	128	131	80	102	160	153	137	182	89	200	54	117
1997	135	134	80	102	134	153	156	177	94	203	40	120
1998	133	138	83	103	134	148	140	175	85	147	37	115
1999	148	119	82	108	117	143	154	160	74	100	39	109
In percentage change												
1990	9.6	14.0	4.0	5.3	6.4	3.7	8.8	6.3	4.9	-0.5	-41.2	6.3
1991	2.2	3.0	4.4	2.7	12.6	5.2	6.4	5.8	1.9	-2.6	-2.1	2.8
1992	1.9	0.4	-22.0	-16.4	4.6	-0.5	-13.4	-7.5	-11.3	-1.2	-17.7	-9.2
1993	-17.9	-5.7	9.0	2.6	-9.8	4.6	-6.2	-17.7	-18.2	-41.8	141.3	-8.2
1994	5.2	0.3	7.1	-2.0	11.3	12.9	14.8	30.9	11.8	61.6	-11.1	9.6
1995	9.5	-6.4	-60.8	-20.2	8.3	-7.9	-10.2	-7.8	-4.3	4.5	-37.1	-13.6
1996	-9.9	10.0	-1.3	2.0	39.1	-2.0	2.2	15.9	1.1	43.8	1.8	3.5
1997	5.4	2.2	0	0	-16.3	0	13.8	-2.8	5.6	1.5	-2.6	2.5
1998	-1.5	2.3	3.7	6.9	0	-3.3	-10.3	-1.2	-9.6	-27.6	-7.3	-4.2
1999	11.2	-13.3	-1.3	4.8	-12.7	-3.4	10.0	-8.6	-13.0	-32.0	5.4	-3.3

Source: CSO, 2000a: 43.

13)

Balance of Payments 1990–1999
[Z$ millions]

Year	1990	1991	1992	1993	1994	1995	1996	1997	1998	1999
Merchandise, net[#]	591,9	292,1	-1,277,1	646,6	1,395,9	767,5	2,489,0	-2,857,4	-2,258,2	9,536,2
Invisible transactions, net:										
Services	-345,3	-1,137,0	-1,788,8	-1,230,6	-2,273,3	-2,183,5	-2,597,2	-3,908,0	-1,034,0	804,2
Investment Income	-871,6	-1,045,5	-1,432,5	-1,633,3	-2,449,6	-2,836,2	-3,099,4	-5,090,8	-8,152,2	-5,438,3
Unrequited Transfers[*]	259.1	331,3	1,435,9	1,312,1	2,199.6	2,485,6	2,267,6	2,625,7	4,817,5	-8,234,0
Balance on Current account	-365,9	-1,559,1	-3,062,5	-905,2	-1,127,4	-1,766,6	-940.0	-9,230,5	-6,626,9	-3,331,9
Capital: Official	166,2	715,4	2,224,1	1,442,9	1,103,9	682,8	665,3	28,6	94,0	-4,097,2
Private	179,1	557,3	-44,4	738,3	1,660,5	2,463,6	-436,8	182,9	1,245,5	3,370,2
Balance on Capital account	345,3	1,272,7	2,179,7	2,181,2	2,764,4	3,146,4	228,5	211,5	1,339,5	-727,0
Unrecorded flow		100,1	265,5	83,7	561,8	440,0	501,0	-189,9	493,4	-2,106,4
Net Balance	-20,6	-386,5	-617,3	1,359,7	2,198,8	1,819,8	-210,5	-9,208,6	-4,794,0	-6,165,3

Source: Calculated from RBZ, 1999:52.

[#] The inclusion under net merchandise of payment for international freight services and gold sold by the Reserve Bank offsets the visible trade imbalance.

[*] Unrequited transfers includes aid to Government, migrant remittances, pension payments and receipts, gifts, maintenance payments, grants and donations.

14)

External Debt Outstanding and Repayments, 1991–1999

[*Z$ millions*]

Year	1991	1992	1993	1994	1995	1996	1997	1998	1999
Long term Debt	12 974	18 001	24 685	31 828	37 255	44 844	76 609	142 943	151 148
Government	9 382	13 999	19 478	25 303	29 336	34 804	58 820	115 478	118 234
Bilateral	3 814	4 553	6 081	7 522	8 854	10 954	18 774	33 017	31 271
Multilateral	2 528	5 177	8 387	11 923	14 106	16 886	28 900	60 766	63 433
Private	3 040	4 269	5 010	5 358	6 377	6 964	11 146	21 696	23 531
SOEs	2 264	2 309	2 837	3 792	4 511	5 199	9 056	20 171	23 857
Bilateral	549	675	953	1 419	1 705	1 910	3 117	11 530	14 192
Multilateral	967	1 086	1 357	1 694	2 052	2 455	4 506	5 775	6 800
Private	747	548	527	679	754	834	1 433	2 866	2 866
Private Sector	1 328	1 693	2 370	2 732	3 407	4 841	8 733	7 294	9 057
Short-term Debt	2 863	2 811	2 973	4 121	3 886	5 995	15 798	24 897	21 010
Total External Debt	15 837	20 813	27 658	35 849	41 142	50 839	92 407	167 840	172 159
In US Dollars	3 136	3 798	3 991	4 290	4 419	4 694	4 966	4 510	4 508
External Debt Repayments									
Government	1 103	1 714	2 511	3 105	2 833	3 528	3 813	7 481	14 969
SOEs	378	638	685	780	834	889	1 074	2 089	3 964
Private Sector	175	454	725	961	957	1 170	1 553	2 670	3 236
Total	1 662	2 805	3 921	4 846	4 625	5 587	6 440	12 240	22 168

Source: RBZ, 1999: 55.

BIBLIOGRAPHY

African Development Bank, [1995[, *African Development Report*, ADB Group, Abidjan, Cote D'Ivoire.

——, [1996], *African Development Report 1996: A Summary*, ADB Group, Abidjan, Cote D'Ivoire.

Agere, S.T., [1986], 'Progress and Problems in the Health Care Delivery System', in Mandaza, I., [ed], *Zimbabwe The Political Economy of Transition 1980-1986*, Codesria Books, Dakar, pp.355-376.

Amin, S., [1964], *The Class Struggle in Africa*, African Research Group, Report No. 2, New England Free Press.

——, [1994a], 'Fifty Years is Enough', *SAPEM*, 8, 2, pp.33-39.

——, [1994b], 'The Issue of Democracy in the Contemporary Third World', in Ulf Himmelstrand, Kabiru Kinyanjui and Edward Mburugu [eds], *African Perspectives on Development*, James Curry Ltd, London, pp.320-335.

Arrighi, G., [1973a] 'Labor Supplies in Historical Perspective: A Study of the Proletarianization of the African Peasantry in Rhodesia', in Arrighi, G., and Saul, J.S., *Essays on the Political Economy of Africa*, Monthly Review Press, New York, pp.180-234.

——, [1973b], 'The Political Economy of Rhodesia', in Arrighi, G., and Saul, J.S., *Essays on the Political Economy of Africa*, Monthly Review Press, New York, pp.336-377.

Astrow, A., [1983], *Zimbabwe: A Revolution that Lost Its Way?*, Pitman Press, UK.

Auret, D., [1995], *Urban Housing: A National Crisis?*, Mambo Press, Gweru.

Barraclough, S., [1990], 'Democracy, Socialism and Development', Paper presented to the Third World Forum Seminar, Zambezi

Falls, Zimbabwe, June 27-30. [copy available in SAPES Trust library].

Bates, R.H., [1981], *Markets and States in Tropical Africa*, University of California Press, Berkeley.

——, [1994], 'The Impulse to Reform in Africa', in Widner, J.A, [ed], *Economic Change and Political Liberalization in Sub-Saharan Africa*, The John Hopkins University Press, Baltimore.

Bayart, J.F., [1993], *The State in Africa: The Politics of the Belly*, Longman, New York.

Beach, D., [1994], *The Shona and their Neighbours*, Blackwell Publishers, Oxford.

Bello, W., [1994], *Dark Victory. The United States, Structural Adjustment and Global Poverty*, Pluto Press, London.

Berg, E., [1981], *Accelerated Development in sub-Saharan Africa: An Agenda for Action*, The World Bank, Washington D.C.

Berman, B., [1992], 'Up From Structuralism', in Berman, B., and Lonsdale, J., [eds], *Unhappy Valley Conflict in Kenya and Africa*, James Currey Ltd, London.

Bhebe, N., [1989], 'The Nationalist Struggle, 1957-1962', in Banana, C.S., [ed], *Turmoil and Tenacity. Zimbabwe 1890-1990*, The College Press, Harare.

Bienefeld, M., [1989], 'The Lessons of History and the Developing World', *Monthly Review*, 41, 3, July-August, pp.9-41.

——, [1995], 'Structural Adjustment and the Prospects for Democracy in Southern Africa', in Moore, D.B. and Schmitz, G.J., [eds], *Debating Development Discourse Institutional and Popular Perspectives*, Macmillan Press Ltd, London, pp.91-128.

Bijlmakers, L.A., Basset, M.T., and Sanders, D.M., [1998], *Socioeconomic Stress: Health and Child Nutritional Status in Zimbabwe at a Time of Economic Structural Adjustment. A three year longitudinal study*, Nordiska Afrikainstitutet, Research Report No. 105, Uppsala.

Bird, G., [1996], 'The International Monetary Fund and developing countries: a review of the evidence and policy options', *International Organisation*, 50, 5, [summer], pp.477-511.

Bond, P., [1990], 'Preserving Inequality: The World Bank in Zimbabwe', *Multinational Monitor*, 11, April, pp.9-11.

——. [1998], *Uneven Zimbabwe A study of Finance Development and Underdevelopment*, Africa World Press Inc., Asmara, Eritrea.

Booth, K., [1991], 'Security and Emancipation', *Review of International Studies*, 17, pp.313-326.

Botchwey, K., Collier, P., and Gunning, J.W., [1998], *External Evaluation of the Enhanced Structural Adjustment Facility*, IMF, Washington, January.

Bourdillon, M.F.C., [1993], *Where are the Ancestors? Changing Culture in Zimbabwe*, University of Zimbabwe Publications, Harare.

Brand, C., [1994], 'The Communal Lands Re-organisation Programme in Zimbabwe', *Review of Rural and Urban Planning in Southern and Eastern Africa*, 1, pp.53-74.

Brand, V., Mupedziswa, R., and Gumbo, P., [1995], 'Structural Adjustment, Women and Informal Sector Trade in Harare', in Gibbon, P., [ed], *Structural Adjustment and the Working Poor in Zimbabwe*, Nordiska Afrikainstitutet, Uppsala, pp.132-212.

Bratton, M., [1994], 'Land Redistribution, 1980-1990', in Rukuni, M., and Eicher, C.K., *Zimbabwe's Agricultural Revolution*, UZ Publications, Mambo Press, Gweru, pp.70-86.

Brautigam, D.A., [1994], 'What Can Africa Learn from Taiwan? Political Economy, Industrial Policy, and Adjustment', *The Journal of Modern African Studies*, 32, 1, pp.111-138.

——, [1995], 'The State as Agent: Industrial Development in Taiwan, 1952-1972', in Stein, H., [ed], *Asian Industrialisation and Africa*, St Martins Press, New York, pp.145-182.

Breman, J., and Mundle, S., [eds], [1991], *Rural Transformation in Asia*, Oxford University Press, New Delhi.

Brenner, R., [1976], 'Agrarian Class Structure and Economic Development in Pre-Industrial Europe', *Past and Present*, No. 70, February, pp. 30-75.

——, [1977], 'The Origins of Capitalist Development: a Critique of Neo-Smithian Marxism', *New Left Review*, 104, pp.25-92..

Breslin. E.D., [1994], 'USAID, the State, and Food Insecurity in Rural Zimbabwe', *The Journal of Modern African Studies*, 32, 1, pp.81-110.

Browne, R.S., [1992], 'Alternative Policy Frameworks for African Development in the 1990s', in Nyang'oro and Shaw, T.M., *Beyond Structural Adjustment in Africa: The Political Economy of Sustainable Growth and Development*, Praeger, New York, pp.71-82.

Bruce, J.W., [1990], 'Legal issues in Land Use and Resettlement – Background Paper', in *Zimbabwe Agricultural Sector Memorandum*, World Bank, Washington D.C.

Bush, R, and Cliffe, L, [1984] 'Agrarian Policy in Migrant Labour Societies: Reform or Transformation in Zimbabwe?', *Review of African Political Economy*, 29, pp.77-94.

Byres, T.J., [1991], 'The Agrarian Question and Differing Forms of Capitalist Agrarian Transition: An Essay with Reference to Asia', in Breman, J., and Mundle, S., [eds], *Rural Transformation in Asia*, Oxford University Press, New Dehli, pp.3-66.

Callinicos, A., [1991], *The Revenge of History*, Polity Press, Cambridge.

Central Statistical Office [1994], *Census 1992*, Government Printers, Harare.

——, [1997a], *Zimbabwe 1997 Inter-Censal Demographic Survey Report,* Government Printers, Harare.

——, [1997b], *Statistical Yearbook 1997*, Government Printers, Harare.

——, [1997c], *National Accounts 1985-1996*, CSO, Harare.

——, [1998a], *Poverty in Zimbabwe*, Harare.

——, [1998b], *Statement of External Trade 1990-97*, Harare, August.

——, [1998c], Quarterly Digest of Statistics, Harare, December.

——, [2000a], Quarterly Digest of Statistics, Harare, March.

——, [2000b], Quarterly Digest of Statistics, Harare, December.

Centre of Concern, [2000], 'Quotes', *News and Notices for IMF and World Bank Watchers*, 2, 3, Fall edition.

Chakaodza, A.M., [1993], *Structural Adjustment in Zambia and Zimbabwe. Reconstructive or Destructive?*, Third World Publishing House, Harare.

Chavunduka, G.L., [1982], *Report of the Commission of Inquiry into the Agricultural Industry*, Government Printers, Harare.

Cheater, A.P., [1984], *Idioms of Accumulation. Rural Development and Class Formation among Freeholders in Zimbabwe*, Mambo Press, Gweru.

——, [1986], *Social Anthropology: An Alternative Introduction*, Mambo Press, Gweru.

——, [1990], 'The Ideology of 'Communal' Land Tenure in Zimbabwe: Mythogenesis Enacted?', *Africa*, 60, 2, pp.188-206.

——, [1991], 'Rural Development and Peasant Alienation?', *Zambezia*, 18, 2, pp.89-104.

Chenaux-Respond, M., [1993], *Gender based Land Use Rights in Model A Resettlement schemes of Mashonaland, Zimbabwe*, Rudecon Zimbabwe P/L, Harare.

Chidzero, B., [1993], 'Restructuring the Economy: An Interview with Bernard Chidzero', *The Courier* [Africa-Caribbean-Pacific-European Community], 139, pp.42-45.

——, [1994], 'Macroeconomic Adjustment and Trade Liberalisation', in Rukuni, M., and Eicher, C.K., *Zimbabwe's Agricultural Revolution*, UZ Publications, Harare, pp.277-288.

Chimombe, T., [1986], 'Foreign Capital', in Mandaza, I., [ed], *Zimbabwe The Political Economy of Transition 1980-1986*, Codesria Books, Dakar, pp.123-140.

Chipika, S., [1995], *Economic Reform and Small-scale Enterprises in Zimbabwe: An Indigenous Enterprise Empowerment Strategy*, Intermediate Technology Development Group, Harare.

Chipika, S., and Chisvo, M., [1997], *Economic Reform and Small holder Communal Agricultural Development in Zimbabwe: a Literature Review Paper*, Intermediate Technology Development Group, Harare.

Chomsky, N., [1991], 'The Struggle for Democracy in a Changed World', *Review of African Political Economy*, 50, pp.12-20.

——, [1997], *World Orders, Old and New*, Pluto Press, London.

Chossudovsky, M., [1997], *The Globalisation of Poverty. Impacts of IMF and World Bank Reforms*, Third World Network, Malaysia.

Clarke, D.G., [1980], *Foreign Companies and International Investment in Zimbabwe*, Mambo Press, Gweru.

Cliffe, L., [1986], *Policy Options for Agrarian Reform in Zimbabwe*, FAO, Rome.

——, [1991], 'Were they Pushed or did they Jump: Zimbabwe and the World Bank?', *Southern African Report*, March.

Cockett, R., [1994], *Thinking the Unthinkable: Think-tanks and the Economic Counter-Revolution*, Harper Collins, London.

Cole, D.L., and Cole, J.S., [1994], 'Tobacco Research and Development', in Rukuni, M., and Eicher, C.K., *Zimbabwe's Agricultural Revolution*, UZ Publications, Mambo Press, Gweru, pp.234-244.

Cooper, F., [1993], 'Africa in the World Economy', in Cooper, F., Isaacman, A.F., Mallon, F.E., Roseberry, W., and Stern, S.J., [eds], *Confronting Historical Paradigms. Peasants, Labour and the Capitalist World System in Africa and Latin America*, The University of Wisconsin Press, Madison.

Cousins, B., Weiner, D., and Amin, N., [1992] 'Social Differentiation in the Communal Lands of Zimbabwe', *Review of African Political Economy*, 53, pp.5-24.

Cummings, R.J., [1992], 'A Historical Perspective on the LPA', in Nyang'oro and Shaw, T.M., *Beyond Structural Adjustment in Africa: The Political Economy of Sustainable Growth and Development*, Praeger, New York, pp.29-46.

Curtin Knight, V., [1990],'Zimbabwe a Decade after Independence', in *Current History*, May, pp.201-227.

Dashwood, H.S., [1996], 'The Relevance of Class to the Evolution of Zimbabwe's Development Strategy, 1980-1991', *Journal of Southern African Studies*, 22, 1, March, pp.27-48.

Davis, R., and Sanders, D., [1987], 'Stabilisation Policies and the Effects on Child Health in Zimbabwe', *Review of African Political Economy*, 38.

Deve, T., [1997], 'War Veterans: The Forgotten People?', *SAPEM*, 10,11, Aug 15-Sept 15, pp.8-9.

Dollar, D., and Svensson, J., [1998], *What Explains the Success or Failure of Structural Adjustment Programmes?*, Policy Research Working Paper 1938, Development Research Group, Macroeconomics and Growth, The World Bank, Washington D.C., June.

Drinkwater, M., [1989], 'Technical Development and Peasant Impoverishment: Land Use Policy in Zimbabwe's Midlands

Province', *Journal of Southern African Studies*, 15, 2, pp.287-305.

Dunlop, H., [1972], 'Land and Economic Opportunity in Rhodesia', *Rhodesian Journal of Economics*, 6,1, pp.1-18.

——, 'Development in Rhodesian Tribal Areas', *Rhodesian Journal of Economics*, 8,2, pp.177-189.

Duggan, W.R., [1980], 'The Native Land Husbandry Act of 1951 and the Rural African Middle Class of Southern Rhodesia', *African Affairs*, 79:pp.227-239.

Elliot, J., [1991], 'Environmental Degradation, Soil Conservation and the Colonial and Post Colonial State in Rhodesia/Zimbabwe', in Dixon, C., and Heffernan, M.J., *Colonialism and Development in the Contemporary World*, Mansell, London.

English, E.P., and Mule, H.M., [1996], *The African Development Bank*, Lynne Rienner Publishers, Colorado.

Fanon, F, [1963], *The Wretched of the Earth*, Grove Press, New York.

First Merchant Bank, [1997], *Quarterly Guide to the Economy*, June.

——, [1998], *Quarterly Guide to the Economy*, December.

Friedman, M., [1980], *Free to Choose*, Harcourt Brace Jovanovich, New York.

Fukuyama, F., [1989], 'The End of History?', *National Interest*, 16, [summer], pp.3-18.

——., [1992], *The End of History and the Last Man*, The Free Press, New York.

Galbraith, J.K., [1991], *A History of Economics*, Penguin Books, England.

Gaidzanwa, R.B., [1988], *Women's Land Rights in Zimbabwe*, Dept. of Rural and Urban Planning, University of Zimbabwe, Occasional Paper No.13, August.

Garbett, G.K., [1966], 'The Rhodesian Chief's Dilemma: Government Officer or Tribal Leader?', *RACE*, No.8, pp.113-128.

Gemini Survey, [1991], *Micro and Small-scale Enterprises in Zimbabwe. Results of a Countrywide Survey*, USAID Technical Report No. 25.

George, S., [1992], *The Debt Boomerang. How Third World Debt Harms Us All*, Pluto Press, London.

——, [1993], 'The Debt Question', in Lundestad, G., and Westad, O.A., [eds], *Beyond the Cold War: New Dimensions in International Relations*, Scandinavian Uni. Press, Norway.

George, S., and Sabelli, F., [1994], *Faith and Credit. The World Bank's Secular Empire*, Westview Press, Boulder, USA.

Gibbon, P., [1995], 'Introduction: Structural Adjustment and the Working Poor in Zimbabwe', in Gibbon, P., [ed], *Structural Adjustment and the Working Poor in Zimbabwe*, Nordiska Afrikainstitutet, Uppsala, pp.7-57.

Gill, S., and Law, D., [1988], *The Global Political Economy. Perspectives, Problems and Policies*, Harvestor and Wheatsheaf, Great Britain.

Gill, S., [1993], 'Neo-liberalism and the Shift Towards a US-centred Transnational Hegemony', in Overbeek, H., [ed], *Restructuring Hegemony in the Global Political Economy*, Routledge, London.

Godwin, P., and Hancock, I., [1993], *'Rhodesians Never Die' The Impact of War and Political Change on White Rhodesia*, 1970-1980, Oxford University Press, New York.

Government of Southern Rhodesia, [1955], *What the Native Land Husbandry Act means to rural Africans and to Southern Rhodesia. A five year plan that will revolutionise African agriculture*, Government Printers, Salisbury.

Government of Zimbabwe, [1983], *Progress Report on the Intensive and Accelerated Resettlement Programme*, Department of Rural Development, Harare.

Government of Zimbabwe/MLARR, [1986], *Communal Lands Development Plan, Government Printers*, Harare.

Government of Zimbabwe, [1991a], *A Framework for Economic Reform 1991-1995*, Ministry of Finance, Economic Planning and Development, January.

——, [1991b], *Second Five-Year National Development Plan*, Ministry of Finance, Economic Planning and Development, December.

——, [1994], *Budget Statement*, Ministry of Finance, Economic Planning and Development, Harare.

Government of Zimbabwe/Land Tenure Commission, [1994], *Report of the Commission of Inquiry into Appropriate*

Agricultural Land Tenure Systems, Government Printers, Harare.

Government of Zimbabwe, [1996], *Public Expenditure Review*, Heads of Ministries Business Retreat, Montclair Casino Hotel.

Government of Zimbabwe/MPSLASW, [1996], *1995 Poverty Assessment Study Survey Preliminary Report*, Government Printers, Harare.

Government of Zimbabwe, [1998a], *Zimbabwe Programme for the Economic and Social Transformation 1996-2000*, Ministry of Finance, Economic Planning and Development, Harare.

Government of Zimbabwe/MPSLASW, [1998b], *1995 Poverty Assessment Study Survey Final Report*, Government Printers, Harare.

Government of Zimbabwe, [1998c], *Land Reform and the Resettlement Programme Phase two: a Policy Framework Document*, Government Printers, Harare, September.

——, [2001], 'Health Sector Reforms in Zimbabwe', ZANU-PF web site – www.zanupfpub.co.zw, 16/03/01.

Greider, W., [1997], *One World Ready or Not: The Manic Logic of Global Capitalism*, Simon and Schuster, New York.

Grilli, E.R., [1993], *The EC and the Developing Countries*, Cambridge University Press, Hong Kong.

Handford, J., [1976], *Portrait of an Economy. Rhodesia Under Sanctions*, Mercury Press, Salisbury.

Hardin, G., [1993], *Living within Limits*, Oxford University Press, Oxford, UK.

Hawkins, A.M., [1994], 'Lessons of Adjustment from Zimbabwe', in Kapoor, K., [ed], *Africa's Experience with Structural Adjustment. Proceedings of the Harare Seminar, May 23-24, 1994.*, World Bank Discussion Papers 228, Washington D.C., pp.48-52.

Herbst, J., [1989], 'Political Impediments to Economic Rationality: Explaining Zimbabwe's Failure to Reform its Public Sector', *The Journal of Modern African Studies*, 27, 1, March, pp.67-84.

Hewitt, A., [1989], 'ACP and the Developing World', in Lodge, J., [ed], *The EC and the Challenge of the Future*, Pinter, London.

Himmelstrand, U., [1994] 'Perspectives, Controversies and Dilemmas in the Study of African Development', in Himmelstrand, U.,

Kinyanjui, K., and Mburugu, E., [eds], *African Perspectives on Development*, James Curry Ltd, London, pp.16-36.

Iliffe, J., [1987], *The African Poor. A history*, Cambridge University Press, Cambridge.

——, [1989], 'The Origins of African Population Growth', in *Journal of African History* [review article], 30, pp.165-169.

ILO/SAMAT, [1995], *Report on the Design of Policies and Programs for Growth and Employment Promotion in the Non-Formal Sectors of Zimbabwe*, ILO, December [Copy available in IDS library].

IMF, [1997], *Zimbabwe—Recent Economic Developments*, Country Report No: 97/59, Washington D.C., July.

Jackson, J.C. and Collier, P., [1988], 'Incomes, Poverty and Food Security in the Communal Lands of Zimbabwe', Occasional Paper, Department of Rural and Urban Planning, University of Zimbabwe.

Jansen, D., and Muir, K., [1994] 'Trade, Exchange Rate Policy and Agriculture', in Rukuni, M., and Eicher, C.K., *Zimbabwe's Agricultural Revolution*, UZ Publications, Mambo Press, Gweru, pp.175-187.

Jayne T.S., [1991], *Structural Adjustment and Food Security in Zimbabwe: Strategies to Maintain Access to Maize by Low-Income Groups during Maize Market Restructuring*, Ministry of Lands, Agriculture and Rural Resettlement, Harare.

Jayne, T.S., Chisvo, M., and Rukuni, M., [1994]. 'Zimbabwe's Food Insecurity Paradox: Hunger Amid Abundance', in Rukuni, M., and Eicher, C.K., *Zimbabwe's Agricultural Revolution*, UZ Publications, Mambo Press, Gweru, pp.289-303.

Jayne, T.S., and Rukuni, M., [1994], 'Managing the Food Economy in the 1990s', in Rukuni, M., and Eicher, C.K., *Zimbabwe's Agricultural Revolution*, UZ Publications, Mambo Press, Gweru, pp.374-390.

Kadenge, P., Ndoro, H., and Zwizwai, B., [1992], 'Zimbabwe`s Structural Adjustment Programme: The First Year Experience', in Mwanza, A., [ed], *Structural Adjustment Programmes in SADC*, SAPES Books, Harare, pp.168-197.

Kadhani, X.M., [1986], 'The Economy: Issues, Problems and Prospects', in Mandaza, I., [ed], *Zimbabwe The Political*

Economy of Transition 1980-1986, Codesria Books, Dakar, pp.99-122.

Kanji, N., and Jazdowska, N., [1993], 'Structural Adjustment and Women in Zimbabwe', *Review of African Political Economy*, 56, pp.11-26.

Kanyenze, G., [1996], 'The Impact of Economic Stabilisation on the Wage Structure in Zimbabwe: 1980-90', in Harvey, C., [ed], *Constraints on the Success of Structural Adjustment Programmes in Africa*, Macmillan Press Ltd, London.

Kapoor, K., [1994], 'The World Bank Perspective of ESAP in Zimbabwe', Paper presented at the ILO Workshop on Cooperative Development and ESAP, February 22.

Kaseke, E., Dhemba, J., and Gumbo, P., [1997], *Transferring Resources to Poor Households. The case for Social Safety Nets in Zimbabwe*, Ministry of Public Service, Labour and Social Welfare/UNICEF, Harare.

Kennedy, P., [1994], 'Political Barriers to African Capitalism', *Journal of Modern African Studies*, 32, 2, pp.191-213.

Kiguel, M., and Jones, C., 1995, 'Adjustment in Africa: Reforms, Results and the Road Ahead', in Kapoor, K., [ed], *Africa's Experience with Structural Adjustment. Proceedings of the Harare Seminar, May 23-24, 1994.*, World Bank Discussion Papers 228, Washington D.C., pp.7-27.

Kim, K.S., [1995], 'The Korean Miracle [1962-80 Revisited: Myths and Realities in Strategies and Development', in Stein, H., [ed], *Asian Industrialisation and Africa*, St Martins Press, New York, pp.87-144. .

Kramer, E., [1998], 'A Clash of Economies: Early Centralisation Efforts in Colonial Zimbabwe, 1929-1935', *Zambezia*, 25, 1, pp.83-98.

Kriger, N.J., [1992], *Zimbabwe`s Guerilla War. Peasant Voices*, Cambridge University Press, Cambridge.

Kropotkin, P., [1899] [1974 ed], *Fields, Factories and Workshops Tomorrow*, George Allen and Unwin Ltd, London.

Kujinga, Z and Makoni, K, [1996], *Poverty in the ESAP Era. The Case of a Commercial Farming Community*, Silveira House, ESAP Monitoring Project, Harare.

Laidler, M., [1993], 'EC-Zimbabwe cooperation: a tradition of solid support', *The Courier* [Africa-Caribbean-Pacific-European Community], No. 139, May-June, pp.49-50.

Lang, T., and Hines, C., [1993], *The New Protectionism*, Earthscan Publications Ltd, London.

Lehman, H., [1990], 'The Politics of Adjustment in Kenya and Zimbabwe: The State as Intermediary', *Studies in Comparative International Development*, Fall, 25, 3, pp.37-72.

Leys, C., [1995], 'Confronting the African Tragedy', *New Left Review*, 204, March/April, pp.33-47.

——, [1996], *The Rise and Fall of Development Theory*, James Currey Ltd, London.

Logan, B.I., and Mengisteab, [1993], 'IMF-World Bank Adjustment and Structural Transformation in Sub-Saharan Africa', in *Economic Geography*, 69, 1, January, pp.1-24.

Luxemburg, R., [1951 ed], *The Accumulation of Capital*, Routledge and Kegan Paul International, London.

MacGarry sj, B., [1993], *Growth? Without Equity?*, Silveira House Social Series/Mambo Press, Gweru.

——, [1994], *Land For Which People? Some Unanswered Questions*, Silveira House Social Series/Mambo Press, Gweru.

——, [1998], *A Rural Poverty Datum Line 1996 Hurungwe Area*, The Catholic Commission for Justice & Peace/Mambo Press, Gweru.

——, [1999], *The Poverty Trap*, Final draft to be published by Mambo Press, Gweru.

——, [2000], *Zimbabwe and the International Financial Institutions*, unpublished paper, Silveira House, Harare.

Magadzire, G.S.T., [1994] 'Smallholder Agriculture under ESAP: Challenges and Prospects', in ZFU/Friedrich Ebert Foundation seminar papers, *The Future of Smallholder Farming under ESAP*, Kadoma Ranch Motel, November 2-3.

Makone, I., [1994], 'Marketing Procurement of Produce', in ZFU/Friedrich Ebert Foundation seminar papers, *The Future of Smallholder Farming under ESAP*, Kadoma Ranch Motel, November 2-3.

Makoni, S., [2000], 'State of the Zimbabwe Economy', Address by the Minister of Finance and Economic Development to the ZANU-PF Special Congress, 16 December.

Makumbe, J.Mw., [1996], *Participatory Development The case of Zimbabwe*, UZ Publications, Harare.

Mandaza, I., and Sachikonye, L.M., [1991], 'Introduction The Zimbabwe Debate on the One-Party State and Democracy', in Mandaza, I., and Sachikonye, L.M., [eds], *The One-Party State and Democracy The Zimbabwe Debate*, Sapes Books, Harare, pp.1-17.

Mandaza, I., [1991], 'The One-Party State and Democracy in Southern Africa: Towards a Conceptual Framework', in Mandaza, I., and Sachikonye, L.M., [eds], *The One-Party State and Democracy The Zimbabwe Debate*, Sapes Books, Harare, pp.19-41.

——, [1995], 'The State and Politics in Zimbabwe', *SAPEM*, 8, 6, March, pp.31-32.

——, [1997], 'A Country in Crisis?', *SAPEM*, 10,11, Aug 15-Sept 15, pp.4-7.

Mandebvu, M., [1997], 'The Next Stage: The World Bank Group and ZIMPREST', *SAPEM*, 10,11, Aug 15-Sept 15, 11-14.

Mariga, I.K., [1994], 'Cotton Research and Development', in Rukuni, M., and Eicher, C.K., *Zimbabwe's Agricultural Revolution*, UZ Publications, Mambo Press, Gweru, pp.219-233.

Marquette, C.M., [1997], 'Current Poverty, Structural Adjustment, and Drought in Zimbabwe', *World Development*, 25, 7, pp.1141-1149.

Martin, D. and Johnson, P., [1981], *The Struggle for Zimbabwe,* Monthly Review Press, London.

Marx, K., [1978 ed], *Capital. A Critique of Political Economy*, Progress Publishers, Moscow.

Masanzu, F., [1994], 'Agriculture and ESAP', in ZFU/Friedrich Ebert Foundation seminar papers, *The Future of Smallholder Farming under ESAP*, Kadoma Ranch Motel, November 2-3.

Mashingaidze, K., [1994], 'Maize Research and Development', in Rukuni, M., and Eicher, C.K., *Zimbabwe's Agricultural Revolution*, UZ Publications, Mambo Press, Gweru, pp.208-218.

Masuko, L. and Nyoni, D., [1993], *Decentralisation Policy in Zimbabwe: Impact on Local government Performance*, IDS Monographs, University of Zimbabwe, Harare.

Mengisteab, K., and Logan, B.I., [1990] 'Implications of Liberalisation Policies for Agricultural Development in Sub-Saharan Africa', *Comparative Political Studies*, 22, 4, January, pp.437-457.

Mengisteab, K., [1992], 'Responses of Afro-Marxist states to the crisis of socialism: a preliminary assessment', *Third World Quarterly*, 13, 1, pp.77-87.

Mhishi, S.G., [1995], 'A critical analysis of the Resettlement Programme in Zimbabwe', ZFU/Friedrich Ebert Foundation seminar papers, *Resettlement Programme in Zimbabwe Options for the Future,* Harare Sheraton Hotel, March 16.

Mhone, G., [1992], 'Communal Agriculture in Atrophy', *SAPEM*, 5, 12, September, pp.20-23.

——, [1995], 'Dependency and Underdevelopment: The Limits of Structural Adjustment Programmes and Towards a Pro-Active State-Led Development Strategy', *African Development Review*, 7, 2, pp.51-85.

Mkandawire, T., [1985], *The Informal Sector in the Labour Reserve Economies of Southern Africa with Special Reference to Zimbabwe*, Working Paper No.1, ZIDS, UZ.

——, [1994a], 'Adjustment, Political Conditionality and Democratisation in Africa', in Cornia, G.A., and Helleiner, G.K., *From Adjustment to Development in Africa. Conflict, Controversy, Convergence, Consensus?*, St. Martin's Press, New York, pp.155-173.

——, [1994b], 'The Political Economy of Privatisation', in Cornia, G.A., and Helleiner, G.K., *From Adjustment to Development in Africa. Conflict, Controversy, Convergence, Consensus?*, St. Martin's Press, New York, pp.192-213.

Mlambo, A.S., [1997], *The ESAP The Case of Zimbabwe 1991-1995*, UZ Publications, Harare.

Mnangagwa, Hon. E.D., [1989], 'Building on a Firm Foundation. Constitutional developments in Zimbabwe, 1987-1990', in *Parliamentarian*, 70, July, pp.127-131.

Mohamad, M., 1999, 'Our Region, Ourselves', *Time*, May 31, pp.18-21.

Moore, D.B., [1991], 'The Ideological Formation of the Zimbabwean Ruling Class', *Journal of Southern African Studies*, 17, 3, September, pp.472-495.

——, [1995], 'Development Discourse as Hegemony: Towards an Ideological History – 1945-1995', in Moore, D.B. and Schmitz, G.J., [eds], *Debating Development Discourse Institutional and Popular Perspectives*, Macmillan Press Ltd, London, pp.1-53.

Moyo, J. N., [1992], 'State Politics and Social Domination in Zimbabwe', *The Journal of Modern African Studies*, 30, 2, pp.305-330.

Moyo, S., Moyo, N.P., and Lowenson, R., [1985], *The Root Causes of Hunger in Zimbabwe – an overview of the nature, causes and effects of hunger, and strategies to combat hunger*, ZIDS working papers, IDS, UZ, September.

Moyo, S, and Skalnes, T, [1990], *Zimbabwe`s Land Reform and Development Strategy: State Autonomy, Class Bias and Economic Rationality*, Research Papers, Institute of Development Studies, U.Z., Harare.

Moyo, S., [1991], *Zimbabwe`s Agrarian Reform Process: Lessons or Domino Strategies?*, Discussion Papers, Institute of Development Studies, Harare.

Moyo, S. and Page, H., [1992], *A Review of the Class and Gender Basis of Agricultural Extension Services in Zimbabwe`s Communal Areas*, Discussion Papers, Zimbabwe Institute of Development Studies, Harare.

Moyo, S., [1994], 'Land Tenure Bidding Among Black Agrarian Capitalists in Zimbabwe', *Southern African Political and Economic Monthly*, 7, 8, May: 37-40.

——, [1995], *The Land Question in Zimbabwe*, Sapes Books, Harare.

Moyo, T., [1998], 'Capital Markets and the Wheels of Fortune', *Southern African Economist*, March, pp.7-9.

Mswaka, T.E., [1994], 'A Land Tenure System for Zimbabwe: A Businessman's Perspective', Paper prepared for the conference *Land Tenure Systems and their Impact Upon Economic Development*, Harare Sheraton, 28-29/06/94.

Mudimu, G., [1994], 'Possible strategies for Smallholder Sector', in ZFU/Friedrich Ebert Foundation seminar papers, *The Future of Smallholder Farming under ESAP*, Kadoma Ranch Motel, November 2-3.

Mugabe, R.G., [1989], 'The Unity Accord: its promise for the future', in Banana, C.S., [ed], *Turmoil and Tenacity. Zimbabwe 1890-1990*, The College Press, Harare, pp.336-359.

Mugwetsi, T. and Balleis S.J., P., [1994], *The Forgotten People. The living and health conditions of farm workers and their families*, Silveira House Social Series/Mambo Press, Gweru.

Muir, K., [1994], 'Agriculture in Zimbabwe', in Rukuni, M., and Eicher, C.K., *Zimbabwe's Agricultural Revolution*, UZ Publications, Mambo Press, Gweru, pp.40-55.

Mukora, C.M., [1992], 'The Significance of Current Farm Designations in Zimbabwe', *SAPEM*, 7, 1, October, pp.42-43.

Muzulu, J., [1996], 'The Structural Adjustment Implications of Real Exchange Rate Depreciation on the Manufacturing Sector in Zimbabwe', in Harvey, C., [ed], *Constraints on the Success of Structural Adjustment Programmes in Africa*, Macmillan Press Ltd, London.

Muzvidziwa, V.N., [1997], 'Masvingos's double rooted female heads of households', *Zambezia*, 24, 1, pp.97-123.

Myint, H., [1975] 'Agriculture and Economic Development in the Open Economy', in Reynolds, L.G., [ed], *Agriculture in Development Theory*, Yale University Press, New Haven.

Mwanza, A. M., [1992], 'Theory and Practice of Structural Adjustment Programs', in Mwanza, A.M., [ed], *Structural Adjustment Programmes in SADC*, SAPES Books, Harare.

——, [1992], 'Structural Adjustment Programmes in SADC. What Have We Learned?', in Mwanza, A.M., [ed], *Structural Adjustment Programmes in SADC*, SAPES Books, Harare.

Ncube, M.N., [1994], 'Epochs of Economic Structural Adjustment in Zimbabwe and Their Social Dimensions, 1965-95', in Shepherd, G.W. jnr., and Sonko, K.N.M., [eds], *Economic Justice in Africa. Adjustment and Sustainable Development*, Greenwood Press, Westport, pp.175-187.

Ncube, W., [1991], 'Constitutionalism, Democracy and Political Practice in Zimbabwe', in Mandaza, I., and Sachikonye, L.M.,

[eds], *The One-Party State and Democracy The Zimbabwe Debate*, Sapes Books, Harare, pp.155-177.

Ndlela, D.B., [1986], 'Problems of Industrialisation: Structural and Policy Issues', in Mandaza, I., [ed], *Zimbabwe The Political Economy of Transition 1980-1986*, Codesria Books, Dakar, pp.141-164.

Ndoro, H., [1996], 'The Informal Sector in a Decontrolling Formerly Socialist Economy', in Mhone, G.C.Z, [ed], *The Informal Sector in Southern Africa. An Analysis of Conceptual, Research and Policy Issues*, Sapes Books, Harare, pp.21-53.

Nicholle, W.H.H., [1971] 'The Development of the Subsistence Sector. What is being done in Rhodesia?', *Rhodesian Journal of Economics*, 5, 4, pp.1-8.

North, D, [1981], *Structure and Change in Tropical Africa*, W.W. Norton, New York.

Nyangoni, C., and Nyandoro G., [1979], *Zimbabwe Independence Movements*, Rex Collins, London.

Nyawata, O.I., [1988], 'Macroeconomic Management, Adjustment and Stabilisation', in Stoneman, C., [ed], *Zimbabwe's Prospects. Issues of Race, Class, State and Capital in Southern Africa*, Macmillan, London, pp.90-115.

Okoth-Ogendo, H.W.O., [1993], 'Agrarian Reform in Sub-Saharan Africa: An Assessment of State Responses to the African Agrarian Crisis and Their Implications for Agricultural Development', in Basset, T.J., and Crummey, D.E. [eds], *Land in African Agrarian Systems*, The University of Wisconsin Press, USA.

Oni, S.A Prof., [1997], *Impact of ESAP on the Communal Areas of Zimbabwe*, Friedrich-Ebert-Stiftung, Harare.

Onwuka, R.I., [1989], 'Beyond Lome 3: Prospects for Symmetrical EurAfrican Relations', in R. I. Onwuka and T. M. Shaw [eds], *Africa in World Politics: Into the 1990s*, Macmillan, Hong Kong.

Ould-Mey, M., [1994], 'Global Adjustment: implications for peripheral states', *Third World Quarterly*, 15, 2, pp. 319-336.

——, [1995], 'Democratisation in Africa: The Political Face of SAPs', *Journal of Third World Studies*, 12, 2, pp.122-158.

Pamacheche, E., [1996] 'Economic Policy Development and Poverty Alleviation', *The Political Economy of Poverty in Zimbabwe*, I.D.S. Policy Dialogue Series No: 1, U.Z., Harare.

Phimister, I., [1988], *An economic and social history of Zimbabwe 1890-1948*, Longman, New York.

Polanyi, K., [1944], *The Great Transformation*, Farrar and Rinehart Inc., New York.

Poverty Reduction Forum, [1997], *The National Budget and Poverty Reduction*, Institute of Development Studies, UZ, Harare.

——, [1999], *Towards a Pro-Poor National Budget: Recommendations for the 1999 National Budget*, UNDP/PRF/IDS, UZ, Harare.

Rakode, C, [1995] 'The Household Strategies of the Urban poor: Coping with Poverty and Recession in Gweru, Zimbabwe', *Habitat International*, 19, 4, pp.447-471.

Raftopoulos, B., [1992], 'Beyond the House of Hunger: Democratic Struggle in Zimbabwe', *Review of African Political Economy*, 54 & 55, pp.59-74, 57-66.

Ranger, T.O., [1985], *Peasant Consciousness and Guerilla War in Zimbabwe*, James Currey Ltd, London.

——, [1993], 'The Communal Areas of Zimbabwe', in Basset, T.J., and Crummey, D.E. [eds], *Land in African Agrarian Systems*, The University of Wisconsin Press, USA.

Rasmussen, R.K., and Rubert, S.C., [1990], *Historical Dictionary of Zimbabwe* [2nd ed], The Scarecrow Press, Inc., Metuchen, New Jersey.

Ravallion, M., and Chen, S., [1996], *What can New Survey Data Tell us About Recent Changes in Living Standards in Developing and Transitional Economies?*, Background Paper to the World Development Report 1996, Poverty and Human Resources Division, Policy Research Department, the World Bank, Washington D.C.

Renfrew, Dr. A., [1992], *ESAP & Health*, Silveira House Social Series No. 3, Mambo Press, Gweru.

——, [1994a], *Quarterly Economic and Statistical Review*, March-June.

——, [1994b], *Quarterly Economic and Statistical Review*, September-December.

——, [1995], *Annual Report*, RBZ, Harare.

——, [1997a], *Quarterly Economic and Statistical Review*, March-June.

——, [1997b], *Quarterly Economic and Statistical Review*, September-December.

——, [1997c], *Annual Report*, RBZ, Harare.

——, [1998], *Annual Report*, RBZ, Harare.

——, [1999], *Quarterly Economic and Statistical Review*, September-December.

Riddell, R.C., [1981], *Report of the Commission of Inquiry into Incomes, Prices and Conditions of Service*, Government Printers, Harare.

——., [1990], 'Zimbabwe', in Riddell, R.C., [ed], *Manufacturing Africa*, James Currey, London, pp.337-411.

——, [1993], 'The Future of the Manufacturing Sector in Sub-Saharan Africa', in Callaghy, T.M., and Ravenhill, J., [eds], *Hemmed in: responses to Africa's economic decline*, New York, pp.215-247.

Rifkind, M.L., [1972], 'Land Apportionment in Perspective', *Rhodesian History*, no. 3, pp.53-62.

Robinson, P. B., [1998], *Macroeconomic Performance During ESAP – An Essay on Iatrogenic Economics*, Paper prepared for the International Conference, 19-21 August 1998, organized by the University of Zimbabwe Department of Economics and the Professional Development and Training Programme in Economics Project.

Rosewarne, S., [1992], 'Toward a New European Regime of Capital Accumulation?', in B. Nelson, D. Roberts and W. Veit [eds], *The European Community in the 1990s*, Berg Publishers Inc., Oxford.

Rotberg, R.I., [2000], 'Africa's Mess, Mugabe's Mayhem', *Foreign Affairs*, 79, 5, September/October, pp.47-61.

Roth, M., and Bruce, J.W., [1994], *Land Tenure, Agrarian Structure and Comparative Land Use in Zimbabwe: options for land tenure reform and land redistribution*, Madison Land Tenure Centre, University of Wisconsin, August.

Rukuni, M., [1994], 'The Evolution of Agricultural Policy: 1890-1990', in Rukuni, M., and Eicher, C.K., *Zimbabwe's Agricultural Revolution*, UZ Publications, Mambo Press, Gweru, pp.15-39.

Rukuni, M., and Jayne, T.S., [1995], Alleviating Hunger in Zimbabwe: Towards a National Food Security, UZ.

Rukuni, M., [1998], 'Land Reform in Zimbabwe: Dimensions of a Reformed Land Structure', Paper prepared for the conference *The Land Reform Challenge: An Economic and Social Perspective*, organised by the Economic Advisory Project [Friedrich Ebert Stiftung and the Zimbabwe Economics Society], Miekles Hotel, Harare, 27/02/98.

Sachikonye, L.M., [1995a], 'Industrial Restructuring and Labour Relations under ESAP in Zimbabwe', in Gibbon, P., [ed], *Structural Adjustment and the Working Poor in Zimbabwe*, Nordiska Afrikainstitutet, Uppsala, pp.38-131.

——, [1995b], 'From 'Equity' and 'Participation' to Structural Adjustment: State and Social Forces in Zimbabwe', Moore, D.B. and Schmitz, G.J., [eds], *Debating Development Discourse Institutional and Popular Perspectives*, Macmillan Press Ltd, London, pp.178-200.

——, [1997], 'Labour's Quest for a Better Deal', *SAPEM*, 11, 9, December, pp.9-10.

——, [1998], 'The Crisis of Governance in Zimbabwe', *SAPEM*, 11, 5, March, pp. 8-9.

Sahn, D.E., Dorosh, P.A. and Younger, S.D., [1997], *Adjustment Reconsidered Economic Policy and Poverty in Africa*, Cambridge University Press, Cambridge.

Saul, J.S. and Wood, R., [1971], 'African Peasantries', in Shanin, T., [ed], *Peasants and Peasant Societies*, Penguin Books Ltd, England.

Schatz, S.P., [1996], 'The World Bank's Fundamental Misconception of Africa', *The Journal of Modern African Studies*, 34, 2, pp.239-247.

Schmidt, E., [1996], *Peasants, Traders, and Wives. Shona Women in the History of Zimbabwe, 1870-1939*, Baobab Books, Harare.

Schmitz, G.J., [1995], 'Democratization and Demystification: Deconstructing 'Governance' as Development Paradigm', in Moore, D.B. and Schmitz, G.J., [eds], *Debating Development*

Discourse Institutional and Popular Perspectives, Macmillan Press Ltd, London, pp.54-90.

Schumacher, E.F., [1993], *Small is Beautiful*, Blond and Briggs Ltd, London.

Scott, E.P., [1995], 'Home-Based Industries: An Alternative Strategy for Household Security in Rural Zimbabwe', *The Journal of Developing Areas*, 29, [January], pp.183-212.

Sen, A., [1990], 'Food, Economics and Entitlements', in Eicher, C.K., and Staatz, J.M., [eds], *Agricultural Development in the Third World*, John Hopkins University Press, Baltimore, pp.189-203.

Shopo, T.D., [1986], 'The Political Economy of Hunger', in Mandaza, I., [ed], *Zimbabwe The Political Economy of Transition 1980-1986*, Codesria Books, Dakar, pp.223-241..

Sibanda, A.E, [1988], 'The Political Situation', in Stoneman, C., [ed], *Zimbabwe's Prospects. Issues of Race, Class, State and Capital in Southern Africa*, Macmillan, London, pp.257-283.

——, [1990], 'The Lancaster House Agreement and the Post-Independence State in Zimbabwe', Discussion Paper no.9, ZIDS, UZ, Harare.

Sibanda, M.J., [1989], 'Early Foundations of African Nationalism', in Banana, C.S., [ed], *Turmoil and Tenacity. Zimbabwe 1890-1990*, The College Press, Harare, pp.25-49.

——, [1996], 'What Government Has Done to Date to Reduce Poverty', *The Political Economy of Poverty in Zimbabwe*, I.D.S. Policy Dialogue Series No: 1, U.Z., Harare.

Silveira House, [1998], *Micro Enterprise Development* [final draft], Silveira House, Harare.

Skalnes, T., [1993], 'The State, Interest Groups and Structural Adjustment in Zimbabwe', *Journal of Development Studies*, 29, 3, April, pp.401-428.

Staatz, J.M. and Eicher, C.K., [1990], 'Agricultural Development Ideas in Historical Perspective', in Staatz, J.M. and Eicher, C.K., [eds], *Agricultural Development in the Third World*, The John Hopkins University Press, Baltimore.

Stein, H., [1995], 'The World Bank, Neo-Classical Economics and the Application of Asian Industrial Policy to Africa', in Stein,

H., [ed], *Asian Industrialisation and Africa*, St Martins Press, New York, pp.31-53.

Stenflo, G. A. [1993], *Poverty in Zimbabwe 1990–1991 Report from a Short Term Mission to the Central Statistical Office*, Harare, November 9-December 19.

Stoneman, C., [1978], 'Foreign Capital and the Reconstruction of Zimbabwe', *Review of African Political Economy*, 11, January-April, pp.62-83.

——, [1988], 'The Economy: Recognising the Reality', in Stoneman, C., [ed], *Zimbabwe's Prospects. Issues of Race, Class, State and Capital in Southern Africa*, Macmillan, London, pp.43-61.

Stoneman, C., and Cliffe, L., [1989], *Zimbabwe. Politics, Economics and Society*, Printer Publishers, New York.

Stoneman, C., [1992], 'The World Bank Demands its Pound of Zimbabwe's Flesh', *Review of African Political Economy*, 53, pp.94-96.

——, [1993], 'The World Bank: Some Lessons for South Africa', *Review of African Political Economy*, 58, pp.87-98.

Strange, S., [1986], *Casino Capitalism*, Basil Blackwell Ltd, London.

——, [1987], 'The persistent myth of lost hegemony', *International Organisation*, 41, 4, [Autumn], pp.551-574.

——, [1988], *States and Markets*, Pinter Publishers, London.

Streeten, P., [1993], 'Markets and States: Against Minimalism', *World Development*, 21, 8, pp.1281-1298.

Szeftel, M., [1998], 'Misunderstanding African Politics: Corruption and the Governance Agenda', *Review of African Political Economy*, 76, pp.221-240.

Takavarasha, T., [1994], 'Agricultural Pricing Policy', in Rukuni, M., and Eicher, C.K., *Zimbabwe's Agricultural Revolution*, UZ Publications, Mambo Press, Gweru, pp.153-174.

Takavarasha, T. and Sibanda, L., [1994] 'The Intended Impact and Outcome of the Economic Structural Adjustment Programme on the Smallholder Farming Sector', in ZFU/Friedrich Ebert Foundation seminar papers, *The Future of Smallholder Farming under ESAP*, Kadoma Ranch Motel, November 2-3.

Tandon, Y., [1990] 'Zimbabwe and Uganda: A Contrasting Record', in Mahjoub, A. [ed], *Adjustment or Delinking?*, Zed Books, London.

Thomas, S.J.A., [1992], 'An Estimate of Communal Land Population Density in the Natural Regions of Zimbabwe', Zimbabwe Trust, Occasional Paper 1, Harare.

Triffin, R., [1978], 'Reshaping the International Monetary Order', *International Social Science Journal*, 30, 2.

Tshuma, T., [1997], *A Matter of {In}justice: Law, State and the Agrarian Question in Zimbabwe*, Sapes Books, Harare.

UNDP/PRF/IDS, [1998], *Zimbabwe Human Development Report 1998*, Institute of Development Studies, University of Zimbabwe, December.

UNICEF, 1993, *Findings from the Third Round of Sentinel Surveillance for the Social Dimensions of Adjustment*, Ministry of Public Service, Labour and Social Welfare, Harare.

USAID, [1997], *Agricultural Policy Analysis Project Phase 111, Final Evaluation: Zimbabwe Grain Marketing Reform Support Program and Grain Marketing Reform Research Project*, USAID, September [copy obtained from the Australian High Commission, Harare].

van Onselen, C., [1976], *'Chibaro' African Mine Labour in Southern Rhodesia, 1900-1933*, Pluto Press, London.

von Hayek, F., [1944], *The Road to Serfdom*, University of Chicago Press, Chicago.

Waterbury, J., [1999], 'The Long Gestation and Brief Triumph of Import-Substituting Industrialization', *World Development*, 27, 2, pp.323-341.

Watkins, K., [1994a], 'GATT: a Victory for the North', *Review of African Political Economy*, 59, pp.60-66.

——, [1994b], 'Adjustment in Africa', in Kapoor, K., [ed], *Africa's Experience with Structural Adjustment. Proceedings of the Harare Seminar, May 23-24, 1994*, World Bank Discussion Papers 228, Washington D.C., pp.130-140.

Weiner, D., Moyo, S., Munslow, B., and O'Keefe, P., [1984], 'Land Use, Agricultural Productivity and the Agrarian Debate in Zimbabwe', ZIDS Research Papers, UZ.

Weiner, D., [1988], 'Land and Agricultural Development', in Stoneman, C., [ed], *Zimbabwe's Prospects. Issues of Race, Class, State and Capital in Southern Africa*, Macmillan, London, pp.63-89.

Weisbrot, M., Naiman, R., and Kim, J., [2000], 'The Emperor Has No Growth: Declining Economic Growth Rates in the Era of Globalization', Centre for Economic and Policy Research [www.cepr.net], Washington, 27 November.

Weitzer, R., [1990], *Transforming Settler States. Communal Conflict and Internal Security in Northern Ireland and Zimbabwe*, University of California Press, England.

Wheelwright, T., [1995], 'Political Economy. Past, Present and Future', *Social Alternatives*, 14, 3, July, 41-44.

Williams, W.A., [1972], T*he Tragedy of American Diplomacy*, Dell Publishing, New York, N.Y.

Williamson, J., [1993], 'Democracy and the 'Washington Consensus'', *World Development*, 21, 8, pp.1329-1336.

Wolf, E.R. [1969], 'On Peasant Rebellions', in Shanin, T., [ed], [1971] *Peasants and Peasant Societies*, Penguin Books Ltd, England, pp. 264-274.

Worby, E., [1995], 'What Does Agrarian Wage-Labour Signify? Cotton, Commoditisation and Social Form in Gokwe, Zimbabwe', *The Journal of Peasant Studies*, 23, 1, October, pp.1-29.

World Bank [1989], *Sub-Saharan Africa. From Crisis to Sustainable Growth*, The World Bank, Washington D.C.

——, [1991], *Zimbabwe Agricultural Sector Memorandum* [vol.II], The World Bank, Washington D.C.

——, [1994a], Adjustment in Africa: Reforms, Results and the Road Ahead, Oxford University Press, New York.

——, [1994b], Governance The World Bank's Experience, The World Bank, Washington D.C.

——, [1995], *Zimbabwe Achieving Shared Growth, Country Economic Memorandum* [vol.1 and 2], Report No: 13540-Zim, Macro, Industry and Finance Division, Southern Africa Department, Washington D.C., April 21.

——, [1996], *Understanding Poverty and Human Resources in Zimbabwe: Changes in the 1990s and Directions for the Future*, The World Bank, Washington D.C., December.

——, [1997a], *World Development Report 1997. The State in a Changing World*, Oxford University Press, New York.

——, [1997b], *Memorandum of the President of the International Development Association to the Executive Directors on a Country Assistance Strategy of the World Bank Group for the Republic of Zimbabwe*, Southern Africa Department, Report No: 16541-ZIM, May 1.

Young, C., [1994], 'Democratisation in Africa: The Contradictions of a Political Imperative', in Widner, J.A, [ed], *Economic Change and Political Liberalization in Sub-Saharan Africa*, The John Hopkins University Press, Baltimore.

ZCTU, [1996], *Beyond ESAP. Framework for a Long-term Development Strategy in Zimbabwe Beyond the Economic Structural Adjustment Programme*, Radix Consultants, Harare.

Zimbabwe Farmers Union, [1997], 'COTTCO Goes Private', *Zimbabwe Farmer*, July, p.8.

ZimNews, [2001], 'The New Scramble for Africa – ZANU-PF's grand strategy for regional domination', 8/01-16/01/01, www.zwnews.com

Zuckerman, E., [1991], 'The Social Costs of Adjustment', in Thomas, V., Chhibber, A., Dailami. M., and de Melo, J., [eds], *Restructuring Economies in Distress. Policy Reform and the World Bank*, Oxford University Press, New York, pp.247-275.

Zvobgo, R.J., [1986], 'Education and the Challenge of Indepedendence', in Mandaza, I., [ed], *Zimbabwe The Political Economy of Transition 1980-1986*, Codesria Books, Dakar, pp.319-354.

Newspapers

The Sunday Times [Zimbabwe]
The Sunday Mail [Zimbabwe]
The Herald [Zimbabwe]
The Financial Gazette [Zimbabwe]

The Daily News [Zimbabwe]
The Zimbabwe Independent
The Zimbabwe Mirror
The Zimbabwe Standard

The Mail & Guardian [SA]

The Age
The Australian
The Sydney Morning Herald

The New York Times
The Washington Post
The Chicago Tribune

The Guardian Weekly
The Independent [UK]
The Observer [UK]

Index